Inclusion in Early Childhood Settings

Second Edition Children with Special Needs in Canada

Inclusion in Early Childhood Settings

Second Edition   Children with Special Needs in Canada

INGRID CROWTHER
University College of the North

Pearson Canada
Toronto

Library and Archives Canada Cataloguing in Publication

Crowther, Ingrid, 1944–
  Inclusion in early childhood settings : children with special needs in Canada / Ingrid Crowther.—2nd ed.

Includes index.
ISBN 978-0-13-208202-0

  1. Inclusive education—Canada. 2. Early childhood education—Canada. 3. Early childhood special education—Canada. 4. Special education—Canada. I. Title.

LC4019.2.C76 2010   371.9'046   C2009-901707-5

ISBN-13: 978-0-13-208202-0
ISBN-10: 0-13-208202-0

Vice President, Editorial Director: Gary Bennett
Editor-in-Chief: Ky Pruesse
Editor, Social Sciences and Humanities: Joel Gladstone
Marketing Manager: Loula March
Senior Developmental Editor: Patti Altridge
Production Editor: Kevin Leung
Copy Editor: Carol Anderson
Proofreader: Susan Broadhurst
Production Coordinator: Janis Raisen
Composition: Laserwords
Art Director: Julia Hall
Cover Design: Anthony Leung
Cover Image: Harald Eisenberger, GettyImages

  6 7   14 13 12

Printed and bound in Canada.

Brief Contents

Contents

Preface

The term "special needs" for this book has been chosen deliberately. Many jurisdictions in Canada not only use and are familiar with this term, but also receive funding based on the identification of special needs.

This text has been written to introduce the early childhood educator to working with children with special needs. Many students lack expertise in this area and may have had limited experiences with children with special needs. Thus, this text endeavours to:

- Dispel biases by presenting real children with real problems through photographs, interviews and scenarios
- Create excitement about working with children with special needs in inclusive settings, through identification of real-life success stories with children, practitioners and students in the field
- Portray introductory concepts that are critical to interacting with children and families with special needs
- Instill understanding that all of us have strengths and weaknesses
- Provide relevance to what students are learning about children with special needs
- Provide an active approach that looks at child care in the context of inclusiveness, avoiding classifying children by their needs but rather dealing with them as individuals
- Provide information in charts and tables to encourage students to look up and find information quickly

Many of the current texts in the field of children with special needs provide information about dealing with identification, discussion of causes and theoretical intervention strategies. That sort of approach is not inclusive. It does not give individuals knowledge about how children should be treated or what strategies could be implemented. In contrast, this text aims to help in other ways, such as:

- Promoting a change of attitude about working with children with special needs
- Providing individuals with information and references in practical, accessible formats such as charts, lists, photographs, graphs and diagrams
- Involving learners in active participation through such strategies as utilizing the support website at Pearson for additional information, student exercises, class participation exercises and community-based exercises
- Involving learners in realistic and meaningful experiences to gain new understanding about inclusive settings
- Linking learners to relevant internet references to help them find pertinent up-to-date information
- Creating a forum for discussion

Organization

The information in this text is presented in a user-friendly way. The flow of information starts with the child and family through the use of photos, scenarios, individual education plans or portfolios, and interviews. The theoretical components are woven around the interaction patterns of children and adults, the inclusive program and the learning environment. Thus the focus is on the child, the family and the practitioner, but the broader focus of the community at large is also included.

Typical aspects of the book's content include discussion of every child's right to learn through play; an overview of the types of programs for children with special needs in Canada; identification of the major disabilities from a Canadian perspective; information on how to organize an inclusive child care environment; specific guidelines for setting up inclusive environments to foster communication, play, positive interactions, motor activities, social, emotional and cognitive growth; and a discussion of Canadian issues related to the care of children with special needs.

Special Features

- **Website** featuring Weblinks, to support and enrich the information in the text and including:
  - Forms, charts and observational tools for convenient replication.
  - Please access the website at **www.pearsoned.ca/text/crowther**.
- **IPPs and individual portfolios**—Actual individual program plans are provided, with instructions on how to develop them. Also included are samples of individual portfolios, another strategy to develop individualized programming for children with special needs (see Chapter 5).
- **Voices**—Chapter 11 is devoted to issues concerning inclusive care in Canada, and features comments from all of those involved: staff members, parents, directors, consultants and children.
- **Reflections**—These recurring features present relevant personal insights from the author and other professionals in the field, and direct students toward their own insights.
- **Floor plans** of successful inclusive learning environments.
- **Appendix**—SpeciaLink Child Care Inclusion Practices Profile, Principles Scale and Recommendations for Inclusive Care.
- **CourseSmart**—CourseSmart is a new way for instructors and students to access textbooks online anytime from anywhere. With thousands of titles across hundreds of courses, CourseSmart helps instructors choose the best textbook for their class and give their students a new option for buying the assigned textbook as a lower cost eTextbook. For more information, visit www.coursesmart.com.

Changes to the Second Edition

- Updated information.
- A new website that links students directly to related websites, to enrich and broaden the information found in the text. and to provide easy access to additional resources.
- Chapters have been edited to include more charts and tables for easy referencing.
- Additional information about autism and attention deficit order has been expanded and is included in a number of relevant sections of the book.

ACKNOWLEDGMENTS

I would like to acknowledge the children and families across Canada who helped in the creation of this text, especially Jordan, Susan, Gabriella and Christopher. In addition, I would like to acknowledge the help of the following individuals: Sharon Hope Irwin, executive director of SpeciaLink and Dr. Arlene Young, psychologist; and the following for their invaluable insight during the review process: Shirley Bainbridge, Karla Baxter-Vincent, Janet Berezowecki, Cindy Brandon, Karen Chandler, Lana-Lee Hardacre, Susan Hartwell, Dawn Loran, Ann McDonald, Margaret H. Patten, Jane Proudlove, Janice Quade, Dawn Wojkowski, and Christine Wojcik.

I would also like to include special thanks to the staffs of the following inclusive centres: Capilano College Child Care Centre, Vancouver; Child Development Centre, Whitehorse; Cedar Road Aboriginal Head Start Program, Prince Rupert, British Columbia; Loyalist College Curriculum Lab Preschool, Belleville, Ontario; Berwick Child Development Centre, Vancouver; and Brite Beginnings, Edmonton. I would like to extend my appreciation to both SpeciaLink and the Childcare Resource and Research Unit for their permission to include the valuable information on special needs children contained in the appendices.

My special thanks go out to the reviewers who made many helpful suggestions that have been incorporated into the text. Their work helped make the process of reviewing and editing much easier and resulted in a much better book.

DEDICATION

I would like to dedicate this text to Dr. Harold Goldsman, who has spent a lifetime selflessly working to improve the quality of life for the children and families of his communities; and Ross Smithrim, who, with the help of his family, overcame a number of handicapping conditions to successfully complete a college diploma program, and used his creative talents to support the children and families in his community.

1 Setting the Stage

CHAPTER

"Inclusion, as a value, supports the rights of all children, regardless of their diverse abilities, to participate actively in natural settings within their communities. A natural setting is one in which the child would spend time had he or she not had a disability. Such settings include but are not limited to home, family, play groups, child care, nursery schools, Head Start programs, kindergartens, and neighbourhood school classrooms" (Hope Irwin, Lero & Brophy, 2000:5).

Learning Outcomes

After studying this chapter, you will be able to:

1. Identify the importance of the right to play for all children.
2. Discuss causes of bias and appropriate strategies to mitigate bias.
3. Describe the main reasons for individual differences.
4. Describe the strategies needed to set up an inclusive environment.
5. Explain the importance of forming collaborative partnerships.

Photo 1.1

Photo 1.2

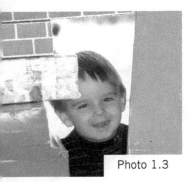

Photo 1.3

Photo 1.4

Children's Right to Play

Play is the most powerful means of learning for young children. When children actively explore the environment, using all of their senses, they gain skills to:

- Communicate with each other (Photo 1.1)
- Learn about the world around them (Photo 1.2)
- Develop physically, emotionally, socially and mentally (Photo 1.3)
- Learn to solve problems (Photo 1.4)
- Make meaningful decisions (Photo 1.5)
- Build upon what they already know (Photo 1.6)
- Gain self-confidence in their ability to act (Photo 1.7) (Crowther, 2003; IPA World, 2004)

The right to play has long been supported by international organizations such as the United Nations. Article 31 of the UN Convention on the Rights of the Child identifies the critical role of play in every child's life:

1. Parties recognize the right of the child to rest and leisure, to engage in play and recreational activities appropriate to the age of the child and to participate freely in cultural life and arts.

2. Parties shall respect and promote the right of the child to participate fully in cultural and artistic life and shall encourage the provision of appropriate and equal opportunities for cultural, artistic, recreational and leisure activity (Covell, 2001:176).

Further, in Article 13 the charter defines the child's right to freedom of expression: ". . . this right shall include freedom to seek, receive and impart information and ideas of all kinds, regardless of frontiers, either orally, in writing or in print, in the form of art, or through any other media of the child's choice." (Covell, 2001:168).

Photo 1.5

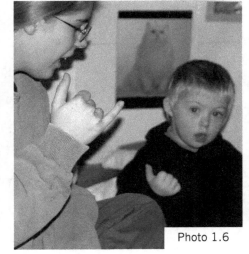

Photo 1.6

The right of children to learn through play is supported by most of the relevant legislation. However, what constitutes play for young children, especially children with special needs, is often interpreted differentially (see Reflection on page 7). Children with special needs must have the same rights as all other children. Therefore, the focus of care for these children should be on:

- Equal opportunities to participate in all learning activities (Photo 1.8)
- Facilitation of equal opportunities by organizing learning spaces effectively in a way that provides opportunities to solve problems and engage in active choices
- Accessibility of materials and equipment to all children (Photo 1.9)
- Observation, in order to identify where adaptations may be needed
- Active participation in indoor and outdoor activities (Photo 1.10)

Photo 1.7

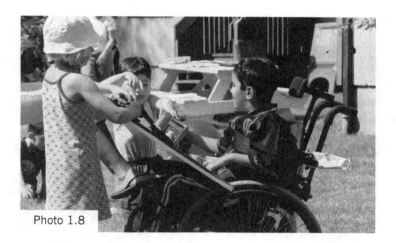

Photo 1.8

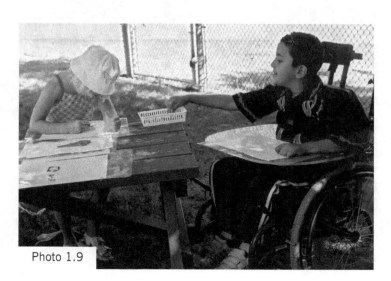

Photo 1.9

Photo 1.10

- Development of schedules that support regularly occurring indoor and outdoor play, and monitoring and adapting all learning areas to provide maximum opportunities for active involvement of all children
- Provision of opportunities to make personal choices and decisions (Photo 1.11)
- Organization of the learning environments to set up learning experiences that foster independent interactions with peers, materials and equipment.
- Provision of learning experiences and materials that are developmentally appropriate and age appropriate (Photo 1.12)
- Awareness of the developmental abilities of all children, in order to provide appropriate learning materials and experiences

Photo 1.11

Photo 1.12

From the Author   Reflection

In centres across Canada I have often observed children with special needs engaged in structured, teacher-directed activities. Here is a relevant example of an observed interaction:

During free play activities, Nancy, a four-year-old, was sitting at a table with one of the early childhood educators. Under the guidance of the adult, Nancy was encouraged to trace letters on a piece of paper. This activity was provided because Nancy needed to improve her fine-motor skills.

Careful observation of the activity identified a number of developmentally inappropriate practices. Nancy was trying to trace letters with her left hand. This process obscured much of what she was tracing because her arm and hand covered most of the area she was working on. She was also holding her pencil with a palmar grasp, which made it very difficult for her to follow the printed example. Nancy used a full-arm movement to try to accomplish her task, which further inhibited her ability to trace the letters appropriately. The result of her attempts was poor. She did not produce clear, recognizable letters. The letters extended beyond the area of the page. Nevertheless, she was rewarded with a "Good job!" at the end of the activity.

This activity was totally inappropriate for Nancy. If the intent was to improve her fine-motor control, the activity could have been arranged in a number of ways that would have been more rewarding and appropriate to her. She should have been working on a larger surface to accommodate her palmar grasp and whole-arm movement. Better activities to help her control and refine her arm movement would include filling and dumping play. Her fine- and gross-muscular control could be enhanced through activities such as moulding clay, or painting or drawing. Most importantly, Nancy was robbed of an opportunity to engage in a meaningful activity that was directed by her and that supported her individual development.

Unfortunately, proactive legislation that supports the rights of children with special needs does not exist in Canada. "While all provinces and territories have made some provision for the inclusion of children with special needs, in no jurisdiction is it illegal to exclude a child from a child care on the basis of disability or other special needs. And while many provincial officials and child care consultants have worked diligently to make inclusion a reality in their jurisdiction, written policies, training requirements, and resource allocation seldom suggest systematic, stable support for inclusion" (Hope Irwin et al., 2000: xiii). It therefore falls upon individual child care centres to include children within their programs, often without the resources or support to do this.

Inclusion

Inclusion respects the child's right to learn through play in his or her natural environment. For children with special needs, inclusion includes the following considerations:

1. No child may be excluded from a program or from any part of a program for reasons of disability;
2. Children's attendance in any one program should be proportionate to the number of cases of special needs occurring in the general population;
3. The child's right to play is respected and fostered;
4. Children are encouraged to participate in all parts of the program;
5. Families are encouraged to participate as full partners; and
6. The promotion of inclusive care is embraced by all partners. (adapted from SpeciaLink, 2004)

Attitudes, Values and Beliefs About Inclusive Care

The interactions between young children and adults are often based on our knowledge about children, our understanding of their strengths and needs, and our own personal experiences. Too often, our perceptions about children influence how we interact with them and also may act as a barrier to inclusion. It is therefore very important to clarify any points of bias or commonly held misconceptions.

1. Bias

"Bias is a point of view or inclination that manifests itself through favouritism, dislike, or fear toward someone because of that person's particular looks, behaviour, or lifestyle. A bias can be conveyed to another through nonverbal, verbal, and physical interactions. In other words, one's point of view is clearly reflected by one's attitude and actions" (Saderman Hall & Rhomberg, 1995: 2).

Bias occurs regularly in everyday life. Individuals are influenced by what they see, hear, feel and smell. For example, Jesse is a 12-year-old boy of mixed heritage: His mother is Aboriginal and his father is from Pakistan. His nickname on the Aboriginal reserve where he lives is "Little Terrorist." He is often asked why he does not wear his hair tied up and covered in a top knot. Many children are discouraged from playing with him. Jesse often comes home in tears, or states that he has a stomach ache and does not want to go to school.

Not all experiences lead to such a strong bias. Many instances of bias are much more subtle. For example, Marianna believed that Fisher-Price toys were the best toys to buy for her infant. When questioned why she believed this, she said that magazines and television ads seemed to indicate that they were.

When one centre was faced with including a child with disabilities, some of the families did not want the child included and expressed their opposition. They did not inquire about the special need, nor were they interested in discussing the topic. The fears expressed were that:

- Less time would be available to spend with their child, because the child with special needs would demand more time from the two regular staff
- Less money would be available to spend, because most of the resources would be needed to buy expensive equipment for just one child
- Children would pick up the negative behaviours modelled by this child
- Children would be hurt by the child's aggressive behaviours

The staff ultimately decided not to accept the child, because too many families threatened to move their children to another centre should the child be accepted.

2. Sources of Bias

Any bias, including bias about children with special needs, can arise from a number of sources. The degree of bias an individual may hold is dependent on many factors, including:

- Knowledge about child development and special needs
- Experiences with individuals with special needs
- Physical indicators, such as the appearance of an individual
- Belief systems, such as ideas about how children learn or should be treated
- Socioeconomic status, which is an indicator of the social and economic values an individual holds
- Cultural influences that lead to certain ways of thinking and behaving
- Designation of roles, such as male and female, parent or teacher
- Determinants such as skin colour or ethnicity
- Family dynamics
- Health status

A) KNOWLEDGE BASE Knowledge is one of the critical factors in anyone's ability to make informed decisions about how to interact with any child, how to select materials and resources, and how to develop a quality learning environment. Consider the following examples:

Two individuals were asked to identify what they thought of when they heard the phrase "children with special needs." Melanie, a first-year student in an Early Childhood Education program, responded: "You can usually tell if the kids are special needs by the way they look, like a Down's syndrome child or a child in a wheelchair. A lot of them are hyper, like disturbed kids, and they are hard to deal with. Most kids with special needs require a lot more work and attention. It would be hard to have them in a regular program with normal kids." Melanie clearly demonstrated her bias in several ways:

- She seemed to think that a child can be diagnosed based on the child's appearance. Although this might be true of some children, it is untrue of most (see Reflection).

Reflection

For the Student

Look at the photographs presented at the beginning of the chapter. How many children could you identify as special needs simply by looking at them? Melanie obviously had limited experiences with children with special needs. Her experience and knowledge were based on physical characteristics and the perceived behaviours of children with special needs. Reflect upon what you have seen or heard about children with special needs. What are some of the influences that might have caused Melanie to believe as she did?

Reflection

For the Student

Read over some of the scenarios above and below (reflections about Nancy, Jeremy and Archibald). How many of these children showed similar behavioural characteristics? Reflect on some of the children you know. How many of these children show some of the characteristics of the children in the scenarios? Why is it dangerous to generalize about the behaviour of children?

- She also felt that most children with special needs share a behavioural characteristic: hyperactivity. All young children are active. Few children are actually diagnosed as hyperactive.
- Melanie also felt that working with children with special needs required more work. The amount of work required is not based on special needs alone. All children require more attention and work at some times than at others. Not all children with special needs require a consistently large amount of attention.
- Melanie felt that it would be difficult to provide inclusive care. In fact, providing inclusive care should be very rewarding, not difficult. As with any child, the environment should be set up to accommodate the individual child's strengths and needs. When children are together in an inclusive setting, they learn to appreciate each other's strengths and weaknesses, and learn that everyone has some special needs.

The second person asked to identify what she thought of when she heard the phrase "children with special needs" was Arlene, a child psychologist. She answered: "All children have special needs. They are all individuals. I recognize that there is a code to identify the various types of disabilities, but children should be children. However, we should look at children as individuals who have different likes and dislikes, learning styles, and strengths and needs. The challenge is to try to gain insights into what the child understands so that we can interact in positive ways to help his or her optimum growth and development." It is evident from

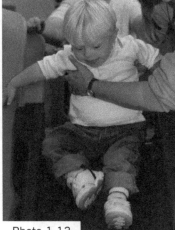

Arlene's quote that she has a lot of knowledge and experience with children with special needs. She understands that:

- All children are unique individuals
- All children have special needs
- Adults need to interact with children based on their developmental levels
- Adults need to engage in positive interactions

B) EXPERIENCE WITH CHILDREN WITH SPECIAL NEEDS When Josh started attending a nursery school program, the staff had no previous experience with children with special needs. As a result, Josh was treated as "special." One staff member was always near him to help him. All interactions with Josh were positive, but he had few opportunities to actively explore and interact with materials in the environment independently. For example, when Josh tried to use the climber, one adult helped him up and another adult held him as he slid down the slide (Photo 1.13). This type of interaction can quickly lead to dependency. Josh's parents decided to take him to a different nursery school.

Photo 1.13

The staff in the new setting had experience in interacting with children with special needs. Josh was encouraged to participate independently. Josh thrived in this environment. He soon participated fully in all activities, independently (Photo 1.14).

The staff at the first centre were clearly biased about his abilities. They had decided that Josh needed careful supervision and help.

C) PHYSICAL INDICATORS Jeremy was born with cerebral palsy. He is able to walk by himself but lurches from side to side. Since Jeremy is very unsteady on his feet, people often try to help him walk. When Jeremy tries to tell them that he can walk by himself, he is most often not understood, as his speech is slurred and hard to understand.

Photo 1.14

This bias is clear. Jeremy looks unstable. He might fall and hurt himself. He needs to be helped.

D) BELIEF SYSTEMS It is a relatively new approach to include children with special needs in settings within their neighbourhoods or in settings of choice. This approach is based on the belief that inclusion is a system that removes barriers so children may participate in all aspects of their life (Child Care Advocacy Association of Canada Fact Sheet, 2004). In the past, belief systems advocated partial to total segregation of children with special needs.

E) SOCIOECONOMIC STATUS Socioeconomic status dictates what a family can or cannot afford to do. Often, lower-income families cannot give their children the same stimulation or experiences that families with higher incomes can. When children from low-income families are not as well dressed, or do not have the same experiences as children from high-income families, sometimes negative assumptions are made about the care low-income families give their children. For example, Archibald, a three-year-old boy, often came to school with torn, dirty clothes. His hair was not combed, and his hands and face were dirty. He did not settle into routines easily. If crossed, he would scream, throw his toys, and sometimes bite or kick. The staff rarely saw his parents. He was usually dropped off by various extended family members. The staff tried to contact the family in writing and by phone, but these attempts were unsuccessful. The staff assumed that the family did not care and that they did not use appropriate guidance techniques at home.

F) CULTURAL INFLUENCES Throughout much of our country's past, children with special needs were often hidden away. Parents often placed children with special needs in institutions. More recently, a movement to keep these children living at home also saw them segregated into specialized schools or classes. Today, the view is that it is better to integrate children into settings within their neighbourhoods.

Each of these three approaches was supported by the dominant Canadian cultures of the time. Huge institutions were built to house children with special needs for the rest of their lives. As society's values shifted toward keeping children at home, special schools were built and special classes were equipped and opened. It is only recently that most of the dominant cultures across Canada embrace inclusion as the most appropriate methodology for caring for young children with special needs.

Reflection   *For the Student*

"The nature of developmentally appropriate practices allows for the inclusion of children with great variation in development within the same setting. Even in a group of young children without disabilities, of the same age, children can be as much as two years apart developmentally" (Udell, Peters & Piaza Templeman, 2001:34). Reflect upon this statement. Have you noticed this age spread in abilities in a group of children?

For the Student   Reflection

Reflection

Josh also has a role. His role as a child within the program is also open to bias. What bias might be attributed to Josh?

G) DESIGNATION OF ROLES Individuals have various roles they engage in every day. Each role carries its own bias. For example, Josh's mother was most concerned with developing his independence. This dictated her choice of program. The staff at the day care were more concerned with his safety. Subsequently, the interactions between Josh and the staff increased his dependency on adult intervention. Additionally, Josh's father served in the army and was often out of the country. As a result, Josh's mother's role was as primary caregiver of Josh and as the person responsible for most of the decisions concerning his care and education.

H) RACIAL AND SIMILAR DETERMINANTS, SUCH AS SKIN COLOUR OR ETHNICITY Often perceptions of a child's abilities are based on the experiences, beliefs and values formed by individuals about children from diverse backgrounds. These perceptions may lead to prejudice regarding beliefs formed based on skin colour, ethnicity or race and to false expectations (Allen, Paasche, Langford & Nolan, 2007; Wilson, 2008). This observation is especially true if the child comes from a geographic area that is thought to include higher numbers of children with special needs.

I) FAMILY DYNAMICS The types of interactions that occur within the home and family attitudes toward a child all have a profound impact on the child. Children who live in abusive or neglectful environments often do not receive the optimal attention and stimulation needed for healthy growth and development. As a result, these children live under constant stress and may exhibit many of the signs and symptoms of children with special needs. "A child who misses positive stimulation or is subject to chronic stress in the first years of life may have difficulty overcoming a bad early start" (McCain & Mustard, 1999:52).

Often these children are labelled as children with special needs. The practitioner doing the labelling usually relies on someone else to provide the quality programs that these children need. However, if the child is enrolled in a program that is nurturing and of high quality, much of this early negative impact can be mitigated. "The evidence is clear that good early childhood development programs that involve parents or other primary caregivers of young children can influence how they relate to and care for children in the home and can vastly improve outcomes for children's behaviour, learning and health in later life. The earlier in a child's life these programs begin, the better. These programs can benefit children and families from all socioeconomic groups in society" (McCain et al., 1999:52).

J) HEALTH STATUS Children who are medically fragile or often ill, or who live with family members who are ill, may also have a poorer head start. It is hard to stimulate someone who is not feeling well to be involved in active play. It is equally hard for someone who is not feeling well to have enough energy to stimulate a child.

Reflection

Reflection   *For the Student*

Your health is critical to your ability to provide active and stimulating programs for young children. Reflect upon your energy level when you are not feeling well. How will this affect the children in your care? What strategies can you use to ensure your own well-being?

These children may also exhibit symptoms of special needs. As in the example above, a warm and nurturing child care program can provide the appropriate stimulation that is needed. Caregivers of young children need to take care of themselves in order to have the required energy to provide a healthy, stimulating program for the children in their care.

3. Anti-Bias Defined

The prefix "anti-" means "against," so taking an anti-bias approach "means taking a stand against unfair treatment associated with one of the areas of diversity where bias may exist" (Saderman Hall et al., 1995:2). All individuals operate within the biases that are set by the times in which we live, the environment in which we have been raised or work, and our social system. It is therefore not possible to be free from bias. "We will always have preferences, but to act on them in an exclusionary manner constitutes a bias" (Saderman Hall et al., 1995:3). Adults working in inclusive settings must be aware of their personal biases and be prepared to overcome barriers that are imposed by a biased approach.

4. Strategies to Mitigate Personal Bias

Most of the types of biases referred to above can be mitigated by developing and using a number of strategies:

- Reflective practices and discussions, such as those featured in this chapter (see Table 1.1)
- Active listening strategies (see Figure 1.1 on page 16)
- Appropriate self-care practices—Caregivers who feel tired or unwell may see things more negatively, resulting in negative interactions with children or other staff. Caregivers should ensure that they are healthy and well rested by getting regular sleep, regular health-care checkups and appropriate nutrition and exercise.
- Strategies to create an atmosphere of mutual respect for everyone—This includes children, families, other professionals and other staff. Applying reflective practices (see Table 1.1) and active listening (see Figure 1.1), developing lines of open communication with all partners and sharing information in a confidential, trustful manner will help set the stage for mutual trust and respect.

- Strategies to organize an inclusive learning environment (see section on elements of inclusive environments, p. 16)
- Identification of and elimination of subjective terminology that leads to bias in all observations, written documents and reports
- Organization of workshops with all team members—families, other professionals, community members and staff—to identify bias and to make recommendations toward elimination of biased perspectives

TABLE 1.1 **REFLECTIVE PRACTICES**

Stop and reflect	Think about what you have observed or heard. Do you have enough information? Can you make an unbiased interpretation based on what you have observed or heard?
Check your own feelings	How do you feel about what you have seen or heard? If you are feeling anxious or resentful, reflect upon why you feel this way. Do not respond until you have clarified how you feel. Try some of the other strategies below prior to responding.
Clarify	**Paraphrase**—Repeat what has been said to you in your own words. You might start with, "I understand that . . . " or "I believe you said . . . " **Pararead**—Repeat to yourself what you have read. You might write it down in your own words. Check what you have written against the original. If in doubt, clarify your perception in person.
Understand	Do you understand the information presented? Do you need to expand your knowledge with further research before you can interpret the information?
Mutual understanding	Are all individuals in agreement with the information? Are there differences? If there are differences, what steps must be taken to come to agreement?
Summarize	Summarize all of the information presented. Check to see that all the salient points have been covered.

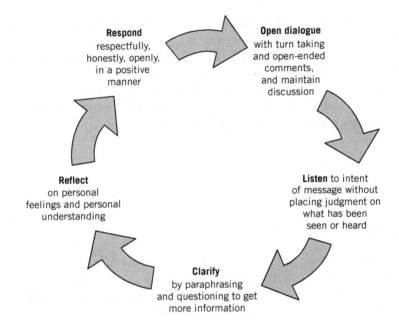

FIGURE 1.1
Active Listening Strategies

Elements of Inclusive Environments

1. Reasons for Individual Differences

The abilities of children in any age group vary greatly. This variance is the result of a number of factors, including

- Differential rates of development—Children generally pass through similar stages of development. However, not all children pass through the same stage at the same age or for the same amount of time. Some children may even skip a stage. For example, Jordan was a late talker. He used gestures and single words until he was three. He then started to talk in complete sentences.
- Accidents, problems during pregnancy or birth, identifiable genetic defects, chromosomal abnormalities, developmental delays and exposure to abuse and neglect
- Genetic disposition—Heredity seems to influence intelligence, specific abilities, specific aspects of personality and some specific psychopathologies, such as schizophrenia or depression. It is important to remember that the environment also plays a strong part in shaping the individual. "Children also mold their own environments by the choices they make—what they do and with whom—and their genetic makeup influences these choices. . . . A child who has inherited artistic talent may spend a great deal of time creating 'masterpieces' in solitude, while a sibling who is athletically inclined spends more time playing ball with others. Thus not only will the children's abilities (in, say, painting or soccer) develop differently, but their social lives will be different as well" (Papalia, Wendkos Olds, & Duskin Feldman, 2001:84).

- Background experiences—Children need appropriate stimulation and learning experiences, especially in the early years. These early experiences are critical to future success. "It is clear that the early years from conception to age six have the most important influence of any time in the life cycle on brain development and subsequent learning, behaviour and health. The effects of early experience, particularly during the first three years, on wiring and sculpting of the brain's billions of neurons, last a lifetime" (McCain et al., 1999:2).
- Quality of the learning experiences—The High/Scope Perry Preschool Program has been long acknowledged to be an excellent program. The outcomes for individuals who have attended the program have been tracked longitudinally. The results are illuminating: "More than 40 years of scientifically based research by the High/Scope Perry Preschool Program has found that adults born into poverty who participated in a high quality, active learning preschool program at ages three and four have a greater chance of experiencing more positive adulthood than individuals who do not" (High/Scope Research Foundation, 2004:2). By age 27, the group of adults who had attended the Perry School Preschool, as compared with a control group, had:

  - 63% fewer habitual criminals in the group
  - 68% fewer arrests for drug dealing
  - 21% fewer relying on social-service support systems
  - 31% more high school graduates
  - Almost twice the number of home owners
  - Three times as many individuals earning $2000 (US) or more per month
  - Significantly higher achievement and literacy scores (High/Scope Research Foundation, 2004:1)

- Societal values and beliefs about raising and educating children—All children are unique. Children are shaped "by the many contexts in which the child lives—family, school, community, country, world" (Schickedanz, Schickedanz, Forsyth & Forsyth, 2001:xx).

Therefore, in any quality child care setting, a large number of elements must already be considered. These elements are similar in inclusive settings and are examined in the following section.

2. Organization of Learning Spaces to Encourage Active Participation

A) ACCESSIBILITY Active play involves making choices and decisions. In order for children to make these choices, the environment must be arranged in a way that encourages and enables children to navigate within the environment, so that they can find and use relevant materials and engage in appropriate learning experiences. To ensure accessibility, placement of materials and traffic flow need to be considered.

- Placement of materials—Since an environment that includes children with special needs may have especially broad age and developmental spans, corresponding equipment and materials must compensate for this. A system should be put in place that encourages children to find the appropriate materials they can use successfully. Table 1.2 outlines some ideas for the organization of materials.
- Traffic flow—The environment should be organized to encourage children to move from one area to another without difficulty, as shown in Figure 1.2 on page 21. Some areas, such as the carpentry area, should be out of the traffic flow area (Area F). Other areas, such as drama (Area J) and blocks (Area B), should have large spill-out areas. These areas need lots of room for the play to extend into.

Photo 1.15

Outdoor play areas should also have clear pathways to encourage children to try different skills. In Figure 1.3 (see page 24), concrete pathways encourage riding. Access points to all of the climbing apparatus are via ramps starting from the concrete platforms. There are a variety of ways to get onto the apparatus: crawling, climbing or riding. All equipment is either totally or partially accessible to wheelchairs, and fully accessible if the child is mobile.

Some areas should be close to each other to encourage the use of materials in different areas. When areas are within visible range, children will start to use materials from one area in another area. This is especially important for children who are younger, either in age or by developmental delay. These children need to be able to scan the area to see what they might wish to use. For example, in Figure 1.2, the carpentry area is close to the creative art area. Children can easily take the structures created in carpentry to the creative art area to decorate (Photo 1.15).

The medium and large climbers are joined by ramps, platforms and gently rising stairs. Children can traverse from one area to the other above ground. This often leads to more dramatic play. For example, a group of preschoolers were pretending that the large climber was a space station and the small climber was the space shuttle. The connecting platform was a tunnel they had to crawl through to get from one place to the other. One of the children in a wheelchair was also actively involved in this play. He was able to get to the platform but not to the higher parts of either climber. His job was to open and shut the "air gates" to make sure that individuals would not "choke and die 'cause they have no air."

Most areas outside are wheelchair accessible. The terrain has been set up to maximize usability at various skills levels, with ramps, ladders, poles, concrete riding paths, gently rising stairs, grassy areas and sand areas. Children can safely ride, run, climb or jump, irrespective of their individual abilities.

The flooring between areas in Figure 1.2 is flush. This prevents tripping and also provides unobstructed access for a wheelchair to move from the carpeted to tiled areas.

All shelves that are not against walls are a child-friendly height. This increases ease of supervision and also makes it easier for children to see areas that they might wish to participate in.

Materials and shelves could be colour coded to provide easier visibility for children with visual impairments. Labels should include symbolized forms, pictorial labels and Braille to make it easier for children to make their own choices.

TABLE 1.2 **ORGANIZATION OF MATERIALS**

Organization	Description
Install open shelves	• Heavy items should be on the bottom shelf, easy to access. • Lighter items can be stored on higher shelves. • Child can see and access materials readily.
Provide transportable containers 	• Providing various containers (baskets, caddies, buckets, bags, cases) with handles helps children to transport items from one area to another. • If needed, provide containers that can slip onto handlebars of a walker, or sit on the tray of a wheelchair.
Organize by type 	• Materials should be stored by type. This allows children to easily find and return the materials they wish to use. • Clear plastic containers are ideal, as the child can see what is in the container.
Label by picture and word 	• Labelling helps children identify, find and return materials easily. • Labelling should include the picture and the word and/or, if appropriate, an outline of the object.
Use storage consistently	• Storage needs to be consistent. When materials are rotated, similar materials should appear on the same shelf.
Create a system that indicates ease of use	• The system could be as simple as easiest toys at the bottom and hardest ones on the top. • Storage could be colour coded: red for easiest, green for hardest. Both shelves and toys should be colour coded. This works well for items such as puzzles.
Ensure success	• If a child picks a toy that is too difficult to manage, he or she may become frustrated and leave all the pieces lying around. If trays, baskets or boxes are provided, the child is encouraged to put all the pieces in the storage container and put the container back on the shelf. In this way the child learns that it is OK to feel frustrated, but the materials still need to be put away. Additionally, often another child will come and complete the activity.
Store rotational materials accessibly	• There needs to be accessible well-organized storage for rotational materials. When a child wants an item, a staff member should be able to access it quickly and efficiently.

Photo 1.16

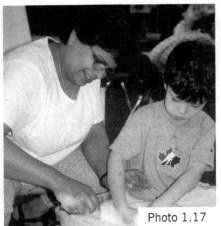

Photo 1.17

Ensure that the overall tone of the room does not distract from the activities or the children's work. Extensive use of colour could distract children who have high activity levels or who are easily distracted. A display of children's creative efforts should provide the colour on the walls and other display areas. Reserve the use of colour for children's creations.

Supervision in the outdoor play area should be highly visible. However, staff members need to be stationed at different positions on the playground so that they can interact in a timely manner in case of dangerous play. For example, Troy, an active four-year-old, wanted to climb over the railing. Melanie was close enough to him to remind him to stay on the platform.

Some parts of the indoor area, such as the sand area, are on the floor to encourage accessibility for all children (see Photo 1.16). Other areas can be changed to accommodate the needs of children as the need arises. A platform can be used to raise or lower the level of play as needed. For example, Keegan was reluctant to use the water table because there were too many children around it. He was much more comfortable engaging in water play when the activity was more individual and located closer to the ground (see Photo 1.17).

The outside play area is more difficult to adapt because it is a permanent structure. However, care has been taken to add various levels of access to ensure maximum accessibility. Additionally, there is enough space to add mobile equipment as needed.

B) SAFETY CONSIDERATIONS Both indoor and outdoor areas shown in the figures have been set up to maximize the safety of all children. The following strategies were employed:

- Smooth flooring was used to prevent tripping and give easier access to children using walkers or wheelchairs.
- Some of the materials may be more dangerous for some children. For example, Dillon, a four-year-old, liked to put items in his mouth. The staff consequently placed the smaller items on higher shelves so that they were not accessible to the children, reducing the chance of an injury caused by choking.

FIGURE 1.2

Indoor Learning Environment

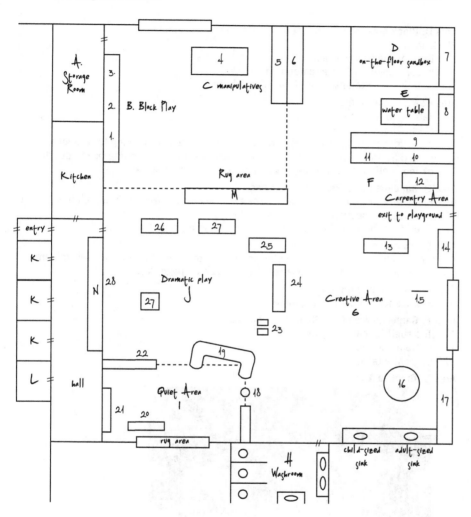

Please refer to the key on the next page.

FIGURE 1.2

Continued

Area B: **Block Area** (see Photo 1.14 on page 11)
Block shelf
1. Bottom shelf for wooden blocks
2. Second shelf for lighter cardboard blocks
3. Rotational materials—out of reach of children

Area C: **Manipulative Area**
4. Table and four chairs
5. Manipulative shelves
    a) Bottom shelf: lacing cards, large beads, easy puzzles, stacking toys, tracks, Duplo
    b) Middle shelf: small beads, small vehicles, sorting trays, sorting bears, puzzles
    c) Top shelf: sorting shapes, Lego, floor puzzles, small blocks

Area D: **Sand Area** (see Photo 1.16 on page 20)
6. Floor-level large-vehicle parking—The floor has lines drawn on it and pictures of the vehicles are mounted on the back of Shelf 5.
7. Shelf for sand toys: fences, digging toys, moulding toys, logs

Area E: **Water Play**
The water table changes from a regular water table to a low platform with several large water containers for individual use (see Photo 1.17 on page 20).

8. Storage for pouring toys
9. Storage for bubble-making materials

Area F: **Carpentry Area** (see Photo 1.15 on page 18)
10. Top shelf for carpentry tools
11. Bottom shelf for wood
12. Carpentry table

Area G: **Creative Area**

13. Shelf with three-dimensional materials: dough, mixtures, clay, tools for dough and clay
14. Drying rack
15. Double-sided easel
16. Table with four chairs
17. Creative shelf—bottom shelves for children's use; top shelves for rotational materials

Area I: **Quiet Area**

FIGURE 1.2
Continued

18. Plant
19. Snake
20. Book shelf
21. Quiet games for concentration, such as puzzles, matching games
22. Small wall with plants on top

Area J: **Dramatic Area**
23. Cradles
24. Baby-bath area (see Photo 1.18)
25. Couch
26. Stove
27. Dress-up clothes
28. Child-sized kitchen cabinets

Area K: **Offices**

Area L: **Staff Lounge**

Area M: **Music Area** (see Photo 1.19)

Area N: **Cubbies**

Photo 1.18

Photo 1.19

When children asked to use these items, they were brought down and supervision was provided.
- The arrangement of the room maximizes the ability of staff members to
  supervise the room readily. In the outside spaces, staff members station themselves so that they are closer to the main activities.
- The riding spaces outside incorporate common safety rules. The riding path is
  wide enough to accommodate two vehicles. Children are encouraged to drive
  on the right side of the road. Stop signs and crosswalks have been placed on the
  pavement to prevent accidents and enforce road safety rules (see Figure 1.3,
  Area A).
- Sand has been placed under all climbing equipment. The sand is raked daily to
  remove debris.

FIGURE 1.3

Inclusive Outdoor Space

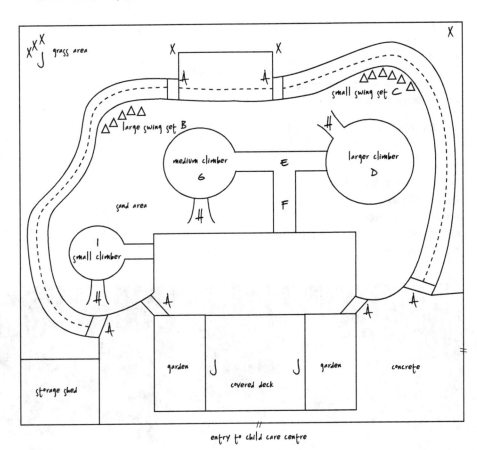

A: Crosswalks and stop signs

B and C: Swing sets

△:   Child-height cedar hedge

D: Large climber—wheelchair accessible to lower platform; upper platform has a playhouse; access by ramp, ladders and poles; also includes a slide

E: Platform connecting two climbers—wheelchair accessible

F: Ramp to reach platform

G: Medium climber—wheelchair accessible, access by ladders, gently sloping stairs, chain ladder, pole and climbing rope

H: Slides

I: Small climber—totally wheelchair accessible, access by ramps, gently sloping stairs

J: Benches

X: Mature trees

- The areas at the back of the swings are protected by a child-height cedar hedge, to prevent a child from accidentally running into the swing.
- The outdoor space is protected from the wind by a cedar fence and from the sun by a covered deck and a number of trees (Figure 1.3, Area X).

C) DISPLAY SPACES Display areas serve a dual purpose. They should be set up to attract children's attention. Areas may be set up to provide a point of interest, tweak the children's curiosity or focus on current activities. Children also need room to display their creative efforts, both two- and three-dimensional. For example, a group of preschool children had been interested in the insects they had seen outside. They created a mural through painting and printmaking. This mural was hung in the corner of the room and a platform was added in front of it. Children collected the plastic insects and some natural materials to place on the platform. They engaged in a number of activities—dramatic play using the insects, matching the insects to the insects in their mural and setting up an environment for the insects.

Through this activity the children learned in several ways:

- They learned to respect each other's efforts. Some of the children were able to make clear prints; others created more of a smudge. Some children were able to paint recognizable insects; others could not. Two children, Elsa and Michael, actively participated in this activity. At one point, Elsa watched Michael paint. Michael was covering an area in green paint. Elsa told him she thought green was a good choice because it looked like grass.
- They were able to use something they created to continue with the activity. The children matched the insects to the outlines they had created.
- They saw that their creations were valued. Children gain pride in their achievements when their work is appropriately displayed. When the families came to pick up their children, they asked about what had been created. Elsa promptly described all the parts she had created. Keegan just looked over to the display and smiled.
- They helped in the set-up of the activity. When children have opportunities to help organize their learning environment, they tend to take a greater interest in the activity.

Displays can also be used to continue expanding children's learning. At three years of age, Jordan was communicating using gestures and some single words. He had been one of the children very interested in creating the mural. Anita, one of his teachers, noticed his interest in the mural. She started to talk to him about some of the things she saw. Jordan and Anita took turns pointing out some of the insects in the mural and some of the plastic ones and naming them. Anita was thrilled when Jordan pointed to the snail and said "red snail."

D) SEPARATION OF LEARNING SPACES Spaces need to be separated according to their uses. Table 1.3 identifies some of the criteria that need be considered.

TABLE 1.3   **CRITERIA FOR SEPARATION OF SPACES (FIGURES 1.2 AND 1.3)**

Criteria	Description
Safety	• Areas such as carpentry should be situated away from the flow of traffic to avoid accidents while using tools (Figure 1.2, Area F). • Accidental collisions on playground equipment can be prevented by separating swings and the bottom of slides from major traffic areas (Figure 1.3, Areas B and C). • Kitchen and eating areas should be located away from washroom areas (Figure 1.2). • Sand needs to be confined to a corner to limit spilling (Figure 1.2, Area D).
The need to be alone	• Area should be protected from intrusion so that children can be alone by choice (Figure 1.2, Area I). • Use a sign to protect areas from intrusion, such as a "Do not disturb" or a stop sign.
Messy areas	• Messy areas such as sand, water and creative area should be on a tiled floor and near the water source to facilitate clean-up.

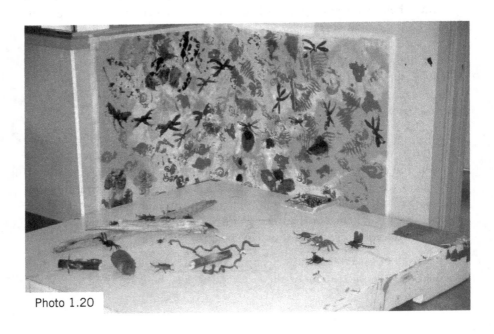

Photo 1.20

E) SPECIALIZED AREAS Specialized areas are set up to meet the changing needs of children. Some examples of this type of area might include:

- Expanded sensory activities—These areas are often set up to provide soothing alternatives to children who at times may be experiencing stressful situations, may find it difficult to control their behaviour or may need to practise skills in other, less threatening ways. Some examples of extended sensory activities include:
  - Flour or coloured sand on different coloured surfaces to trace, draw or manipulate
  - Finger painting with different textures
  - Playdough or clay to pound or mould
  - Dry materials such as sand, beans, peas or rice to manipulate, fill and empty or pour
  - Water to pour, fill and empty or create bubbles

- Dramatic areas that encourage children to express their feelings in safe, non-threatening ways—The dramatic area often provides a safe outlet to express feelings that may otherwise not be expressed. Some examples of extended dramatic activities include:
  - Dress-up
  - Puppet play, with hand or finger puppets
  - Play with dolls and stuffed toys

- Areas that follow the special interests of children—Any program for children should be based on the observations of children's interests, strengths and needs. The learning experiences emerge from these observations. This is called an emergent curriculum. Simply defined, it means that the adult bases his or her interactions on the child: The child takes the lead. A good example of this approach is shown in Photo 1.20. The teacher followed the children's lead by:
  - Realizing that the children wanted to complete their art activities and so encouraged them to continue the activities outside.
  - Encouraging children to bring unfinished activities outside to complete.
  - Providing appropriate space outside (in the shade, protected from traffic flow).
  - Ensuring that the activity was accessible to all the children.

F) STORAGE OF CHILDREN'S LEARNING MATERIALS Children need to be able to make choices and solve their own problems. Appropriate storage is a key factor in children's ability to be involved in active play. Table 1.4 identifies aspects of storage that should be considered.

G) DEVELOPMENTALLY APPROPRIATE AND AGE-APPROPRIATE PRACTICES "Developmentally appropriate practice is based on knowledge about how children develop and learn. As Katz states, 'In a developmental approach to curriculum design, . . . [decisions] about what should be learned and how it would best be learned depend on what we know of the learner's developmental status and our understanding of the relationships between early experience and subsequent development' (1995, 109). To guide their decisions about practice, all early childhood teachers need to understand the developmental changes that typically occur in the years from birth

TABLE 1.4   **ASPECTS OF STORAGE THAT ENCOURAGE ACTIVE PLAY**

Storage Aspect	Importance
Organization by type	• When materials are organized by type, children learn to make connections about how things fit together. These connections are part of the real world. Language, math and science are categorized into groupings and sub-groupings (classification). • Materials organized by type also encourage children to find the specific items that they need to encourage their specific learning activity.
Predictability	• Children should be able to make the connection between what the materials are and where they are found. For example, materials generally are stored in the area that makes it easy for children to find the required items. Plastic pails and shovels are stored in the sand area and blocks in the block area. • However, some materials can be used in more than one area. This means that the same materials should either be stored in two areas, or in close proximity to each other. For example, large trucks are suitable for sand or block play. If these are stored close to both areas, they can be used as needed in either area (Figure 1.2, Item 6). These vehicles are parked in a parking-lot configuration. This further enhances the predictability of the storage of materials. Children can identify vehicle parking.
Clear labelling	• Materials should be labelled by word or sign, and picture or outline. This clearly identifies what is to be found in the storage container and where it needs to be returned to when the child is finished using it. It also encourages the child to start to make the connections between symbols and written words.
Appropriately-sized, clear containers	• Too many items in a container will cause the child to dump out all materials to find what is wanted. This often leaves a mess. It also distracts the child from his or her play, as clean-up is usually required. • Predictable containers should be used. For example, if children are involved in sorting activities, one might store all the same-sized bears of different colours in one container. If children are interested in

TABLE 1.4 **CONTINUED**

	creating patterns, these bears should be stored in containers that contain bears of the same size and colour, such as a container of red bears or blue bears of the same size. • Baskets or caddies allow a collection of materials to be moved to other areas.
Consistency	• Children need to know where to find the materials and what system of organization is used. Frequent changes in where to find materials or how they are stored causes confusion and disrupts the long-term learning experiences of children. For example, Danny had been interested in playing with the large dinosaurs in both the block and sand area. They had been stored between the two areas in clear bins. The staff decided to change the bins and store vehicles there, instead. Danny looked for the dinosaurs in the regular spot. When he did not find them, he wandered aimlessly around the room. When asked what he wanted to do, he signed, "dinosaurs." He was told that the dinosaurs were put away, and it was time to play with the cars. Danny finally went to the book area and looked at some books about dinosaurs.
Accessibility	• Low, open shelves should be used to facilitate accessibility of materials. • Containers should be light enough to carry or move. • Small shelves on wheels can be easily moved from area to area. • Baskets or caddies allow collection of materials to be moved to other areas. • Materials should be stored logically within the specific learning area.

Storage separate from play area	• Toys should be stored separately from the play area. When toys are stored within the play area, such as the sand toys in the sandbox, the area becomes cluttered. The result could be any of the following:
	
	   • The toys take up so much space that there is no room to be creative.
	
	   • Toys get broken.

TABLE 1.4 CONTINUED

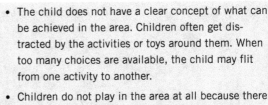

- The child does not have a clear concept of what can be achieved in the area. Children often get distracted by the activities or toys around them. When too many choices are available, the child may flit from one activity to another.
- Children do not play in the area at all because there is not enough space and there is no clear concept of what might be accomplished there.
- Children may get the clearly inappropriate message that it is all right to leave a mess.

through age 8 and beyond, variations in development that may occur, and how best to support children's learning and development during these years." (National Association for the Education of Young, 2006).

Age-appropriate practices ensure that the decisions made about program practices are appropriate for the chronological age of the child, irrespective of his or her developmental level. A four-year-old with a developmental delay of two years should be playing with toys that are appropriate for a four-year-old but with the appropriate developmental skill level. For example, this child should use a regular-rhythm instrument during music and movement times instead of a toddler or infant rattle.

All inclusive learning environments should be organized to reflect developmentally appropriate and age-appropriate practices. Both developmentally and age-appropriate practices are guided by the following principles:

- Knowledge of child development guides the application of all practices—This knowledge helps early childhood educators be sensitive to typical variations in child behaviours.
- Interaction of all domains: physical, social, emotional, language and cognitive—"Development in one domain influences and is influenced by development in other domains" (Gestwicki, 2007:8). Caregivers must recognize the need to provide experiences to the whole child rather than trying to remediate only certain skills.
- Varied approaches to facilitate learning for all individuals—Strategies that work for one child may have to be adapted to the needs of a second child. For example, Jeremy identifies items verbally, in sentence structure with many descriptive words. In contrast, Dillon uses a combination of single words and sign language.
- Observation of children—"Observation is the cornerstone of effective teaching. Teachers and child care providers usually base intervention and curriculum planning decisions on careful observation of children's developmental needs." (Trawick-Smith, 2003:8) For example, had the staff observed Danny's interest in dinosaurs, they would have used his interest to continue to provide and enhance his skills through dinosaur play.
- An emergent curriculum—Structure is provided in the organization of the learning environment and planning of that environment based on the observed strengths and needs of the children. See the example of insect activity on page 25.

- Partnerships—Teachers and other professionals, families and children are active partners in providing learning experiences for children. When individuals collaborate toward a common goal, children benefit from a consistent approach at school, at home and (if needed) during therapy.
- Inclusiveness—All children actively participate in all learning activities.

In summary, inclusive, developmentally and age-appropriate learning environments and practices focus on how each child learns, bearing in mind that each child is the best judge of what he or she needs to learn at a given time. "Effective early childhood instructional practices emphasize child-initiated, child-directed play activities, based on the assumption that young children are intrinsically motivated to learn by their desire to understand their environment" (Udell et al., 2001; Freiberg, 2001).

H) RESPECT FOR DIVERSITY All children have unique and diverse needs. "Diverse needs" refers to "variations in the needs or play and the learning styles of children of various cultural groups. For example, children of different cultures will have unique ways of learning or interacting with others, and in no group of students will all individuals be alike" (Trawick-Smith, 2003:11). Respecting diversity includes:

- Creating an atmosphere that encourages children to feel good about themselves and their identity
- Organizing the learning environment to respect the diversity of the children in the program and within the setting of the program by providing experiences, materials and displays that represent diversity
- Incorporating special social or cultural events within the learning environment
- Incorporating anti-bias materials in all learning activities within the playrooms, such as various markers or crayons to represent skin tones of different ethnic groups, and pictures and toys of individuals with handicaps
- Establishing an environment of mutual respect for all individuals: children, families, staff and other professionals
- Modelling behaviours that foster understanding and respect for diversity
- Providing a flexible program that meets the needs of all children and their families

I) APPROPRIATE ROUTINES Routines should centre on the basic needs and safety of children. Routines should be:

- Flexible about individual differences—For example, children should go to the bathroom as needed, and not as a timetabled event.
- Consistent—Children need to learn that there are things that occur on a regular schedule. Consistent routines include washing hands after toilet visits, messy play or meal times; cleaning up toys when one is finished with an activity; and putting scraps in the garbage.
- Regular—Children also need to have certain activities occur on a regular basis. This helps the child learn to know what to expect. For example, creating a timetable that includes flexibility, consistency and regularity helps children predict and sequence their activities during the day.

FIGURE 1.4
Example of a Timetable in an Inclusive Setting

Time	Activity	Description
7:00–8:00	Arrival	• Greeting of children and family members
		• Family members help children remove outdoor clothes and settle in for free play activities
		• Family members discuss pertinent information about the children's activities at home, how the children are feeling and any additional information
		• Family members sign children in and fill in information forms as needed
		• Family members tell children that they are leaving
	Snack	• Breakfast snacks are left out for children who have not had breakfast
	Free Play	• Active play within environment
9:00–11:30	Group Music	• Group music and movement activity
	Washroom	• Washroom routines and getting dressed to go outside
	Outdoor play	• Free play activities
11:30–12:30	Lunch time	• Washroom routines before and after lunch
		• Children set table for lunch
		• Lunch
		• Preparation for sleep time: story time, set-up
12:30–2:30	Sleep time	• Activities for non-sleepers
2:30–3:00	Washroom/Snack	• Quiet activities for non-sleepers and early risers
3:00–4:30	Indoor activities	• Transition to go outside
4:30–5:30	Outdoor play and free play activities	• Outdoor group physical activity, free play
5:00–5:30	Dismissal	• Family members pick up children
		• Staff member discusses child's day with family members
		• Family members sign out child, read over comments about child's day

J) APPROPRIATE SCHEDULING The schedule for children within an inclusive program should be flexible, consistent and regular. An example of a timetable is presented in Figure 1.4.

K) ADAPTATIONS AND ACCOMMODATIONS All learning environments for children will need to be adapted at times to accommodate the child with special needs.

Accommodations may have to be made to include strategies for changes or adaptations to the environment and program in order to meet specific needs. These needs could be categorized as follows:

- Communication—Verbal, symbolic, body language such as gestures or signing, and formal devices such as the use of symbol boards

- Physical—Adapting physical space to accommodate children using wheelchairs or walkers; providing specialized equipment to aid activities such as drawing and eating; and adding adaptive devices to help individuals become more independent, such as door switches and light switches at child's level
- Cognitive—Developmentally and age-appropriate materials and equipment to encourage active participation
- Social—Strategies for active play with opportunities to engage in solitary and group play
- Emotional—Establishing a climate that is respectful and encourages recognition of the strengths and needs of all children

Collaborative Partnerships

One of the most critical factors in any inclusive setting is the need to collaborate with the many individuals who are involved with children, especially children with special needs. This team of individuals should always include children, parents, family members, early childhood educators, resource consultants and child support workers, to share expertise and knowledge about the child. Other professionals may join the team at other times, depending on the needs of the child. These professionals could include medical professionals, and specialists such as speech and language therapists or physical therapists, psychologists or child support workers.

The collaborative approach ensures that the unique needs of each individual are supported in the context of that child's family and community (see Figure 1.5).

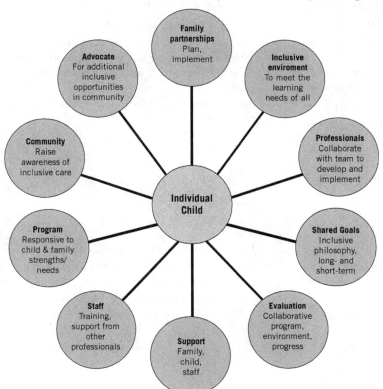

FIGURE 1.5

Collaborative Approach

SUMMARY

Inclusive care is more than a philosophy. It is the right of every child. Research has clearly identified the benefits of inclusive care (Schweinhart & Weikart, 1986). These benefits include:

- Educational benefits
- Social benefits for all individuals
- Cost savings
- Societal benefits (McCarthy, 2001)

Concern about the benefits of including children with special needs also has been expressed regarding:

- The lack of resources to cope with children with high needs
- The lack of training of early childhood educators to cope with inclusive practices
- The fear that the disabling condition might be so severe as to negate the benefit of inclusion

Most jurisdictions within Canada offer support to children and families with special needs. However, in most instances this support is only provided if the child has been diagnosed with a special need. This means that children very early in life are identified and subsequently labelled. Some of the conditions with which children are commonly labelled today include attention deficit, autism and cerebral palsy.

Often the condition becomes more important than the child. For example, the child is treated as a child with cerebral palsy. Justin, a six-year-old with cerebral palsy, was enrolled in the Boy Scout Cub program. He was using a walker and a wheelchair to navigate. The Cubs planned a weekend winter camping trip at a regional educational outdoor facility. When the parents of Justin were approached, they were surprised to hear that Justin was to be included. The father volunteered to participate in the activities. Justin was very excited. He had attended the outdoor facility with his grade one class. He had heard about the outhouse that a porcupine had chewed a hole into. He had not seen the outhouse because he had been left behind with his teacher assistant in the outdoor class-room while the rest of the children explored the outdoor spaces.

Justin's father fitted his walker with skis. A group of children and one adult walked to the outhouse. A tobog-gan was taken in case Justin needed to rest. It took Justin and the children an hour to get to the outhouse. He walked the whole way by himself. He agreed to let the children take turns pulling him back on the toboggan. The whole Cub pack rejoiced and celebrated Justin's efforts.

This example clearly illustrates that:

- Some individuals limit children's efforts by their perception of what a child can do.
- Children can achieve their own goals if permitted.
- Adaptations in time and equipment may need to be made.
- All children benefit from and enjoy the success of an individual's achievement.

KEY POINTS

Children's right to play

- Through active play, children gain skills in commu-nication and all developmental domains, learn to solve problems, make decisions, build on what they already know and gain self-confidence
- Active play is supported by the UN Convention on the Rights of the Child

Bias

- Bias influences how we use all of our senses
- Bias results from lack of knowledge, experience, our perceptions of an individual, our belief sys-tems, cultural influences, roles, family dynamics, health status and socioeconomic status

Anti-bias

- Anti-bias means taking a stand against the unjust treatment of individuals
- The anti-biased approach includes reflective practices, active listening, appropriate self-care practices, creating an environment of mutual respect and creating an inclusive environment

Inclusive environments

- Creating inclusive environments requires knowledge of individual differences
- Learning spaces must be organized according to many principles: accessibility, traffic flow, display spaces, safety aspects, separation of learning spaces, need for areas of specialization, children's storage, developmentally and age-appropriate practices, respect for diversity, routines, scheduling and adaptations and accommodations

Collaborative partnerships

- The team of individuals should include all children, families, staff, resource consultants, child support workers and, depending on the child's need, medical professionals, specialists, therapists and psychologists

EXERCISES

1. The UN Convention on the Rights of the Child identifies the critical role of play in every child's life. Reflect on children's right to play as presented at the beginning of the chapter. How does Reflection affect your philosophical viewpoint? Do you see this right to play equally applied to all children within day care settings? Explain why or why not.

2. Look over the list of possible causes of bias.
   a) Identify which ones could apply to you.
   b) What strategies could you employ to mitigate the bias identified?

3. Observe a group of children within a preschool environment engaging in fine-motor tasks. What similarities and differences do you observe in the group of children? How might you account for these similarities and differences?

4. Visit a preschool setting. Draw floor plans of the indoor and outdoor environments. Using the criteria for organizing the environment identified on pages 17–33, pinpoint what changes should be made to both floor plans to accept children with a variety of special needs—physical, social, cognitive and emotional.

5. Using Figure 1.5 on page 33, identify the individuals within your community that should become part of the partnership. For each individual, explain his or her role.

REFERENCES

Allen, K., Paasche, C., Langford, R., & Nolan, K. (2007). *Inclusion in Early Childhood Programs: Children with Exceptionalities.* Fourth Canadian Edition. Toronto: Thomson Nelson.

Child Care Advocacy Association of Canada Fact Sheet. (2004). What Do We Mean By Inclusion. Child Care Advocacy Association of Canada [online]. Available at www.ccaac.ca/pdf/resources/factsheets/inclusion.pdf [11/08/08].

Covell, K. H. B. (2001). *The Challenge of Children's Rights for Canada.* Waterloo, ON: Wilfrid Laurier University Press.

Crowther, I. (2003). *Creating Effective Learning Environments.* Scarborough, ON: Nelson Thomson Learning.

Freiberg, K. E. (2001). Educating Exceptional Children. *Annual Editions.* Thirteenth Edition.

Gestwicki, C. (2007). *Developmentally Appropriate Practices: Curriculum and Development in Early Education.* Third Edition. Clifton Park, NY: Delmar Thomson Learning.

High/Scope Research Foundation (2004). High/Scope Perry Preschool Program. High/Scope Research Foundation [online]. Available at www.highscope.org/Content-.asp?ContentId=1.

Hope Irwin, S., Lero, D., & Brophy, K. (2000). *A Matter of Urgency: Including Children with Special Needs in Child Care in Canada.* Wreck Cove, NS: Breton Books.

IPA World (2004). The International Play Association [online]. Available at www.ipaworld.org.

McCain, M., & Mustard, F. (1999). *Early Years Study Final Report.* Toronto, ON: Publications Ontario.

McCarthy, M. (2001). Inclusion of Children with Disabilities: Seeking the Appropriate Balance. *Annual Editions Educating Children with Special Needs.* Thirteenth Edition, 8–11.

National Association of Young. (2006). Developmentally Appropriate Practice in Early Childhood Programs [online]. Available at www.naeyc.org/about/positions/dap3.asp [06/01/09].

Papalia, D., Wendkos Olds, S., & Duskin Feldman, R. (2001). *Human Development.* Toronto, ON: McGraw Hill.

Saderman Hall, N., & Rhomberg, V. (1995). *The Affective Curriculum: Teaching the Anti-bias Approach to Young Children.* Scarborough, ON: International Thomson Publishing.

Schickedanz, J., Schickedanz, D., Forsyth, P., & Forsyth, G. (2001). *Understanding Children and Adolescents.* Fourth Edition. Needham Heights, MA: Allyn & Bacon.

Schweinhart, L., & Weikart, J. (1986). Lasting Differences: The High Scope Preschool Curriculum Comparison Study Through Age 23. *Early Childhood Education Research Quarterly* 1, 15–45.

SpeciaLink. (2004). The National Centre for Child Care Inclusion [online]. Available at www. specialinkcanada. org/home_en.html [02/06/08].

Trawick-Smith, J. (2003). *Early Childhood Development: A Multicultural Perspective.* Upper Saddle River, NJ: Pearson Education Inc.

Udell, T., Peters, J., & Piaza Templeman, T. (2001). From Philosophy to Practice in Inclusive Early Childhood Programs. *Annual Editions Educating Exceptional Children.* Thirteenth Edition, *2001/2002,* 32–36.

Wilson, L. (2008). *Partnerships.* Toronto, ON: Thomson Nelson.

2 Inclusive Care in Canada

CHAPTER

Chapter Outline

"Children with special needs are often excluded from child care in Canada. Despite the acknowledged role high quality early child care and education has in promoting children's development, most governments in Canada have failed to fully capitalize on the opportunities to use child care programs as a developmental resource for children with special needs. Moreover, exclusion of children with special needs from child care often means that their parents cannot participate in paid employment, or receive the kinds of support that could assist them as parents" (Hope Irwin, Lero & Brophy, 2000:xxi).

Learning Outcomes

After studying this chapter, you will be able to:

1. Describe various legislative requirements for children with special needs in Canada.

2. Identify reasons to explain why there is a lack of inclusive care in Canada.

3. Describe an inclusive setting. How is it similar to any quality setting? How is it different?

4. Describe the core elements of a quality inclusive setting.

5. Identify and describe the various program options for families and children with special needs in Canada.

6. Discuss the skills needed by an early childhood educator to provide inclusive care.

Introduction

Care for children with special needs in Canada is often haphazard and inconsistent (see Table 2.1). Many jurisdictions lack appropriate guidelines, policies or proactive legislation that addresses the inclusion of children with special needs. This often means that children may be prohibited from attending regular programs. Without appropriate guidelines, adequate resources are hard to obtain. When programs have been adequately resourced, the result has been a positive experience for all involved: children, families and staff (Hope Irwin et al., 2000:xiv). Adequate resources include staff training, additional support staff as needed, structural modifications of the physical environment and time to work in collaboration with all families and other professionals.

Additionally, one of the components of high-quality care is the amount of education and training early childhood educators receive (Mayer, 1994; Doherty-Derkowski, 1994; Goelman, Doherty, Lero, LaGrange & Tougas, 2000). It is most disconcerting to note that in most jurisdictions in Canada, there are no additional training requirements for the staff in inclusive centres (see Table 2.1). With adequate training, the child care professional is in a much better position to understand and apply that understanding to:

- Organizing inclusive environments that meet a variety of developmental levels and ages
- Providing learning activities that challenge a variety of developmental levels and ages
- Adapting and modifying the environment, materials and learning experiences to reflect the needs of all the children
- Developing skills in collaborating with families and other professionals
- Establishing partnerships to enhance the opportunities for children with special needs within their neighbourhood communities

It is difficult to get an accurate picture of what services for children with special needs are available on a national level. Statistics are available, however, for the percentage of children with special needs requiring services across Canada. These percentages are as follows:

- 1.6% of children under the age of 4
- 3.7% of children aged 5 to 9
- 4.2% of children aged 10 to 14 (Government of Canada, 2002)

"The rate of disability among younger children in Canada is lower than it is for adults. This is partly because some disabilities in children have not yet been detected and also because the majority of disabilities are acquired after childhood" (Government of Canada, 2002:1).

Information about how many children are diagnosed with special needs and how many children are in inclusive care in a specific jurisdiction is not readily available. However, this information can be gleaned from some representational studies: *You Bet I Care!* (Goelman et al., 2000) and *A Matter of Urgency* (Hope Irwin et al., 2000). These representational studies were conducted on a sampling of day care centres

TABLE 2.1 **LEGISLATIVE REQUIREMENTS IN CANADA**

Jurisdiction	Training of Staff	Description
Alberta	Not required	• Inclusive Child Care Program of Alberta provides for inclusive care • Funding depends on the needs of the child and the type of services needed • Funding may differ per region, and may or may not be available to child care facilities and for specialist consultation
British Columbia	Basic ECE training; special needs training	• Supported Child Development (SCD) Agency provides information and services for developmental delays, disabilities in physical, cognitive, communication or social/emotional and behavioural areas • Supported child care agencies provided with consultant services and support workers • Special needs supplement provided by the Ministry of Children and Family Development
Manitoba	Consultation provided by Children's Special Services; no special training required for staff	• Integration of children into child care settings • Support paid to the child care facility and additional support provided if children are diagnosed with physical, cognitive or developmental delays • Children with behavioural disabilities and who are medically fragile supported by Child Day Care Organization • Grants available for renovations, equipment, materials, staff training and professional service • Children placed by Children's Special Services
New Brunswick	No special training required for staff	• Children identified as special needs if there has been a confirmed diagnosis at birth or developmental issues after birth, or if there are family risk factors • Children with special needs placed in Integrated Day Care Centres • Integrated Day Care Centres supported by funding for child with special needs and for support workers
Newfoundland	No special training required for staff	• No written policy established • Provision for children with special needs in one regulated centre exclusive to children with special needs • Centre funded by Health and Community Services • If eligible, welfare allowance paid to parents to hire support worker
Northwest Territories	No early childhood training requirements	• No segregated child care programs • Extra support to child care providers • Additional support available if eligible, based on financial needs assessment and medical referral
Nova Scotia	No special requirements	• Funding support for inclusive care • Funding eligibility based on evidence of special needs • Centres have designated number of spaces for children with special needs • Additional spaces dependent on grant availability

TABLE 2.1 **CONTINUED**

Jurisdiction	Training of Staff	Description
Nunavut	No early childhood training requirements	• No segregated child care programs • Support provided to child care centres through daily operating grants • Size of operating grant dependent on age of child and area centre is located in; preschool child with identified special need receives 50% increased funding • Health and Children's Initiatives provide funding for adaptive equipment or support worker • Parents eligible for fee subsidy after financial needs assessment and medical referral
Ontario	Resource consultants require ECE diploma and post-secondary program in working with children with special needs; no additional training requirements for child care staff	• No written policy established • Support provided for integration and inclusion • Resource teachers work for agencies and provide services to children in child care settings • Support offered for staffing equipment, supplies and services to child care centres • Level of service depends on identified need and local service model
Prince Edward Island	No additional training requirements for child care staff	• No segregated child care programs • Grants provided to centres based on training and experience of staff to be hired • Documentation such as social need required for additional grants • Funding covers additional staff to lower staff ratio
Quebec	No special requirements	• Policy in place to encourage inclusion • One-time grant available with a diagnosed need approved by ministry
Saskatchewan	No special requirements	• Three types of grants are available: individual inclusion grants to licensed centres and family homes to include children with a delay or risk of a delay; a referral is needed, but not diagnosis; minimum of 20 hours of attendance required enhanced accessibility grant to help cover the cost of including children; child must be diagnosed and require significant support, and parents must be employed training and resource grants per child as well as adaptive equipment grants • Inclusion grants are approved for one year, whereas accessibility grants are approved for six months

TABLE 2.1 CONTINUED		
Jurisdiction	**Training of Staff**	**Description**
The Yukon	No special requirements	• Regulation specifies mainstreaming • Special needs are designated through assessment of the child by child care professionals • Plans must be developed through consultation with families, staff and other professionals • No segregated child care programs are available • Whitehorse Child Development Centre provides intervention programming resources and supports across the Yukon and operates as an outreach mobile unit • Funding is provided dependent on the special need and may include adaptive equipment, transportation, programming support or additional staffing • Fee subsidies for children with special needs available

Adapted from Friendly, Beach & Turiano, 2002

in pre-selected regions, not all day care centres in all regions. The outcomes were then generalized to be representative of Canada. The studies identify the following statistical information:

• Centres that did not have any children with special needs enrolled ranged from a low of 18.7% (Manitoba) to a high of 50% (Newfoundland and Labrador).
• The number of centres with at least three children with special needs enrolled was highest in Manitoba: 45.9% (Hope Irwin et al., 2000).

This statistical information is significant. It means that less than half of the children in Canada have access to inclusive care. One of the problems with a representational study is that the results can reflect either over-or under-representation. If it is true that even more children with special needs are denied access to inclusive care, then the problem is even more dismal than reported. It is critical to obtain more specific provincial and territorial information about:

• The number of children diagnosed
• The number of children considered eligible to receive additional supports and funding for special needs
• The type of services provided
• The number of children receiving support and funding

According to the most recent study on child care in Canada (Friendly and Beach, 2004) specific statistics of children with special needs have been identified in provinces and territories across Canada. These statistics (see Table 2.2) give a more detailed picture of special needs.

TABLE 2.2 **CHILDREN WITH SPECIAL NEEDS IN CANADA, BY PROVINCE**

Jurisdiction	Age of Children			
	0–4	5–9	10–14	Total
Alberta	1.8%	4.5%	5.1%	3.9%
British Columbia	2.0%	3.9%	4.7%	3.6%
Manitoba	1.9%	4.3%	4.8%	3.8%
New Brunswick	1.3%	4.1%	4.4%	3.4%
Newfoundland	1.5%	3.9%	4.1%	3.3%
Northwest Territories	Information not available			
Nova Scotia	1.3%	4.3%	5.3%	3.8%
Nunavut	Information not available			
Ontario	1.6%	4.0%	4.8%	3.5%
Prince Edward Island	2.3%	4.0%	4.1%	3.5%
Quebec	1.3%	2.5%	2.4%	2.1%
Saskatchewan	1.7%	3.2%	4.3%	3.2%
The Yukon	Children using technical aid: 78 Children with speech difficulties: 91 Children with developmental handicaps: 35			

There are a number of reasons for the seeming lack of inclusiveness in child care centres across Canada. Some of these reasons stem from:

- Legislation and policy that make it illegal to exclude children with special needs are lacking. As a result, individual child care facilities can choose whether to include or exclude children with special needs (Hope Irwin et al., 2000:xiii).

Additionally, some of the reasons for non-acceptance of children with special needs were expressed by individual child care centres. These reasons included:

- Insufficient and inconsistent funds to provide services to children with special needs
- Continual cutbacks in funding for child care in general
- Lack of appropriate resources
- Existing facility not accessible without modification to the physical structure
- Staff lack training to offer inclusive programs
- Lack of clear governmental directives
- Lack of availability of child care spaces in individual centres (Friendly, 2008; Childcare Research and Research Unit, 2008; OECD, 2006)

Reflection

From the Author   Reflection

As I have travelled extensively across Canada from one coast to another, from the isolated communities of the north to the large urban centres of the south, I have seen many encouraging sights. I have visited many child care centres across Canada and talked to many individuals responsible for the provincial or territorial legislation of child care. I have observed and photographed a total of 52 centres, of which 40 had children with special needs enrolled. The support to centres that I observed ranged from exceptional to minimal. I saw the following elements of quality:

- Many jurisdictions had developed written policies, training requirements and resource allocations for the inclusion of children with special needs.
- Many child care centres across Canada included children with special needs, even when adequate funding was not available.
- Many centres had a long history of including children with special needs. I visited one centre that had been in operation for 30 years and had always had a policy to accept children with special needs.
- Twenty-one of the centres observed were adequately resourced to provide appropriate care for children with special needs.
- Strong leadership has emerged to move toward more inclusive care (Hope Irwin, 2004; Voices 4 Children, 2003; Friendly, Beach & Turiano, 2002).

Despite the somewhat gloomy picture presented nationally, there are many encouraging signs in all jurisdictions. "A large majority of front-line child care centre staff and centre directors in our sample believe that children with special needs should have the right to attend child care programs, and that legislation should be passed to prevent their exclusion. 89.5% feel that most child care centres would be willing to include children with special needs if adequate resources were in place to support their efforts." (Hope Irwin et al., 2000:xv) There are many centres across Canada that have, and continue to accept, children with special needs, despite the lack of adequate funding or resources. "In our opinion, it is a credit to this workforce that they have reached the level of commitment despite the lack of clear policy directives from the governments and in the face of insufficient funding, inadequate staffing and resources, and the general lack of support for inclusive care" (Hope Irwin et al., 2000:xv).

Challenges of Inclusive Practices

Including children with special needs may provide additional challenges. These challenges may be grouped into two types: those that are relatively easy to overcome and those that require more in-depth consideration.

Some of the challenges of working in an inclusive setting may require extra time and effort but can be more readily overcome:

- Attitudes toward children with special needs—Some staff or families may be reluctant to include children with special needs because they do not understand the value of including these children. This requires a change of attitude. Changes of attitude do not occur overnight, but they do occur when individuals are given information (workshops, research findings, readings) that clearly identifies the value of inclusion. Additionally, when all individuals are given opportunities to observe the effectiveness of the process and see the value to all children involved, attitudes change. This can be done through including families as partners and documenting learning experiences of the children that show the value of inclusion.
- Time—There is a perception that children with special needs will require more one-on-one attention. However, if the environment is structured in ways that encourage active play for all children, this time can be significantly reduced. Some children with special needs will need more one-on-one intervention. This intervention is generally needed for children with more severe disabilities who lack the ability to fend for themselves and therefore need someone to help them. These children can usually receive additional help. In most jurisdictions the possibility of an additional support worker is possible.
- Specific needs—Often staff members feel that they do not know enough about a child with special needs. What needs to be remembered is that a child is a child first. All children have special needs. Knowledge of child development and observation will help to structure the learning activities to be inclusive of all children.
- Structural obstacles—Often, structural changes may need to be made to the existing environment to make it more accessible. One-time funding opportunities are available to meet these needs.

Other challenges are more difficult to overcome:

- Lack of funding—This may lead to an inability to purchase the specialized equipment or materials needed. Available funding may not provide for hiring individuals who have the additional training to support children with special needs. Since funding is provincial or territorial, stronger advocacy is needed to change funding requirements. Many centres are involved in fundraising and rely on volunteer workers to help overcome this challenge.
- Lack of specific education—One of the quality indicators of inclusive early childhood settings is adequate education. Individuals with education on inclusive care will be much more confident in their abilities and bring greater understanding to their work with the children and families. Although some information can be gained by independent research, there needs to be greater advocacy to encourage adequate education requirements for all early childhood educators.

Reflection

> *From a Staff Member*   **Reflection**
>
> I can still remember the first child with special needs who we had in our program. I remember how apprehensive I was. I did not recognize that I had any special abilities or knowledge of how to interact with this child. I also wondered how I was going to interact with the family.
>
> At first, it did seem to be more time consuming and a lot more work. However, I gradually began to realize that much of the time and effort that I was putting in was really due to my own fears. For example, I always wanted to protect him from falling when he was on the climber. I never worried about the other children in the same way. As I became more relaxed, I also realized that this child played along with the other children effectively as long as the materials and activities supported his skills and ability level.
>
> I have learned so much and am so grateful for this first opportunity. I don't think that I could ever work in settings that do not include children with special needs. We all gain: children, staff, families and society as a whole.

Types of Programs for Children with Special Needs

1. Inclusive Programs

"Leigha, the five-year-old daughter of one of the authors, recently asked, 'Mom, will Kaelies always have possibilities?' Since she was just a year old, Leigha has attended a child-care program that actively includes children with disabilities, and she was trying to understand her friend Kaelies's disabilities. While she confused 'possibilities' and 'disabilities,' Leigha innocently identified the main reason for creating inclusive early education programs: to create normalized expectations for children with disabilities among the nondisabled" (Hanline & Daley, 2004:42).

Teaching children in an inclusive setting is not as difficult as it seems. It requires that the early childhood educator look at best practices for teaching young children and the principles of setting up an inclusive environment (see pages 17–33). Best practices involve setting up a program for young children that:

- Emerges based on the observed interests, strengths and needs of the children
- Is supported by learning through active play
- Encourages children to become active partners in constructing their own learning
- Is supported by trained, sensitive and caring adults
- Is developed in collaborative partnerships among children, families, early childhood educators and other professionals

What does an inclusive setting look like? The basic premise of inclusive environments is that the majority of children progress through the same developmental stages irrespective of disability (Hanline et al., 2004). Early childhood education programs already provide a wide range of learning experiences for young children. Children in any grouping are unique individuals with a range of abilities and skills. For example, in a typical toddler setting in Ontario, one might expect to find children aged 18 to 30 months. The difference in skills and abilities between the 18-month-old and the 30-month-old toddler will be quite pronounced. The materials in the environment will reflect these differences. For example, in one toddler group the range of abilities for cutting skills ranged from toddlers who had never cut with scissors to toddlers who could cut a piece of paper in half. Consequently, two types of scissors were available: first scissors (spring-loaded scissors that are squeezed to cut) and safety scissors (child-sized scissors with blunt ends). Additionally, close supervision was provided when the toddlers were cutting to reinforce appropriate cutting habits such as keeping scissors on the table and redirecting a toddler to cutting when the scissors were put into his or her mouth.

The adaptations for most children with special needs are readily made. The child care provider must carefully identify the skills and abilities of the child to provide the expanded range of materials and activities needed. Children with special needs have the right to actively participate in the same core learning experiences found in all quality early childhood settings. In fact, the casual observer often cannot point out the children with special needs in an inclusive setting. Children who are actively engaged in a variety of learning experiences are hard to distinguish from each other.

Harms, Clifford and Cryer have developed three inclusive rating scales—infants and toddlers, preschool children and school-aged children—that identify the core learning areas within quality early childhood settings. Children with special needs are included in all three scales. These scales identify core requirements for any quality early childhood setting. Core elements that are evaluated include space and furnishings, personal care and routines, language and reasoning, learning activities, interactions, program structure, and parents and staff.

A) SPACE AND FURNISHINGS In any environment, there are critical factors to ensure the children's comfort and safety. The elements that need to be considered include:

• Lighting—How much natural light is required? Although many of the jurisdictions in Canada recognize the need for natural lighting, many of them do not have formal guidelines. According to the Illuminating Engineering Society, windows should make up at least 20 percent of wall space (Hawkins & Lilley, 1992).

What learning activities require natural light? Reading and writing should be placed near natural light. If possible, activities that involve the use of colour, such as drawing and painting, should also be conducted in natural light, where the colours are more natural.

There is mounting research that links hyperactivity, decreased productivity and poor health to the use of standard fluorescent lighting (Liberman, 1991; Hathaway, 1994; Crowther, 2007). Substituting full-spectrum fluorescent lighting with ultraviolet enhancement (the type of lighting closest to natural sunlight) has been shown to increase growth, development and student productivity, and to decrease absenteeism and depression due to seasonal affective disorder (SAD).

Children with visual impairments have a higher need for adequate lighting. For these children, extra lighting may be needed for darker areas of the room. Colour coding could be used to attract attention to specific learning areas.

- Colour—Colour has also been shown to produce certain behavioural responses. Colour can be used to soothe and calm or to stimulate and excite. Colours like red, orange and yellow are used to stimulate and excite, whereas colours like blue or green can relax, comfort and soothe individuals. "Light is required for our cells to function normally, and individual colours affect them by causing changes in growth and behavior. It therefore affects our system at a cellular level, and the vibrational patterns giving us life, holding us together" (Chiazzari, 1998:16).

- Noise—Children engaged in active play make a lot of noise through their interactions with each other and the materials within the learning environment. The early childhood educator needs to find the balance between encouraging the natural enthusiasm of children and protecting the children from too much disruptive noise. For example, Jordan, a three-year-old, had been carrying the unit blocks over to the manipulative area. He dropped the blocks by accident as he was walking over the tiled floor. He immediately sat down on the tiled floor and started to stack his blocks to a certain height. He then knocked them down and clapped his hands in delight at the sound it made. Other children, who had been playing in other areas, quickly ran over to see what Jordan was doing. The noise level disrupted the children's attention, causing them to stop the activities they had been engaged in. This example clearly shows how children's attention can easily be refocused by a change in noise level. Continued exposure to high levels of noise can become disruptive to children's concentration and play activities.

Noise levels can be minimized by using some simple techniques:

- ○ Sound buffers—Materials such as carpets, upholstered furniture, padded dividers, acoustic tiles, grassy areas and hedges can absorb and minimize noise.
- ○ Protective surfaces in noisy areas—The block area should be carpeted to reduce the noise of falling blocks. Carpentry tables can be covered with a firm foam surface to decrease the noise of hammering.
- ○ Quiet areas—Separating the noisier aspects of a room, such as the block area, from the reading area helps children to monitor their own need to find a quieter space. Placement of large pillows or cushions in the area can further reduce noise levels (see Figure 1.2, page 21).

- ○ Music—Music can be used to calm and soothe children. "[M]usic has proven to reliably alter young children's moods in the classroom. Helping them overcome anxiety and stress, calming them so that they can focus on a task, and enlivening their bodies sufficiently to maintain alertness, music works its magic whether or not the children consciously pay attention to it" (Campbell, 2000:165).

Noise levels become particularly stressful for some children. Children who are sensitive to loud noises, children who are easily distracted (such as those with attention or hyperactivity disorders) and children who find it harder to concentrate will find noisy environments particularly difficult to deal with.

- Indoor and Outdoor Floor Space—All children need learning areas that can be negotiated freely. Children with special needs may have physical mobility problems, such as lack of coordination in their movements; may require assistive devices to move about, such as walkers or wheelchairs; or may need the security of having stable learning spaces. The learning area should be organized to maximize all children's active exploration.
- Ventilation—Appropriate ventilation is important. It refreshes the air within the room. Stale air leads to lethargic behaviour. If possible, a good air filter attached to the furnace will also help to eliminate some contaminants in the air to reduce the effects of conditions such as asthma.
- Temperature—The room temperature needs to be comfortable for active exploration and play. The suggested temperature is around 20 degrees Celsius. This is especially important for young children who are less active. These children have less ability to regulate their body temperature through exercise. One of the leading causes of accidents is exposure to scalding water. Figure 2.1 identifies how quickly children can receive a burn from water that is too hot.
- Overall Repair—The environment should be well maintained to provide for the safety of all children. Floors and walls should be clean and free from debris, clutter and impediments such as raised tiles or carpet edges, as these can cause tripping. This is especially important for children who may have poor coordination or balance because of a special need.

FIGURE 2.1

Water Temperatures That Cause Scalding

Temperature of Water	Time to Cause a Bad Burn
66°C (150°F)	2 seconds
60°C (140°F)	6 seconds
52°C (125°F)	2 minutes
49°C (120°F)	10 minutes

Source: Pediatric Advisor, 2004

- Organization of Learning Areas—Inclusive program spaces need to be organized to include the core learning areas, as identified in Table 2.3, ensuring that they meet these standards:
  - All materials and equipment are accessible for active play for all children, with additional materials available for rotation.
  - Learning areas such as blocks or music are well defined, do not interfere with each other and are easily supervised.
  - Materials are organized to maximize the independence of all children through techniques such as labelling by picture and word and open, sturdy shelves.
  - Enough child-sized furniture is present that features appropriate adaptations for children with special needs.
  - Soft furniture or soft accessories such as pillows, rugs or stuffed toys appear in various parts of the room for relaxation.
  - A space for privacy is protected from intrusion by a sign or non-intrusion rule.
  - Spaces exist for the display of children's work.
  - Indoor and outdoor spaces are available for daily gross motor activity with a variety of gross motor equipment that is suitable for different skill development levels.

B) PERSONAL CARE AND ROUTINES Personal care routines include arrival and departure, meal time, sleep and rest, toilet visits or diapering and health-related practices such as handwashing or toothbrushing. In an inclusive environment, these routines need to be flexible to meet the individual needs of each child. Some of these routines, such as handwashing, meal time and sleep time, should be predictable so that the child learns to associate each part of the routine with the next logical step. For example, when I arrive, I take off my coat and boots, and put them in my cubbies. After I have gone to the toilet, I wash my hands.

C) LANGUAGE AND REASONING Children need to have a variety of books and games for activities using both receptive language (understanding the message that has been communicated through speech, signing or symbols such as written words) and expressive language (expressing one's thoughts or ideas through verbal language, signing or symbols such pictures). These activities should be suitable for a variety of skill levels and interests.

D) LEARNING ACTIVITIES The types of learning activities that should be included in a quality centre are listed in Table 2.3. Children need to have the full range of activities to develop holistically. The learning activities provided should represent a balance of active or quiet play, activities for concentration or relaxation, and group or individual play.

E) INTERACTIONS The environment needs to be set up to encourage appropriate, safe interactions with all individuals and the materials within the learning spaces. Interactions between children and staff should be used to develop children's self-confidence, skills and abilities, foster their interest and enhance their self-esteem. Positive guidance techniques and appropriate social skills should be modelled to encounrage children to learn appropriate patterns of behaviour and to interact positively with each other and adults.

F) PROGRAM STRUCTURE Much of the program structure is dependent on the daily scheduling. The following points should be considered:

- Does the daily schedule provide structure and predictability? Some events, such as meal or sleep time, should occur regularly every day. This gives all children a sense of personal control because they can predict what will occur during certain times of the day. Many children with special needs require these structured times to develop a sense of a regular, predictable sequence. This repetition and regularity help children to anticipate and respond appropriately to regularly occurring events in their daily lives.
- Is the daily schedule flexible enough to meet all children's needs? If a child is hungry at nine o'clock, does he have to wait until ten o'clock, the scheduled snack time? If a child is actively engaged in a positive learning experience, does he or she have to stop to join a group activity? Does the child who is quick to dress himself or herself have to wait 20 minutes for all children to get ready to go outside?
- Does the schedule provide a balance between free play and structured group activities such as music and movement?
- Are there opportunities for children to participate in activities individually, in small groups or in large groups?

G) PARENTS AND STAFF Interactions with families and other professionals should be built on the principles of cooperation and partnership. All individuals should be recognized as equal partners in planning for children's growth and development.

It is also very important to recognize that a quality program must adequately meet the needs of the staff. Some of the following questions should be considered and addressed:

- Do staff members have a private space to withdraw to, relax in and store personal belongings?
- Do staff members have access to training, resources and professional development opportunities?
- Do staff have separate washroom facilities?

Table 2.3 identifies the core learning areas that should be included for various age groups.

2. Aboriginal Head Start Programs

"Aboriginal Head Start Program (AHS) is a Health Canada-funded, early intervention strategy for First Nations, Inuit and Métis children and their families living in urban centres and large northern communities. Aboriginal Head Start projects provide structured half-day preschool experiences by meeting their spiritual,

Photo 2.1

TABLE 2.3 **CORE LEARNING AREAS IN INCLUSIVE ENVIRONMENTS, BY AGE GROUPINGS**

Infant/Toddler	Preschool	School-Age
• Books and pictures	• Books and pictures	• Arts and crafts
• Eye-hand coordination	• Fine-motor activities	• Music and movement
• Active physical play	• Art	• Blocks and construction
• Art	• Music and movement	• Drama/theatre
• Music and movement	• Blocks	• Language/reading activities
• Blocks	• Sand and water	• Math/reasoning activities
• Pretend play	• Dramatic play	• Science/nature activities
• Sand and water play	• Nature/science	• Cultural awareness
• Cultural awareness	• Math/numbers	• Space for gross-motor play
	• Use of TV, video or computers	• Space for privacy
	• Promoting acceptance of diversity	
	• Space for gross-motor play	
	• Space for privacy	

Sources: Harms, Cryer & Clifford, 1990; Harms, Clifford & Cryer, 1998; Harms, Vineberg Jacobs & White, 1996

emotional, intellectual, and physical needs" (Public Health Agency of Canada, Division of Childhood and Adolescence, 2003:1).

Aboriginal children are often more disadvantaged than other children in Canada. Poverty is the single most disabling factor. According to the Canadian Council on Social Development,

- 52.1% of Aboriginal children are poor.
- Aboriginal children are four times more likely to be hungry.
- Aboriginal children have more health problems (Canadian Council on Social Development, 2003).

It is therefore not surprising to find that AHS programs typically focus on a more global approach in six primary program areas, which are discussed on the following pages.

A) CULTURE AND LANGUAGE The environments of children in AHS programs reflect the cultural aspects of their community. Children's learning activities reflect the cultural events of their community. Typical activities may revolve around activities such as fishing, hunting or special festivals. Children also build upon their particular Aboriginal language. Through these activities, children develop a positive sense about themselves as Aboriginal children. High self-esteem is a critical factor in an individual's approach to learning. This is often the first step in any intervention strategies. Children who have a positive self-esteem will embrace new learning readily, with initiative and enjoyment.

B) EDUCATION AND SCHOOL READINESS Aboriginal Head Start Programs recognize the importance of play in establishing life-long learning skills. Emphasis is placed on:

- Initiation of learning by children
- Ensuring that learning experiences are enjoyable
- Developmentally and age-appropriate learning experiences, materials and equipment
- Respect for each individual child

C) HEALTH PROMOTION "The purpose of the Health Promotion Component is to empower parents, guardians, caregivers and those involved with AHS to increase control over and improve their health. More specifically, the projects will encourage practices for self care, working together to address health concerns, and the creation of formal and informal social support networks. The ultimate goal is for those involved with AHS to take actions that contribute to holistic health" (Public Health Agency of Canada, Division of Childhood and Adolescence, 2003:3).

Healthy children come from healthy families. This approach recognizes the need to include family members if healthy practices are to be implemented. To be effective, good practices leading to good nutrition and effective self-care should be extended beyond the child's time in the program. They need to become an integral part of his or her whole life, in preschool and at home.

D) NUTRITION Nutrition also includes all aspects of a child's life. Children are provided with healthy foods to meet their nutritional needs while in the program. Staff and families receive education to improve their understanding of the relationship between healthy nutrition, behaviour, learning and development. Meal times provide opportunities to learn about nutritious foods, and to share and socialize.

E) SOCIAL SUPPORT Assistance is provided to families for these purposes:

- To increase awareness of community resources and services through such means as resource pamphlets, articles, books, referral information, workshops and community-resource listings
- To facilitate access to community resources and services through direct referrals or provision of contact information
- To empower families to access services and resources within their communities by providing appropriate resource information, by guiding individuals through the help-access process and by encouraging families to seek help when needed

F) PARENTAL AND FAMILY INVOLVEMENT Involvement of families is the cornerstone of all quality programs. "Drawing families into full partnerships allows teachers to demonstrate their respect of the preeminent place of the family in children's lives. As the schools support family efforts, maximum communication between parents and teachers is essential to facilitate understanding and respect for the contribution of each party. Children benefit from greater consistency in their guidance, as teachers and parents work together to plan for major socialization and academic tasks" (Gestwicki, 1999:311). There are several ways in which AHS programs involve the parents, including these:

- Direct involvement in the program—Family members volunteer time every month on a regular basis to help within the program.
- Special events—Family members help organize special events such as celebration feasts or prepare Aboriginal dishes.
- "Parents may bring forth special gifts" (Public Health Agency of Canada, Division of Childhood and Adolescence, 2003:4)—This is an opportunity to share special talents and culturally important skills with children. For example, in one program an elder brought a variety of drums into the child care program and taught the children to drum. This was followed by another elder who taught the children simple dances to the beat of the drum.

In summary, AHS programs follow an inclusive philosophy that provides an early intervention strategy in support of the holistic development of Aboriginal children within their community.

3. Support Programs

Families with children with special needs can access support in a number of ways:

A) MEDICAL SUPPORT Often the family's first contact when obtaining advice about their child is through their physician. Families may be worried about their child's progress. Physicians can diagnose certain physical conditions such as cerebral palsy or failure to thrive. Physicians may also be able to provide general guidelines of children's "normal development." If children do not seem to meet these guidelines, the physician may refer the families to other professionals such as physiotherapists, speech and language pathologists or psychologists.

B) SUPPORT GROUPS When families and child care providers are suddenly faced with the need to provide appropriate care for children with special needs, they often feel lost and isolated. As a result, families of children with specific disabilities have formed support groups, both informal and formal, to share information and to support each other. An example of a support group that has expanded to provide support to families and other professionals is the Saskatchewan Cerebral Palsy Association. The services provided by this organization include:

- Supporting children with cerebral palsy and their families
- Developing and implementing programs such as swim programs or loaner programs
- Providing assistance in obtaining grants for the purchase of equipment for educational purposes

- Providing a resource library of materials such as books, magazines or videos
- Sharing information on available resources, treatments and services
- Advocating for research on the prevention and treatment of cerebral palsy
- Advocating for increased services and access to services
- Promoting education and public awareness through workshops and special events
- Exchanging information through the publication of a regular newsletter
- Working with other groups and associations to provide referral and support services (Saskatchewan Cerebral Palsy Association, 2004)

4. The Role of Government

For children to be accepted into a program that is subsidized for children with special needs, there must be a diagnosis of special need and/or a referral to access these services. In most jurisdictions, the eligibility for services or funding is set by the government, and in most cases, the ministry responsible for children and families sets these criteria.

British Columbia provides a good example of a jurisdiction in which services for children are provided through a centralized system. The Ministry of Children and Family Development is the provincial body responsible for providing funding for services for children with special needs. To be eligible for these services, the following criteria are used:

- IQ criteria—The child is diagnosed with an IQ of 70 or below.
- Diagnosis—The child has been diagnosed with autism spectrum disorder.
- Total Dependence—The child has been diagnosed with "severe disabilities that require long term medical supports and services and can be expected to cause extensive costs in maintaining the child at home. Severe disabilities is currently defined as total dependence for eating, toileting, washing, and dressing" (Wakeham, 2000:3).

Staff members help families access funding through the Ministry of Children and Family Development and help them with the process:

- The social worker—This person is responsible for helping find the appropriate services and resources for the child with special needs.
- The intake worker—This is a social worker who helps families complete the initial intake process. The intake worker collects relevant information, makes referrals and sends this information to the social worker, to ensure appropriate placement.

A number of services are available to families in British Columbia, some of which may also be accessed in other Canadian jurisdictions:

- Home programs—These programs provide financial support to families to cover these expenses:
    - Approved medical equipment expenses
    - Repair and maintenance of equipment

- ○ Medical supplies and drug coverage
- ○ Medical transportation
- ○ Exceptional therapy costs
- ○ Dental and medical plans
- ○ Respite care

- • Services of specialists, such as:
  - ○ Behaviour consultants
  - ○ Family support homemakers
  - ○ Specialized helpers to assist in setting developmental goals for children

- • Child Care Resource and Referral Services

5. Centralized Support Services

The Supported Child Care program in British Columbia is a centralized access point for child care services for children with special needs. For families and the community, the advantage of a centralized organization is that all the service information and resources are accessible at one location. This saves both time and effort in locating the appropriate services for a child with special needs. Supported Child Care consultants (who may be referred to as resource consultants in other jurisdictions) perform these functions:

- • Helping the family access child care that meets the child's and family's needs
- • Supporting child care providers by sharing information and suggestions on how to provide inclusive care to children
- • Providing short-term staffing support
- • Organizing workshops for families and child care providers
- • Visiting child care settings (Wakeham, 2000:15)

Children with special needs may be placed in any of a variety of licensed centres that may or may not be subsidized. These include family child care facilities, group child care centres, the child's own home, out-of-school programs and preschool programs.

6. Specialized Services

Some children, depending on their needs, may require specialized services from other professionals. Table 2.4 gives an overview of some of these services.

7. Additional Programs

A) PLAY THERAPY Active play is the basis of play therapy. Children express themselves most readily through play. "Play is the child's symbolic language of self-expression and can reveal (a) what the child has experienced; (b) reactions to what was

TABLE 2.4   **SPECIALIZED SERVICES**

Specialized Service	Description
Medical	Services provided by community health nurses, orthoptists, physicians or pediatricians to help diagnose possible health problems such as failure to thrive, or sight or hearing problems
Communication	Services provided by speech and language pathologists to children with language delays, or other speech or communication problems
Nutrition	Services provided by nutritionists to help plan and implement appropriate nutritional programs
Mental health	Services provided by psychologists, psychiatrists and mental health workers to support a child's emotional health and well-being
Physical needs	Services provided by physiotherapists to help plan and implement physical activities with children and to suggest specialized exercises and equipment

experienced; (c) feelings about what was experienced; (d) what the child wishes, wants or needs; and (e) the child's perceptions" (Landreth, 2002:18).

In any play situation, children express their past experiences and demonstrate their knowledge about the world around them. Careful organization of materials and learning experiences can present opportunities for observing the child's emotions, actions and experiences. This allows the therapist to respond to what has been expressed. "The selection of a variety of appropriate toys by the therapist can facilitate a wide range of feelings-oriented expression by children. Thus, children are not restricted to discussing what happened; rather, they live out at the moment of play the past experiences and associated feelings" (Landreth, 2002:19). Through this process, the therapist then responds to and plans appropriate intervention strategies for the child.

In any child care setting, play therapy is used to some degree, and activities are set up that encourage both active play and quiet, relaxing activities. For example, Benjamin was able to relieve his feelings of frustration by engaging in sensory finger-painting activities (Photo 2.2). Danielle was able to relieve her feelings of stress by representing her "monsters" in more cheerful representations (Photo 2.3).

Additionally, early childhood educators, through careful observation, may glimpse the first signs of problems. For example, Jonathan's father died in a car accident. He seemed to be handling the situation well, and to be quite at ease in telling everyone that his father had died. A few weeks later, however, the staff

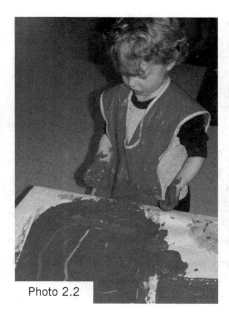

Photo 2.2

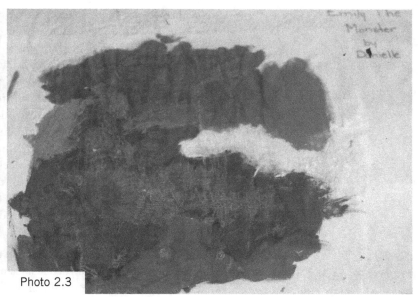

Photo 2.3

noticed that his paintings started to change. He would paint intricate pictures, then cover the entire picture with black paint. When asked why he was doing this, he answered: "This is what my daddy sees. They put him into the ground. He can't see anything anymore." The staff told the boy's mother what was happening. She replied that she had noticed that Jonathan seemed quieter and more withdrawn at home. She decided to send Jonathan to a play therapist.

B) INFANT STIMULATION/DEVELOPMENT PROGRAMS Infant stimulation programs, also known as infant development or early intervention programs, are provided for infants who have been diagnosed as developmentally delayed in one or more major skill areas or are diagnosed as being at risk for developmental delays. This type of program supports families by providing some or all of the following options:

- Home-based programs to help families expand their knowledge and skills about overall growth and development
- Home-based or centre-based programs to help families plan and implement learning activities that enhance the infant's social, emotional, physical and cognitive development
- Consulting services to provide information about:
  ◦ community resources, such as medical, social or educational services
  ◦ family connections or support groups
  ◦ lending libraries of toys, adaptive equipment, books or other resources, such as information about activities that stimulate an infant

C) WITHDRAWAL PROGRAMS In some cases, a child may require specialized help in addition to inclusive care. This specialized care may be provided within the child care facility or may require the family member to take the child to that service. In either case, the child is withdrawn from the regular program to attend the specialized session. Examples of this type of withdrawal program include speech and language therapy or physical therapy. Often, the need for specialized equipment drives the need for a withdrawal type of program.

In most preschool settings, it is up to the parents to take the children to a withdrawal program. This may cause additional hardships for families, because time off work is needed and the children miss part of their day at the preschool. In some of the larger, more regularly funded centres, the specialists may spend a certain amount of time during the week within the centre itself. The centre is equipped with the needed resources for the specialized help. Of course, children still miss a part of their program. Often the specialists can offer guidance to the staff on how to provide some of the needed additional specialized help within the classrooms.

D) SEGREGATED PROGRAMS Segregated programs are programs that are established based on specific needs of children, such as autism or giftedness. The idea of these programs, based on the belief that the child will benefit more from a specialized program, is to group children with like needs together. In most cases, segregated programs for - children with special needs are within the school system, in separate education classes or schools. The rationale for segregated settings is based on these beliefs:

- A child with a severe disability will not gain any benefit from an inclusive setting.
- The child may be so disruptive that the education of other children is impaired.
- The costs are too high to include children with special needs in regular settings (McCarthy, 2002:9).
- The child may need specialized resources that are not available within an inclusive setting.
- The staff does not have the appropriate training to manage children with severe disabilities.

On the opposing side, individuals argue that the benefits of inclusive care far outweigh the restrictive practices of segregated care. The rationale for integrated settings is based on these arguments:

- Every child, irrespective of ability, has the right to participate in the educational setting within his or natural environment. This view is supported by the Canadian Charter of Rights.
- The National Association for the Education of Young Children has found that inclusion does work. It identifies the following characteristics of children in inclusive settings:
  - Increased acceptance and appreciation of diversity
  - Better communication and social skills
  - Greater development in moral and ethical principles

- ◦ Warm and caring friendships
- ◦ Increased self-esteem (National Association for the Education of Young Children, 2002:2–3)

- Studies such as *A Matter of Urgency* also report positive findings. "The results of our study indicate that Canadian child care centres when appropriately resourced, can and do include children with special needs, and have substantial positive impacts on their development" (Hope Irwin et al., 2000:xv).
- All high-quality programs for young children are dependent on sufficient funding. In Canada, there is a growing concern about the quality of child care, including inclusive care. Many of the studies point out that a lack of support, funding, training and adequate policies undermines high-quality care. In high-quality programs, including inclusive programs that receive adequate funding and support, quality child care for all children is provided and the benefits are substantial and long-lasting. Refer to the Perry Preschool study, on page 17 (Schweinhart & Weikart, 1986; McCain & Mustard, 1999; Goelman et al., 2000).

Skills of Early Childhood Educators

Research clearly shows that training of the early childhood educator is the key to successful inclusive learning environments (Hope Irwin et al., 2000; Goelman, et al. 2000). Training components should focus on:

- Specific techniques for working with children with severe disabilities
- Increased awareness about inclusive care, in order to eliminate fears, misinformation and negative attitudes about children with special needs
- Provision of best practices in an inclusive setting
- Fostering self-confidence, in order to adapt and modify the environment to meet all children's needs

Most skills that are needed are the same ones that any early childhood educator relies on when working with young children, such as empathy, sensitivity, knowledge of child development and nurturing skills. In addition, the early childhood educator needs to develop skills in the following areas:

- Organizing the environment to provide materials and choices that span a broad age range and range of developmental abilities
- Organizing the environment to provide security and safety to all children
- Developing learning experiences that are based on the individual strengths and needs of children
- Establishing routines that are flexible, predictable and consistent
- Varying approaches and techniques based on observation of children's individual learning styles, interests and abilities

- Working collaboratively with families and other professionals to facilitate observations, planning of learning experiences and evaluation of achievements, and to develop strategies to maximize children's chances of success

According to another study on inclusion in Canada (Hope Irwin, Lero & Brophy, 2004), additional characteristics should be considered. These characteristics relate to self-confidence, experience and education:

- Self-confidence—To be effective practitioners in an inclusive setting, adults need to build confidence and skills in:
  - Teamwork
  - Meeting individual children's strengths and needs
  - Research, to identify sources of information and support

- Experience with children with special needs—Staff could ask to observe inclusive centres or pursue staff exchanges in order to become more knowledgeable about specific children with special needs.
- Education—Staff should further their knowledge through attendance at conferences, specific courses, seminars or workshops related to inclusion.

SUMMARY

Anyone who wants to work with young children should be aware that this includes working with children with special needs. In most cases, the child with special needs is included with children in his or her community. However, since services vary from jurisdiction to jurisdiction and also from centre to centre within each jurisdiction, child care providers must become knowledgeable about these areas:

- Regional legislative requirements or guidelines for children with special needs
- Local resources and support services
- Accessible funding
- Support networks
- How to advocate for the children and families within their care

KEY POINTS

Identification of how many children have special needs
- Lower percentages of children with special needs are identified in young children
- Specific statistics on type of services and number of children receiving services are not readily available

- Somewhere between 18.7% and 50% of centres in Canada do not accept children with special needs

Legislative requirements for working with children with special needs
- Training requirements range from no training at all to quite specialized training
- Funding for children with special needs is dependent on a diagnosis of needs in most jurisdictions
- Support to centres through grants and funding allocations is dependent on the assessed needs of the children

Reasons for non-inclusiveness
- Lack of funding and resources, training and child care spaces are the main reasons

Inclusive programs are developed on the principles of
- Best practices
- Active play
- Accessibility of all materials and learning activities
- Organization of learning environments to include age-appropriate access to all core curricular elements: books and pictures, fine- and gross-motor activities, dramatic play, nature and science activities, math and numbers, sand and water, cultural diversity, art, music and movement, blocks, TV and computers
- Observation of children's interests, skills and abilities
- Provision of materials and experiences based on a wide range of skills and abilities
- Recognition of individual safety needs

Aboriginal Head Start programs
- Holistic, inclusive approach
- Consist of six elements: culture and language, education and school readiness, health promotion, nutrition, social support and family involvement

Support programs
- Include medical support groups both informal and formal, centralized agencies; the services of specialists, child care resource and referral services; and supported child care

Role of government
- Sets legislation, policies and guidelines
- Sets criteria for funding, usually diagnosis of special need
- Hires qualified individuals to aid families through the application and placement process

- Provides funding for home programs, specialist programs, referral services, supported child care services and specialized services for medical, communication, nutrition, mental-health and physical needs

Centralized services
- Provide all services in one location, such as collection of information, assessment of needs, placement of children, support to children within placement and support to day care facilities

Play therapy programs
- Use active play as the central basis of therapy
- Therapist sets up materials and experiences to observe children's interactions in order to plan and implement intervention strategies
- Child care centres utilize play therapy techniques when setting up learning experiences to include sensory activities, soothing activities and opportunities to be alone

Infant stimulation programs
- Provide opportunities for families with infants diagnosed as at risk or developmentally delayed to learn about and participate in programs that serve to enhance infant development

Withdrawal programs
- Individual children are withdrawn from programs to receive specialized help such as speech and language or physical therapy

Segregated programs
- Children with special needs are placed based on a specific need, in rooms or buildings separated from other children

Skills of early childhood educators
- Training in specific techniques needed for children with severe disabilities; awareness about inclusive care and best practices; and self-confidence in ability to provide inclusive care
- Skill in organizing multi-level skill-based environment; providing a safe environment; establishing appropriate routines; and observing children's strengths, needs, learning styles, interests and abilities

EXERCISES

1. Describe how legislation influences the types of services provided to families and children with special needs.

2. Reflect upon the reasons given for not including children with special needs, as outlined on page 60. Which of these reasons have some validity? What changes would need to be made to the present service–delivery system to address these reasons?

3. Identify the benefits of inclusive settings.

4. Look over the section on Space and Furnishings on pages 48–51. Which of the elements discussed have particular relevance to children with special needs? Explain why you feel this way.

5. Identify what program options are available in your community for children with special needs. Discuss whether these services are adequate. What other services should be provided?

6. Reflect upon your own skills as an early childhood educator. What additional skills do you think you still need to be an effective early childhood educator in an inclusive setting? How might you gain these skills?

REFERENCES

Campbell, C. (2000). *The Mozart Effect for Children*. New York, NY: HarperCollins Publishers Inc.

Canadian Council on Social Development. (2003). Aboriginal Children in Poverty in Urban Communities: Social exclusion and the growing racialization of poverty in Canada. [online]. Available at www.ccsd.ca/pr/2003/aboriginal.htm [18-7-2003].

Chiazzari, S. (1998). *The Complete Book of Color*. Boston, MA: Element Books, Inc.

Childcare Research and Research Unit (2008). Early Childhood education and care in the 2008 federal election: Updates [online] Available at http://action.web.ca/home/crru/rsrcs_crru_full.shtml?x=121428 [16/09/2008].

Crowther, I. (2007). *Creating Effective Learning Environments*. Scarborough, ON: Nelson Thomson Learning.

Doherty-Derkowski, G. (1994). *Quality Matters: Excellence in Early Childhood Programs*. Toronto: Addison-Wesley.

Friendly, M. (2008). Canada's Legacy of Inaction on Early Childhood Education and Child Care. Childcare Research and Research Unit [online]. Available at http://action.web.ca/home/crru/rsrcs_crru_full.shtml?x=121380 [05/05/2008].

Friendly, M., & Beach, J. (2004). *Early Childhood Education and Care in Canada*. Toronto: ON: Childcare Resources and Research Unit.

Friendly, M. Beach, J. & Turiano, M. (2002). Early *Childhood Education and Care in Canada*. Toronto: ON: Childcare Resources and Research Unit.

Gestwicki, C. (1999). *Developmentally Appropriate Practices*. Second Edition. Scarborough, ON: Nelson Canada.

Goelman, H., Doherty, G., Lero, D., LaGrange, A., & Tougas, J. (2000). *You Bet I Care! Caring and Learning Environments: Quality in Child Care Centres Across Canada*. Guelph, ON: Centre for Families, Work and Well-Being, University of Guelph.

Government of Canada (2002). Chapter 6: Young Children with Disabilities in Canada. The Well Being of Canada's Young Children: Government of Canada [online]. Available at http://socialunion.gc.ca/ecd/2002/b-5.htm [16-8-2004].

Hanline, F., & Daley, S. (2004). "Mom, will Kaelie Always have Possibilities?" *Annual Editions Educational Psychology*, Nineteenth Edition, 42–45.

Harms, T., Clifford, R., & Cryer, D. (1998). *Early Childhood Environment Rating Scale.* Revised Edition. New York, NY: Teachers College Press.

Harms, T., Cryer, D., & Clifford, R. (1990). *Infant/Toddler Environment Rating Scale.* New York, NY: Teachers College Press.

Harms, T., Vineberg Jacobs, E., & White, D. (1996). *School-Age Care Environment Rating Scale.* New York, NY: Teachers College Press.

Hathaway, W. (1994). Non-visual Effects of Classroom Lighting on Children. *Educational Facility Planner, 23,* 12–16.

Hawkins, W., & Lilley, H. (1992). *CEFPI's Guide for School Facility Appraisal.* Columbus, OH: The Council of Educational Facility Planners International.

Hope Irwin, S. (2004). SpeciaLink: The National Centre for Child Care Inclusion. SpeciaLink [online]. Available at www.specialinkcanada.org.

Hope Irwin, S., Lero, D., & Brophy, K. (2000). *A Matter of Urgency: Including Children with Special Needs in Child Care in Canada.* Wreck Cove, NS: Breton Books.

Hope Irwin, S., Lero, D., & Brophy, K. (2004). *Inclusion: The Next Generation in Child Care in Canada.* Wreck Cove, NS: Breton Books.

Landreth, G. (2002). *Play Therapy: The Art of the Relationship.* New York, NY: Brunner-Routledge.

Liberman, J. (1991). *Light Medicine of the Future.* Santa Fe, NM: Bear & Company Publishing.

Mayer, D. E. (1994). *National Statement on Quality Child Care.* Ottawa, ON: Child and Family Canada.

McCain, M., & Mustard, F. (1999). *Early Years Study Final Report.* Toronto, ON: Publications Ontario.

McCarthy, M. (2002). Inclusion of Children with Special Needs. *Annual Editions, Educating Exceptional Children,* Thirteenth Edition, 8–11.

National Association for the Education of Young Children (2002). The Benefits of an Inclusive Education: Making It Work. National Association for the Education of Young Children [online]. Available at www.naeyc.org/resources/eyly/1996/07.asp [28/8/2004].

Organization For Economic Co-Operation and Development. (2006). *Starting Strong II: Early Childhood Education and Care.* France: OECD.

Pediatric Advisor (2004). Burn Safety: Hot Water Temperature. University of Michigan [online]. Available at www.med.umich.edu/1libr/pa/pa_hotwatr_hhg.htm [24/8/2004].

Public Health Agency of Canada, Division of Childhood and Adolescence (2003). Aboriginal Head Start (AHS): Program Overview. Public Health Agency of Canada [online]. Available at http://www.phac-aspc.gc.ca/dca-dea/programs-mes/ahs_overview-eng.php [11/11/2008].

Saskatchewan Cerebral Palsy Association (2004). Saskatchewan Cerebral Palsy Association [online]. Available at www.members.shaw.ca/saskcpa [1/8/2004].

Schweinhart, L., & Weikart, J. (1986). Lasting Differences: The High Scope Preschool Curriculum Comparison Study Through Age 23. *Early Childhood Education Research Quarterly* 1, 15–45.

Voices 4 Children (2003). Fact Sheet #18: Children with Special Needs. Child and Family Canada [online]. Available at www.cfc-efc.ca/docs/vocfc/00018_en.htm [7/8/2004].

Wakeham, J. (2000). *Connections: A Resource Guide for Families with Children with Special Needs* (Rep. No. September, 2000). Vancouver, BC: Developmental Disabilities Association.

3

CHAPTER

Who Are the Children with Special Needs?

"One important fact is that all children pass through the same stage of development. They learn to do the same things in the same order. Some go more quickly, some more slowly, some more erratically than others with lots of stops and starts and certainly the final level of achievement is different, but there are things that every child will do." (Macintyre, 2002:9)

Learning Outcomes

After studying this chapter, you will be able to:

1. Identify historical changes to the field of special education, and explain the significance of modern attitudes toward individuals with special needs.

2. Explain what behavioural and emotional disorders are and how they affect a child's growth and development.

3. Discuss how poor physical health may affect children's skills and abilities.

4. Identify the various types of physical disabilities and discuss how each disability affects the child's ability to function within early childhood settings.

Introduction

Society has always influenced the way we view and treat individuals with special needs. Institutions such as churches and governments, as well as culture and economic circumstances, influence our belief and value systems. Over time, changing beliefs about how individuals with special needs should be treated and educated have reflected broader social trends.

In most cultures before the seventeenth century, children and adults with special needs were regarded as inferior beings. The children were mistreated and abused, and in some cultures their differences were seen as the sign of the devil. Families who had children with special needs tried to hide them away. Often they were abandoned, put in an asylum for the insane or even put to death.

From the mid-seventeenth century on, there was a growing trend toward more humane treatment. But it was not until the nineteenth century that education for children with special needs was born. Children started to attend special schools for the deaf, the blind and the mentally retarded. In Canada, the first of these schools opened in Montreal in 1831. This school for the deaf was forced to close five years later because of lack of funding, however. By 1848, permanent residential schools became firmly established. Families who had infants with a diagnosed special need such as Down's syndrome were often advised to place their child in an institution. Other children were placed in an institution when they got older and families found it more difficult to maintain them at home (Winzer, 1999).

Reflection

From a Teacher

I have been a junior and senior kindergarten teacher. I realized how important a good early start was and often wondered what kind of start children with special needs would have. I always felt that these children, in particular, often did not get the same chance as their more "normal" peers. The school board I was working for required that I had training in special needs before I could teach in a class for trainable retarded children. I decided to take the course during the winter semester. One of our assignments was to visit an institution in our area and write a report on our experiences.

We arrived on a Saturday morning. I was interested in the young children, so I was escorted to a locked ward for the preschool children. I cannot describe my shock in what I saw. The ward was arranged with several sleeping rooms along one side. Some of these held cribs, others had low beds. These small rooms opened to a large common room. There was a circular rug in the middle of the room. Under the adult-height windows were some adult-sized chairs and benches. At one end of the room, a TV set was showing Saturday morning cartoons. Some of the children were sitting in front of the TV. Many of the children were in their diapers or still in pajamas. Some were rocking back and forth, and others just sat staring blindly ahead. A few children were strapped into wheelchairs. Some of the children were still in their cribs. At one end of the room there was a toy box filled with toys, a bookshelf filled with an assortment of children's books, and two tables and chairs. Some attempts had been made to brighten the room. Pictures of nursery-rhyme characters had been hung on the walls around the room. I was only there for 10 minutes, but I saw very few adult–child interactions during that time.

I was then taken to the children's school room. This room had more materials, but predominantly materials geared to school-readiness activities, such as alphabet and number cards. When I asked if the children could go outside to play, the answer was, "Only in good weather."

I had not imagined that children could live in such an austere environment. What happened to the concepts of warmth, cuddling and stimulation? This was 1972, not 1872. How could anyone do this to a small child?

In 1906, special education classes were started in public schools in Canada. These were segregated classes within some schools for children with physical disabilities. By the 1940s, special education classes had expanded greatly, to include a variety of other disabilities. Additionally, some school boards established segregated schools for children with special needs.

During World War II, women were added to the workforce in large numbers. This resulted in the establishment of day care centres across Canada. Most of these facilities were closed after the war.

The 1960s brought increased change in social attitudes. "Social attitudes toward education, care, and training of individuals who are exceptional usually reflect more general cultural attitudes toward the obligation of society to its individual citizens" (Winzer, 1999:32). This led to philosophies that placed value on the individual. Accordingly, the educational needs of individuals were also looked at and acknowledged. More special education classes evolved. Children were diagnosed for placement, usually based on an IQ test.

During the 1970s early childhood education started to flourish as more women entered the job market. Early identification became important. Programs such as Head Start and early intervention programs flourished. School systems and some day care centres started to move toward mainstreaming (placing children with special needs within segregated classrooms of elementary schools) and integration (placing children with special needs in classrooms for certain subjects, such as physical education, music and art). In some jurisdictions, children with special needs started to be integrated into regular day care programs, often with a support worker assigned to the child.

Reflection

Reflection   *From a Special Education Class Teacher*

In the mid-1970s, I was honoured to be able to teach in an experimental class of six children, in what was then called a class for trainable retarded children. The class was placed within an elementary school rather than in the school for the "Mentally Retarded." Children in my class ranged in age from four to eight. The special needs represented in the class included physical disabilities, what was then diagnosed as severe mental retardation, behavioural problems and significant language delays. The classroom had very few materials that I thought were developmentally appropriate or provided an adequate number of choices for active play. The children did not participate in the regular recess programs. In fact, some children outside the special needs class were afraid of the children in it.

Within two months, the classroom changed. Children could participate in active play. With the help and support of the rest of the school, all children also participated in the regular recess program. They could go out by themselves and come in by themselves. The children formed active friendships with their peers. Some of the children were even integrated into the music programs within the primary divisions. One of the children had been labelled as "untestable." I did not believe this diagnosis, and with great difficulty managed to convince the psychometrist to retest him. She was amazed to find that not only could he be tested, but that now he tested in the mildly retarded range. Today I am very pleased to note that this experiment was so successful that more of the young children were moved into similar classes around the system, and some of the younger children were actually placed in some of the day care programs.

The 1980s brought a stronger legislative focus on education. Many jurisdictions passed legislation that paved the way for inclusive care. Today, the right to inclusive education has become the norm within all Canadian jurisdictions. However, not all jurisdictions reinforce the concept of inclusion through policies, funding or other supports.

In all areas, children with special needs still face many hurdles that other children do not. In all jurisdictions in Canada, to obtain funding for support, children with special needs:

- Must be diagnosed with special needs by a recognized practitioner, such as a doctor or a psychologist.
- Must be diagnosed with the special need that is funded within the jurisdiction; for example, in Ontario, a child with special needs is defined as "a child who has physical or mental impairment that is likely to continue for a prolonged period of time and who as a result thereof is limited in activities pertaining to normal living as verified by objective psychological or medical findings." (Government of Ontario, 1997:R1.1).
- May forfeit the right to attend the family's day care program of choice.

As a result, children with special needs still do not receive equitable treatment. These children must have a confirmed diagnosis to receive support and funding for quality care. Funding arrangements are usually based on a categorical system, which labels the child with a specific disability in a broad category, such as communication disorders, physical disabilities or impaired health, developmental disabilities, behavioural disabilities, intellectual delays or disabilities or sensory disabilities (Allen, Paasche, Langford & Nolan, 2002; Freiberg, 2005). The categorical approach has several problems:

- Not all jurisdictions recognize all the categories. For example, the definition in Ontario does not cover behavioural or sensory disorders. Children with these disorders will find it difficult to receive the funding and support they need.
- The label often becomes a self-fulfilling prophecy. The child who was labelled as untestable was placed in a "trainable retarded class." It was assumed that because he could not be tested, he had a very low IQ, and as a result he was placed in a program with children of equally low IQs. As later testing showed, he was testable and did have a much higher IQ than expected (see Table 3.1).
- Children may be refused service because the staff feels that the support is lacking or that they are not sufficiently trained to accept a particular special need.

Having special needs in one or more areas profoundly affects all aspects of a child's development. For example, a child with a physical disability will find it harder to explore the environment freely. This makes it more difficult for him or her to gain first-hand knowledge about the particulars of that environment. Consequently, the child has fewer opportunities to form mental representations, with the result that both cognitive and language development could be delayed. It will also be much harder for the child to form a good concept about his or her own body, the functions of various body parts and the position of the body in relationship to other things within the environment. This may affect how the child perceives himself or herself.

The impact of a need in any one domain is like a domino effect: It affects all other areas because of the close interconnections of all developmental domains. To mitigate some of these effects, careful observation, early intervention and holistic care and treatment are required.

All children have special needs at one time or another. For example, at the age of three, Michael had not started to talk. He was referred to a speech and language pathologist. A program was set up for him within the preschool environment. But when Michael did start to speak, he amazed everyone because he spoke in full sentences. Many children print letters backwards when they first start to write; however, as children mature, they learn to print letters appropriately. Within any quality program, the children continue to be involved in active play. The adults recognize the needs and adapt the materials, equipment and strategies to reflect the children's strengths and needs at that particular time.

Some children need more help than others. Depending on the severity of the need, some children may need more assistance, some adaptive equipment or greater

TABLE 3.1 ADVANTAGES AND DISADVANTAGES OF LABELLING CHILDREN

Advantages of Labelling	Disadvantages of Labelling
• Labels help children with special needs access services, funding and other supports. • Labels may help children access specialized equipment or instruction, such as Braille equipment or standing frames. • Labels may help families understand and deal with the problems of having a child with special needs. • Labels may help increase awareness and knowledge of individuals with special needs. Adults will often question or research information that they are not familiar with. • Labels may provide a common language for communications among professionals.	• Labels draw attention to one characteristic of the child. Often as a result of diagnosis, a program is then imposed that centres on the special need rather than looking at the whole child. The child's strengths may be completely overlooked. • Labelling ignores the fact that children are unique and do not fit neatly into fixed categories. • The label will not predict individual needs. For example, what does the label "Down's syndrome" mean? It is not helpful in setting up a program for that child. The child must first be observed for unique characteristics, such as interests, strengths and needs, before an appropriate plan can be created for him or her. • Labelling can lead others to infer that the diagnosis is accurate. An incorrect diagnosis could lead to inappropriate placement and programming. • Making an accurate assessment of a young child's special needs is difficult. Many of the standardized tests are not reliable or valid. • Labelling may lead to teasing by peers. • Labelling may lead to unrealistic expectations. Adults may concentrate on the remediation of needs and ignore the child's right to play. • Labelling may lead to needlessly lower expectations for the child. If the expectation is that the child cannot do a task, the opportunity may never be given to him or her. • For a child labelled "gifted," the label may burden the child with unrealistically high expectations.

adaptation to their program. To access funds to provide for all of the children's needs, caregivers must have children assessed and diagnosed with a special need. Classification for children with special needs is not precise. It tends to lump children together into arbitrary categories based on perceived needs. For example, Jordan was diagnosed with an overall developmental delay, but his teachers noticed that his gross-motor skills were not delayed. He reached the same milestones as other children of his age.

Some of the major categorical systems used in different jurisdictions throughout Canada are identified below. These types of systems are not geared to inclusivity.

They tend to label children and place them in categories, focusing on the need rather than the child. "In naming, a specific term is attached to something or someone. It is a powerful process that carries many messages about perceived value and human relationships" (American Association on Mental Retardation, 2002:5). However, it is important for students learning about children with special needs to know about the major categories for children with special needs, in order to:

- Identify appropriate resources such as equipment, materials, toys and information about children with special needs.
- Apply for relevant funding.
- Become aware of varying strategies for effective interactions and appropriate program planning.
- Interact effectively with families and other professionals.

Children with Behavioural and Emotional Disorders

Children with behavioural or emotional disorders may exhibit feelings such as sadness, fear, anger, guilt, self-stimulation or anxiety that change the way they behave and interact with others. (Freiberg, 2004:111). Before making a judgment on a child's behaviour, however, it is important to remember that all children can and do exhibit many of the behaviours listed in the charts below. Some of these behaviours can often be explained by:

- Age—The younger the child, the more likely it is that he or she will demonstrate some of these behaviours. For example, it is not unusual for a toddler to become seemingly defiant as he is trying to establish his autonomy. This is a normal behaviour that all toddlers go through.
- Stress—Many children may become irritable and uncooperative when they perceive stress in others or are stressed themselves. For example, may parents can attest to the fact that trying to leave the house on time in the morning can become very stressful. Their children seem the most uncooperative at this time.
- Tiredness—When tired, children often become more irritable, cranky and less cooperative.

It is when a behaviour persists on a regular basis over time that a diagnosis by a trained professional should be made. Behavioural and emotional disorders can include a wide range of disabling conditions, such as the ones described below.

1. Most Common Behavioural Disorders

The three most common types of behavioural disorders have many commonalities, but also significant differences. It is important to understand both similarities and differences in order to best meet the needs of the individual and groups of children (see Table 3.2).

TABLE 3.2   **COMPARISON OF BEHAVIOURAL DISORDERS**

Type of Disorder	Description
Oppositional Defiant Disorder (ODD)	Affects about one to ten children under 12 years, with boys outnumbering girls by two to one. Children with ODD • Are easily upset—angered, irritated or annoyed—which often leads to temper tantrums • Get into frequent arguments with adults • Have difficulty complying with requests or rules • Blame others for their own problems • Have low self-esteem
Conduct Disorder (CD)	Affects about 5–15% of school-aged children, with boys outnumbering girls by four to one. Children with CD • Exhibit aggressive behaviours, both verbal and physical, toward children, other individuals and/or materials. • Have disruptive behaviours, including temper tantrums, arguments and constant interruptions • Can be deceitful or thieving • Have difficulty complying with rules
Attention Deficit Hyperactivity Disorder (ADHD)	Affects from 2–5% of children, with boys outnumbering girls by three to one; ADHD is the second-most common mental health problem in children. Children with ADHD • Have a short attention span • Are easily distracted • Continually interrupt • Are inattentive • Are impulsive • Are constantly physically active, often squirming or fidgeting

A) CAUSES OF COMMON BEHAVIOURAL DISORDERS   The exact causes of ODD, CD and ADHD are unknown, although research has identified a number of risk factors, including:

• Gender—More males than females exhibit behavioural disorders. There is no conclusive research that links causes to genetics or to background socialization experiences.

- Temperament—Children who exhibit some of the behaviours listed in Table 3.1 or are hard to manage in the early years are more likely to be diagnosed with a behavioural disorder in later years.
- Brain variations—Often, structural and functional variations in brain wave patterns can be detected for children with ADHD.
- Environmental causes—Maternal smoking, alcohol consumption and substance abuse during pregnancy, a difficult birth, prematurity, a low birth weight, a brain injury and early deprivation are often cited as risk factors.
- Family life—Children living in homes with dysfunctional families have an increased risk of developing a behavioural disorder.
- Problems in learning—Children with intellectual difficulties are twice as likely to be diagnosed with some form of behavioural disorder.

2. Additional Behavioural and Emotional Disorders

A) ANXIETY OR WITHDRAWAL Not all children resort to anti-social behaviours. Some may express their anxiety by withdrawing from situations. This is much more difficult to deal with because:

- People assume that the child is shy.
- The child may be perceived as a loner.
- The behaviour is less noticeable because it is not an obvious problem that needs to be dealt with.

3. Pervasive Developmental Disorders

Pervasive developmental disorders (PDDs) are associated with stereotypical, repetitive behaviours and difficulties with social interactions and with communication. There are five kinds of PDD. The most common is autism. The remaining conditions—Asperger's syndrome, childhood disintegrative disorder, Rett disorder and pervasive development disorder–not otherwise specified (PDD-NOS)—occur rarely and therefore will be covered in less detail (see Table 3.3).

A) AUTISM The syndrome of autism is a severely incapacitating and life-long disability. It is best described as a neurological dysfunction. However, the exact nature or type of dysfunction has not yet been determined (Autism Treatment Services of Canada, 2006).

At present, there is no known cure for autism. Although claims regarding "cures" have been made, they have not been substantiated. Research indicates that the most successful method for treating and educating autistic individuals involves structured and intensive behavioural interventions. Through these, autistic individuals can be assisted to fulfill their unique potential and lead happier and more productive lives (Autism Treatment Services of Canada, 2006).

B) SCHIZOPHRENIA Since schizophrenia is extremely rare in children under the age of 12, childhood schizophrenia will not be covered in this text apart from the following

TABLE 3.3 PERVASIVE DEVELOPMENTAL DISORDERS

Disorder	Description
Autism	Affects three to six of every 1000 children, with three to four more boys than girls affected. Autism is a brain disorder that often reveals itself before the age of 3. Autism is defined by highly repetitive, stereotypic behaviours and impaired abilities to • learn; • communicate; • interact with others; • engage in social interactions; • develop and sustain interests; • sustain attention; and • handle changes to routines. A recent increase in the number of diagnosed cases may be the result of • improved diagnosis; • better criteria for diagnosis; or • a realization that early intervention can mitigate some of the adverse effects of autism for some children.
Asperger's syndrome	Affects 60 individuals per 10 000. Asperger's is usually diagnosed after age 3 and is more common in boys than in girls. The disorder is defined by • repetitive or obsessive routines or rituals; • sensitivity to sensory stimulation—light, textures, certain tastes and sounds; • poor social skills; • problems with motor skills—uncoordinated, delayed, awkward; • food vocabulary and grammar skills; • language problems—difficulty understanding variations in meaning and body language; • few facial expressions; and • difficulty in reading cues and expressions of others.

TABLE 3.3   **CONTINUED**

Disorder	Description
Childhood disintegrative disorder	A rare condition that affects 3–4-year-olds who had developed normally to age 2

The disorder is defined by

• normal development to age 2; and

• a significant loss of expressive and receptive language skills, social skills, especially the ability to adapt, play skills, bowel control and motor skills. |
| Rett disorder | Affects mostly females; rare in males. Rett disorder is a genetic disorder that causes developmental arrest or failure of brain maturation; it is a neurodevelopmental disorder. Up to 50% of children with Rett's are ambulatory (capable of walking).

Rett disorder is defined by:

• a deceleration of growth of the head;

• small hands and feet;

• stereotypical hand movements;

• cognitive impairment;

• problems socializing; and

• few to no verbal skills. |
| Pervasive development disorder–not otherwise specified (PDD-NOS) | A condition in which some but not all features of Pervasive Developmental Disorder are identified. |

definition: "Unlike children with autism, those with schizophrenia typically have a later age of onset of their problem, show less intellectual impairment, display less severe social and language deficits, develop hallucinations and delusions as they get older, and experience periods of remission and relapse" (Mash & Wolfe, 1999:411).

4. General Characteristics

Children with behavioural or emotional disorders may exhibit the following general characteristics:

• An inability to learn that cannot be explained by intellectual, sensory or health factors
• An inability to build or maintain satisfactory interpersonal relationships with peers and teachers
• Inappropriate types of behaviour or feelings under normal circumstances
• A general pervasive mood of unhappiness or depression
• A tendency to develop physical symptoms or fears associated with personal or school problems (Jolivette, Stichter & McCormick, 2002:118).

Children with Cognitive Disabilities

Children with cognitive disabilities are characterized by limitations in a number of abilities, including intellectual functioning and the ability to adapt behaviours in social, conceptual and practical skills (American Association on Mental Retardation, 2002). A number of labels have been, and continue to be, applied to this group of disabilities: mental retardation, intellectual delays, cognitive delays and, sometimes, developmental delays.

Children may have any one of a number of symptoms, some of which may also be part of normal development. The younger the child and the more restrictive the early experiences, the more likely it will be that the child exhibits some of these symptoms.

Young children develop at different rates and in different ways. Each individual is unique. During the early years, young children learn the most they will learn in a lifetime. The young brain is remarkably active in forming numerous connections and "wiring" between these connections to help the individual master and transfer learning and skills in many situations. As a result, care should be taken to look at any symptoms in the context of the child's age, experience and present setting. Possible symptoms are identified in Table 3.4.

The American Association on Intellectual and Developmental Disorders (AAIDD) has developed a classification system for children with cognitive disabilities that is widely used. The original classification system developed by The American Association on Mental Disabilities (now AAIDD) focused on the severity of the delays. According to this type of scale, children are tested, given an IQ score and then placed in an appropriate category. IQ scores are formal measures of intelligence that place children on a scale from non-competent to gifted. These are the categories of mental retardation identified from IQ testing:

- Mildly retarded—IQ score of 55–70
- Moderately retarded—IQ score of 40–55
- Severely retarded—IQ score of 25–40
- Profoundly retarded—IQ score below 25

Recently, the AAIDD has begun to adapt its classification system for individuals with cognitive disabilities. This classification system looks at the adaptive behaviours needed to function appropriately within different settings. The new classification system is being created in collaboration with a wide range of participants and in light of research and subsequent changing viewpoints about the best, most holistic way to treat individuals with this condition. "[W]e are in the midst of discussion about the nature of intelligence; the relationship between intelligence and adaptive behavior; the implementation of the supports paradigm; the best way to conceptualize disabling conditions; the impact of consumer and reform movements; and the effects of terminology upon individual lives" (American Association on Mental Retardation, 2002:xiii).

TABLE 3.4 **COGNITIVE DISABILITIES**

Symptom	Example
Difficulty understanding directions	Damian was participating in an obstacle course. The children were asked to proceed in one direction only. Damian consistently tried to do the obstacle course in the reverse direction after completing it.
Difficulty learning new skills	Bill, a four-year-old, had been in the same day care situation since he was two. The centre encouraged all children to recognize their own names. The staff had posted pictures and the children's names in many locations such as personal hooks and personal displays. Bill consistently needed help to find his picture and name.
Difficulty remembering directions or skills previously learned	Leona found it difficult to remember where materials she had used previously were kept, despite the fact that materials were in labelled containers (picture and word) and in a consistent location that was also labelled. She consistently asked where the materials were or returned them to an incorrect spot. When gently reminded where the toy belonged, she would hit her head and say, "I forgot."
Need for additional help to complete tasks	Timmy consistently needed help to put toothpaste on his toothbrush.
Immature reaction or inappropriate response in social situations	A group of preschool children had been reading stories and discussing how to be empathetic. One of the children, Jamie, was very sad when he arrived one morning. He shared that his dog had been hit by a car and died. When Rodney heard this, he seemed to understand that something was wrong. He ran over to Jamie and gave him the "high-five" sign.
Delays in other domains: physical, emotional, social and language	Stevie was diagnosed as cognitively developmentally delayed. As well, this four-year-old used single words to communicate and found it difficult to master age-appropriate fine-motor tasks such as putting on his own shoes or stacking blocks more than three high.

1. AAMR Assumptions Regarding the Classification System for Cognitive Disabilities

The classification system used by AAMR considers a number of points. These include:

- Limitations in present functioning must be considered within the context of community environments typical of the individual's age, peers and culture.
- Valid assessment considers cultural and linguistic diversity as well as differences in communication, sensory, motor and behavioural factors.
- Within an individual, limitations often coexist with strengths.
- An important purpose of describing limitations is to develop a profile of needed supports.
- With appropriate personalized supports over a sustained period, the life functioning of the person with mental retardation generally will improve (AAIDD, 2002).

Most jurisdictions in Canada utilize the old classification system developed by AAIDD before 1992. However, they also advocate for inclusive care and support it to some degree. This represents a direct conflict between ideology and policy and provides support for the recommendations outlined in the study *A Matter of Urgency* (Hope Irwin, Lero & Brophy, 2000). Canada needs to develop policies and adopt guidelines that support inclusion.

2. Communication Difficulties

Just as children with special needs are categorized by their need, the domains of development are also categorized. In most systems, communication is regarded as part of the cognitive domain.

Communication is made up of three distinct components that are connected and dependent on each other (see Figure 3.1). Receptive communication refers to an individual's ability to understand what has been transmitted through verbal communication, body language and/or other means, such as symbolized form or signing. Physical communication refers to an individual's ability to transmit signals by facial expressions and other body language, such as shrugging the shoulders or using hand movements. Physical communications are culturally determined. For example, in some Asian cultures it is impolite to have direct eye contact with the speaker, which is in direct contrast to Western custom. Expressive language refers to an individual's ability to express himself or herself verbally or physically, including signing or using augmentative devices (devices that help an individual to communicate a message using devices such as symbol boards or talking computers) so that the message can be understood by others.

Children may experience difficulties in one or all of the communication areas. Difficulties in the receptive communication area are described in Table 3.5.

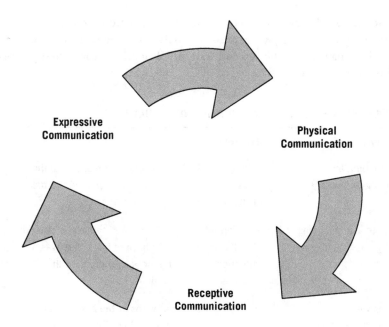

FIGURE 3.1
Communication Components

TABLE 3.5 RECEPTIVE COMMUNICATION DIFFICULTIES

Difficulty	Example
Understanding the meaning of words	Jeremy was sitting beside Jonas. Jonas asked him to pass the shears. Jeremy looked around the table. He obviously understood that he was asked to find something and pass it to Jonas. He did not understand the word "shears." Jonas noticed his difficulty. He walked over, picked up the shears and said, "See, these are shears. They're kinda like scissors."
Understanding and following directions	The children were listening to instructions prior to entering the gross-motor room. "Find a circle and jump inside the circle." As Dillon entered the room, he stopped and looked around. He then started to jump around the room. Dillon had either not heard all of the instructions, he had forgotten what he had been told, he was able to focus on only one part of the instructions or he simply did not understand what was required. As he observed the children, he picked up that jumping was a requirement, so he jumped around the room.
Understanding the meaning of conversations or dialogues	Nancy was listening to the story of Goldilocks and the three bears with a group of her peers. Throughout the story, the child care provider asked questions about what was happening. Nancy was eager to answer but did not answer any questions correctly.

Difficulties in the expressive communication area are much more difficult to diagnose. Children's ability to express themselves is dependent on a number of factors. They may have difficulty with one or all of the factors. These factors are described in Table 3.6.

TABLE 3.6 **EXPRESSIVE COMMUNICATION DIFFICULTIES**

Difficulty	Example
Understanding and responding to messages	Jeremy (see Table 3.5) could not respond to the message because he did not understand the meaning of the word "shears."
Inability to ask questions correctly	Jennifer, a five-year-old, wanted to have another drink of milk. She said, "Me have milk." There was no inflection in her tone, nor any indication that this was a request for more milk.
Problems with the use of various parts of speech	Jetta consistently put verbs at the beginning of her dialogue, as in "Jump, me" or "Go fast, me."
Delayed use of language	Jordan, a three-year-old, communicates verbally in one- or two-word utterances using correct intonation patterns.
Morphology (how words are built) prefixes (a part of speech placed in front of a word to change the word's meaning, such as "in-" or "re-") suffixes (a part of speech placed at the end of a word, such as "-ly" or "-ness").	Children may avoid using any prefixes or suffixes. This may not be an actual inability to use prefixes or suffixes, but the result of inappropriate modelling: Many adults tend to omit the "-ly" suffix. It is quite common to hear, "Come quick," instead of "Come quickly."
Phonology—using the 44 phonemes (the smallest unit of speech sound). Phonological difficulties arise from articulation disorders, and voice, fluency or physical disorders of the speech mechanisms. Second-language learners may have difficulty with English phoneme sounds.	Nancy, a seven-year-old said, "De nake mall" ("The snake is small").

TABLE 3.6 CONTINUED

Difficulty	Example
Blending the sounds of the alphabet into words (phonics)	Some children cannot take individual letter sounds and put them together to make a word. For example, the word "cat" can be broken down into the individual letter sounds: c-a-t. When these sounds are verbalized separately, some children cannot put the sounds together to create the word "cat."
Using beginning or ending consonant sounds	Some children cannot distinguish differences in individual sounds or distinguish them from the whole word. Similar sounds, such as "d" and "t" or "b" and "d," are easily confused.
Distinguishing vowel sounds	This is much more difficult because there are two types of vowel sounds to distinguish—short and long—both of which come with a set of rules and exceptions. And inability to distinguish vowel sounds can become complicated for a child who has difficulty following directions or sequences or with remembering.
Difficulty in identifying and using appropriate language specific to the context of various situations (pragmatics)	Lily, a four-year-old, told her caregiver to "Shut up." Her caregiver responded that this was not a polite way to say this. Lily thought about it and replied, "Shut up, please?"

3. The Impact of Culture on Communication

The use of physical communication is culturally and experientially dependent. It can also be individualistic. Children's ability to express themselves physically depends on their ability to perceive messages through body language, their physical ability to imitate appropriate body language and their ability to understand and use body language. Here are some typical examples of children who use a different type of body language:

- Dillon nodded when he meant No, rather than Yes.
- Melanie waved at people if she wanted them to go away, or if she wanted to be alone.
- Markus put his hands on top of his head when he was frustrated.

In addition to the possible disabilities described above, there are also a number of specific language disorders. These include aphasia, an inability to communicate effectively using verbal language because of difficulty in comprehension or production difficulties, and apraxia, an inability to communicate verbally because the child cannot effectively use the muscles that control speech sounds.

Some children may simply not be able to learn through verbal communication, and so they will need to be involved in nonverbal communication. There are some early warning signs of children who are in this category:

- The infant does not make early vocalizations or sounds, such as cooing or babbling.
- The infant started to coo and babble but stopped.
- The infant or toddler continues to coo, but using vowel sounds only.
- The child does not express any words.
- The child is not talking.
- The child does not follow simple directions.
- The child shows no evidence of recognizing familiar objects in the environment by pointing to them or following requests to get them.
- The child is difficult to understand.
- The child does not combine words into sentences or phrases.
- The child cannot relate experiences or tell stories in a relevant sequence.
- The child does not seem to understand verbal dialogue.

4. Advanced Cognitive Abilities

Children who fall into this category are often also referred to as intellectually superior, gifted or talented. These children have abilities that are advanced compared with other children of the same age. The identification of giftedness is difficult because:

- The identification is dependent on the particular values and beliefs about what abilities should be recognized as exceptional. Is the child only gifted if he or she is exceptional overall? Can a child be gifted in only one or two areas? What value is placed on giftedness in different areas, such as art, music or academic achievement?
- Various jurisdictions have different criteria for measuring giftedness. Is it measured by an IQ score? Is it on the basis of a diagnostic assessment in a particular area?
- Giftedness is somewhat of a subjective assessment in the early years. For example, Christopher started to talk in full sentences by the time he was 18 months old. He also used "big" words. He was continually identified as bright. He certainly had an advanced skill in language, and, since this was a very observable skill, assumptions were made about his general abilities.

Some of the behaviours that children who are gifted might exhibit are included in Table 3.7.

5. Learning Disabilities

"'Learning disabilities' refer to a number of disorders that may affect the acquisition, organization, retention, understanding or use of verbal or nonverbal information. These disorders affect learning in individuals who otherwise demonstrate at least

TABLE 3.7   BEHAVIOURS OF GIFTED CHILDREN

Behaviour	Example
Extensive vocabulary and advanced communication interactions	Christopher, a two-year-old, was on a field trip to a department store. He was touching some of the clothes as he was walking by. When asked to please not touch, he responded, "Will the sales clerk get annoyed with me if I touch the clothes?"
Creativity in approaching tasks, such as using materials symbolically when materials are not readily available	Olivia, a four-year-old, built a zoo. She used rectangular blocks to make fences. When she ran out of these blocks, she used wedges. She said, "There are gaps. The animals might escape." She experimented and discovered that she could create rectangular shapes by putting two wedges together. Olivia also said that she was going to create a "terrain" to make the zoo "more realistic." She created hills within her enclosure by placing boxes of various sizes in the enclosure and then putting a brown blanket on top of these. She also created a moat by using blue material to drape inside the fence she had created.
Ability to solve problems independently	Billy wanted to test which of the bottles held more water. He thought that the tall, skinny bottle would hold the most water. Billy collected a funnel, a measuring cup and some linking cubes. For every cup he poured into the bottle, he added one of the linking cubes. When he was finished, he could compare which bottle held more water visually. Billy was amazed to find that the shorter bottle held more water. He repeated his experiment to make sure that it was "absolutely true."
Perception of the world from another individual's perspective	Emily, a toddler, saw another toddler fall and hurt herself. Before the adult could get to the injured child, Emily was already there. She said, "That hurt." She hugged the child and managed to calm her down.
Transference of learning from one situation to another	Jarred had discovered that he could create different colours of paint when he was fingerpainting. He had discovered that yellow and red make orange. When he was at the paint station, he decided to experiment to create different colours. He was delighted to realize that he could create shades of colours and new colours.

TABLE 3.7 CONTINUED

Behaviour	Example
Divergent thinking ability (ability to think of a variety of ways to solve a problem)	Braelyn and Yasmine wanted to test how fast the little cars could travel. They decided that they could test and discuss the speed of the cars in the following ways: • Pushing them quickly on a flat, clear surface • Testing them on the ramp they had built • Creating a new ramp that was higher • Creating a new ramp that was steeper • Using hollow cardboard tubes of varying lengths to roll the cars down

average abilities essential for thinking and/or reasoning. As such, learning disabilities are distinct from global intellectual deficiency" (The Learning Disabilities Association of Canada, 2004:1).

Children who experience learning disabilities may have difficulty in a variety of areas. These are identified in Table 3.8.

TABLE 3.8 LEARNING DIFFICULTIES FOR CHILDREN WITH LEARNING DISABILITIES

Difficulty	Example
Oral language skills	Charlie, a five-year-old, liked to tell stories. His stories would ramble on and on. He combined several stories into one oral narrative: "I got a dog. And mommy went to the dentist. And yesterday I hmmm. I like ice cream."
Overall language skills	Jessica, a six-year-old, often confused words. She might ask for a shovel but in reality want a pail, or she might ask for something by saying, "I want hmmm, hmmm, thing, you know," and make a motion to describe the action of the object in the air.
Visual spatial processing	Janie, a four-year-old, found it difficult to put a simple puzzle together. She would turn the piece around and around and try to force it into a specific spot.
Visual sensory-motor problems	Jeremy at age three had very poor coordinated movements. He ran with a jerky, awkward gait. He often lost his balance and fell. Jeremy also showed poor visual spatial processing. He was observed walking into walls or furniture.

TABLE 3.8 **CONTINUED**

Difficulty	Example
Visual perceptual tasks	At age four, Olanda found it difficult to match two objects that were the same. She also found it hard to match a real object to a picture, such as a toy dog to a picture of a similar dog. Jeremy found it difficult to track a rolling object. He would chase a ball as it started to roll away, but stop chasing it because he lost the ball from his visual perspective.
Visual–motor integration	Eight-year-old Jonathan found it difficult to try to grab the crib toy within his reach above him. He would swat at it, until he managed to grab it by chance.
Memory	Alex often forgot simple sequential tasks. When he arrived in the morning, he would need reminders to take his coat off, hang it on the hook, take his boots off and put his slippers on.
Attention span	When Dillon arrived in the morning, he would visit four areas of interest within a 10-minute time span.
Fine-motor control	At four, Jakob had great difficulties with fine-motor activities such as stringing beads, holding scissors to cut and pasting items on a piece of paper. He generally avoided the painting and drawing areas of the preschool room.

Many other learning disabilities do not surface until children start elementary school. At this time, additional difficulties may surface in children's ability to solve mathematical problems, to read and to write.

Children with Impaired Health

Impaired health can be identified as a special need if the disease or condition—such as AIDS, diabetes, asthma, allergies or cystic fibrosis (a genetic condition that affects the respiratory and digestive systems)—affects daily functioning in that individual's life.

These conditions affect children, families and staff in the following ways:

- Children may need to take medication, and it may change their behaviour to make learning more difficult. The effects could include such behaviours as drowsiness, inattentiveness or lack of motivation.

- Children may be absent because of illness, which may increase family stress levels because there are few options for sick–child care.
- Children may need a variety of sophisticated interventions. Staff may need training to gain the knowledge to implement these procedures, such as knowing when and how to give an EpiPen to counteract an allergic reaction. This may create more stress on the staff because of the heightened responsibility for the safety of that child.
- There may be ethical problems and fears associated with some conditions such as AIDS.

High rates of absenteeism caused by impaired health may also affect other domains, such as social or cognitive development.

1. Cystic Fibrosis

Cystic fibrosis is a condition that is genetic and affects the respiratory and digestive systems. It is treated by medication and by diet. The physical manifestations of this condition include:

- Failure to gain weight
- Slow growth pattern
- Chronic episodes of pneumonia or bronchitis

2. Diabetes

There are two types of diabetes. Type 1, insulin–dependent diabetes, is the most common in young children; Type 2, non-insulin-dependent diabetes, is most common after the age of 40. Type 1 diabetes can be treated by insulin intake, diet and exercise. The symptoms of children with diabetes are usually controlled by the medication. Sometimes a diabetic emergency is caused by a low or high sugar imbalance. Symptoms of a diabetic emergency include:

- Dizziness, drowsiness and confusion
- Rapid breathing
- Rapid pulse
- Feeling or looking ill

It is important to know what type of imbalance is evident—low or high sugar—because the treatment, such as giving a child more sugar, may cause a more severe reaction. If the condition is unknown, immediate consultation with a medical emergency authority is essential.

3. Allergies and Asthma

Allergies may also affect a child's performance. Allergies may be caused by genetic factors or by a large range of substances, such as pollen, stings or dust. They may be controlled by medication and by trying to minimize contact with the allergy-causing agent. Some common signs and symptoms of allergies include:

- Rashes, hives or itching
- Complaints of a tight feeling in chest or throat
- Swelling of specific areas of the body
- Wheezing
- Weakness, dizziness or confusion
- Feelings of nausea
- Vomiting

Asthma is a condition that obstructs the bronchial passages by narrowing or swelling the tubes or by clogging the tubes with mucus. Asthma may be controlled by a variety of drugs, usually administered by an inhaler. Common symptoms of an asthma attack include:

- Wheezing
- Violent coughing
- Shortness of breath

4. AIDS

Acquired immune deficiency syndrome (AIDS) is caused by a virus that attacks and disrupts the immune system. In most childhood cases, the HIV virus is transmitted to the fetus by an infected mother. It may also be transmitted through contaminated blood, such as a blood transfusion, or through abusive sexual contact. Children who suffer from AIDS have no defences to combat disease and are prone to eventual fatal infections and cancers.

Children with Physical Disabilities

Physical disabilities generally affect a child's ability to move effectively. Other domains such as cognitive, social, emotional or language may or may not be affected. Physical disabilities may be present at birth or caused by accidents, in particular, trauma to the head.

There are a number of physical disabilities that affect the child's ability to move around the environment effectively. Some children may need total support to help with any kind of movement. These children may have to be moved from one location to another with physical assistance. Other children may be able to navigate with minor assistance by using crutches or braces. Some children may not need assistive devices to walk, but may find it difficult to coordinate muscles smoothly, resulting in a lurching, disjointed gait. They may also find it difficult to keep their balance and will need clear, smooth passageways to navigate successfully.

Fine-motor skills may also be ineffective, and children may need to use assistive devices such as Velcro straps on spoons, paint brushes or pencils. All fine-motor utensils need to be checked to ensure effective use. The child's ability to hold and move the utensils should dictate the adaptations needed.

1. Cerebral Palsy

Cerebral palsy is an an orthopedic condition (a condition that involves the skeleton, joints and muscles). This is one of the most common conditions in young children with disabilities. Children with cerebral palsy find it difficult to coordinate muscle movements and therefore to maintain an appropriate posture or to balance effectively for movement. Cerebral palsy may be classified by the number of body parts that are impaired and by the type of brain damage that has occurred, as well as the subsequent motor patterns that are evident.

Spastic cerebral palsy refers to children who have suffered damage to the motor cortex of the brain. These children will have difficulty controlling voluntary movement. The condition is characterized by slow and difficult movement, poor coordination and weak, hypertonic muscle tone (normal muscle tone is excessively tense).

The primitive reflexes that an individual exhibits at birth continue to be involved as the child grows. These reflexes are automatic and involuntary. Children may continue to exhibit primitive reflex movements, such as the rooting reflex, the startle reaction, the stretch reflex, the asymmetrical tonic neck reflex, protective extensive reactions and righting reactions.

Children with cerebral palsy will be affected in a number of ways:

- They will experience difficulty in reaching developmental milestones because they have little control over their muscles.
- They will need to learn to use braces or other assistive devices to walk.
- They may develop a multi-disabling condition affecting some or all other developmental domains.
- They may have difficulty communicating effectively because of impaired motor function of the speech organs.
- They may have visual or auditory problems.
- They may have deficits in the tactile senses, causing decreased ability to feel pain, pressure or temperature.

2. Hearing Impairments

"Hearing loss is silent, painless, and invisible, one of the least recognized and most misunderstood disabilities. Severe and profound hearing loss (deafness) is a low-incidence condition; however, milder forms of hearing impairment (hard of hearing) are widely prevalent" (Winzer, 1999:324).

Hearing loss is defined in terms of the individual's ability to distinguish the intensity of loudness over several frequencies. This is usually measured in decibels, the smallest measurable difference in loudness intensity between sounds. Hearing impairment is subsequently categorized into mild, moderate, severe or profound hearing loss. An individual with a mild hearing loss may have difficulty hearing faint sounds that are far away. An individual with a moderate hearing loss may find it difficult to follow conversations, especially in group situations. An individual with a severe hearing loss needs a hearing aid to understand language and will need speech and language training. With a profound hearing loss, individuals may hear loud sounds but cannot understand speech sounds.

Hearing is a critical component of the development of speech and language. Infants who are deaf will babble, but much later than other children—usually after they start to observe the movement of the lips and mouth, between six and ten months of age. The babbles produced by these infants are the labial sounds: sounds produced by the lips and mouth (Schickedanz, Schickedanz, Forsyth & Forsyth, 2001). Infants who are deaf will not respond to the normal soothing or interactive techniques used by family members, such as singing or sound games. As a result, families may attribute the infant's behaviour to other causes.

Children who suffer deafness or hearing loss will have some degree of difficulty. Predictable difficulties include:

- Inability to communicate using spoken language and consequent dependence on others around them to learn alternative means of communication
- Difficulty in interpreting the feelings and emotions of others, as many of these are portrayed through tone of voice
- Possible difficulty in acquiring early cognitive experiences through active exploration, unless care is taken to provide enriched opportunities through the other senses

Children who suffer from a loss of hearing or partial loss of hearing can still live active, normal lives. Their environment must be adapted to provide numerous opportunities to learn through alternative sensory experiences. Alternative communication strategies must also be provided, both to the child and to those individuals the child is in contact with.

3. Limb Deficiencies

Limb deficiencies may involve the loss of parts of limbs, such as toes and fingers, or the loss of a total limb, such as an arm or leg. Children may be born with this condition or suffer the loss due to an accident. A lost partial or total limb may be replaced by a prosthesis that allows the child to function relatively normally with some adaptations, such as ramps or gradually rising stairs on climbing equipment.

4. Muscular Dystrophy

Muscular dystrophy is an inherited condition, typically occurring in boys, that is associated with the degeneration of muscle fibre. Symptoms may not become evident until the child starts to walk. As the muscle tissue deteriorates, the child will find it difficult to climb stairs, and increasingly more difficult to walk effectively.

Many children will be confined to a wheelchair by the time they are eight years old. This condition is associated with a shorter lifespan and is usually not associated with other disabilities.

5. Spinal Cord Damage

Damage or injury to the spinal cord will result in muscular damage below the point of injury, manifested by partial or total paralysis. As with other physical disabilities, children may need to use assisted devices for walking or may require a wheelchair. They may also have little control over bowel and urinary functions.

Spina bifida is a defect in the vertebrae that protect the spinal cord. The effects of spina bifida can range from minimal to severely disabling. Children may suffer neurological damage that results in delays in or impairment of growth and development. A resulting paralysis of the lower body may make it necessary for children to walk using assistive devices or in more severe cases to need a wheelchair. Children may have some perceptual and cognitive disabilities.

6. Tourette's Syndrome

Tourette's syndrome is characterized by involuntary muscle movement, such as sporadic twitches or tics. Additional symptoms may include hyperactivity (higher motor activity levels than normal for children of this age), short attention span, increased impulsive behaviour and restlessness.

7. Visual Impairments

Visual impairment is categorized by the severity of the loss: mild, moderate or severe. Vision is measured by two factors: the ability to see from a distance and visual acuity (clarity of vision). Normal vision is reported as 20/20 vision.

Infants whose visual acuity is impaired or completely lacking will find it more difficult to actively explore their environment. The motivation to move is not as strong when visual stimulation is missing. As a result, motor milestones may be delayed. Additionally, early symbolic and social play are limited. Both types of play are highly reliant on the visual senses. It is hard to use objects or actions symbolically when they cannot be seen.

Children may also experience difficulties with communication skills, as they will not be able to pick up visual cues such as body language or facial expressions. Interaction patterns may also be impaired. The body language of individuals who cannot see may differ from that of sighted people. For example, some of the cues that signal interest include smiling, eye contact or varied facial expressions. These may be missing totally, and this may interfere with peer social interactions.

Children with visual impairments need to learn about their world by relying on their other senses. These children can develop normally in all other areas if great care is taken to build their confidence in themselves and their environment so they can actively explore, and if children are provided other ways to learn than through visual stimulation.

Children at Risk

Risk factors that threaten early childhood development include biological and environmental conditions that may increase the likelihood of problems in physical, social, emotional, social or cognitive development. Risk factors include poverty, inadequate nutrition, child abuse, exposure to substance abuse and environmental factors.

1. Poverty

"In 1989, one in seven Canadian children lived below the poverty line. A unanimous, all party resolution, however, set out to change that. Child poverty would be eliminated by the year 2000. Twelve years on, the ratio stands at one in five, or a 43 percent increase. In human terms, the difference translates into approximately 500 000 more children living in poverty." (Martin, 2002).

Children who live in poverty are vulnerable in all developmental areas. Poor families have few resources to spend on stimulative materials, appropriate nutritious foods and appropriate shelter, and often have less time to spend with children because of long working days. "Income seems to be strongly related to children's physical health, cognitive abilities, and school achievement in the early grades even after controlling for a number of other parental characteristics, and these effects of income are most pronounced for children who experience persistent and extreme poverty." Brooks-Gunn and Duncan also suggest that the timing of poverty is important. "Low income during the preschool and early school years is more predictive of low rates of high school completion than low income during later childhood and adolescence" (Behrman, 1997:9; Brooks-Gunn & Duncan, 1997).

2. Nutrition

The two most common problems in early childhood development that may not be identified as special needs are obesity and undernourishment. These conditions are often caused by unhealthy eating habits, but both obesity and undernourishment may also be caused by a diagnosable medical or psychological condition. Obesity may also result from a lack of appropriate physical exercise.

When children are so obese that it affects their physical activity, their social and physical development may lag. Children who are obese find it more difficult to keep up with their peers, may be teased and may be excluded. For example, Jonathan was a child who was obese as an infant. This made it very difficult for him to reach the normal physical developmental milestones. At 16 months of age, he had made no attempts to stand or pull himself to a standing position. The family finally sought medical help. With an appropriate diet, Jonathan not only lost weight but became physically more active. By the time he started in a toddler play-group program, he had almost reached all of his physical milestones.

Children who are undernourished consume too few calories for healthy growth and development. Reasons for undernourishment may include a specific disability such as fetal alcohol syndrome or severe cerebral palsy. Some children may have difficulty chewing or swallowing. A number of children in Canada may suffer from malnutrition because of poverty. Undernourishment may cause lack of appropriate growth and development. Children who do not meet the daily nutritional requirements may be listless, hard to motivate or seem tired all the time. For healthy growth and development in all domains, appropriate nutrition is paramount.

3. Exposure to Child Abuse

Child abuse in any form, whether physical, sexual or emotional abuse, or neglect, leaves a lasting effect on the developing individual, particularly in the early years. "It is clear that the early years from conception to age six have the most important influence of any time in the life cycle of brain development and subsequent learning, behaviour and health. The effects of early experience, particularly during the first three years, on wiring and sculpting of the brain's billions of neurons last a lifetime" (McCain & Mustard, 1999:7). Unfortunately, "wiring and sculpting" are affected not only by appropriate experiences, but also by inappropriate ones. A PET scan of the brain of a child who has been abused will show significantly less activity in the temporal lobes of the brain. Brain growth is stunted by any form of abuse. "As a result, regions in the cortex and in the limbic system (responsible for emotions, including attachment) are 20 to 30 percent smaller in abused children than in normal kids" (Begley, 1997:32).

Brain development in the early years goes through periods when the brain is more sensitive to stimulation. "There are windows of opportunity for these sensitive periods. For attachment, the window closes at 18 months; for self-regulation at 24 months; and syntax at three to four years. Once a window closes, the potential for growth, differentiation and connection is much less. However, that does not mean that no further connections will be made—but to bring about change after windows of opportunity have lowered is fighting biology and like trying to swim upstream against a current" (Steinhauer, 1999:15).

Children who have been abused in the early years will suffer permanent damage, for a variety of reasons:

- First, they will have difficulty regulating their feelings. They will be more negative, will smile less and may be more sullen or withdrawn.
- They may be more aggressive, show greater frustration and have fewer strategies to deal with their frustration.
- They may develop patterns of ADHD behaviours such as hyperactivity, short attention spans and distractibility.
- They are likely to be less empathetic toward peers.
- If abused as an infant, the child's ability to form strong attachments is also impaired. This will interfere with the ability to form positive relationships with peers in later years.
- All of these factors lead to eventual difficulty in the school years. These children tend to have difficulty learning and seek high levels of approval from their teachers (Steinhauer, 1999).

A) SYMPTOMS OF CHILD ABUSE "Child abuse occurs when a parent or guardian or caregiver mistreats or neglects a child, resulting in injury, or significant emotional or psychological harm or serious risk of harm to the child" (National Clearinghouse on Family Violence, 1997).

It is crucial that symptoms of the various forms of child abuse are recognized. Provincial law requires that all forms of suspected child abuse must be reported. Since many of the symptoms of child abuse can also be attributed to other reasons, careful observation and documentation are required. Table 3.9 outlines the possible symptoms of child abuse.

TABLE 3.9   POSSIBLE SYMPTOMS OF CHILD ABUSE

Type of Abuse	Possible Symptoms
Emotional	Children may exhibit some of the following behaviours: • poor self-image, lack of self-confidence • inappropriate behaviour patterns towards adults, peers and/or materials • withdrawal from activities or children or adults • physical and/or verbal aggression • exaggerated compliance and submission • delayed social skills • poor growth patterns; failure to thrive in infants • developmental and cognitive delays • lack of self-initiative • reluctance to engage in play activities
Neglect	Children may appear to be: • constantly hungry; may try to steal food • in poor health, with frequent illnesses • exhibiting a number of dental problems, such as cavities • tired and lacking in energy • dressed inappropriately for various weather conditions • dressed in clothes that are torn, dirty and or ill-fitting • showing poor growth patterns; failure to thrive in infants • demanding or overly demonstrative for physical attention • dirty and unkempt • exhibiting a physical injury that has not been treated

TABLE 3.9   CONTINUED

Type of Abuse	Possible Symptoms
Physical	Children may: • have unexplained injuries, such as bruises, burns, welts or broken bones • become upset if asked to explain injuries, or refuse to let an adult look at an injury hidden by clothes • wear clothing to hide signs of abuse even if that clothing is inappropriate for weather conditions (such as wearing long-sleeved sweaters in hot weather) • be fearful of certain situations, such as going home or of being touched • show fearful behaviours when an adult is within their proximity, such as ducking down when an adult approaches at a certain angle • be overly demanding or aggressive • be withdrawn and compliant • be frequently absent • talk about physical violence during play or dramatize violence using dolls or puppets
Sexual	Children may: • engage in dramatic play that portrays sexual acts • show knowledge of and use sexual terms that are not age appropriate • engage in self-stimulating behaviour, such as masturbation, and self-exploration • complain of pain in throat, abdomen or genital area • exhibit physical symptoms, including difficulty walking or sitting, genital discharge and swelling or bleeding • exhibit behaviours such as wetting or soiling self, being overly clingy or seeming to revert to behaviours more appropriate to younger chidlren • be excessively rebellious or aggressive • be excessively compliant • show signs of depression • resist undressing or being undressed • talk about what has happened to them that relates to sexual assault

Source: Public Health Agency of Canada (2005); Manitoba Services and Housing (2003)

4. Exposure to Substance Abuse

Children who have been exposed to substance abuse in the fetal stages may exhibit a number of physical and behavioural differences. The most commonly studied areas of substance abuse are alcohol, tobacco and drugs, such as cocaine and heroin.

Symptoms are generally associated with the particular type of abuse.

The most common syndrome associated with drug abuse is fetal alcohol syndrome. "Fetal alcohol syndrome refers to a physical and mental birth defect that may develop in individuals whose mothers consumed alcohol during pregnancy. It is an organic brain disorder which is characterized by central nervous system involvement, growth retardation, and characteristic facial features" (Graefe, 2003:13). According to Graefe (2003), the symptoms are specific to different ages of the child:

- Infancy—Infants may have problems bonding, be irritable, have erratic sleep patterns or cry a lot. Many infants fail to thrive, which may be tied to feeding difficulties and a weak sucking reflex. Infants may have overall muscle weakness and tend to be highly susceptible to illness. Additional symptoms include sensitivity to touch, sound and sights, and slowness to reach developmental milestones.
- Preschool—Preschoolers tend to be highly sociable but indiscriminate with relationships. They tend to have poor motor control and a low attention span. They are easily distracted and may be hyperactive. Poor eating and sleeping habits are still evident. Delays may be noted in language development and in the ability to understand dangerous situations. They do not respond well to routines or verbal warnings, and may be prone to temper tantrums.

Smoking during pregnancy also causes a number of potential problems. "Over 2500 chemicals have been identified in cigarette smoke. Most likely, the majority of the adverse effects are attributed to two main ingredients: nicotine and carbon monoxide. During pregnancy, these chemicals decrease the oxygen available to the growing fetus, and increase fetal blood pressure" (Goldberg, 2002:1). Potential problems include low birth weight, fetal and neonatal mortality, increased incidence of sudden infant death syndrome and spontaneous abortions. "The increase in carbon monoxide coupled with the decreased oxygen resulting from nicotine constricting the mother's capillaries affects brain development, which causes later deficits in learning and memory. Researchers have found that lung damage to the offspring can last into adulthood" (Schickedanz et al., 2001:75).

Drug addiction during pregnancy results in addiction in the fetus and the newborn to the drug used. The newborn experiences drug-withdrawal symptoms at birth, including irritability, extreme sensitivity to touch, tremors, feeding problems, diarrhea and vomiting. Later effects may include impaired or excessive motor activity, impaired information-processing ability, difficulty in self-regulatory behaviours, impulsiveness and less responsiveness to stimulation.

KEY POINTS

Historical viewpoints

- Societal values and beliefs reflected in changing attitudes toward education of children with special needs
- Rise of institutional care from 1831 to 1970s
- Segregated settings from 1906 to present day
- Inclusive care in the 1990s

Behavioural and emotional disorders

- Feelings and emotions influence behaviour and interactions
- Conduct disorders—Aggressiveness, disruptive behaviours
- Anxiety/withdrawal—Withdrawing from stressful situations
- Attention deficit hyperactivity disorder—Impulsiveness, short attention span, inattentiveness, increased physical activity
- Pervasive development disorders—autism: avoidance of human contact, self-stimulation, fixation

Cognitive disabilities

- Difficulty following directions, learning new skills, remembering or responding appropriately to others or situations in other domains
- Classification system AAIDD—Mild to profound retardation
- Reform of AAIDD to reflect supports, individuality, sensitivity and personalized supports needed
- Communication difficulties—Receptive, expressive and body language difficulties; evident in difficulty with discerning meaning of words, following directions, engaging in communication; difficulty with syntax, morphology, phonology, phonics and pragmatics
- Advanced cognitive abilities—Giftedness dependent on value and belief system, subjective in early years, difficult to measure; signs include enhanced vocabulary, creativity in approach to tasks, independence in problem solving, perception of other perspectives, ability to transfer knowledge and skills, and ability to think divergently

- Learning disabilities—Difficulty with skills in oral language, overall language, visual spatial skills, visual motor memory, perceptual tasks, visual–motor integration, memory, attention span and fine-motor control

Impaired health—Identified as a special need if the disease or condition affects the daily functioning of that individual

- May result in need to medicate or provide other specialized interventions
- May pose ethical problems
- May result in increased absenteeism
- May lead to developmental delays or social-adjustment problems

Physical disabilities

- Cerebral palsy—Difficulty with coordination of muscle movement with continued primitive reflex behaviour; difficulty with reaching motor milestones, mobility without assistive devices, communication, visual and auditory channels, and tactile senses; may have multiple disabling conditions
- Hearing impairment—Classified from mild to severe; difficulty in communication, interpretations of feelings and emotions, and acquiring cognitive skills
- Limb deficiencies—Loss of single limb, part of a limb or multiple limbs
- Muscular dystrophy—Gradual deterioration of muscle fibre
- Spinal cord damage—Paralysis or partial paralysis below point of injury
- Tourette's syndrome—Hyperactivity with involuntary muscle movements such as twitching and tics
- Visual impairment—Classified from mild to severe; may be delayed in reaching motor milestones; difficulty with symbolic and social play, communication skills, self-confidence and peer interactions

Children at risk

- Poverty—Lack of appropriate stimulation, materials, shelter or nutrition leaves young children vulnerable in all domains

- Nutrition—Inappropriate nutrition can lead to obesity or undernourishment
- Exposure to child abuse—Child abuse affects brain development, resulting in lasting problems in ability to regulate behaviour or form appropriate social relationships

- Symptoms of child abuse—emotional/psychological, neglect, physical, sexual
- Exposure to substance abuse—Includes alcohol, tobacco and drugs; children develop abnormal behaviour patterns and health problems

EXERCISES

1. Trace the historical steps in the evolution of the field of early childhood education. Explain how the current philosophical viewpoint has evolved.

2. Refer to Table 3.1 on page 72. There are far more disadvantages to labelling children than advantages. Reflect on your personal feelings. Where do you agree most strongly? Least strongly? Explain why.

3. What positive guidance techniques would you draw upon to help a child who is having difficulties handling his or her behaviour?

4. Reflect on the following scenario: A new child has been registered in your toddler program. When you first meet Damian, he refuses to look at you or greet you. He cringes away from your touch, sits in the corner and rocks while flicking his fingers in front of his eyes. How do you feel? What are some strategies you

might need to develop to help you interact with this child?

5. Identify what kinds of problems you might expect with children with (a) communication disabilities and (b) learning disabilities. What could you do to minimize the problems listed?

6. What strategies might you have to develop to include a gifted child within a preschool program?

7. A child with cerebral palsy who is using braces and crutches has enrolled in your program. Refer to the floor plan in Chapter 1 (page 21). What additional adaptations might be needed to accommodate this child?

8. How might you minimize the effects of poverty within a day care setting? How would you involve families? What resources might you need to gather?

REFERENCES

Allen, K., Paasche, C., Langford, R., & Nolan, K. (2002). *Inclusion in Early Childhood Programs: Children with Exceptionalities*. Third Canadian Edition. Scarborough, ON: Thomson Nelson.

American Association of Intellectual and Developmental Disabilities (AAIDD). (2002). Definition of mental Retardation [online]. Available at www.aamr.org/Policies /faq_mental_retardation.shtml [01/08/2008].

American Association on Mental Retardation (2002). *Mental Retardation Definitions, Classifications, and Systems of Supports*. Washington, DC: American Association on Mental Retardation.

Autism Treatment Services of Canada. (2006). What is Autism? Autism Treatment Services of Canada [online]. Available at www.autism.ca/whataut.htm [01/08/2008].

Begley, S. (1997). How to Build a Baby's Brain. *Newsweek, 28*, 28–32.

Behrman, R. E. (1997). Children and Poverty: Analysis and Recommendations. *The Future of Children in Poverty*, 7[2], 1–161.

Brooks-Gunn, J., & Duncan, G. (1997). The Effects of Poverty on Children. *The Future of Children and Poverty* 7[2], 55–72.

Freiberg, K. E. (2004). Emotional and Behavioral Disorders. *Annual Editions Educating Exceptional Children*, Sixteenth Edition.

Freiberg, K. E. (2005). Educating Exceptional Children. *Annual Editions, 16*. Guilford, CT: McGraw-Hill/Dushkin.

Goldberg, B. (2002). Smoking in Pregnancy. Baby Corner [online]. Available at www.thebabycorner.com/pregnancy/info/preg0046.html [29-8-2004].

Government of Ontario. (1997). Day Nurseries Act. R.R.O. 1990, Reg. 262.

Graefe, S. (2003). *Living with FASD: A Guide for Parents*. Vancouver, BC: Ben Simon Press.

Hope Irwin, S., Lero, D., & Brophy, K. (2000). *A Matter of Urgency: Including Children with Special Needs in Child Care in Canada*. Wreck Cove, NS: Breton Books.

Jolivette, K., Stichter, J., & McCormick, K. (2002). Making Choices—Improving Behavior—Engaging in Learning. *Teaching Exceptional Children, 34*, 24–29.

Macintyre, C. (2002). *Play for Children with Special Needs*. London, UK: David Fulton Publishers.

Manitoba Services and Housing. (2003). Protecting Children from abuse and Neglect [online]. Available at www.gov.mb.ca/fs/childfarm/child_protection.html [06/01/09].

Martin, A. (2002). Child Poverty in Canada. PoliticsWatch News [online]. Available at www.politicswatch.com/child_poverty.htm.

Mash, E., & Wolfe, D. (1999). *Abnormal Child Psychology*. Belmont, CA: Wadsworth Publishing Company.

McCain, M., & Mustard, F. (1999). *Early Years Study Final Report*. Toronto, ON: Publications Ontario.

National Clearinghouse on Family Violence. (1997). Abuse of Children with Disabilities [online]. Available at www.phac-aspc.gc.ca/ncfv-cnivf/familyviolence/html/nfntsdisabl_e.html [06/01.09].

Public Health Agency of Canada. (2005). Publications from the child maltreatment [online]. Available at www.phac-aspc.gc.ca/cm-vee/public-eng.php#rep [06/01/09].

Schickedanz, J., Schickedanz, D., Forsyth, P., & Forsyth, G. (2001). *Understanding Children and Adolescents*. Fourth Edition. Needham Heights, MA: Allyn & Bacon.

Steinhauer, P. (1999). How a Child's Early Experiences Affect Development. *Interaction* 13[1], 15–21.

The Learning Disabilities Association of Canada. (2004). Learning Disability Defined. The Learning Disabilities Association of Canada [online]. Available at www.ldac-taac.ca.

Winzer, M. (1999). *Children with Exceptionalities in Canadian Classrooms*. Scarborough, ON: Prentice Hall Allyn and Bacon.

4 The Inclusive Learning Environment

CHAPTER

"Inclusion is a term used to describe the ideology that each child, to the maximum extent appropriate, should be educated in the school and classroom he or she would otherwise attend. It involves bringing support services to the child (rather than moving the child to the services) and requires only that the child will benefit from being in the class (rather than having to keep up with the other students" (Council for Exceptional Children, 2008).

Learning Outcomes

After studying this chapter, you will be able to:

1. Discuss the key components necessary to foster children's learning in an inclusive environment.
2. Explain how variables such as colour, the size and number of children in each learning area, light and maintenance of the learning areas affect children's activities and learning.
3. Analyze and discuss the various dimensions that are critical in the organization of inclusive settings.
4. Identify and discuss how the various core learning areas have been adapted to meet the needs of all children.
5. Define and explain what the relevant adaptations are and why they are critical to maximize learning.
6. Discuss what skills adults need to set up inclusive environments.
7. Define and discuss the role of an adult in an inclusive environment.

Introduction

The environment is a key component in fostering children's learning. In an inclusive environment, the range of abilities, the diversity of the group of children, the various learning styles and the varying needs of the children make the task of appropriate organization complex and challenging. Early childhood educators must consider all aspects of the environment to meet the needs of the children. All

TABLE 4.1   ADAPTATIONS

Adaptation	Description	Example
Spacing	Creating space to allow access to materials, equipment or learning areas	• Individuals in wheelchairs or using walkers
Removal of barriers	Providing ramps or adaptations to equipment to provide access	• Pavement connecting areas outside for wheelchair access • Clear floors to prevent tripping or falling • Wedges to provide smoother access from different flooring types, such as rug to tile
Range of materials	Provide choices for various skill and ability levels	• Range of puzzles, from simple to complex • Range of writing tools suitable for palmar to tripod grasp
Labelling system	Pictures, symbols, Braille or colour schemes to help the child locate learning areas and locate and return materials	• Cars in parking lots on the floor with a picture and word of the car
Adaptive devices	Devices that provide greater independence	• Baskets to hang on wheelchairs • Switches to operate doors or lights • Symbol boards to enhance communication
Flexibility	Routines and activities to respect child's ability to complete tasks	• Different starting times for transitions • Continuation of activities from indoor to outdoors or over several days
Stability	Structured environment that encourages predictability and comfort in knowing where things are	• Changes are in choices of materials and/or equipment; learning areas remain stable
Collaborative planning	Families, professionals and staff members develop individual program plans that identify the individual child's strengths and needs, set goals and objectives, list strategies and evaluate the progress of the child regularly	• Individual program plans • Individual service plans • Individual portfolios

dimensions of the learning environment must relate to the growth and development of all children, as outlined in Table 4.2. In essence, the early childhood educators "set the stage" for learning.

The inclusive learning environment is not substantially different from other environments. The central focus is on encouraging active play. The key differences are in the adaptations that have been made (see Table 4.1).

TABLE 4.2   ASPECTS OF OPTIMAL CHILDREN'S LEARNING ENVIRONMENTS

Environments	Optimal Aspects
Learning spaces that foster emotional development	• Secure, safe environment to encourage active exploration • Spaces for individual and group play to encourage child to recognize and respect personal feelings and the feelings of others • Organization that encourages independence • Materials and toys that represent diversity to foster understanding of self and others
Learning spaces that foster social development	• Organization of learning spaces to encourage individual, small-group or large-group interactions • Organization to provide opportunities to practise a variety of role-play situations • Materials and equipment that encourage individual or group play • Organization to support the growth of respect and cooperation with each other
Learning spaces that foster cognitive development	• Encouragement of a variety of skills such as problem solving, decision making, divergent thinking, transferring knowledge and skills from one situation to another, and experimenting with materials and equipment
Learning spaces that foster physical development	• Open spaces to practise gross-motor skills such as running, crawling, riding or balancing • Equipment that encourages development of motor skills such as strength, endurance, agility, balance and coordination • Materials to encourage fine-motor development to refine grasps, eye–hand coordination and skill development such as constructing, painting, drawing, cutting and pouring
Learning spaces that foster language development	• Materials and equipment that encourage children to talk about their play, as in dramatic role-play situations • Materials that foster language development, such as books, word games, picture games, videos, computers, photographs, pictures and puzzles
Learning spaces that foster individual development	• Adaptations to meet individual needs, such as a large variety of learning materials to meet a wider age range of abilities, or adaptations to the physical environment to facilitate active choices • Materials, organization and equipment to encourage individual and group learning activities

Setting the Stage

"The physical elements of a learning environment help to create a psychological climate of ambiance. Whether the message is overt or symbolic the physical environment communicates information about the kinds of behaviors and performances expected of children" (Winter, 1999:135). It is critical that adults think about the messages that the organization of the learning environment is sending. A number of variables can either impede or facilitate learning.

1. Use of Colour

Colour, as discussed in Chapter 2, page 49, can be used to soothe or excite children's activities. Careful consideration must be given to the colours used in the environment.

The use of bright, primary colours in rugs or furniture will place emphasis on the rugs and the furniture, as these items will stand out in the environment. Children's learning activities will be de-emphasized. In fact, these colours might also serve as a real detractor to the children's activities. Many of the materials and toys are colourful. For example, materials such as Lego or Duplo blocks are usually in bright, primary colours. When these are used on a bright surface, or a colourful rug, the materials tend to blend in and are hard to pick out. This makes the activity much harder to accomplish. In addition, children who have difficulty with visual figure ground (ability to pick out individual items from a background, such as that shown in Photo 4.1), or with any visual problems, will find this task almost impossible. When children work on bright table surfaces, with materials such as coloured paper and various colours of crayons and markers, these are also difficult to pick out. The bright surfaces also reflect light and may lead to eye strain. This affects the ability of the child to be creative and to sustain activity.

When the walls are brightly coloured, it is hard to display children's work appropriately. Their creative efforts become lost in a sea of colour. When too much colour exists within the learning environment, children may become distracted more easily, find it harder to settle into a routine or may tend to avoid certain areas altogether.

Photo 4.1

For example, in an integrated preschool room, the following colour scheme was used: One wall was painted a bright red, with colourful depictions of the alphabet and associated pictures marching across the middle of the wall. Two bookshelves in dark blue were placed at right angles to this wall to create a book corner. The cushions in the area were bright yellow and red. The rug in the block area was an alphabet rug in yellow with brightly coloured letters, numbers and pictures in various squares. The other three walls were painted in a darker blue. The overall effect gave the impression of a dark, dull day. The room seemed very small. The furniture was in variations of primary colours: yellow, red and blue. Within this environment, the following behaviours were observed within one hour:

- Children were wandering around. Some children were running and had to be reminded to walk (eight times).
- No children were observed in the book area.
- Children only used blocks that were of a natural colour.
- There was a high noise level in the room. Children became progressively noisier during the hour of observation. The lights were flicked on and off four times to remind the children to settle down.
- The papers that children chose to draw on tended to be large and white or off-white.

I eventually noticed that one child had created an area of calm for himself. He was sitting under a table and hidden from view by a bright tablecloth. When I peeked under the tablecloth, he placed his finger on his lips to say, "Shhh!" He also whispered, "You can come and draw with me if you like." I crawled under the table to sit with him. The atmosphere was much cozier and the noise was somewhat diminished. When I emerged from under the table, one of the staff members explained that this child worked there most of the time. I asked why she thought he did that. The answer was that he was very bright, but that he did not like interacting with other children very much. The staff did not seem to realize the effect that the environment had on the children.

From the Author   Reflection

One of the integrated settings I observed left a memorable impression on me of what *not* to do. When I entered the preschool room, I became overwhelmed with the bright profusion of colours. The effect of the colours was worsened by the bright sunlight streaming in. It hurt the eyes! I was also overwhelmed with a sense of disorganized bedlam. Children were in continual motion. The noise level was overpowering. The learning areas were in disarray. Toys had been left scattered on brightly coloured rugs. These toys were hard to pick out because they blended in so well with the background. There was no area that had been created to provide a relief from the over-stimulation of senses.

One child, who was visually impaired, brought the beads over to the rug area. She accidentally dropped the beads. She sat down to try to find them, spreading out her hands to try to feel the beads. She eventually gave up and found another activity.

The observer questioned the staff to find out if these were normal behaviours during free-play activities. The staff indicated that these behaviours were fairly typical. When asked why this particular colour scheme had been chosen, the staff responded that children liked primary colours. When asked if they liked the colour scheme themselves, some staff members indicated that they did not find it restful.

In contrast, another inclusive setting had decided to de-emphasize the background colours and emphasize the children's activities. In this centre, all the walls were a very pale green. The furniture was natural wood, and the floors and rugs were neutral colours. The children's creative efforts dominated the walls and display areas. When you entered this room, your eye was immediately drawn to what the children had accomplished. None of the behaviours observed in the first example were evident in the second setting.

Colour schemes should be carefully selected to ensure that:

- The focus is on children's creative efforts through displays of their art work, photographs or documentation of their activities.
- The colour does not interfere with the children's ability to accomplish their activities.
- Colour is used to enhance children's ability to relax and concentrate on learning activities.
- Colour is selected to promote an appropriate atmosphere of learning and relaxation.
- The choice of colour promotes the development of aesthetic appreciation.

2. Size of the Learning Area

The nature of the activity should dictate the size of the learning area. A simple system can be used to define the size of any learning area (Shipley, 2008; Crowther, 2007).

- Simple units—A simple unit is one play space. Children involved in individual play such as working on a puzzle, reading a book or painting use simple units.
- Complex units—A complex unit is made up of four spaces. Children involved in complex units are usually involved in some sort of group play such as parallel play (play beside another child, using similar materials but not sharing ideas or materials) or associative play (children share materials and ideas, but may continue to be engaged in an individual play activity). Children use complex units when they are involved in learning areas such as sand, water or carpentry.
- Super units—Super units are made up of eight play spaces. Dramatic play and block play usually involve super units. Larger spaces are needed because block play can spread over a larger area, and dramatic play often utilizes a number of larger pieces of equipment and furniture or may involve larger groups of children.

In a flexible environment, depending on the children's interactions or needs, the size of the play area may change. For example, a single unit may change to a more complex unit because children have decided to work on a larger puzzle together or because a child with a wheelchair in a simple unit needs more room to navigate in. In contrast, a complex unit can become a single unit if, for instance, sand play is provided in individual containers on a platform or on a tabletop.

3. Number of Children per Learning Area

The number of children in a play area should be flexible. Children who are actively involved in play should continue to play together without interruption. Consider the following examples:

In the first example, a symbolized form of four stick figures on a piece of paper was mounted on the sandbox. Five children were playing there. The children were emptying and filling containers of sand. Each child had a container and a scoop. The children were talking to each other about how full their containers were: "Mine is almost full." "Mine is overflowing." One child, Josh, signed, "Full." Amie, another child, promptly signed back and verbalized that his was fuller than hers.

Rachel, a staff member, walked over to the area. She indicated that there were too many children in the sand centre. She asked one of the children to count the stick people. She then said, "See, you counted four. How many individuals are there here?" Josh signed, "Four." She responded that that was not correct; there were five people. Rachel stated that there were too many people and that one child had to leave. She asked who had joined the activity last. The children continued with their filling and dumping activity. She finally arbitrarily selected one child to leave, assuring that child that she could come back when there was room.

In this situation, the adult has not realized the value of the children's play. All children were actively involved. All children were communicating effectively with each other. Each child had found enough space and materials to engage in the sand activity without causing a problem for another child. This type of arbitrary assignment and reinforcement of rules is developmentally inappropriate and cheats children of valuable learning experiences. It is developmentally inappropriate for two reasons:

- Most young children do not make the connection between symbols (stick figures) and the number of children engaged in an activity. There were enough materials for five children to use, and therefore there was room enough to play. The young child sees the world from his or her own perspective.
- Since the play was peaceful and appropriate, asking one child to leave was inappropriate. What was the message given? The children may have concluded that the activity they were involved in or the way they were interacting was inappropriate. It would be difficult for a child to find any other reason for disrupting his or her play.

In the second, more positive example, at a water centre, great excitement was being expressed. A group of six children had discovered that they could cover the water table with bubbles and then hide items in the water under the layer of bubbles.

They had also discovered that by using straws, they could blow away the bubbles to create a clear space to see and find the objects hidden. Their enthusiasm attracted other children. Harmon rolled over in his wheelchair. He consistently asked to see, but the children were too excited to hear him. Joyce, the early childhood educator, walked over and said, "Harmon would like to join you." The children promptly moved over and made room for Harmon to participate. The table might have been too crowded for that many children, but since this was a valuable learning experience for the children and since the children were interacting appropriately, there was no reason to disrupt their play.

In summary, the number of children that can participate in a learning activity should depend on three factors:

- The interest of the children—If children are actively engaged, then obviously they have made a decision on how to utilize the space effectively.
- The type and number of materials available (although the number of materials can quickly be increased if needed)—Sometimes a small group of children can be very innovative in using materials perceived to be suitable for just one individual. For example, three children were using a small six-piece transport puzzle. They created a road out of small blocks to pretend to drive the vehicles along. The puzzle frame was utilized as a parking lot.
- The type of interaction—If children are interacting appropriately, they should not be disturbed. If there is a problem, this situation can be used as a problem-solving situation. Note how Joyce prompted the children to solve the problem to include Harmon. In the following situation, Melanie, an early childhood educator, used the situation to encourage the children to solve a problem: Jordan joined a group of four children who were creating strings of beads. He found a long pipe cleaner to use, but could not find an individual container of beads. He grabbed a container from another child. She promptly shouted that it was hers and grabbed it back. Melanie heard the child and asked all of the children what the problem was. Joseé said that Jordan was grabbing beads. Melanie looked at Jordan and asked him what he would like to do. He pointed to his pipe cleaner. "I see," said Melanie, addressing all of the children. "Jordan would like to put some beads on his pipe cleaner." Jordan nodded. Andrew replied, "There's none more." Melanie said, "We seem to have a problem. Jordan would like some beads but can't find any. How could we solve this problem?" The children thought about it and then decided that each of them could give a few beads to Jordan.

4. Type of Lighting

Appropriate lighting is important in many activities where children need to use their visual skills more effectively than usual (see the discussion in Chapter 2, pages 48–49). The need for adequate lighting for children who have visual impairments is even more critical. Any visual work will be greatly enhanced if it takes place near natural light, or if additional light is provided—such as floor lamps or table lamps—to improve the quality of the light in all areas of the room. Additional lights also help the children learn to select the amount of light they need by turning lights on or off.

5. Maintenance of the Learning Environment

An environment should be aesthetically pleasing. This means that walls, furniture and floors should be clean and free of scratches, dents or holes. Tables should be tidied and cleaned after use. If the environment is left in a messy state, the wrong messages are imparted to children (Photo 4.2). They learn that:

- leaving a mess is appropriate
- someone else is responsible to tidy up
- areas that are unattractive or have no room in which to engage in meaningful activity should be avoided
- some learning activities are not valued
- independent action or problem solving is not a requirement

All children need to be engaged in a regular routine. This is an excellent way to expand their sequential skills in a natural way. When I engage in an activity I need to pick up after myself, clean the table and put the materials back where they belong. Consistent expectations not only help children to become more independent, but also encourage growth and development in all skill areas.

6. Additional Dimensions

In summary, the environment in an inclusive setting plays a critical role. The environment can act as a "teacher." Adults need to carefully consider all aspects of the environment to create learning spaces that are appropriate for all children. There needs to be collaboration among families, teachers, other professionals and children to design, change and evaluate the physical learning environment.

Additional dimensions should also be considered in the effective organization of learning environments (Crowther, 2007; Winter, 1999; Harms, Clifford & Cryer, 1998). These dimensions are described in Table 4.3.

Photo 4.2

TABLE 4.3   DIMENSIONS OF THE LEARNING ENVIRONMENT

Dimension	Description	Importance
Softness	Created by the use of soft furniture and items such as large pillows, carpets or grassy surfaces	• Provides opportunities for relaxation
Hardness	Created by use of blocks and ground surfaces such as tiled floors or pavement	• Encourages a different type of play, such as stacking, riding or running
Open-ended materials	These materials, such as blocks, painting or beading, can be used in a variety of ways to construct or explore.	• Provide children with a variety of ways to accomplish tasks • Encourage problem solving
Closed learning materials	These materials, such as puzzles, dominoes or nesting cups, can usually be used in only one way	• Help children develop specific skills, such as patterning, matching or sorting
Intrusion	Children can join others in ongoing play (such as small or large group play); provides a flexible change from simple to complex or super units of space	• Encourages children to interact with each other in small and large groups
Seclusion	Encourages privacy; created by the careful placement of bookshelves or small loft areas, or the transformation of large boxes into a playhouse with a no-interruption rule	• Helps children get away from the pressures that result from continual interaction with peers
Tasks ranging from simple to complex	Range of materials to meet various developmental levels; for example, puzzles range from single-knob puzzles to interlocking puzzles with a background picture to interlocking puzzles with no background picture, to interlocking puzzles with ever-increasing numbers of pieces	• Encourage children to progress at their own rate and speed • Provide opportunities to scaffold tasks, a guided process that gradually removes external prompts or help
Low mobility	Scheduled time for less-active play, such as looking at books or drawing both indoors and out	• Gives children time to relax • Encourages thinking and concentration
High mobility	Space available to engage in active play such as running, riding or building both indoors and out	• Provides opportunities to build gross-motor skills • Provides opportunities to exercise

TABLE 4.3   CONTINUED

Dimension	Description	Importance
Safety	Children need to be able to explore safely; for example, when infants start to crawl, they need to be assured that they can navigate around the environment without fear of injury from sharp objects on the floor or from falls down stairs	• Encourages independence • Builds skills
Safe risks	Learning involves taking risks; for example, infants need to learn to crawl not only on flat surfaces but also up and down stairs	• Encourages growth and development through active exploration
Accessibility	All items that can be used safely should always be accessible through a system of child-sized open shelves and clearly labelled containers	• Encourages increased independence • Encourages problem solving
Inaccessibility	Materials such as cleaning products or medication should be locked away. Some materials may be dangerous to some children, such as small beads that might be swallowed by children mouthing objects. Items should be placed out of reach but accessible visibly. This way, children may ask for the items and staff can supervise the activity.	• Creates a safe environment • Increases self-confidence to explore independently
High stimulation	Colours such as red or yellow attract children. The use of photographs, posters or children's work adds interest to the environment. Novel materials or experiences provide opportunities for movement and increased motivation to engage in new learning.	• Attracts children to an activity • Increases children's attention span • Provides opportunities to make choices
Low stimulation	Soothing colours (pale shades, greens and blues), low noise levels and a set-up protected from visual distractions such as dividers or shelves used to separate area from other areas in the room	• Provides opportunities for relaxation and solitude • Helps develop the ability to increase concentration skills

TABLE 4.3   **CONTINUED**

Dimension	Description	Importance
Predictability	Routines and set-up of the learning environment should follow a regular pattern that children can anticipate. For example, children generally arrive and leave at the same time. Lunch and sleep or rest times should occur at regular intervals. Similarly, routines such as always taking shoes off before lying down for a nap and washing hands after going to the washroom should be established	• Helps children gain comfort and familiarity with the setting • Helps children know where to find things and when to expect changes
Unpredictability	Unpredictability can be introduced by using a variety of materials in a variety of settings, such as rolling balls down different surfaces both indoors and out	• Helps children learn to cope with uncertainty • Helps children make and test predictions
Familiarity	Familiarity is established by maintaining the core learning areas in relatively static positions. Changes made in the learning environment should involve children	• Helps children gain a sense of security in knowing where things are • Helps children gain a sense of ownership as they help create change
Novelty	Novelty can be introduced through the use of new materials/equipment, going on field trips, guests and visitors in the child care settings Use familiar objects in new ways	• Helps children maintain interest • Expands learning • Enhances motivation

Putting the Pieces Together

The creation of inclusive learning areas must be undertaken in light of all the topics covered in the previous chapters, such as children's right to play, the elements of core learning areas, the strengths and needs of all children and the various dimensions of individual learning areas.

The following information draws upon actual observed learning areas in a variety of inclusive environments across Canada. Areas have been included based on the core learning areas as described in Table 2.3, page 53. Representation is included from all age groups. Individual centres have not been identified, to ensure confidentiality of the children with special needs who participated in these inclusive settings.

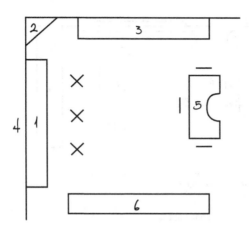

FIGURE 4.1
Books and Pictures

Key

1. Bookshelf
   - picture books and board books on bottom shelf
   - easy-to-read books on middle shelf
   - books suitable to read to children on top shelf
2. Stuffed toys

3. Manipulative shelf
   - puzzles, matching games, board games
   - easiest materials on bottom shelf
   - hardest materials on top shelf
4. Window above bookshelf
5. Table with three chairs, wheelchair accessible
6. Adult-sized couch
X Large cushions

1. Books

In the preschool setting shown in Figure 4.1, the book corner has been set up on the opposite side of the noisier areas, such as blocks, sand and water. This corner has been designated as a quiet area for concentration and manipulation.

One of the children, Jamie, uses a wheelchair with a basket attached to the side. Jamie wheeled himself directly to the bookshelf (Figure 4.1, area 3). He took a book from the second shelf, put it in his basket and went over to the table. He navigated his wheelchair under the table, took out his book and started to look at it. When he had finished looking at the book he returned it to the bookshelf.

Children also read books outdoors. A quiet sheltered area is set up for reading in the corner of the playground. The area has soft plastic cushions on the ground covered by a blanket. It is protected from the wind. In winter, the area is in full sunlight. Children may collect books in baskets to take outside to read (Photo 4.3).

2. Fine-Motor Activities

In the preschool setting shown in Figure 4.1, the environment is adapted and organized based on the emergent interests of children and the observations made by the staff. The staff made the following observations about the children:

- They were interested in animals and in small vehicles.
- They were sorting and patterning the materials. For example, one child lined up all the red cars.
- They used the beads infrequently.

Photo 4.3

FIGURE 4.2

Fine-Motor Activities

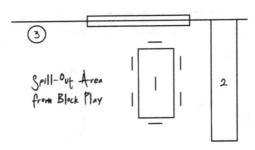

Spill-Out Area from Block Play

Key
1. Manipulative table with six chairs
2. Manipulative shelf
   a) bottom shelf
      • blocks, unit blocks, small cubes
   b) second shelf
      • accessories, tracks, vehicles, people
   c) third shelf
      • large beads, 3 puzzle racks, one-piece knobbed puzzles, interlocking with background picture, 12 or more interlocking pieces
      • sorting bears, one container of each: blue, red, yellow, green
      • two large bowls and 4 dishes: blue, red, yellow, green
3. Display area

Photo 4.4

As a result of these observations, the manipulative area was organized as shown in Figure 4.2. Since two of the four-year-old children put most of the materials in their mouths, the small animal and vehicle beads were only placed on the table when a staff member could supervise the area directly. When there was no direct supervision of the children in this area, these beads were moved to a shelf that was out of the children's reach. Children could ask to use these beads but could use them only when supervised.

The staff continued to observe the children in the manipulative area. Examples of these observations on manipulative materials are listed in Figure 4.3. These observations identified the type of manipulative activity the child was engaged in and the type of learning strategy used. Based on these observations, the staff was satisfied with the revisions made to the manipulative materials. They also added a display area (Figure 4.2, area 3) to document the children's progress and to use the documentation to encourage continued activity. The staff also decided to add milestone documentation to the display area in the hall outside. Dillon's first beading effort was posted in this area.

Additional opportunities to increase fine-motor development were available in other parts of the room. Staff observed the children's continued interest in using crayons, markers and pencil crayons. A table was set up with a variety of paper and writing tools in organized containers. Children could decide what to use and how to use these materials.

3. Art

The creative art area in another preschool room has a variety of activities available, including painting, sculpting, cutting and pasting, and drawing (see Figure 4.5).

FIGURE 4.3

Examples of Observations of Manipulative Activities

Dates: Oct. 7, 9, 10, 11
Key: R = random, **S** = sorting, **P** = patterning
Setting: beading activities

Child's Name	Type of Activity	Comments
Timmy	R, R, R, R	Stringed using gimp Used only vehicle beads
Marcia	P: ABAB pattern P: AABBAABB pattern S: Elephants of different colours S: Zoo animals of different colours	Uses animal beads Fills length of gimp
Dillon	R: Used pipe cleaners R: Poured beads onto plate, then started to bead on pipe cleaner R: Put one train bead on gimp	Filled more than one pipe cleaner When Dillon put bead on gimp immediately ran to teacher to show what he had done

FIGURE 4.4

Frequency Count of Interests of Group of Children

Dates: Oct. 6, 7, 8, 9, 10
Key: t = tally, ++++ = bundle of five tallies

Activity	Number of Children Observed	Coments
Tracks and small vehicles	++++ ++++ ++++ ++++ ++++	Dillon dumps bears into bowls, gets a scoop from the sand area and scoops them onto the plates, then dumps back into bowls. Usually repeats activity at least three times.
Puzzles	++++ ++++ ++++ III	Jeremy has tried the vehicle puzzle five times. He puts the pieces on the tray, waits for someone to finish it, looks at it, dumps it out and tries to fit the pieces in. He refuses help from peers or adults.
Matching games	III	
Matching bears	++++ ++++ ++++ ++++ ++++	
Small blocks	++++ ++++ III	

FIGURE 4.5

Art Activities

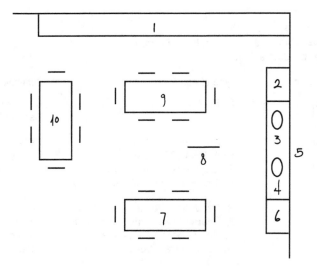

Key

1. Storage shelf
   - Bottom 3 shelves hold materials of choice for children to access
     - paper of various types
     - decoratives materials: buttons, cotton balls, glitter, scraps of material and cloth
     - natural materials: pine cones, seeds, sand, stones
     - playdough and playdough tools
     - scissors, glue
     - drawing materials: pencils, crayons, markers
     - brushes: different sizes and shapes
   - Top shelves
     - rotational materials or materials that can only be used with supervision; children request

2. Drying rack
3. Child-sized sink
4. Adult-sized sink
5. Adult-height lockable shelves
6. Three-dimensional display shelf
7., 9., 10. Tables for creatve art work: fingerpainting, painting, cut and paste, dough or clay, drawing and writing
8. Double-sided easel

The art area is in a corner of the room, on a tiled floor with access to water for both children and adults. Adults actively participate in creative art efforts.

The art area is a popular learning area. Children experiment with the materials in a variety of ways and for a variety of purposes. Art provides all children with opportunities to actively participate at their own level, regardless of ability. Some children simply engage in art for the sheer pleasure of watching colours explode under their fingertips. Other children experiment with and try different techniques to increase their understanding of the world around them. Others create with a specific purpose in mind. The following examples capture only some of the many possibilities.

- Josh and Ted collected all the materials they needed to make their own play-dough (Photo 4.5). Both boys had learned to make playdough in the past. They got out the large bowls. They went to the storage bins and got a cup of flour and a quarter cup of salt each. To facilitate this process, staff had placed the correct size of cup in each bin. Next, each boy got a small container of water. The boys mixed their playdough (Photo 4.5). When they had added too much water, they added more flour to "make it less wet." Eventually they asked for the fruit-flavoured drink crystals to add colour and a fruity smell to their playdough. Josh and Ted not only gained a skill, they also became more independent and developed greater confidence in their abilities.

Photo 4.5

- Benjamin had been playing in the block area. He had created an elaborate structure for his animals. When he left to get some more animals, some of the other children changed the structure. Benjamin reacted instantly. He shouted at the children and told them to leave. When they did not leave he tried to pull them away from the structure. Michael, the early childhood educator, immediately went over to the children. He gently reminded Benjamin to tell the other children what he had wanted to do. Benjamin shouted, "I did. They didn't listen." He then promptly burst into tears. Michael suggested that perhaps Benjamin should find a soothing activity until he calmed down. He also told Benjamin that he would post a "Do Not Disturb" sign until they could all solve this problem.

  Benjamin immediately went to the creative area and started to fingerpaint (Photo 4.6). He created a variety of designs, covered them up and recreated them. He eventually stopped crying. When he was satisfied with his efforts, he put his work on the drying rack, washed his hands and said he was ready to "talk calmly." Benjamin was able to engage in sensory experiences to find relief from a personally frustrating experience.

- Many children visit the creative area for the pure enjoyment of creating. It is an area that encourages children to create free of restrictions and expectations. Braelyn had started to glue buttons to her paper. She decided to change the colour both of her buttons and the paper to "enhance the brightness of my efforts." She was pleased to note that she could paint the buttons to change the colours (Photo 4.7). Braelyn was disappointed when some of the colour dropped off her buttons. But she also noticed that some of the colour stuck to the buttons, and that this colour seemed to be mixed with the glue. She promptly mixed some glue and paint. She was very pleased when this time the colour stuck to her buttons.

Photo 4.6

- Dillon had watched Benjamin fingerpainting, but when asked if he wanted to join in, he quickly indicated that he didn't. Anne noticed his interest. She knew that Dillon regularly used the flour to create playdough. Ann quickly set up a table with flour on it, sat down and drew some lines. She described what she was doing. Dillon came and watched. He soon started to draw lines and shapes in the flour. He continued with this activity over several days. Dillon could use an alternative material for a result similar to the fingerpainting (Photo 4.8). Anne

Photo 4.7

Photo 4.8

had recognized Dillon's interest and reluctance to fingerpaint and provided him with an acceptable alternative.

- Danielle often talked about monsters. She refused to look at books about them. Much of her artwork represented monsters (Photo 4.9). She often represented the monsters in bright, cheerful colours, and almost always identified them by female names. When asked why she painted the monsters in this way, she replied, "Happy." The staff knew that Danielle was experiencing a stressful time at home. They surmised that this was her way of coping with her stressful situation.

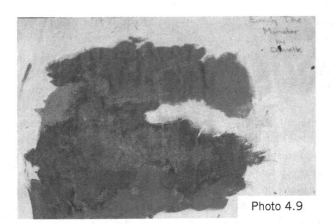

Photo 4.9

4. Music and Movement

Music activities provide excellent opportunities to explore and discover skills associated with such musical concepts as sound, rhythm, beat and volume, both individually and in groups. Young children from very early ages enjoy creating sounds. One need only observe any infant with a rattle, a toddler with pots and pans or a preschooler with sticks on the ground or on a pail enjoying the sounds they create.

The music area in this preschool setting (Photo 4.11) was organized on a shelf adjacent to the block area. This organization allowed children to spill out into the block area if necessary for group or movement activities.

The staff noticed varying degrees of musical skill in the children. The children aged 3 to 5 ranged in ability from being able to beat out the rhythm of a known tune to creating sounds with various instruments (Photo 4.10).

The staff provided the appropriate number and types of rhythm instruments. Not only did abilities range in music, but also in physical competence. The area was organized to fully encourage participation by all children (Photo 4.11).

5. Blocks

Another preschool centre found that they were forced into a more inclusive approach when one of their children, Keith, arrived with a broken leg and crutches one morning. Keith usually started in the block play area. But on that morning, Keith quickly became frustrated because the blocks on the bottom shelf were too

Photo 4.10

Photo 4.11

Photo 4.12

Photo 4.13

Photo 4.14

heavy for him to move and the lighter blocks were too high for him to retrieve. The staff decided to make some quick changes to the block area, but they also decided to look at this area more closely to see what overall changes could be made. During their discussions, the staff also realized that the children really did not use the area effectively.

To make the block area more accessible, they decided to leave the heavy unit blocks on one shelf at the bottom, but to add some of the lighter blocks to the bottom shelf on the other side. They created labelled bags for the unit blocks and hung these on hooks on the wall beside the building block shelf (see Figure 4.6). The staff thought that this arrangement would be more accessible for all children, as two toddlers were enrolled within the preschool setting.

The next morning, the staff eagerly awaited the arrival of the children. They were happy to note that not only was Keith able to effectively build with the blocks again, but the toddlers were also starting to stack the cardboard blocks (Photo 4.12).

6. Sand

Sand play is a naturally sensory activity. Children of all ages and adults enjoy the sensation of sand running through their fingers (Photo 4.13). Sand activities can be provided in a variety of ways to meet the needs of all children.

- Sandbox on the floor (see Figure 1.2, page 21) or ground outside—Venice is ladling sand into her bucket using a full palmar grasp (Photo 4.14). The success of this activity has been enhanced by providing a ledge to place her pail on, so that she can concentrate on the action of filling. She would find it difficult at her stage of development to hold the pail and fill it at the same time. The success of her digging and filling activity has been further enhanced by providing her with a ladle that has a shorter handle. This increases her ability to get the sand into the pail.
- Sand on a platform—The placement of the sand on a platform provides greater accessibility to the activity (Photo 4.15). Children find it easier to access the sand because there is no lip to obstruct access. As well, children can kneel or sit on the ground to access the sand activity.
- Sand in individual containers on the table—Putting sand on the table makes almost all types of play possible: solitary play (playing alone without interacting with others), parallel play (playing beside others, and with similar materials, but without interaction), associative play (playing with others, sharing materials and ideas, but continuing with own activity; Photo 4.16) and cooperative play (play toward a common goal that involves planning, role designation and the sharing of ideas and materials). Therefore, this activity becomes very inclusive. Children at different social levels can interact effectively. For example, children who have not yet developmentally learned to share do not need to: All materials are duplicated.

FIGURE 4.6
Block Area

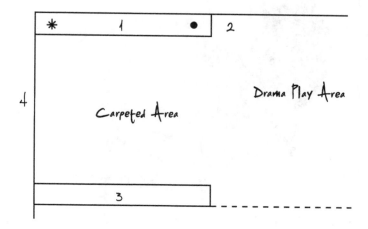

1. Block Shelf
   - First Shelf: ✳ large hollow wooden blocks
     - ● cardboard and foam blocks
   - Second Shelf: accessories, small cars, tracks, fences, natural materials such as pine cones, wooden rounds
2. Hooks for bags with unit blocks
3. Vehicle Shelf: large vehicles on bottom shelf, construction books on top shelf
4. Pictures of children engaged in block play

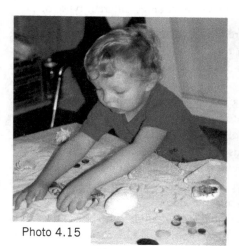

Photo 4.15

Photo 4.16

Photo 4.17

- Alternatives—Using alternative materials for sand gives children opportunities to transfer knowledge and skills from one setting to another. Examples of sand alternatives include dried seeds such as peas or rice, shredded paper (see Photo 1.1, page 4) and snow (Photo 4.17).

7. Water

Like sand activities, water activities are also naturally soothing. Children are fascinated by the various aspects of water, such as movement and bubbles, and will spend much time exploring both sensory and conceptual aspects (Photo 4.18). Water is also like sand in that it can be provided in various ways to encourage different types of play.

- Water table—Dillon and Autumn are taking turns at the water table pouring water into the water wheel to make it turn (Photo 4.19). As one child pours, the other child watches the wheel turn. The water table has been adapted to ensure the success of the children's activity by providing a clear Plexiglas centre to rest containers on. The clear surface provides opportunities to continue to observe what is happening to the water. The Plexiglas surface also leaves hands free to pour and observe. This type of activity encourages associative play.
- Water containers on a platform—This type of set-up (see Photo 1.17, page 20) encourages a variety of types of play: solitary, parallel, associative and cooperative. Children can engage in the type of social activity most comfortable to them using the supportive materials around them.
- Water in individual containers on the table—The children had been on a field trip to the ocean. They had collected many items. The children and their families continued to collect relevant items and bring them to the preschool. Individual clear tubs were set up to encourage children to recreate their "ocean experience." Michael chose his items to place into his tub from a variety of items kept on a shelf beside him (Photo 4.20). He explored various aspects of

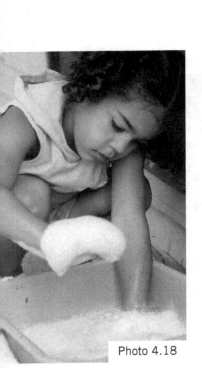

Photo 4.18

Photo 4.19

Photo 4.20

the activity by putting things into floating shells, dropping things into the water to watch them splash and stirring the water with his hands to watch the objects move. The activity was adapted to make it more successful for him. The tub was the size of the small table and therefore accessible from all sides. A towel covered the table to soak up any spilled water. A drying rack was placed on the shelf to encourage children to facilitate additional learning about water, but also to facilitate clean-up.

- Alternative water experiences—Some of these experiences could include blowing bubbles of various sizes (Photo 4.21), walking in the rain (Photo 4.22) or observing flowing water outside (Photo 4.23).

Photo 4.21

Photo 4.22

Photo 4.23

8. Dramatic Play

In one inclusive toddler setting, the children had been interested in picnics. They had had picnics outside on the playground. The toddlers were also interested in housekeeping activities. The organization of the dramatic play area represented their interests.

The organization ensured maximum successful participation of the toddler group. The area was made more attractive by adding familiar items to the toddlers' environment. The canopy that had previously covered the outside picnic area was brought inside. To attract the children's attention, icicle lights were hung from the edges of the canopy (Photo 4.24). Some of the children were crawling, some were cruising (walking while holding on to furniture) and the rest were walking independently. The furniture that was added was accessible to all groups. In addition, the tables and chairs were sturdy enough to allow children to pull themselves up to a standing position.

The staff also created a dramatic play area outside. A large mirror was positioned securely on the fence and dress-up clothes, large material pieces and scarves were set up beside the mirror (Photo 4.25).

9. Nature and Science

Nature and science activities tie into most of the learning areas in the children's environments. Children learn about the natural world around them in various ways:

- Mixing materials to create playdough—They learn about consistency and how to change it (Photo 4.5, page 119).
- Mixing colours when painting to create new colours (Photo 4.6, page 119)
- Experiencing natural events, such as rain and snow (Photos 4.22 and 4.17)

Photo 4.24

Photo 4.25

Photo 4.26

- Creating bubbles by adding soap to water and stirring (Photo 4.18) or by blowing (Photo 4.21)
- Learning about how materials perform differently if wet or dry (Photos 4.15 and 4.16)

Often, children discover things that fascinate them. Although the magnets had been in the science area previously, they had not attracted much attention. Mario found one of the magnets under the carpentry bench. He was delighted when he found that a nail had stuck to it (Photo 4.26). The children immediately became interested in how magnets work and what is attracted to magnets, and began actively exploring the environment to find things that the magnet would attract.

The staff set up a special magnet area in the room, with the active involvement of the children. The children thought they needed to have baskets to "collect things to test." They also decided that they needed some way of showing which things were attracted to the magnets and which were not. The children finally decided that they would put the things that were attracted to a magnet on the green paper, because green means go, and things not attracted on the red paper, because red means stop (see Figure 4.7). The staff helped create documentation panels in the area that children could refer to. These panels included photographs and comments about the children's activity.

When one of the children mixed up all the items on the table, Mario told him he would help him get them back in the right place. Dillon and Mario picked up all the pieces and put them in a basket. They next took turns testing each piece. Mario would remind Dillon where the piece belonged: "That's not attracted. It stops the magnet, so put it on red."

10. Math and Numbers

In one preschool program, math and number activities were used across the curriculum in all areas. Table 4.4 identifies the types and distributions of these materials.

FIGURE 4.7

Magnet Area

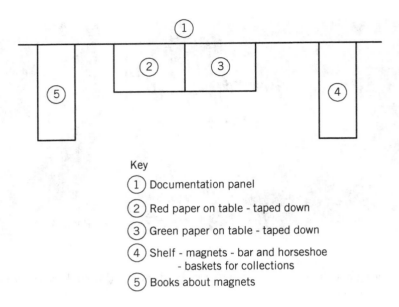

Key

① Documentation panel

② Red paper on table - taped down

③ Green paper on table - taped down

④ Shelf - magnets - bar and horseshoe
      - baskets for collections

⑤ Books about magnets

11. TV, Video and Computers

Television watching and the use of computers is a disputed field. Much of the research talks about the hazards of technology in early childhood settings. However, there are also benefits. The issue is really one of appropriate use and adult monitoring.

"Computers should be used in developmentally appropriate ways beneficial to children, and like any other tool they can also be misused. There is considerable research pointing to the positive effects of technology on children's learning and development. That research also indicates that computers supplement and do not replace highly valued early childhood activities, and materials, such as art, blocks, water, books, exploration with writing materials, and dramatic play" (National Association for the Education of Young Children, 2005:1).

Similar comments may be made about the benefits of watching television. There are a number of appropriate television programs that can become part of the healthy development of young children. "Children need a variety of activities for healthy development and television can be a fun and educational part of a child's daily routine, if managed properly" (Media Awareness Network, 2005:1).

12. Space for Gross-Motor Play

Outdoor play is one of the important indicators of the quality of a program. Among the programs surveyed for this book, there seemed to be a general recognition that gross-motor play was an important activity. Additionally, most centres scheduled regular activities outdoors. All centres had appropriate outdoor play areas, and a few also had indoor gym areas. For a more detailed description, see Chapter 8, pp. 278–281.

TABLE 4.4 **SUPPORTIVE MATERIALS FOR MATH AND NUMBERS**

Area	Materials	Activities
Books	• Base, G. (2001). *The Watering Hole*. Toronto, ON: Random House. • Bateman, R. (1998). *Safari*. Toronto, ON: Madison Press Ltd. • Dale, P. (2000). *Big Brother Little Brother*. Cambridge, MA: Candlewick Press. • Davis, A., and Petrièiæ, A. *The Enormous Potato*. Toronto, ON: Kids Can Press. • Krebs, L., and Cairns, J. (2003). *We All Went on Safari: A Counting Journey Through Tanzania*. Cambridge, MA: Barefoot Books. • Selman, M., and Donnelly, M. (1995). *Big Tracks Little Tracks*. New York, NY: HarperCollins Publishers.	Children used these books to: • Count objects, animals, etc. • Compare sizes • Compare items the child was using to items in a book Books were found in the book corner, but also in the manipulative beading section and the science corner to support current interests.
Manipulatives	• Counting bears • Sorting trays of various colours • Colour tiles • Shape tiles • Peg boards (small knobs and large knobs) • Beads: animal and vehicles available on request, large beads of various sizes, colours and shapes gimp and long pipe cleaners for ease of stringing • Puzzles: single pieces, large and small knobbed pieces, interlocking pieces • Lacing cards • Small cubed blocks • Light table with clear glass shapes of various sizes and colours • Dominoes: with pictures and numbers • Interlocking tracks for small cars and trains • Small vehicles and trains • Duplo blocks	Children engaged in: • Patterning activities—Child creates a pattern that is repetitive, such as red bear, blue bear, red bear, blue bear, an ABAB pattern. • Seriation activities—Child lines up materials according to size, such as small bears to large bears. • Matching activities—Child places exact duplicate of objects side by side, for instance matching two large bears, or two dominoes with six dots each, end to end. • Sorting activities—Child places a number of materials with similar characteristics together, such as lining up all the red bears on a red tray. • Counting—For instance, how many beads on a string, how many cars in a row, how many pegs on a peg board. • One-to-one-correspondence—Child places one object onto another object, for instance, one bear on one circle or one shape per hole.

TABLE 4.4 **CONTINUED**

Area	Materials	Activities
Sand/water	• Digging and pouring tools, such as scoops, spoons, measuring cups and containers to pour or scoop into • Measuring tools, such as measuring cups or spoons • Scales	• Measuring activities—Which is heavier or lighter: placing water containers or sand containers on the scale to see which has more or less, or is heavier or lighter • Associated vocabulary: equal to, more than, fewer, most • Counting activities—Such as how many scoops in a pail • Comparison activities—Such as more full of water, more sand or heaviest
Music	• Bells, drums, tone blocks • Bells of different pitches • Shakers of different volumes	• Beat four times • Walk and follow same beat • Listen and follow a beat • Compare sounds according to volume or pitch
Blocks	• Unit blocks • Hollow blocks • Cardboard blocks • Foam blocks	• Count how many • Compare size—build a tower taller than individual • Compare which is longer, shorter • Associated vocabulary: long, short, heavy, light
Dramatic play	• Setting the table • Making playdough	• One-to-one correspondence—One spoon per plate • Measuring amounts to make playdough
Carpentry	• Nails of various sizes • Wood of various sizes • Hammer	• Measure correct size of nail to hammer into wood • One-to-one correspondence—One nail per hole • Count—Number of times needed to hit a nail into the wood

13. Summary of Adaptations

Overall, the inclusive environment is organized in the same way that any quality environment for young children is organized. The same core learning areas are represented. Adaptations are made immediately to accommodate the needs of any child in the program. Adaptations may be needed to:

• ensure the safety of the children
• ensure accessibility of materials and activity
• maximize success
• accommodate various learning styles
• provide for opportunities for active play

To maximize all children's learning, all of the inclusive settings make relevant adaptations based on the observed strengths and needs of the children. The adaptations made within each core learning area are summarized in Table 4.5.

TABLE 4.5 **SUMMARY OF RELEVANT ADAPTATIONS**

Adaptive Enhancements	Assistive Devices Used
Independence	Accessibility: • A basket was added to a wheelchair to facilitate carrying items to other areas. Organization: • The organization of materials encouraged children to find the appropriate level of difficulty such as finding a book or puzzle that was at their level.
The environment	Adaptations to furniture: • Tables were adapted so that wheelchairs could fit under them Traffic flow: • All learning areas were accessible by wheelchair or other assistive devices. Accessibility: • Furniture such as chairs or couches was placed low on the floor to encourage access by all individuals. • Furniture such as a table could provide access to child in a wheelchair.
Safety	Potentially dangerous objects: • Objects that were potentially dangerous were stored out of reach. • Children could use the objects, such as beads, as long as the staff provided close supervision. • Furniture was sturdy enough for children to safely balance against it or use it to pull themselves up to a standing position.
Varying levels of abilities	Adaptation of materials: • Pipe cleaners, gimp and shorter tools were provided to enhance success of manipulation activities. • Ledges in the water area were provided in order to facilitate filling and pouring activities. • Large bowls and plates were provided in order to encourage filling and dumping activities. • Dress-up clothes used Velcro to make putting them on more manageable for little fingers. • Various levels of materials such as rhythm instruments and books were provided to accommodate individual differences. Limitations: • Some materials were put out in limited amounts in order to maximize the success of the activity, such as flour and water for making playdough. Safety: • Sturdy materials were provided to encourage active participation without fear of breakage.

TABLE 4.5   **CONTINUED**

Adaptive Enhancements	Assistive Devices Used
Adaptations to encourage relaxation	Relaxation: • Soothing activities such as fingerpainting were provided to help children relax. • Soft areas were set up in various parts of the room such as couches, large pillows and carpets. Expression of feelings: • Art activities were used as a way for children to express their feelings (as with Danielle's monsters) and to help them cope with these feelings. Alternative activities: • Activities more acceptable to some children, such as using flour to draw on rather than fingerpainting, were set up.
Recognition of individual differences	Maximizing learning: • Materials were changed in order to maximize children's success, such as providing lighter blocks for ease of building. Individualizing activities: • Greater access was provided by placing some activities on the floor, such as the sand. • Activities were provided in a variety of ways to encourage different types of play activities, such as individual sand and water containers.
Adaptations to maintain/enhance interest	• Materials were added, such as beads, to encourage sorting or patterning activities. • Points of interest were provided to attract attention, such as the canopy and hanging lights (see Photo 4.24 on page 126).

Planning an Inclusive Environment

The adults who planned the inclusive learning environments described above used consistent planning strategies. These included the following steps:

1. Observe the children—To make the learning activities meaningful to the children, the early childhood educator must first be aware of the children's strengths and needs. Observations and relevant adaptations are critical in this process (see Figure 4.3, page 117). All domains should be observed: physical, social, emotional, cognitive and language. Observations also provide valuable information about the need for early intervention strategies. The earlier a need can be identified, the earlier intervention strategies may be implemented. Early intervention often plays a significant role in mitigating some of the negative impacts of a disability (see "Reflection from the Author," opposite).

2. Plan the learning activities and learning environment—Organize the learning spaces based on the observations and interpretations (see "Fine-Motor Activities," pages 115–116).

Joey, my friends' first son, had Down syndrome. The family became actively involved in learning how they could nurture his growth and development. One of the strategies used was to offer Joey enhanced stimulation. The family participated in an infant-stimulation program. Friends and relatives also offered support and relief for the parents. When Joey was two, he was enrolled in an inclusive preschool program. Joey adjusted extremely well to the preschool setting. The family and early childhood educators worked together to provide an appropriate active learning program for the child.

Joey moved from the preschool program into a regular kindergarten program. He handled the transition well and had a successful year. He then progressed to a regular grade one program. Joey handled some aspects of the structured program well. However, he did start to fall behind his age peers with respect to many of the more academic requirements, such as reading and writing. At a case conference it was decided that Joey's gains in social skills and the social benefits to the other children warranted keeping Joey in a regular program with adaptations.

Today, Joey is in grade six. He is still in a special program within a regular classroom but is coping well. He has friends his age and is participating in team sports such as baseball. He is also learning to play the piano. Without the early intervention, I doubt that Joey would have had the same opportunities.

3. Implement the learning activities and spaces.
4. Evaluate and observe—Evaluate if the environment has been effectively set up. If the answers to the following questions are Yes, then few changes and adaptations need to be made at this time:

    a) Are the children using the materials appropriately?
    b) Is the traffic in the learning area appropriate?
    c) Can you identify relevant learning taking place in various learning areas?
    d) Do the children seem to enjoy the activities?
    e) Can children use the materials and equipment independently?
    f) Are a variety of skill levels provided for?
    g) Are the activities accessible to all children?

5. Adapt, revise, change—Adapt and revise where needed. Change if interest is dropping or no interest has been expressed.

In summary, planning children's learning spaces requires a continual cycle of observing, planning, implementing, evaluating and observing, adapting and changing (see Figure 4.8).

Planning Cycle

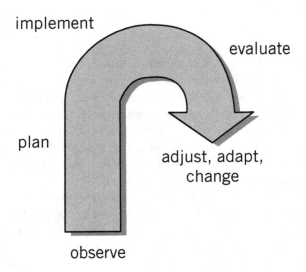

Individual Program Plans

Many different names exist in Canada for individual program plans—individual education plans, functional program plans and family-centred program plans. The development of individual programs provides opportunities to:

- Summarize individual strengths and needs
- Provide short- and long-term developmental goals
- Provide a summary of information about an individual
- Provide recommendations and strategies for successful intervention strategies

An individual program plan is developed collaboratively among family members, children, staff and other professionals. Each individual program plan has a number of phases:

- Collection phase—This includes collecting information from all partners, such as observations and reports from specialists.
- Planning phase—This phase should involve all individuals involved in the process. The following information is developed and agreed upon in a series of meetings:

  ○ Identification of strengths and needs
  ○ Setting long- and short-term goals
  ○ Identification of resources, materials and appropriate strategies
  ○ Support strategies needed to assist all individuals to meet the goals

- Implementation phase—All individuals will implement the agreed-upon strategies.
- Evaluation phase—It is important to set up a system of information sharing that gives all partners opportunities to reflect upon the progress of the child. This facilitates any necessary adjustments or modifications. A regular meeting should be set up to evaluate the progress made in all settings.

The Role of Adults

The adults' role in the inclusive environment is multifold. Some of the topics have already been covered and are summarized in Figure 4.9. One of the key concepts is to establish a collaborative process. Since many individuals are involved in the lives of all children, proceeding collaboratively is critical both to maximizing learning and to organizing successful learning experiences and environments. These individuals include parents, children, family members, staff, other professionals, community agencies and the community. A collaborative system provides opportunities for all of its members to be actively involved at all levels, organizing the environment, evaluating, setting policies and procedures and sharing information. Each member has a key role to play in the life of the child:

- Parents and families—Families are key to the collaboration because they have vital information about their children and first-hand knowledge of their children's physical, social, emotional and cognitive traits (Duckworth & Kostell, 2002). Family members also have the most at stake. They are the individuals with the primary responsibility for their child's health and well-being.
- Staff—All staff members need to have continued support and training to help create inclusive environments for all children.
- Other professionals—At some point in their lives, all children will be involved with other professionals, such as medical personnel or specialists. Children with special needs will be involved with a much greater variety of specialists. The early childhood educator must collaborate with all professionals to ensure that a

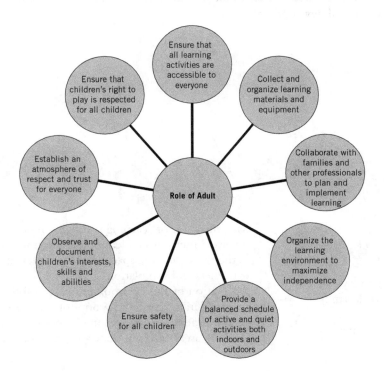

FIGURE 4.9

Role of the Adult in the Learning Environment

team approach is taken to the health, well-being and education of the child. Other professionals can support the staff in developing strategies to help facilitate growth and development in all areas.

- Children—Children need to be recognized as individuals who are active participants in their learning. Adults need to encourage full participation of the children to plan, organize and implement learning activities. Adults should follow the lead of the child.

Staff's efforts need to be supported. The key person to support the staff is the supervisor or executive director. The research clearly shows that a supportive director can make a very positive contribution to inclusive care and to staff morale and motivation (Hope Irwin, Lero, & Brophy, 2000; Hope Irwin, Lero, & Brophy, 2004). Support can be provided through:

- applying for assistance in dealing with particular problems, such as for funding to gain support for another adult on the floor or requesting the services of a specialist to help build effective strategies
- active listening strategies supported by the director and all staff
- engaging in brainstorming sessions with other staff to develop solutions and strategies for common problems
- providing training opportunities through workshops, courses and conferences
- engaging in a collaborative process that encourages and values all members of the team
- providing staff with a private space to withdraw to, as needed
- providing resources to staff to increase their opportunities to engage in personal professional development

SUMMARY

To nurture all children and their families, the inclusive environment must be organized effectively. Effective organization should achieve several ends:

- Respect for the right to learn through play
- Nurturance of all children's individual learning styles
- Establishment of a collaborative process between all individuals involved

- Maximization of learning through a review of all quality dimensions of learning environments, such as the use of colour, space, developmental appropriateness and stimulation
- Adaptation of the environment based on the needs of individuals and groups of children
- Establishment of core learning experiences and learning areas within indoor and outdoor learning environments

KEY POINTS

Aspects of inclusive learning environments
- All aspects must foster emotional, social, cognitive, physical and language development

Setting the stage for inclusive environments—
Elements to consider include the:
- use of colour
- size of the learning area
- number of children in a learning area
- type of lighting
- maintenance of learning spaces

Dimensions of the learning areas
- Softness/hardness
- Open-ended materials versus closed ones
- Simplicity/complexity
- Intrusiveness/seclusion
- High mobility/low mobility
- Risk taking/safety
- Accessibility/inaccessibility
- High stimulation/low stimulation
- Predictability/unpredictability
- Familiarity/novelty

Inclusive core learning areas
- Books
- Fine motor/Manipulatives
- Art
- Music and movement
- Blocks
- Sand
- Water
- Dramatic play
- Nature and science
- Math and numbers
- TV, video and computers
- Gross motor

Relevant adaptations
- To enhance independence
- To adapt the environment for safety
- To provide for varying levels of abilities
- To encourage relaxation
- To recognize individual differences
- To maintain interest

Planning for an inclusive environment
- A cycle of activities starting with observation, then continuing with collaborative planning, implementation, evaluation, and adaptations and/or changes, and then returning to observation to start the cycle again

Role of the adult—Multi-fold:
- Collaborative planning, implementation, evaluation and organization
- Organization of safe learning materials and environment
- Development of team effort with all partners
- Provision of balanced schedule
- Observation and documenting of children's interests, skills and abilities
- Establishment of an atmosphere of respect and trust
- Provision of developmentally appropriate learning activities and materials

EXERCISES

1. Define the key components of a learning environment. Explain the impact each component has on children's learning.

2. Using the chart below, explain the critical nature of each of the components listed in relationship to children's learning.

Components	Description of Critical Nature of Components
Use of colour	
Size of the learning area	
Number of children per learning area	
Type of lighting	
Maintenance of learning spaces	

3. Describe and explain the importance of additional dimensions of effective learning environments as listed on pages 111–114.

4. Compare an inclusive setting to a non-inclusive setting. What similarities do you notice? What differences are evident? Use the chart below to help you with this process.

COMPARISON OF INCLUSIVE AND NON-INCLUSIVE SETTINGS

	Inclusive Setting	Non-inclusive Setting
Type of learning experiences		
Organization of the environment		
Type of learning materials		
Accessibility		
Free choice		

5. Focus on three inclusive organized learning activities as outlined on pages 114–132. Identify what strategies have been used to:
   • provide for the safety of all children
   • provide for accessibility
   • maximize success

6. Reflect on the planning cycle (see Figure 4.8, page 134). Develop a plan of action for a new, inclusive toddler program based on the cycle. How will you gather observations on the children you do not know? What strategies could you use to ensure maximum accessibility? How will you decide on the type of materials to include and the type of effective organization?

7. Describe the role of the adult in any learning environment.

REFERENCES

Council for Exceptional Children. (2008). Inclusion. Council for Exceptional Children [online]. Available at http://www.cec.sped.org/Content/NavigationMenu/NewsIssues/TeachingLearningCenter/ProfessionalPractice TopicsInfo/Inclusion/default.htm [22/02/2008].

Crowther, I. (2007). *Creating Effective Learning Environments.* Scarborough, ON: Nelson Thomson Learning.

Duckworth, P., & Kostell, P. (2002). The Parent Panel. *Annual Editions Educating Exceptional Children,* Thirteenth Edition, 12–15.

Harms, T., Clifford, R., & Cryer, D. (1998). *Early Childhood Environment Rating Scale*. Revised edition. New York, NY: Teachers College Press.

Hope Irwin, S., Lero, D., & Brophy, K. (2000). *A Matter of Urgency: Including Children with Special Needs in Child Care in Canada*. Wreck Cove, NS: Breton Books.

Hope Irwin, S., Lero, D., & Brophy, K. (2004). *Inclusion: The Next Generation in Child Care in Canada*. Wreck Cove, NS: Breton Books.

Media Awareness Network (2005). Special Issues for Young Children. Media Awareness Network [online]. Available at www.media-awareness.ca/english/parents/television/issues_children_tv.cfm?RenderForPrint=1 [30/6/2005].

National Association for the Education of Young Children (2005). Computers and Young Children. National Association for the Education of Young Children [online]. Available at www.naeyc.org/resources/eyly/2001/01.htm [30/6/2005].

Shipley, D. (2008). *Empowering* Children: *Play-Based Curriculum for Lifelong Learning*. Scarborough, ON: Nelson Thomson Learning.

Winter, S. (1999). *The Early Childhood Inclusion Model: A Program for All Children*. Olney, MD: Association for Childhood Education International.

5 Communication Strategies in Inclusive Settings

CHAPTER

"Children develop language at different rates, and in different ways. While you can be confident that a child who is fast to talk and understand is intellectually bright, the opposite is not necessarily true—many children who are slow to talk are also bright. For other children, slowness to speak and understand is a sign of a language disorder or more general problem of development, or perhaps a hearing deficit. Language delays need to be taken seriously, because sometimes—but not always—they point to problems that need early diagnosis and treatment" (Needlman, 2000:1).

Learning Outcomes

After studying this chapter, you will be able to:

1. Identify the components of communication.
2. Describe the importance of language milestones.
3. Identify the range of communicative abilities within an inclusive setting.
4. Discuss the various factors that affect language development.
5. Identify and discuss essential communication strategies and adaptations within inclusive settings.
6. Identify and discuss collaborative relationships to enhance communication.

Introduction

The ability to communicate is one of the most important areas of human development. All living organisms communicate in one way or another. Communications form the cornerstone of receiving, understanding and responding to a multitude of stimuli. "Speech and language are the typical human activities in communication. Language is a system of symbols organized into conventional patterns of meaning. Speech is essentially a mechanical production of language. Other methods than speech may be appropriately employed to express language—sign language and writing, for example. However, while it is possible to possess language and lack the ability to speak, it is not possible to have speech without language" (Winzer, 1999:117).

Communication can be broken down into various components. These components include:

- Receptive language—Understanding the intent of a message or communication (see Figure 5.1). Understanding of communication precedes expression.
- Expressive language—We're using expressive language when we respond to a message or communication, or initiate communication through verbalizations

FIGURE 5.1
Receptive Language

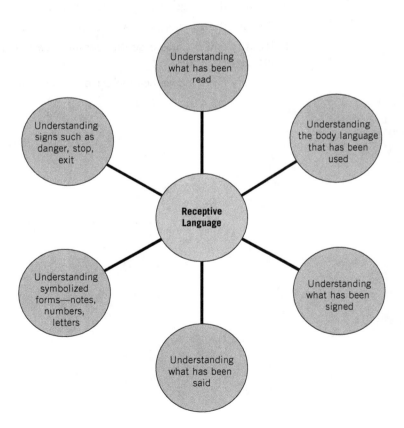

or body language (see Table 5.1). Expressive language is based on the understanding of receptive language development.

- Body language—This means understanding and responding through such physical mechanisms as facial expressions or movement of particular body parts (see Table 5.1).

TABLE 5.1 **EXPRESSIVE AND BODY LANGUAGE**

Type of Communication	Description
Verbal expression	• Using verbalizations such as grunts, squeals or babbling to communicate meaning • Talking in single words or sentences ranging from simple to complex • Using intonation patterns such as raising voice at the end of a question • Telling stories or relating events
Facial expression	• Smiles, frowns, raising eyebrows • Expressions to indicate feelings such as puzzlement, tiredness, anger or surprise
Eye contact	• Eye contact or avoidance of eye contact • Eye movement to look at specific items • Staring at items
Body language	• Flailing of arms and legs to express excitement • Gestures such as waving goodbye • Pointing • Turning head toward source of stimulation • Using ritualistic forms such as shaking head to mean "No" or raising shoulders to express "I don't know." • Physiological signs such as flushing or increased breathing • Blinking • Mouth movements
Alternative modes of communication	• Sign language • Assistive devices such as computers to write, or pictures or symbols to identify what is desired • Writing • Drawing

Development of Language

Language development is universal. All children pass through similar stages, but the rate of acquisition is individual. Most children acquire communication skills in their first three years; however, differences in language development can be related to the supportive environments that children are exposed to. "Differences in language development can be detected in the first years of life and by 24 months, differences in vocabulary words can be detected among children from different classes. This development is strongly related to communicative words spoken to the child during the early period of life. This period of development has a significant effect on later language development and literacy and for males, is related to anti-social behaviour as teenagers. It also appears to be related to IQ, which is influenced by the effects of the care giving environment on experience-based brain development in the early years, particularly the first year" (McCain & Mustard, 2002:12).

Language development is also dependent on brain development. Research points to critical periods of brain development. "This means that the developing brain is best able to absorb language, any language, during this period. This ability to learn a language will be more difficult, and perhaps less efficient or effective, if these critical periods are allowed to pass without exposure to language" (National Institute on Deafness and Other Communication Disorders, 2001:2). Additionally, during the periods of language acquisition, coinciding periods of brain growth spurts become evident. The first of these periods occurs between the ages of one-and-a-half and two years, the age of emergent language abilities, and the second between three and six years, when children start to use their language skills to guide individual behaviours.

Communication and language skills are learned in an interactive environment. As children observe and hear language used appropriately, they will learn to make the connections between what they hear, what they see and how to use this information. To facilitate language development, it is critical to understand how language develops and what to expect at different ages. This knowledge provides opportunities to plan and implement developmentally and age-appropriate programs for children. Developmental milestones are outlined in Figures 5.2A–E. These charts will:

- Help identify children's developmental levels
- Serve as a basis to develop specific observational tools
- Serve as the basis for identifying communication problems or delays
- Provide a quick reference for the selection of appropriate learning experiences for young children

It takes special skills to recognize and respond to the communication signals that very young infants send (see Figure 5.2A). This is difficult because the infant's mode of communication is crying and body language. These signals can easily be ignored or misinterpreted. To respond with sensitivity and understanding, adults need to be familiar with the infant's language milestones.

FIGURE 5.2A

Developmental Language Milestones: Birth to Four Months

Communication Method Used	Description
Differential cry	• Crying changes in intensity to indicate needs such as hunger, pain, discomfort, need for comforting, thirst, frustration, boredom, illness
Making sounds	• Gurgling and a variety of throat sounds
Listening	• Turns head toward auditory stimulation • Looks at face of individual speaking to him or her • Waves arms, hands or legs when spoken to • Stops crying to listen to see if there is a response • Listens to vocalizations
Body language	• Uses eye contact to continue communication • Expresses excitement by waving arms or kicking • Avoids eye contact, turns head away, stops moving or yawns to signal a desire to stop to interact • Uses facial expressions to indicate likes and dislikes
Cooing	• Various vowel sounds such as "eeee" and "oooo" with addition of pitch, volume and intonation patterns
Maintaining communication	• Turns toward sounds or voices and responds appropriately before speaker is in visual range • Imitates cooing, facial expressions and gestures such as waving or shaking the head • Takes turns: listens, then responds, listens again

At the age of four to twelve months, children quickly gain skill in communicating (see Figure 5.2B). Differential crying changes to more deliberate sound patterns that mimic adult speech. Proto-words—verbalizations that sound like words and are accepted as words such as "da-da-da" for daddy—are the start of intentional vocalizations. Real words soon follow.

Communication skills in the twelve-month to two-year age group (see Figure 5.2C) are marked by increasing vocalizations and intentional communications. Children start to use:

• Deictic gestures—Gestures used to communicate infant's intent, such as pointing to or reaching for a desired object

FIGURE 5.2B

Developmental Language Milestones: Four Months to Twelve Months

Language Skill Used	Description
Babbling	• Combinations of vowel and consonant sounds such as "ma-ma-ma-ma" take on the characteristics of adult intonation patterns
Intentional communication	• Speech patterns and sounds resemble native language • Recognizes and responds to own name • Responds to simple requests such as wave goodbye • Imitates and initiates intonation patterns and non-speech sounds such as lip smacking or coughing • Reacts differentially to variations in voice tone expressing anger or happiness and to unknown sounds or sudden, loud noises • Uses differential vocalizations to express feelings: frustration, happiness or fright • Uses babbling, intonation pattern, physical actions to express requests and to get a response • Uses proto-words • Follows simple directions such as pointing to a picture in a book upon request
Listening	• Listens to simple rhymes, songs or music and reacts through movements, gestures or facial expressions
Understanding of words	• Understands meaning of everyday words such as items of clothing, food or body parts (an average of 36 words by 8 months)
Vocabulary	• Uses up to 2–6 words by 12 months

• Representational gestures—Gestures used to symbolize an object, a request or an event, such as supporting side of head with two hands to indicate tiredness

During the preschool years (see Figure 5.2D) there is an explosion of language acquisition. Children gain rapid competence in becoming adept language users. Language is starting to be used to describe, to tell stories and for enjoyment. Also, as children approach the school years, other forms of communication are added to the child's repertoire. Children learn to read, write and use other symbolized forms such as math and music symbols.

FIGURE 5.2C

Developmental Language Milestones: Twelve Months to Two Years

Language Skill Used	Description
Words	• Starts to use babbling to mimic real words • Uses words related to games, routines, food and drink, people, body parts, animal names, clothing, household items, toys and vehicles, as well as prepositions such as "up" and "down" • Confuses words that sound similar, such as "dish" and "fish," until about 20 months • Imitates animal sounds and sound effects such as "yum-yum"
Intentional communication	• Uses gestures to support intentional communication • Uses deictic gestures • Uses representational gestures • Uses joint attention—By 16 months 65 percent of pointing is accompanied by joint attention • Uses underextensions • Uses overextensions • Uses holophrastic speech • Uses telegraphic speech
Listening	• Listens to stories, looking at books as book is read and pointing to pictures when asked
Understanding	• Identifies body parts, familiar objects, toys or animals by pointing • Locates objects when asked to • Uses "yes" or "no" to answer questions • Understands increasing number of words
Vocabulary	• Uses up to 26 words at 13 months • Uses up to 210 words at 16 months • Understands 0–52 words by 12 months • Understands 0–347 words by 16 months • Understands 3–544 words by 20 months • Uses identification—"My ball" or "Look, plane!"
Expression of meaning	• Location—"Daddy here" or "Me on chair" • Nonexistence—"No more" or "All gone" • Negation—"No go" or "No hat" • Ownership—"My cookie" or "Mommy's hat" • Recurrence—"More cheese" or "Again" • Simple sentences—"Daddy drive car" or "Drink milk" • Attribution—"Red car" or "Big ball" • Questioning—"Where ball?" or "What that?"

Adapted from Schickedanz, Schickedanz, Forsyth, & Forsyth, 2001:213.

FIGURE 5.2D

Developmental Language Milestones: Preschool Years

Language Skill Used	Description
Words	Three-year-old: • Expands sentence structure to three or more words • Asks why and what questions repeatedly • Uses comparative words—more, longer, faster • Repeats simple rhymes, finger plays, simple songs • Talks about things not evident—"Mom's car is black." • Describes actions, events, and feelings—"I went to the circus. I liked the clowns." • Maintains conversations by adding comments ("It's a *blue* car."), asking questions ("Why did she jump in the water?"), making suggestions ("Let's read another book.") or answering questions appropriately Four-year-old: • Creates more complex sentences—"I went shopping with mom and we bought a new doll for me and some clothes for my brother." • Asks and answers questions using who, what, why • Identifies words that sound alike—ball and fall • Tells stories or pretends to read to peers • Changes manner of dialogue depending on who is spoken to—for example, simplifying language to speak to younger children
Grammar	Three-year-old: • Uses plurals—dolls, cats • Uses "-ing" endings on verbs • Uses negatives—"not mine" or "no more water" • May overextend grammatical rules—"feets" or "hurted" Four-year-old: • Uses spatial terms—"on," "in" and "under" • Uses prepositions—by the tree, with Mommy • Uses possessive pronouns—hers, his, theirs; and nouns—Mom's • Uses past tense • May continue to overextend grammatical rules – "feets" or "hurted" Five-year-old: • Uses past tense correctly, both regular and irregular forms • Uses "would" and "could"

Communication development in the early school years (see Figure 5.2E) is focussed on refinement of skills, such as increased competence with grammatical structures, reading and writing, and the continued expansion of vocabulary.

FIGURE 5.2E

Developmental Language Milestones: School Years

Language Skill Used	Description
Grammar	Six-year-old: • Uses verb tenses, word order and sentence structure appropriately Seven-year-old: • Understands and follows grammatical rules in conversations and in written form Eight-year-old and older: • Uses increasingly complex grammatical structures correctly
Vocabulary	Six-year-old: • Understands 10 000 to 14 000 words • Learns five to ten new words a day Seven-year-old: • Enjoys learning new words, especially long words • Looks up words in dictionary for meaning Eight-year-old and older: • Continues to increase vocabulary and understand more complex words
Conversations	Six-year-old: • Talks with peers and adults; may interrupt if excited; makes up stories to tell • Uses language to express a variety of feelings: dissatisfaction, frustration, enjoyment or anger • Uses slang and profanities • Uses humour to attract attention—jokes, riddles—and makes up funny stories Seven-year-old: • Speech patterns start to reflect culture and geographical areas • Exaggerates verbalizations; e.g., "My Dad's stronger than a bear." • Language becomes more descriptive with more use of adjectives and adverbs • Conversations become more coherent Eight-year-old and older: • Uses and enjoys word plays • Becomes fluent conversationalist • Talks to friends on the telephone • Imitates colloquial language—slang words, swear words, and curses • Compliments and criticizes others

Sources: Crowther, 2005; Schickedanz et al., 2001; Berk, 2002.

Ranges of Communicative Abilities

In any setting, children will reach developmental milestones at different rates and at different times. They will use language in different ways, understand verbal and/or physical communication differently and respond depending on their ability, age and level of development. The ranges of abilities within inclusive settings can be identified as:

1. Normal range—Children who fall into this range tend to meet developmental milestones (as identified in Figure 5.2 A–E) in all aspects of communication.

2. Gifted range—Children who fall into this category may demonstrate:

   a) Early and extensive language skills
   b) An extensive vocabulary
   c) Use of complex sentence structures
   d) Discussion of elaborate ideas
   e) Creativity in making up stories and telling them
   f) Interest in reading

3. Exceptional range—Children who fall into this range may demonstrate difficulties in a number of areas. These include:

   a) Receptive language abilities—Children may demonstrate difficulties in receptive language abilities. These difficulties may include:
      ◦ Lack of understanding of what is expressed
      ◦ Inability to follow directions
      ◦ Inappropriate or irrelevant responses to auditory signals
      ◦ Lack of attentiveness to auditory expressions shown, for instance, in lack of eye contact, absence of reaction to auditory stimulation or inattention to auditory signals

   b) Expressive language abilities—Children may demonstrate difficulties in expressive language skills. These may include difficulties in:
      ◦ Vocalizing wants and needs
      ◦ Using words and word meanings appropriately
      ◦ Expressing themselves coherently
      ◦ Learning new vocabulary
      ◦ Recalling information

   c) Articulation abilities—Children may mispronounce sounds and words or may stutter.

   d) Attentiveness—Children may have difficulties attending to language activities and interactions. These difficulties may include:
      ◦ Inattentiveness while listening to stories
      ◦ Lack of turn-taking skills while interacting verbally with others
      ◦ Difficulty in attending to conversations
      ◦ Continual interruptions while others are talking
      ◦ Self-stimulating behaviour, such as rocking or flicking of the fingers

- Easy distractibility in communicative settings
- Ignoring of requests or questions

e) Reading and writing abilities—Children may have difficulties with print materials. Difficulties may be evident in the child's ability to:

- Read
- Comprehend what has been read
- Identify differences and similarities between letters and numbers
- Learn the alphabet
- Identify letter sounds
- Spell words
- Perceive the correct order of letters in words

Factors Affecting Language Development

In addition to the potential communication difficulties listed above, children may also experience a number of problems that will reflect on their ability to communicate effectively. These include:

- Structural problems—Some children may have physical problems that interfere with their communication, such as a hearing loss, lack of visual acuity, cerebral palsy, cleft lip or a cleft palate.
- Frustrated behaviours—Children may become frustrated with themselves and others due to an inability to communicate effectively. This may lead to inappropriate behaviours such as withdrawal from interactive situations, physical aggression or temper tantrums.
- Language disabilities—Some children may have a language disorder, such as a language delay or aphasia that has a subsequent adverse affect on academic achievement.
- Learning disabilities—These affect many of the language domains. Children may experience difficulty in:

  - Ability to listen—This not only impairs children's ability to perceive language appropriately, but also impairs their ability to respond appropriately.
  - Expressive language delays or disabilities—Some children tend to have difficulty in using language to express themselves.
  - Articulation problems—Speech may be immature, often unintelligible, with substitutions of inappropriate words, or with some speech irregularities.
  - Difficulty with semantics (word meaning)—Vocabulary repertoire is poor and children fail to understand many underlying concepts or multiple meanings, such as the various meanings of "fork."
  - Difficulties with syntax (rules of how language is put together)—The children's utterances have many grammatical errors. Children often string together a series of unrelated thoughts that ramble on and on repetitively.

- Pragmatics—Children are unable to utilize skills such as recognizing cues or turn-taking, and have difficulty communicating their intent.

- Lack of stimulation—Children who are not stimulated to talk or to listen will often suffer language delays or have a limited vocabulary.
- Restricting conditions—Some conditions such as autism, attention deficit disorder or neurological conditions will result in difficulty in conversing with others.
- Cognitive impairment or delay—The ability to produce and understand language is closely tied to cognitive development. Language learning requires that children form mental representations (mental pictures) of the world around them and learn to associate the words that correspond to these mental images. Any delay in cognition will cause a delay in language acquisition.
- Auditory processing disorders—Some children may have difficulty in decoding auditory speech sounds. These children will have difficulty understanding verbal messages.

Essential Strategies within Inclusive Settings

A number of essential strategies must be considered when setting up an inclusive environment. These include collaboration with partners, observing communication behaviours of children, developing individual program plans or portfolios and planning for an inclusive environment.

1. Collaborative Processes

Collaboration can be defined as several individuals cooperating with each other to work together toward a common goal. The collaborative team consists of the child, family members, staff members and other professionals. The common goal is to improve the communication competence of the child.

A) PARTNERSHIPS WITH FAMILIES Families are the key individuals in the communicative process. Family members are the child's first teachers. Developing fetuses start to react to sounds by 25 weeks through motor activity. "And in the last week of pregnancy, they learn to prefer the tone and rhythm of their mother's voice. In one clever study, mothers read aloud Dr. Seuss's lively book *The Cat in the Hat* to their unborn babies over the last six weeks of pregnancy. After birth, their infants were given a chance to suck on nipples that turned on the recording of the mother reading this book or different rhyming stories. The infants sucked harder to hear *The Cat in the Hat,* the sound they had come to know while still in the womb" (Berk, 2003:91). After birth, continued interactions between the infant and family members lead to increased growth and development of communication skills. Thus, children arrive in child care with a communication competency that is best known to the family members. It is vital that this information is shared and that continued collaboration is encouraged.

Involvement of the family members in all aspects of planned communication and language activity within the child care centre leads to increased:

- Consistency of learning activities for the child
- Ability to transfer language learning from one setting to another
- Increased knowledge about the child's communicative abilities
- Extended expertise—Family members, child, staff and other professionals each bring a different piece of knowledge to the table, all relevant and important
- Inclusive treatment of the child
- Respect for the child and family

B) PARTNERSHIPS WITH OTHER PROFESSIONALS   Children with perceived communication difficulties should be referred to other professionals such as speech and language pathologists. Often this has happened prior to the child's entry into a program. All professionals involved with an individual child need to become part of the working team. Collaboration with other professionals as part of the team leads to:

- Improved diagnosis of strengths and weaknesses
- Improved planning for communicative success
- Inclusive communicative activities that focus on all children's strengths and needs
- Identification of appropriate resources
- Increased use of developmentally and age-appropriate techniques
- A coordinated effort between all individuals: staff, family members, professionals and the child

2. Observing Communicative Behaviours

To ensure the success of planned activities, observation of the child's progress is critical. Accurate and complete information about a child's communicative abilities leads to:

- Improved diagnosis of strengths and needs
- Individual and pertinent planning
- Identification of appropriate strategies and resources
- Collaboration among partners: family members, other professionals and the child
- The ability to plot progress
- Maximizing the success of experiences through use of the child's observed strengths, interests and abilities in the planning and implementation of activities

When a language difficulty is suspected, a screening tool should be used. Screening tools are usually age-specific, geared to infants (see Figure 5.3), toddlers (Figure 5.4) and preschoolers (Figure 5.5). Each tool is further divided into smaller age groups. This makes it easier for the observer to identify a specific age group in

FIGURE 5.3

Screening Checklist for Infants

Age	Skill	Comments
By 3 months	Coos Establishes eye contact Looks at and listens to caregiver Turns toward source of sound Startles at loud or unexpected sounds Reacts by smiling	
By 6 months	Adds babbling to cooing sounds Imitates and initiates sounds Takes turns—listens, responds, listens Reacts differentially to different voices Responds to facial expression	
By 9 months	Uses body language to express intent, such as pointing to a desired object Responds to own name Mimics adult intonation patterns Takes turns during vocal play Responds appropriately to "no" Uses vocalizations during play	
By 12 months	Points to items in environment or books Imitates gestures Demonstrates understanding of simple sentences —For example: "Go out?" Child runs to door Uses proto-words Listens to simple rhymes, music, songs, books Plays games such as peekaboo	
By 15 months	Repeats words, phrases Uses words Uses holophrastic speech Follows simple directions, such as "Get the car"	
By 18 months	Names familiar objects Talks while playing with toys Answers questions by pointing or using words Uses "no"	

order to observe a specific skill set associated with it. When competency in one or more items is identified as lacking, referral to a speech and language specialist should be made. Screening tools help in many ways. They can:

- Confirm or deny the suspicion of language difficulties
- Isolate the type of problem
- Provide a means of sharing information with families, staff and other professionals
- Compare the language of the child to developmental norms to assist with decisions about the next steps

- Form the basis of a referral to a specialist
- Facilitate the development of a specific communication program to meet the strengths and needs of individual children

FIGURE 5.4

Screening Checklist for Toddlers

Age	Skill	Comments
By 2 years	Uses telegraphic speech Locates objects upon request Identifies body parts, familiar objects, animals, people, by naming or pointing Asks questions, such as "Why?" or "What?" Uses descriptive words Repeats simple rhymes, finger plays or songs Initiates and maintains verbal interactions Uses words to indicate non-existence Uses "no" appropriately Uses possessives, such as "my," "Mommy's" Requests more of something	

FIGURE 5.5

Screening Checklist for Older Toddlers and Preschoolers

Age	Skill	Comments
By 3 years	Uses sentences of three or more words Asks questions repeatedly Follows two-step directions, such as "Get your ball in the hall, please" Uses plurals Talks about things not present May overextend grammatical rules	
By 4 years	Uses complex sentences Asks and answers questions Tells stories Uses pronouns: I, me, you, he, she Uses possessives: hers, his, theirs, Mom's Uses spatial terms: on, in, under May overextend grammatical rules	
By 5 years	Explains concepts Talks about past, future, present Uses word endings for irregular verbs	

Sources: Crowther, 2005; Hanen, 2002

3. Individual Program Plan

The individual program plan (IPP) is a written plan that describes the communication program and services required by an individual child. A typical communications IPP will include observations and assessments, identification of strengths and needs, goals and objectives, strategies, implementation activities and evaluation and review. Figure 5.7 is an example of a communications IPP that was set up and implemented in collaboration with the speech and language pathologist, the staff and the family members within the Loyalist College Preschool Curriculum Lab.

The IPP usually starts with a section that identifies a specific communication problem. The identification of this problem has been diagnosed through observations (by family members and staff) and most often is accompanied by a formal assessment by a speech and language therapist. The assessment information is then used to develop a profile of the child that includes strengths, needs, goals and objectives. This profile forms the basis of a plan of action: strategies and implementation activities. The child's progress is tracked through the implementation, and the IPP is reviewed regularly to identify adaptations, additional strategies or new strategies as needed. Simplified, the process can be represented in the flow chart shown in Figure 5.6.

4. Individual Portfolio

Another strategy that is receiving increasing acceptance and use is the creation of an individual portfolio. The portfolio is written as a collaborative process with all individuals involved. Jordan's portfolio was developed collaboratively with Jordan, his family members, the speech and language pathologist and the preschool staff. A communication portfolio particularly lends itself to reporting the progress in speech and language. The portfolio grows with the changing abilities of the child. This serves to give a complete picture over time about a child's abilities. The same information is provided about Jordan, but in a way that tells the story of his progress (see Figure 5.8 on p. 161).

In summary, the portfolio provides an alternative way of capturing a child's abilities over time. The biggest advantage of the portfolio is that the child becomes an active partner in the creation of the portfolio, in the ongoing evaluation of his or her skills and in the tracking of his or her successes and adaptations.

5. Planning for an Inclusive Environment

The IPP or portfolio processes are similar to what should be used when planning activities within an inclusive setting. Planned activities should focus on the strengths, needs and interests of all the children. The activities should be a collaborative effort between all partners: children, staff, families and professionals such as speech creationists, resource consultants and speech and language pathologists.

The steps in the planning process for an inclusive communication environment need to include the following elements: identification of the communication

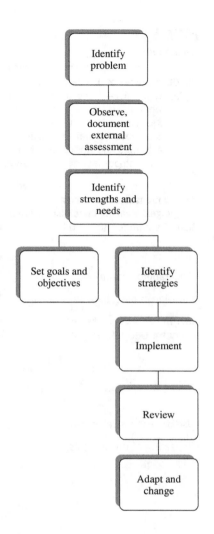

FIGURE 5.6
IPP Process

FIGURE 5.7

Communications IPP

Name: Jordan   **Age:** 2.8
Date: October 5, 2004
Summary of Diagnosis

1. **Diagnosis by Speech Pathologist**
   a) **Expressive language**—Severe speech delay caused by a choroid plexus cyst located near the speech centre of the brain
   b) **Receptive language**—Within high normal range

2. **Observations of Family Members**
   a) **Expressive**—Uses only grunts, pointing and pulling individuals to what he wants
   b) **Receptive**—Family feels that Jordan understands well
   c) **Behaviour**—Jordan and family members are frustrated at his lack of ability to speak

FIGURE 5.7

Continued

---

3. **Observations of Day Care Staff**
   a) **Expressive**—Uses cooing and babbling sounds; grunts; points or pulls staff toward what he wants
   b) **Receptive**—Normal
   c) **Behaviour**—Usually engages in solitary play. He is self-sufficient in choosing his activities and finding his own materials. He is easily frustrated when he is not understood; he cries and withdraws from the situation.

Observations and Assessment
Language Screening Checklist for Jordan (Home)
Date: September 30, 2004   **Observers:** Family members

Skill	Comments
Telegraphic speech	No verbalizations used
Location of objects upon request	Willingly and accurately brings requested item
Identification of body parts, objects, people, animals	Uses pointing to identify all major body parts, common objects around house, family members and friends, farm animals around our farm; especially likes pet cat
Asking questions	Points to items and grunts to indicate he wants them, or pulls one of us to the object and points
Use of descriptive words	Indicates size by hand motion
Repeating of rhymes, finger plays, songs	- Listens to rhymes, finger plays and songs - Smiles, laughs and uses appropriate hand gestures - Favourites: Twinkle, Twinkle Little Star; Pat-a-Cake; Baa, Baa Black Sheep; Head and Shoulders - Brings over nursery rhyme book to have it read to him
Use of words to indicate non-existence	Uses head shake or moves hands back and forth
Possessives	Pats his chest to indicate something is his
Requests for more	Points or pulls person to what he wants; shows empty container to indicate he wants more

Continued

Language Screening Checklist for Jordan (Preschool)
Date: September 25–30, 2004   **Observers:** Jane, Jonathan

Skill	Comments
Telegraphic speech	Uses series of grunts, some babbling and cooing sounds
Location of objects upon request	Brings items requested immediately; also brings items requested of another child
Identification of body parts, objects, people, animals	Uses pointing to identify; seems to understand, plays with animals as well as other children in his group and makes some animals sounds: moo, baa
Asking questions	- Tends to play by himself - Does not indicate what he wants but rather gets it himself - Stops to listen when questions are asked by other children
Use of descriptive words	Shows big, small, tall, long, short, heavy using hand motions
Repeating rhymes, finger plays, songs	First to arrive at story time; uses appropriate body language to support what he has heard
Use of words to indicate non-existence	Empty—looks at container and places hands palms up More—uses sweeping finger motion to indicate more
Possessives	Pulls object toward him, clutching it tightly to his chest
Requests for more	- Points or pulls person to what he wants - Holds container upside down to indicate he wants more to drink - Points to food then plate to indicate he wants more to eat
Behaviour	- Tends to stay away from other children - Cries and withdraws if not understood

Identification of Strengths and Needs

Strengths	Needs
Receptive language skills in normal range	Expand sound production of vowels and consonants
Communicates with gestures	Combine sounds into words
Uses babbling and cooing sounds	Interact with other children to communicate

FIGURE 5.7
Continued

Interests
Interested in books, songs, finger plays
Plays with animals

Goals
Jordan will
1. Increase his vocalizations
2. Develop an expressive vocabulary
3. Interact with other children

Objectives
Jordan will:
1. Use initial sounds every time he requests something or answers questions, such as "mm" for milk
2. Interact with a small group of children with similar interests during free play activities

Strategies
1. Objectives will be implemented at home, within speech therapy sessions and at preschool.
   • Within preschool daily: at meal times, at reading or music and movement times, and during animal play
   • At home daily with similar animals and books, and at meal times
   • At weekly sessions with the speech therapist
2. Jordan's interests will be used to encourage interactions with other children. Strategies:
   • Set up the manipulative area to encourage parallel play with animals
   • Set up a similar play area at home to encourage play with siblings
3. Positive feedback will be given every time Jordan uses vocalizations.
4. Progress will be monitored at home, during therapy and within preschool.
   • Observation evaluations filled in at home and at day care, with the master form kept at day care
   • Observations sent to speech pathologist weekly
   • Team meetings held as directed by speech and language pathologist or as requested by other team members
   • Monthly review of communication plan

Evaluation of Jordan's Progress
Evaluator(s): Jane, Mother

Date	Type of Vocalization	Setting
Oct. 6	Requested milk—"M?"	Snack table
Oct. 6	Listened to Alicia say "Grr." Smiled, picked up another dog and grunted	At home with sister during animal play

FIGURE 5.8

Jordan's Individual Communication Portfolio

Purpose of Jordan's Portfolio

"My name is Jordan. This is my portfolio. It will tell you about me and my communication skills. It will tell you who I am, what I can do and about my interests. This portfolio will help all of us to improve my ability to talk and interact with others."

This portfolio has been developed for Jordan by his grandmother, his teachers and his speech and language pathologist. The portfolio was developed on October 5, 2004. At this time, Jordan was 2.8 years old. He attended a half-day preschool program five mornings a week. He visited a speech and language pathologist once every week.

This portfolio will provide a record of Jordan's communication activities. The portfolio will contain the following sections: Likes and Dislikes, Things That Jordan Does Well, Individual Goals and Objectives, Strategies to Help Calm Jordan, Activities and Evaluation.

The information in this portfolio was gathered with Jordan's help. He initiated many activities such as pointing to or bringing things to indicate what he liked. Any information that was put into the portfolio was always read to him. Jordan often took his portfolio to his speech therapy sessions and home, so he could add information.

What I Like

I like to listen to stories. I like the book Classic Nursery Rhymes.

I like books about animals.

I like to paint on the divider.

I like to build houses for my animals.

FIGURE 5.8
Continued

I like to make necklaces with animal beads.
I like to make necklaces with Shanleigh.

I like to play with Colin.
We like to make tornadoes.

FIGURE 5.8
Continued

I like to play the triangle.

I like playing to "Twinkle, Twinkle, Little Star."

What I Don't Like

I get angry when people don't understand me.

I want people to understand me.

I don't like it when someone takes my things away.

I don't like it when someone breaks my buildings.

I don't like it when some kids don't leave me alone.

I don't like it when my grandmother leaves. I cry.

What I Can Do Well

I understand everything.

I can do the actions to songs and finger plays.

I can make the sounds of animals: "Sssss" for a snake and "Moo" for a cow.

I can make things work. I can do it by myself. This is an "um." I can say some sounds.

FIGURE 5.8
Continued

I can sort. I can sort all the fish and all the farm animals. I can sort all the coloured vehicles: blue cars, red fire trucks and orange planes.

I can clean up by myself. I don't need someone to remind me. I clean up my toys at home.

My Goals

I am going to increase what I can say. I will make more sounds.

I will learn to say words.

I will play with other children.

My Objectives

I will make a sound every time I want something.

I will say short words like "not," and "my."

I will join other children who are doing things I like.

FIGURE 5.8

Continued

What to Do When I Get Upset

When I get upset and cry when my grandmother leaves, I want to wave goodbye from the window.

When I get upset when you don't understand, hug me and try again.

Activities

I want to do things I like.

I like you to tell me when I have done good work.

I want to put shapes on my chart.

I want to mark on paper when I can do something.

I like going to see Ann (speech and language pathologist).

I like to play with Colin and Shanleigh.

Evaluation

1. Tracking Progress

When Jordan used letters or words to interact, the sound or word was added to the chart. Jordan would then place a sticky shape on his chart.

2. Collections

When Jordan presented any work that he then chose to talk about, it was collected and put into his portfolio.

Jordan's Art Work
October 11
Jordan used orange, red, green and blue markers.
He brought his art work to Jane and pointed to and said "o" for orange, "boo" for blue and "gr" for green.

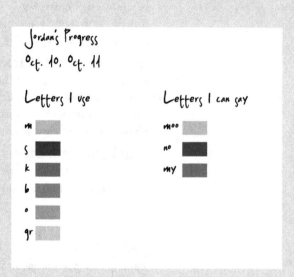

needs, skills, abilities and interests of the children within the program; and possible strategies for implementation. The steps used will reflect the process used in the Loyalist College Preschool Curriculum Lab.

A) IDENTIFICATION OF SPECIFIC COMMUNICATION NEEDS The following conditions were identified within this preschool setting:

- Speech delay (see Jordan's IPP)
- Overall language delay; uses signing to communicate—one child
- Expressive language delay—three children
- Superior communication skills—three children
- Attention deficit disorder—one child

B) COMMUNICATION SKILLS OF CHILDREN WITHIN THE PROGRAM The staff created a milestone graph to indicate the overall communication skills and abilities of the group of children (Figure 5.9). This information was gathered from individual observations of staff, family and assessments from the resource consultant and the speech and language therapist.

C) INTERESTS OF THE CHILDREN Additionally, the staff created a frequency count to identify the most common interests of the children (see Figure 5.10). The staff also created a bulletin board to encourage input from families. The documentation panel (Figure 5.11) was displayed as a bulletin board. The board also served to identify interests and encouraged families to add information.

D) STRATEGIES FOR IMPLEMENTATION The information collected was used to plan the organization of the environment and the specific related language activities. The information gathered about the children's abilities served to help staff understand

FIGURE 5.9

General Range of Communication Skills of the Children in the Program

Area	Range of Skills
Expressive language skills	Babbling, proto-words, holophrastic speech, telegraphic speech, complex sentences, story-telling, explaining concepts
Receptive language	Turns toward voice or sound, listens and uses body language to respond, points to identify, follows simple directions, follows complex directions
Body language	No eye contact, eye contact, uses facial expressions, uses gestures, points or pulls individuals to indicate desire
Signing	Uses sign language to communicate

FIGURE 5.10

Common Interests of Children

Dates: October 2–4
Observers: Jane, Jonathan

Interest Areas	Frequency	Interest Activities	Frequency
Sand	卌 卌 卌 卌 卌 卌 卌 卌 卌 卌 卌 III	Beading: - Animal beads	 卌 卌 II
Water	卌 卌 III	- Vehicle beads	卌 IIII
Carpentry	卌 卌 卌 卌 卌 卌 卌 卌 III	**Baby bathing**	卌 卌 卌 II
		Dinosaur structures	卌 卌 卌 卌
Art	卌 卌 卌 卌 III	Animals in sand play	卌 卌 III
Sculpting	卌 III	Vehicles and tracks	卌 卌 卌 III
Sewing	卌 卌 卌 卌 III	Rhythm instruments	卌 卌 III
Books	卌 IIII	Lego construction	卌 IIII
Quiet	卌 卌 卌 卌 卌 卌 III		
Drama	卌 卌 II		
Music	卌 卌 卌 卌 卌 卌 I		
Blocks	卌 卌 卌		
Gross motor manipulatives	卌 卌 卌 卌 IIII		

the range of language activity that needed to be represented within the environment. This understanding made it possible for staff to:

- Utilize the information on individual IPPs; for example, in Jordan's case, to engage Jordan in daily language activities while he was enjoying his active play of choice and while he was with other children
- Engage in spontaneous language activities as children were engaged in the regular activities of the day
- Plan for language activities in the variety of interest centres—The staff in collaboration with the speech pathologist brainstormed activities that could occur while children were actively engaged in activities around the room
- Use the children's interests to motivate language development as needed
- Provide the resources and materials needed to encourage continued development and interest

i. Strategies to Encourage Expressive Language Activities Activities should be set up in ways to encourage active interactions between children and adults. This can be done by:

- Providing sufficient materials of interest. An example would be duplicate sets of animal beads and vehicle beads, with enough beads to engage more than one child in active play (see Figure 5.12 on p. 171, photo 1).

FIGURE 5.11

How to Display a Bulletin Board

We Like Animals and Cars
Children's Dictation

- We like to use animals in the sandbox.
- We like to make animal environments.
- We construct vehicles from Lego.
- We like to play the rhythm instruments. Shanleigh likes to keep time to "Listen to the Horses Clipping Clopping."

- We like to make long strings of animals or vehicles.
- We like the magnetic animal puzzles.
- Jordan likes the animal books. He just pointed to them.
- We like to make animals swim in the water.

What I Like

What I Like

FIGURE 5.11
Continued

What I Like

"Our horses are galloping. They like to gallop quickly. The Arabian stallion is the quickest. The colts are the slowest."

What We Created

"We collected log rounds, small logs and rocks to create a pond. We used pond animals like snakes, lizards, frogs, turtles and insects. The blue bulletin board is our water."

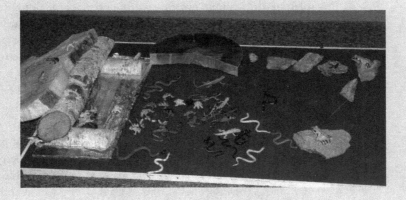

Please Add Photographs or Other Interests to Our Board

Ted likes to use plastercine to make dinosaurs.

Jessica particularly likes the book *Where the Wild Things Are*.

- Providing space to play in close proximity with each other; for instance, using a long, narrow table so that all children can see each other and retrieve materials readily.
- Observing children's play and spontaneously facilitating appropriate expressive language activities. For example, Jane, the early childhood educator, noticed that Jordan and Shanleigh were beading. She sat down near the two children and started to identify the animals that Jordan was putting on his string. She then also verbalized the animal sound. Shanleigh quickly imitated Jane. Jordan became involved as he too started to imitate the animal sounds made. The two children laughed at each other as they put the beads on the string and made the sounds. In this way, two of Jordan's needs were met: his need to interact with other children and his need to vocalize during play.
- Encouraging dialogue with children in a variety of interest centres. Michael was using sea animals and other related materials at an individual water play area (Figure 5.12, Photo 3). Jonathan noticed his activity. He verbally reinforced Michael's activities by labelling the animals he was using: "The crab is sitting at the bottom." He also described the activities that Michael was engaged in: "Oh, look! You put the crab into the shell. The crab and the shell are floating on top of the water." Michael responded by looking at the shell and crab and smiling.
- Becoming aware of the type of language that the adults could reinforce at each area. For example, the staff recognized that some of the children had superior language abilities and also recognized that they did not always have the language expertise in some content areas. Liesl and Hannah had been very interested in the different types of horses (Figure 5.12, photo 4). The staff created a list of all the toy horses available within the centre. They also created a display of the various horses on a bulletin board, along with various books on horses. Pictures of the toy horses were mounted on cards that were labelled so that children could match the picture to the real horse. This gave staff the knowledge and opportunity to label the horses and activities appropriately.
- Providing additional materials to continue children's interests or expand the learning activity. The children's interest was expanded by providing additional animal puzzles. These puzzles also expanded the learning activity by providing opportunities to complete puzzles in an alternative way, by using a magnetized pole. Children gained the opportunity to talk about magnetism. Interest was also expanded, to encourage looking at the details of the pictures of the animals on the puzzle with a magnifying glass. Miranda was able to identify the number of legs the insect had, that a moth had long feelers and that some insects had two wings (Figure 5.12, photo 7). Her excitement sparked the interest of other children. Soon there were a number of children communicating with each other to look for and identify different items.
- Following a set program as developed in collaboration with the speech and language pathologist and the family members. The target sounds for Jordan for the week might be "k" and "s." The pond activity (Figure 5.12, photo 8) presented a wonderful activity to practice the "s" sound, as a variety of snakes were available for this type of play.

FIGURE 5.12

Documentation of Children's Skills and Interests

We are interested in animals.

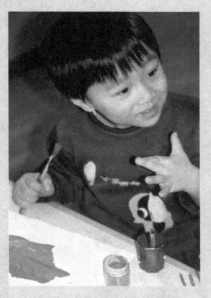

- We like to make necklaces out of animal beads.
- We know the names of the animals and the colours.

- I like to paint the animals, especially the green ones.

- I like to make the water animals float.

- We like to learn more about the various types of horses.

FIGURE 5.12
Continued

- I like to play along to "Listen to the Horses Clipping Clopping."

- I like to look at the animals closer.
- They look larger.
- I can see things like how many legs. I can see the feelers and wings.

- We like to create habitats for our animals and dramatize their activities within the habitats.

FIGURE 5.12
Continued

I Like Building Vehicles

I like:
- big trucks
- long trucks

- Reading related stories about animals to children. Reading provides children with opportunities to:
  - Hear spoken language
  - Make associations between the printed word and the verbalization, or sign language
  - Answer questions verbally or through pointing
  - Gain understanding of words in context and through picture clues
  - Enjoy listening activities

- Providing language materials and activities at various levels that are both age appropriate (appropriate for the chronological age) and developmentally appropriate:
  - Books, including picture books, easy reading books (with large pictures and few words, with words explaining the meaning of pictures), picture dictionaries, research books (books that encourage children to find information for themselves), read-aloud books (books that adults read to children).
  A variety of literature should be provided: nursery rhymes, finger plays, fairy tales, fables, poetry, fiction and non-fiction.
  - Music to listen to, to use musical instruments with, to move to or to sing along with. Songs can include:
    - Simple and repetitive songs, such as "Mary Had a Little Lamb"
    - Action songs, such as "Head and Shoulders" or "I'm a Little Teapot"
    - Action games, such as "Ring Around the Rosie"

- ○ Music or songs to play rhythm instruments to, such as "Listen to the Horses Clipping Clopping"
  - ○ Songs supported by books, where the child can look at the book while listening to the song (Siomades, 1999; Adams, 1973)
- ○ Language games, such as picture dominoes, matching card games, match a sound, rhyming words or what goes together
- ○ Puppets—finger puppets, hand puppets, puppet theatre
- ○ Feely boxes—The feely box is used to hide things in. The child puts his or her hand into the sleeve to find the object in the box and guesses what it is (Figure 5.13). Children can be encouraged to describe what they feel.

ii. Strategies to Encourage Receptive Language Activities   Children need to hear or see (in writing or signing) language used. A child needs to learn to associate the words with items, ideas, events, people or animals. This allows the child to form the mental representations needed to remember and use the words. Strategies to use for children who need to develop receptive language skills include the following:

- When the child is engaged in an activity such as looking at something, pointing at something or playing with something, the facilitator should use this opportunity to talk about what the child is looking at. For example, Ann said to Robert, "Those are red sparkles, red sparkles." This was both verbalized and signed.

  Dillon turned the container of sparkles around repeatedly. Ann: "I see the sparkles are moving!" Dillon stopped and looked at Ann and smiled.

  Dillon spread glue on his creation and shook sparkles on the area. Ann: "The sparkles are sticking to the glue."

  Dillon looked at the area with the sparkles in it. Ann: "Look, this red area is shiny. This one is not." Dillon pointed to the shiny area. Ann: "It is shiny." (Photo 5.1)

FIGURE 5.13

Feely Box

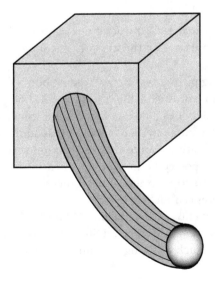

Photo 5.1

- Encourage children to look at books or read books to them. Ann had read a book about insects to the children. Levi had been playing in the sand area. He continually stopped his activity and looked over at Ann and the book she was reading to the other children. When Ann had finished reading the book, Levi went over, picked up the book and looked at it (Photo 5.2). Ann noticed his activity. She followed Levi's lead and verbalized what he was doing. He was counting the ladybugs. Ann counted them aloud to him.
- Use an approach that is multi-sensory. Pritti had set up individual bubble play areas to involve some of the children who normally avoided larger group activities. Keegan was fascinated by the texture of the bubbles. He listened to Pritti describe the activity. He eventually started to feel the bubbles that Pritti held. Eventually, Keegan placed his hands into the bubble mixture and started to explore the bubbles himself (Photo 5.3). When Pritti said she was going to blow some bubbles, Keegan stopped, watched and smiled. He imitated the action immediately.
- Utilize materials that encourage listening—Activities that lend themselves to listening include those shown in Table 5.2.

Photo 5.2

TABLE 5.2 MATERIALS TO ENCOURAGE RECEPTIVE LANGUAGE DEVELOPMENT

Materials	Description
Puppets	Puppet shows tell a story or illustrate a poem, encouraging children to watch and listen. This activity reinforces understanding as children can make the connections between what they hear and the puppets' actions.
Props such as pictures, photographs, flannel board pieces or real objects	Props may be used to encourage children to make the connections between what is said and the words used. For example, telling a story about bears is enhanced by using stuffed-toy bears to illustrate the story.
Language audio card reader	An audio card (picture and word) is fed through the reader. "First children slide an audio card through our reader and listen to a recorded voice. Then they record their own response and listen to the recorded voice" (Wintergreen, 2003:154).
Listening centres	Children can listen to stories or music through earphones while following along in a book.
Rhythm instruments	Children listen and move in accordance to the type of beat that is heard, such as slow, fast, quiet or noisy. Children can take turns creating the beats themselves.
Action songs	Action songs such as "Head and Shoulders" reinforce the words with the corresponding action.

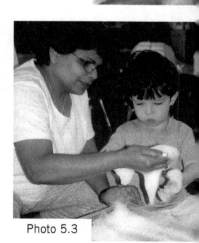

Photo 5.3

• Model appropriate language. Avoid using slang. Enunciate words clearly. Look at the child while speaking. Speak at the appropriate volume and slowly. Use a variety of expressive intonation patterns to speak.

iii. Strategies to Encourage Communication Through Body Language Communication involves a number of different supportive body language signals, including hand movements and gestures, facial expressions, eye contact, body posture and body movement. "Gestures and body language communicate as effectively as words—maybe even more effectively. We use gestures daily, almost instinctively, from beckoning to a waiter, or punctuating a business presentation with visual signals to airport ground attendants guiding an airline pilot into the jetway or a parent using a whole dictionary of gestures to teach (or preach) to a child" (Imai, 1966:1).

Body language varies from culture to culture and from individual to individual. "As the global village continues to shrink and cultures collide, it is essential for all of us to become more sensitive, more aware, and more observant to the myriad motions, gestures, and body language that surround us each day. And as many of us cross over cultural borders, it would be fitting for us to respect, learn, and understand more about the effective yet powerful 'silent language' of gestures"(Imai, 1966:1).

It is most important that caregivers understand and know how to use body language effectively to help communicate with young children. Supportive body language becomes extremely important with very young children or with children who have communication difficulties. Table 5.3 lists various types of North American body language and how they might be used and interpreted. Body signs may be used to:

• Help interpret the behaviour of children
• Express feelings
• Enhance understanding of messages
• Help to model a different communication technique

Table 5.3 provides some general guidelines into various types of body language. However, it is important to be aware that knowledge of the individual will help to interpret how body language is used and what it might mean.

iv. Strategies to Maintain Attention Some children find it difficult to maintain attention. To improve a child's attention span, the caregiver must first have some idea of what a normal attention span for that individual might be and what circumstances lead to increased or decreased attention span. For example, Peter would engage in self-stimulating behaviour, such as rocking and flicking his fingers in front of his face, during all group times. He would listen to an individual story if sitting on someone's lap while they looked at the book together. He also left interest areas when more than three children started to play in that area. It seemed that Peter adjusted better to individual and small group activities. The program needed to be adjusted to accommodate his needs.

TABLE 5.3 **USE OF BODY LANGUAGE**

Message	Types of Body Signs
Approval	• Smile • Getting down to the child's level • Leaning toward the child • Relaxed body posture • Hand gestures such as thumbs up
Respect	• Eye contact (not respectful in Asian cultures) • Allowing personal space as required by the individual child
Puzzlement or lack of knowledge	• Raising eyebrows • Shrugging shoulders • Raising forearms and hands, palms up
Interest	• Smile • Getting down to child's level • Eyes level with child's activity and child
Unhappiness	• Walking or standing with shoulders hunched • Mouth turned down, sad facial expression
Boredom	• Ritualistic behaviour such as swinging legs, spinning around on the floor, gazing into the distance
Defensiveness	• Ridged body posture • Arms crossed on chest
Aggressiveness	• Raised open hand (ready to hit) • Shaking a fist at someone • Angry expression on face
Tiredness	• Rubbing eyes or ears • Hands folded and head rested on folded hands
Warning	• Waving forefinger at someone
Stop	• Hands held up, palm faced outward
Impatience	• Drumming fingers on desk • Tapping foot on floor
Uncertainty	• Pulling hair • Biting nails
Avoidance	• Lack of eye contact
Self-stimulation	• Rocking back and forth • Flicking fingers in front of face
Stop interaction	• Looking away

Strategies used to increase and maintain interest include the following:

- Observing the child to identify his or her interests and skills
- Using the interests of the child to motivate the child to engage in language activities
- Providing appropriate challenges and materials to maintain the activity, such as expanding the language activity of Liesl and Hannah (see Figure 5.12, Photo 4)
- Following the child's lead—Dillon's interest in the sparkle activity (Photo 5.1 on page 175) was enhanced by the adult's interactions. The adult observed Dillon and followed his lead to maintain attention.
- Providing enough time—John had been painting. He was asked to come and listen to a story. He responded that he was not finished and did not want to listen to a story. When the routine was enforced, John threw a temper tantrum. The result was that he did not listen to the story, the other children's time was interrupted and he could not finish his painting. Routines should be set up to meet the needs of the child, not to enforce a strict timeline. The whole negative episode could have been avoided had one of the following strategies been used:
  - Giving John a choice to finish his painting after the story
  - Allowing John to finish his painting and listen to the story from where he was
  - Giving John a choice as to what he wished to do
- Providing appropriate resources to encourage continued interest, such as those provided for Michael during his water play activity (Photo 5.3 on page 175).

Communicative Adaptations in Inclusive Settings

Communication takes many forms. Not all children learn the same way, nor will all children be able to learn in the same way. Table 5.4 identifies some adaptive methodologies that might be used.

Role of the Early Childhood Educator

Early childhood educators have a profound effect on young children's communication development. They are in a key position to coordinate activities between all partners—children, specialists, families and staff—and to maximize the child's success. The key roles of the early childhood educator include:

- Careful observation of children's communicative skills and interests—Jane had observed Hannah and Liesl's interest (Figure 5.12, photo 4). Based on this interest, additional language activities were created.

TABLE 5.4 ADAPTIVE COMMUNICATION

Type	Description
Braille	• Braille is a writing system based on raised dots that will help a child with a visual impairment to read and write.
Signing	• American Sign Language is a visual-spatial language that uses gestures, facial expression such as eyebrow or lip movements and the surrounding space to help in describing individuals or places. • Signed English—Every word in the English language has a corresponding sign. Signed English is similar to spoken English. • Finger Spelling—Each letter of the alphabet has a corresponding sign. Words are spelled out letter by letter.
Pictorial representations	• Pictures familiar to the child give the child the opportunity to communicate desire or choice. This child is indicating that he wants more rice.
Labelling	• Labelling in the environment should include pictures, words and signs such as ASL or Braille. This maximizes the child's ability to independently find and return materials. • Colour coding labels helps to speed up augmentative/alternative communication (AAC). For example, all verb signs might be colour-coded pink.

Augmentative/alternative communication (AAC)	• "ACC is any device or method that improves the ability of a child with communication impairment to communicate effectively" (Ballinger, 1999:1).
	  1. Developmental approach—Provision of intervention strategies based on normal language development; works well with preschool children.
	  2. Ecological inventory—Identification and adaptation of relevant activities within the common environments children spend time in.

Multimodal communication	• Using more than one method of communication, such as verbal and signing; Advantage of greater diversity in approaching language learning.
Adaptive devices	• Adaptive devices help children to communicate with greater ease and flexibility; includes reading, writing and interactions with others. Examples include flashing lights to "grab" attention, or talking books. • Adaptive writing devices to hold writing/drawing tools.

TABLE 5.4   **CONTINUED**

Type	Description
Adaptive technologies	• Recorded speech devices: Child touches picture in order to hear the recorded message. May be used to enhance vocabulary or listen to short stories.
Computer augmentative alternative communication device	• These devices allow individuals to communicate with others through pictorial and/or written communication • Computers with that provide verbal feedback of what has been typed or scanned
Communication software	• This software offer many options, including text to speech, communication boards, vocabulary expansions and sentence building • Functionally speaking devices offer a wide variety of conversational topics in which to engage.
Head pointing or eye-tracking systems	• Allow individuals to navigate using eye or head movements, instead of a standard computer mouse.
Voice activation	• Allows the spoken word to be converted to speech.
Writing pens	• These devices convert writings or drawings done on specialized paper to computer-based writings and drawings.

- Setting up language activities to encourage active play situations within each interest area in the room—For example, the beading area was set up to encourage interactions among the children (Figure 5.12, photo 1).
- Using spontaneous play to create "teachable moments"—Pritti had observed Keegan's reluctance to get involved in larger group activities. Setting up a small water play area encouraged Keegan to participate. She then used this situation to involve Keegan in a spontaneous language activity.
- Setting up displays to document children's learning and activities (Figure 5.11 on page 16B)
- Evaluating children's progress
- Creating an IPP (Figure 5.7 on page 157) or a portfolio (Figure 5.8 on page 161)
- Adapting communication strategies as needed (Table 5.4)
- Providing materials to maintain attention and interest over time—The pond area (Figure 5.12, Photo 8) continued to be active over many weeks. Many spontaneous language activities and "teachable moments" were continued over time.

SUMMARY

Children learn to communicate effectively when:

- Language is modelled appropriately by adults and peers
- Children interact with each other in active play
- There is a consistent approach to learning at home, in therapy and in care
- Alternative strategies are used to facilitate communication as needed
- Learning is fun, based on children's interests
- Individual strengths and needs are acknowledged and planned for

KEY POINTS

Components of communication
- Receptive language
- Expressive language
- Body language

Development of language
- Universal, with individual rate of acquisition
- Critical periods
- Dependent on environment
- Developmental milestones in predictable progression through the ages

Range of communicative abilities in inclusive settings
- Normal
- Gifted
- Exceptional: receptive, expressive, articulate, attentive, reading and writing

Factors affecting language development
- Structural problems
- Frustrated behaviours
- Language disabilities
- Learning disabilities
- Lack of stimulation
- Restricting conditions
- Cognitive impairments
- Auditory processing

Essential strategies within inclusive settings
- Collaborative approach
- Partnerships with other professionals
- Observation
  - Screening tools
  - Language behaviours
  - Importance of observing—For diagnosing problems or skills; planning activities; identification of skills, interests and abilities; plotting progress; preparing referrals; developing plan of action

Individual Program Plan (IPP)
- Written plan of action for an individual
- Contains observations and assessment, identification of strengths and needs, goals and objectives, implementation activities and evaluation

Individual portfolio
- Ongoing, collaboratively created summary about an individual
- Contains purpose, likes and dislikes, abilities, goals and objectives, strategies, activities and evaluation

Planning inclusive learning environments
- Collaborative effort
- Process oriented—Identification of communication needs; children's skills, abilities and interests; implementation strategies

Strategies for implementation
- Expressive language—Encourage active play; observe children's play; interact in planned and spontaneous ways; encourage dialogue between children; reinforce language in all areas; expand materials based on interests; follow guidelines provided by professionals; read to children; provide language materials, music and experiences across different levels of abilities
- Receptive language—Follow child's lead, utilize teachable moments, encourage looking at books, use a multi-sensory approach, utilize a variety of materials that encourage listening, model appropriate language
- Body language—Identify and interpret different types of body language indicating approval, respect, puzzlement, feelings, interest, defensiveness, aggressiveness, tiredness, warning, action, avoidance
- Maintaining attention—Observe, use interests, provide individual challenges, provide enough time, provide the appropriate resources

- Communicative adaptations—Braille, signing, pictorial representations, labelling, augmentative/alternative communication, multi-modal communication adaptive devices

- Role of the early childhood educator—Observing children's interests, strengths and needs; setting up language activities; responding to teachable moments; displaying children's efforts; creating IPP or individual portfolios; adapting communication strategies; maintaining interest over time

EXERCISES

1. Divide the class into three groups. Each group picks a children's story that can be easily dramatized, and then dramatizes the story in one of these ways:
   - Using body language only
   - Without props
   - Using a variety of props

   Identify which technique you enjoyed the most and why.

2. Using the developmental milestone charts on pages 145–149, observe a group of children within a preschool setting. How many children seemed to fit into the normal range? How many were exceptional? What types of exceptionalities could you identify?

3. Discuss what range of communicative abilities might be found in a preschool setting.

4. Reflect upon your own language abilities. Which areas do you excel in? Which areas do you need to work on? How does this compare with children in inclusive settings?

5. Identify the importance of the essential communicative strategies for inclusive settings, utilizing the chart below.

6. Compare the IPP and the individual portfolio. What are the advantages and disadvantages of each? Reflect on which one you might wish to use and why.

7. Utilize the adaptive communication table (Table 5.4 on page 179). Develop an observation tool using this chart. Implement the tool in an inclusive setting. Discuss which strategies seemed most effective and why.

COMPARISON OF INCLUSIVE AND NON-INCLUSIVE SETTINGS

Essential Area	Importance
Collaboration	
Observation	
Individualized programming	
Planning strategies	
Implementation strategies	

REFERENCES

Adams, P. (1973). *There Was an Old Lady Who Swallowed a Fly*. Singapore: Child's Play International Ltd.

Ballinger, R. (1999). How to Get Started. What Is Augmentative and Alternative Communication (ACC)? Available at http://aac.unl.edu/yaack/ [21/09/2004].

Berk, L. (2002). *Infants and Children*. Fourth Edition. Boston, MA: Allyn & Bacon.

Berk, L. (2003). *Child Development*. Canadian Edition. Toronto, ON: Pearson Education Canada Inc.

Crowther, I. (2005). *Child Development Primer*. Scarborough, ON: Thomson Nelson.

Hanen. (2002). Understanding Language Delay and Disorders. The Hanen Centre [online]. Available at www.hanen.org/Hanen2002/pages/Parents/Understand ingLanguageDelay/UnderstandingLanguageDelay.htm [10-11-2004].

Imai, G. (1966). Gestures: Body Language and Nonverbal Communication. California State Polytechnic University, Pomona [online]. Available at www.intranet.csupomona. edu/~tassi/gestures.htm [29-12-2004].

McCain, M., & Mustard, F. (2002). *The Early Years Study*. Toronto, ON: The Founders' Network.

National Institute on Deafness and Other Communication Disorders (2001). Language Developmental Milestones. National Institute on Deafness and Other Communication Disorders [online]. Available at www.comeunity.com/disability/speech [8-11-2004].

Needlman, R. M. (2000). The Importance of Language. drSpock [online]. Available at www.drspock.com/ article/0,1510,4829,00.html [25-9-2004].

Schickedanz, J., Schickedanz, D., Forsyth, P., & Forsyth, G. (2001). *Understanding Children and Adolescents*. Fourth Edition. Needham Heights, MA: Allyn & Bacon.

Siomades, L. (1999). *The Itsy Bitsy Spider*. Honesdale, PA: Bell Books.

Wintergreen. (2003). Wintergreen Learning Materials. Concord, ON: Wintergreen.

Winzer, M. (1999). *Children with Exceptionalities in Canadian Classrooms*. Scarborough, ON: Prentice Hall Allyn and Bacon.

6 Play in Inclusive Settings

CHAPTER

"The universal importance of play to the natural development of the wholeness of children has been underscored by the United Nations proclamation of play as a universal and inalienable right of childhood. Play is the singular central activity to childhood, occurring at all times and in all places. Children do not need to be taught to play, nor must they be made to play. Play is spontaneous, enjoyable, voluntary, and non goal-directed" (Landreth, 2002:9–10).

Learning Outcomes

After studying this chapter, you will be able to:

1. Identify how play affects a child's development.
2. Define the various types and stages of play.
3. Discuss the various stages of play found in inclusive settings and the reasons for a range of developmental play stages.
4. Discuss the importance of establishing a collaborative process with families and other professionals.
5. Discuss the various factors that should be considered when organizing an environment in which children's play is valued.
6. Discuss the importance of observing and documenting children's play.
7. Define and discuss the importance of the following adaptations in inclusive settings: environmental support, material adaptation, simplified activities, children's preferences, special equipment, adult support, peer support, invisible support.
8. Describe the role of the early childhood educator in encouraging active play within children's learning spaces.

Photo 6.1

Introduction to Play

Play is a natural way of learning for all children. Through active play, children lay the foundations of all future learning. "The idea that play is a basic, vital human disposition has long been recognized" (Elkind 2007:4). According to Bodrova and Leong (Koralek, 2004:7), there are a number of principles through which play influences development. Although only four principles will be discussed, there are a number of others. Play affects the child's motivation, facilitates cognitive decentring, develops mental representations and fosters deliberate actions.

1. Play Affects the Child's Motivation

When children can make choices, receive gratification through their efforts and interact in positive situations, a cycle of learning develops. This is particularly important for young children with special needs. These children are often placed into situations in which they are required to engage in activities where they do not have a choice and that may not be developmentally appropriate for them. These situations arise to meet adult expectations for children with special needs to "catch up" to normal development. Children make greater gains when they are left to work in an environment that provides developmentally appropriate choices and engages their interests. For example, one of the goals for Dillon's IPP was to improve his fine-motor skills. Dillon was encouraged to choose his own activities for reaching this goal. He discovered that he could use the large chalk to create marks on the board (Photo 6.1). He experimented endlessly to create straight lines and circles in various colours. When he had covered the area he had used, he erased the shapes and started again. Through this activity Dillon gained:

- Self-confidence in his ability to interact with the materials in his environment
- Practice in refining his fine-motor skills
- Insight into cause and effect relationships—Dillon could see the different marks he made, and he could erase them and start again.
- Confidence in his ability to produce different shapes

2. Play Facilitates Cognitive Decentring

All young children's thinking is centred on their individual perspective. It is difficult for a young child to take on a different perspective. The child is focused on one aspect of his or her perspective and is unable to think about other aspects. For example, Jamie, a three-year-old, had finished a painting. When her grandmother telephoned a little while later, Jamie enthusiastically ran to get her painting. She held it up to the phone and said, "Look at the painting I just finished." Jamie's focus was on her painting. She was talking to her grandmother, and Jamie could see her painting, so she assumed her grandmother could see it too.

Through play, children gradually learn to take on different perspectives. Through this, they are developing the skill of decentred thinking. As children experiment with materials during block or water play or sand play, they gain experience in seeing and manipulating objects from different perspectives. Benjamin decided to try to use the water wheel with sand, instead of water, to see if he could make the wheel turn (Photo 6.2). He was able to transfer learning from one situation to another. Through this activity he gained experience in:

- Observing how different materials cause a similar effect
- Using equipment and materials in different settings effectively
- Seeing the result of individual actions from different perspectives

Through dramatic play, children further develop decentred thinking skills. Children gradually take on different roles during pretend play. As children practise the various roles they take on, they are learning about how to act differently, depending on the role they assume. They gradually learn to coordinate various roles and negotiate the different play scenarios. For example, Jenna, a four-year-old, had been playing the role of a child in the daily living centre. She explained, "I am crying because I want the toy my brother is playing with. I am only pretending to cry. He is only my pretend brother." Later, she decided to switch roles. She became the mother. When her two "children" were arguing about a toy, she said, "There are enough toys for both of you. Timmy, you could find a new bucket." Jenna clearly was able to take on and understand the different roles she assumed.

Photo 6.2

3. Play Develops Mental Representations

"This development occurs as the result of a child separating the meaning of objects from their physical form. First children use replicas to substitute for real objects; then they use new objects that are different in appearance but can perform the same function as the prototype. Finally, most of the substitution takes place in the child's speech with no object present. Thus, the ability to operate with symbolic substitutions for real objects contributes to the development of abstract thinking and imagination" (Bodrova & Leong, 2004:7).

For example, Ben had been very interested in animals. Initially, he played with the animals in different settings, such as sand play or water or block play or the light table. Occasionally he would hold up an animal and look at Yenka, his teacher. Yenka would supply the name. As he looked at books, he was able to point to the animal upon request. Eventually, Ben was able to make the word "lizard," copied from a dictionary card. Ben was gradually forming mental representations of the animals he was playing with. He started by becoming familiar with what the animals looked like: their shapes, textures, colours or sizes. He gradually understood the labels associated with each animal and was finally able to reproduce the label in symbolized form—an outline of the lizard and the printed word (Photo 6.3).

Photo 6.3

4. Play Fosters Deliberate Actions

As children gain experience in play situations, their actions become more deliberate. For example, Melanie, a nine-month-old infant, kicked the mobile at the foot of her bed to make it move and squeak. Melanie would watch and listen. When the sound and movement stopped, she would kick it again. Jake, a five-year-old, knew the rules for snakes and ladders. He would patiently explain them to anyone who wanted to play with him. If other children made mistakes, he would correct them. Because Jake had memorized rules, he was able to monitor the game to ensure that everyone played by the same rules.

In summary, play provides opportunities for children to accomplish many things:

- Learn through making personal choices
- Learn in a natural setting with real materials
- Learn through interactions with others and materials
- Establish positive attitudes toward learning
- Engage in meaningful activity
- Develop autonomy
- Acquire skills associated with cognition, socialization, self-awareness, motor control, language and emotional control

Development of Play

Play develops in an orderly, predictable pattern. Figure 6.1 provides an overview of the social play stages as they develop from one age to the next; Figure 6.2 provides an overview of the cognitive play stages. Many of the stages overlap because children may enter a different stage of play depending on their development, their interactions and the stimulation received. For example, solitary play evolves through the infant years and into the toddler years. As the toddler is given opportunities to play with other children, parallel play evolves. Play stages are cumulative and may continue to exist over time for different purposes.

Not only is it important to know what the various stages are, it is also critical to understand what skills are prevalent at each stage. The type of play changes with age and with the experiences that children have had. Solitary play may be a sensory exploration of a toy by touching, mouthing or throwing. It will continue throughout all ages with a different purpose, such as wanting to be by oneself to read a book. As children develop more and more skills, the purpose of their play will change in accordance with those skills. The toddler may be content to listen to a story or look through a book, whereas the preschool child may start to read words and may pretend to read a story to others.

It is important to understand the development of play in order to facilitate optimal active play situations that meet the needs, interests, abilities and skills of all children. Knowledge of the stages of development enables the child care provider to:

- Provide appropriate materials and resources
- Continue to adapt and change learning environments as needed
- Be sensitive to the needs of all the children
- Maintain an environment of positive social interaction
- Understand how and when interactions are needed

FIGURE 6.1

Social Play

Type of Play	Definition	Example
Onlooker play	Child watches others play without interacting.	Josh watched the children fingerpaint without interaction or joining in.
Solitary play	Child plays alone.	
Parallel play	Children play side by side, using similar materials, but without interacting with each other.	
Associative play	Children play with similar materials, sharing ideas and materials, but engage in personal activities.	

FIGURE 6.1

Continued

Type of Play	Definition	Example
Cooperative play	Children play together toward a common goal, planning their play and designating roles to achieve the goal.	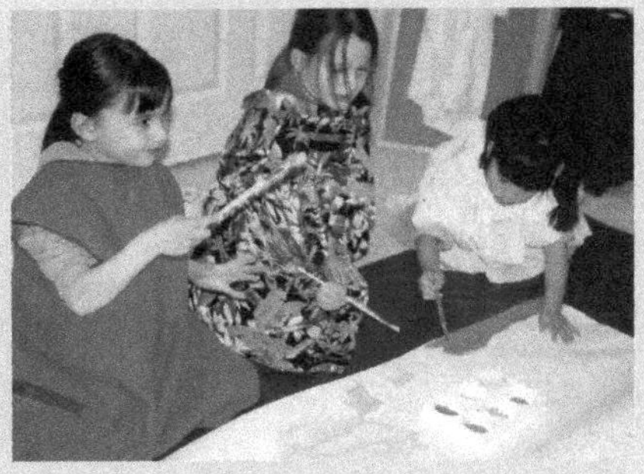

FIGURE 6.2

Cognitive Play Defined

Type of Play	Definition	Example
Functional play	Children repeatedly practise skills through interacting with objects, other individuals and language.	
Symbolic play	Children use one action or object to represent another idea.	Lauren represents sleepy. 

FIGURE 6.2

Continued

Type of Play	Definition	Example
Constructive play	Children use materials or objects to create something.	
Dramatic play	Children create imaginary roles and situations with or without props. **Sociodramatic play** occurs when two or more children are involved in dramatic play situations.	
Games with rules	School-aged children have the understanding of preset rules. They agree to play by these rules.	Competitive sports such as tennis or hockey

Range of Stages of Play

Children in inclusive settings will exhibit all types of play behaviour as identified in Figures 6.1 and 6.2. Children may be engaged in specific play behaviours for a number of reasons, including the ones listed in Table 6.1.

TABLE 6.1 REASONS FOR PLAY BEHAVIOURS

Reason	Possible Result	Example
Developmental ability	Limited ability or experience to engage in tasks	• Developmental delay may cause difficulty to share toys and materials
Physical limitation	Limited access to materials and equipment	• Use of wheelchair may make it difficult to access all activities independently
Background experiences	Limited stimulation	• Environment can be perceived as overwhelming, with too many choices • Lack skills or knowledge to use materials in appropriate ways.
Family values	Devalue the value of play	• Lack experiences in making choices or solving problems • Lack self-initiative
Family expectations	Focus on educational need and directed learning tasks	• Need to learn how to play
Type of disability	Hinders active participation	• Lack of ability to move, communicate or interact may limit degree of active play
Societal pressures	Increasing pressures to prepare children academically	• "Academic training is increasingly replacing imaginative play and experiential hands-on learning in the early years of our children's lives. Education is now seen as a race, and the earlier you start, the sooner and the better you finish. Yet there is no evidence that this push for early academics, such as the effort to have children start reading by age five, produces any lasting advantage for children. If anything, research and experience point in the opposite direction" (Tepperman, 2007).

Strategies to Develop a Play-Based Curriculum

A number of strategies should be considered when an active play-based curriculum is being set up. These may be categorized into collaborative processes and setting the stage for play to occur. As previously discussed, collaboration forms the cornerstone of a quality program. Collaboration among children, staff, families and other professionals not only enriches the knowledge about learning through play, but also ensures congruence among practices in the child's various settings: home, centre-based and therapy-based.

1. Collaboration with Families

When families and child care staff work together toward a common goal, everyone benefits. This may involve initial information sessions with families to promote a play-based approach. Not all family members may understand that play is the cornerstone of early learning. Before the information session, displays and resources to identify the value of play should be set up to attract attention to a play-based curriculum and offer opportunities for individualized research. An information session can be conducted in different settings:

- Individual sessions—These sessions can be part of the intake procedure. The session could include a tour of the facility and an open discussion about the value of play to the child's development. Support documentation (displays and resources) can be used to show how a play-based approach works and how the child's strengths and needs are met.
- Group sessions such as discussion groups or seminars on the topic of play—This gives families an opportunity to further explore the topic of play and to ask staff about concerns that might need to be addressed.

Families play an important part in helping to create a positive learning environment for their children, both at home and at the centre. Families share information about:

- Children's interests—A mechanism needs to be provided to encourage information sharing. This could be done by posting documentation about children's interests on bulletin boards, creating a portfolio of evolving interests (either individual or group) or providing space on daily recording charts that encourage families to record children's interests upon arrival or departure at the centre. Focus on the child's interest ensures that the activities and planning provided are appropriate to that individual.
- Progress in different settings—There needs to be a regular flow of information between families and staff. Families should be encouraged to participate to keep similar observation tools to those the centre uses (see Tables 6.4 and 6.5, pages 207 and 208). Families should have access to the information about their child. A system needs to be developed that ensures confidentiality of individual

children and families but also keeps families informed about their child's progress.

- Concerns—When concerns arise it is best to set up a time to meet, either in a face-to-face meeting or through a telephone call. This should be done immediately, as the longer a concern remains unaddressed, the harder it becomes to deal with it. The tone of the meeting should be respectful and involve active listening. The outcome should involve mutual problem solving to reach a consensus about the action to be taken.
- Celebrations of success—Often, celebrations of successes are forgotten. A celebration of success gives all individuals opportunities to feel good about progress made, validate the child's efforts, acknowledge the efforts of families, staff and other professionals and create a positive atmosphere.

2. Collaboration with Other Professionals

Various types of professionals can play an important role in helping child care practitioners set up an appropriate play-based program for children. These could include specialists such as play therapists, occupational therapists, sand play therapists or music therapists. The therapist is a highly trained individual with specialized skills.

Following is a brief description of the type of services each of these professionals might offer with respect to play and the child with special needs.

A) PLAY THERAPY Play therapy has long been established as a way to encourage children to express their feelings and explore relationships. Play therapy is defined as "a dynamic interpersonal relationship between a child (or person of any age) and a therapist trained in play therapy procedures who provides selected play materials and facilitates the development of a safe relationship for the child (or person of any age) to fully express and explore self (feelings, thoughts, experiences, and behaviours) through play, the child's natural medium of communication, for optimal growth and development" (Landreth, 2002:16).

There are a number of play therapy associations around the world. According to the Canadian Association for Child and Play Therapy:

> It is a therapeutic approach for human service professionals and as stated by Virginia Axline, "provides an opportunity for the child to 'play out' his or her feelings and problems just as, in certain adult therapy, an individual 'talks out' his or her difficulties." A child's self-understanding is one of the goals in this approach. Play Therapy can be used either as a primary or adjunct therapy in settings such as Children's Services, Community Agencies, Psychiatric Centers, Children's Hospitals, Schools, and Women's Shelters (Canadian Association for Child and Play Therapy, 2004:1).

B) THE LUDIC MODEL: OCCUPATIONAL THERAPY In an interview with Francine Ferland, Professor in Occupational Therapy at the University of Montreal, the connections between play and the Ludic Model were discussed. Based on research and her experiences in working with children and families of children with special needs (neurological disorders, physical disabilities, developmental delays and cognitive disabilities), Professor Ferland has developed the Ludic Model ("Ludic" means "related to play") to use with children in occupational therapy settings.

This model was created as a reflection of the importance of play in the life of any child. It is based on research conducted with parents of children with physical disabilities and interviews with the occupational therapists who have worked with these children and with adults who had lived with someone with permanent physical disabilities since birth. The subjects of the research study were individuals with physical disabilities, developmental delays and intellectual deficiencies. The research was conducted after the first publication of the *Ludic Model* and reported in a second edition of the publication (Ferland, 2005).

The Ludic Model embraces the philosophical underpinnings of the child's right to learn through play. Play has three components that relate to all aspects of treatment of the child: assessment, planning a treatment program and implementation. The Ludic Model embraces play in the following ways:

- Nurturing a playful attitude (Ludic attitude)—Play is seen as more than engaging the child in play-like tasks—for instance asking the child to do a task such as drawing shapes with colourful pens on a piece of paper. A playful attitude is what leads to active play—the desire to play, the enjoyment that arises with play and the positive interactions that arise from play. The Ludic attitude is characterized by pleasure, curiosity, a sense of humour and spontaneity.
- Involving the interests of the child—Careful consideration is given to identification of the child's interests. This information is gathered from family members and the therapist's observations, and could include information from the child care centre. Using the child's interests to develop a program is a strong motivator for the child to want to participate, which is necessary to awaken the desire to act and to maintain pleasure in action.
- Involving the child in active play (Ludic action)—Active play involves decision making, problem solving and interacting with materials and other individuals in meaningful ways. When children are actively involved, learning occurs that is relevant to their abilities, is intrinsic or self-motivated (motivation that is internal and expressed by the individual) and leads to greater autonomy. Ludic actions are instrumental components that permit the actions of play.

C) SAND PLAY THERAPY Sand play therapy was first used by Margaret Lowenfeld in 1930. It was further developed by Dora Dalff, who developed the use of sand as a tool for therapy and named it sand play. Sand play is similar to play therapy because it also engages the child in active play through the medium of sand and expresses the child's thoughts and feelings. Sand play has been used extensively in Germany, England and the United States and has had recent acceptance and use in certain jurisdictions in Canada.

During sand play, the therapist observes the child carefully and follows the child's lead as appropriate. According to the Sandplay Therapists of America:

> The essentials of sandplay therapy are a specially proportioned sandtray, a source of water, shelves of miniatures of multitude variety: people, animals, buildings, bridges, vehicles, furniture, food, plants, rocks, shells—the list goes on—and an empathetic therapist who provides the freedom and the protection that encourages children (or adults) to experience their inner, often unrealized, selves in a safe and non-judgmental space. The therapist as a witness is an essential part of the method, but this therapist is in the mode of 'appreciating,' not 'judging,' what the sandplayer does (Bradway, 1999:2–3).

D) MUSIC THERAPY Music therapy has strong historical roots. Many of the ancient philosophers, historians and scientists have alluded to the power of music as a therapeutic agent. Music can evoke different types of moods and can be used to change moods. "Music is a natural and important part of young children's growth and development. Early interaction with music positively affects the quality of all children's lives. Successful experiences in music help all children bond emotionally and intellectually with others through creative expression in song, rhythmic movement, and listening experiences" (The National Association for Music Education, 2008:1). The effects of music are measurable and have been identified by research:

- Music can influence physiological processes, such as speeding up or slowing down the heart rate.
- Music may be used for medical purposes. For instance, classical music is sometimes provided in infant intensive-care units. Studies have found that these infants tend to gain more weight, leave the hospital earlier and have better survival rates.
- Regular, continued experiences with music in early childhood relate to improved competence in many domains: physical, social, language, emotional and cognitive.
- Music can be used to evoke various moods. It can also be used to change moods; for example, to calm a child (Campbell, 2000; Canadian Association for Music Therapy, 2003).

The Canadian Association for Music Therapy defines the term this way: "Music therapy is the skillful use of music and musical elements by an accredited music therapist to promote, maintain, and restore mental, physical, emotional, and spiritual health. Music has nonverbal, creative, structural, and emotional qualities. These are used in the therapeutic relationship to facilitate contact, interaction, self-awareness, learning, self-expression, communication, and personal development" (Canadian Association for Music Therapy, 2003:1).

E) BENEFITS OF COLLABORATION WITH PLAY SPECIALISTS Each of these kinds of specialists is an expert in play with children with special needs. Interactions with these specialists will help the child care staff to:

- Create an atmosphere of calmness and therapeutic value in the classroom—Sand and music are excellent ways to offer relief in times of stress or frustration.

- Organize play areas with appropriate toys and resources—Children will become more independent in making appropriate choices and solving their own problems.
- Gain insight into how to use play opportunities to foster children's well-being and development—Provide opportunities to children that are relaxing, soothing and enjoyable.
- Gain expert advice on how to handle certain behaviours—Examples include fear, withdrawal from situations or lack of interest in play.
- Become more knowledgeable about alternative ways of helping families and children—Early childhood educators will be able to offer a greater variety of choices to families if a referral is needed.

3. Setting the Stage for Play

"When children are playing they are thinking, innovating, negotiating, and taking risks" (Jones, 2004:24). Learning environments should be organized in ways that encourage active play activities by supplying children with appropriate learning spaces, enough time and materials. Child care providers should encourage children to solve problems and provide challenges by presenting children with new problems to solve. These problems should emerge from careful observation of the children's evolving interests, in a spirit of acceptance and appreciation of the children's curiosity about the world around them.

Key considerations for organizing the environment for active play—setting the stage for play—have been described by Crowther (2007). These include observation, materials and resources, program format, "teachable moments," documentation of children's successes, a variety of self-expressive materials, organization of learning spaces and mediation between children (Carr, 2005:4).

A) OBSERVATIONS OF CHILDREN In order to effectively plan play for a group of children, knowledge of the children's usual play behaviour, interests, abilities and frustration levels is critical. Once it is gathered by all team members—other professionals, family members and staff—this information will help early childhood educators plan and organize developmentally appropriate and age-appropriate play experiences for all the children (see "4. Observing Children's Play," pages 206-209).

B) MATERIALS AND RESOURCES To optimize children's success and decrease possible frustration, a number of things should be considered when choosing toys, materials and resources in inclusive settings (Carr, 2005; National Lekotek, Centre, 2005). (See Table 6.2.)

C) PROGRAM FORMAT Often, the format of the program may deter children from engaging in active play. Programs that are too rigid or too open in scheduling tend to inhibit active play. Key components that encourage active play are flexibility and predictability. Adults should carefully consider appropriate strategies for transitions, allot an appropriate amount of time for active play, provide overall stability in day-to-day experiences, observe and interact with children spontaneously, document children's efforts, provide a variety of self-expressive materials,

TABLE 6.2 **MATERIALS AND RESOURCES TO OPTIMIZE SUCCESS**

Category	Clarification of Points
Durability	• Toys and equipment should be tough, in order to withstand active play
Safety	• Materials and equipment should not chip, splinter or break with repeated use • Avoid harmful substances such as lead paint. Larger equipment must be sturdy, to prevent tipping or falling when in use
Potential for various levels of play	• Learning materials should support all levels of play • Learning materials should meet a variety of developmental needs • Play materials should be flexible enough to meet varying types of social or cognitive play
Involvement of more than one sense	• Visual—Different, contrasting colours; clear detail; realistic appearance; movement • Auditory—Interesting sounds • Tactile—Varied textures, contours or surfaces • Smell—E.g., scented dolls (powder scent), scented playdough
Opportunity for success	• Open-endedness—Learning materials can be used in more than one way; no right or wrong way • Avoiding frustration—Opportunities to effectively manipulate or experiment with learning materials
Accessibility	• Learning materials can be accessed and used in various places or positions, such as on the floor, on a table or on a tray while sitting in a wheelchair
Adaptability	• Adjustments to equipment to accommodate different heights, volumes or speeds, such as adjustable paint easels, listening centres with appropriate volume control or a variety of ground surfaces to encourage running or riding at different speeds
Using the child's interest	• Appropriate materials to enhance current interests and abilities
Developmentally and age-appropriate	• Materials should be appropriate for the children's age and developmental levels
Culturally appropriate	• Materials should relate to the culture of the setting by providing items such as storybooks on disabilities, dolls in wheelchairs or pictures of individuals working in communities with disabilities
Self-expression	• Materials should encourage creativity, uniqueness and opportunity to make choices. Children should gain experiences with a wide variety of media (National Lekotek Centre, 2005)
Interactivity	• Variety of interactions should be possible—verbal, body language, individual or group
Simplicity	• Materials should look realistic, be devoid of distracting backgrounds, easy to understand and attractive
Scaffolding	• Materials should encourage skill development, from simple to complex
Cause and effect	• Materials should encourage children to see the result of their actions, such as turning a knob so a light will flash or rolling a toy on the floor or down a ramp
Familiarity	• Materials should be familiar to the children's experiences and backgrounds

organize the learning spaces to encourage active play and mediate between children as needed.

- Transitions—Transitions should be kept simple and to a minimum. Major transitions, such as from indoor to outdoor play, meal times, sleep times or dismissal, should be carefully considered. Ample warning should be provided and children should be included through such techniques as actions, songs and providing additional help, and through the use of visual or auditory cues.
- Time to complete tasks—Ensure that there is enough time for all children to complete activities. At least one hour of free play in the morning and in the afternoon should be considered. Provide opportunities to complete activities over time by creating storage for projects in progress.
- Predictability—Children should get a good sense of what is happening next. There needs to be a schedule that establishes continuity from day to day. In this way, children can gradually learn to anticipate and get ready for the next routine.
- Stability—Continual, massive changes, such as total room changes to the environment to accommodate new themes, should be avoided. Children need the security of knowing where things are and how to find them. Changes and adaptations should be made based on the children's abilities and interests. These changes should involve the children and should not affect the overall organization of the room.

D) "TEACHABLE MOMENTS" Teachable moments occur when an early childhood educator observes children's play and identifies a situation that can be used to increase interactions between children or foster growth and development. For example, Jamie had been watching Dillon draw on the chalkboard (see Photo 6.1, page 186). Both boys tended to be involved in solitary play. Kaya asked Jamie if he wanted to draw on the chalkboard. Kaya created a set of chalk similar to Dillon's and brought it over to the chalkboard, telling Dillon that Jamie also wanted to draw on the board. Both boys continued to draw. Kaya had created an opportunity for the two boys to be involved in parallel play.

E) DOCUMENTATION OF CHILDREN'S SUCCESSES Documentation of children's successes is important in several ways. It serves to inform visitors, other professionals and families of the children's accomplishments, and it also reinforces the value of play as a primary mode of learning. Additionally, children's efforts are acknowledged and documented. This leads to increased pride in achievement and may motivate children to continue with current activities or move on to new challenges.

Documentation of children's achievements also helps the adult to recognize the significance of even small achievements and the importance of sharing these achievements with family members. For example, Jeremy, a teacher in a class of children diagnosed with learning disabilities, reported: "One of my profound moments in teaching occurred when I called one of the parents of Scott, an eight-year-old child with dyslexia, to inform the parents that Scott had created a poem on the new voice-activated computer. Scott and I had decided to submit this poem to a children's magazine and needed his parents' agreement. I had not met Scott's parents before. Neither parent had attended the parent night in the fall. When I called the mother during lunch hour, I politely introduced myself. Her response was very abrupt. I explained what Scott had achieved and what he wanted to do with this achievement. There was a long silence. Eventually she responded: 'You mean you called me to tell me something good about my son? In all the years that Scott has been in school, first preschool, then kindergarten and now elementary school, we have never been called about something he has done well.' I was stunned. I thought back over the number of times that I contacted family members and had to admit that it was usually because of a problem that had occurred. This was a teachable moment for me. I have since then strived to share as many of the successes as I can in as many ways as I can. I have found that the results have been most rewarding. I now teach happier children, have more supportive families and enjoy my job so much more."

Several types of documentation could be used. Two of the most common are documentation panels and portfolios. Both techniques involve all partners: children, families, staff and other professionals. The purpose of both documentation panels and portfolios is to clearly identify the activities the children have been engaged in and the learning that resulted, and to be open to adding additional information as the learning activity continues to evolve. Examples of the two techniques are shown in Figures 6.3 and 6.4.

These sample pages from a portfolio followed a field trip to look for signs of spring. They include the children's expression through art and dictations about the signs of spring. The children decided what to include. One of the advantages of a portfolio over a documentation panel is that children can take the portfolio home to show to families. Individual copies can also be provided at the families' request.

F) VARIETY OF SELF-EXPRESSIVE MATERIALS Communication is central to all interaction. There are many forms of expression. The Reggio Emilia approach to education talks about the "Hundred Languages of Children" (Malaguzzi, 1997). Communication can take many forms—verbal, written, symbolic, signing, artistic, body language or music. It is essential to provide materials that engage children in a variety of ways to express themselves (see Table 6.3 on page 204). It is also children's fundamental right to have their personal way of expression acknowledged, understood and valued.

FIGURE 6.3

Example of One Part of a Documentation Panel

Ideas About Signs of Spring

The information was gathered from the children. Ideas were communicated through verbalizations, pointing to pictures and signing. The list was expanded over several days. Sometimes the child and a family member or other professional would add items to it.

growing things	ice disappears	ride our bikes
snow melts	put winter things away	spring cleaning
gets warmer	play outside longer	collect things
rain	see things on the ground	work in the yard
sing spring songs	birds come back	insects come out
animals come out		

FIGURE 6.3
Continued

Ideas About Signs of Spring

The children decided that they would like to go on a field trip to gather signs of spring.

We found many signs of spring.

Katie found pussy willows. "They are fuzzy."

"I discovered that the ground is soggy. When you step on it water seeps over your boots."

Anastasia found a flower: "Yellow." Braelyn said, "It's a dandelion, Anastasia, and it's actually a weed."

Yasmine was excited that the ice had disappeared from the river. She said, "I see shells, stones and tiny little fish."

FIGURE 6.4

Sample Pages of a Project-Based Portfolio

What We Learned About Spring

Children learned to represent their ideas in different ways. They used different media: crayons, oil pastels, glue, different coloured foil scraps and play dough. They were able to articulate various concepts about spring verbally, in writing, through signing and by providing visual cues:

- changing weather patterns—rain and snow, what to wear, observing rain on the window
- effects of temperature—melting
- new growth—flowers
- activities related to spring—splashing in puddles

Danielle drew a picture of rain. She signed that her picture was about "rain falling."
When Jordan heard Danielle's message, he ran to get a pair of boots, an umbrella and a raincoat.
Damian saw the boots and said, "In the spring there are puddles. I like to splash in puddles."

Jenna had been fascinated with watching raindrops run down the window pane. She traced their path with her fingers. She said, "Shiny." Later she created her own raindrops. She used a paste brush to create a circle of glue on her paper. Then she added scraps of shiny foil to the circles of glue.

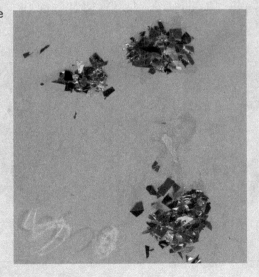

FIGURE 6.4

Continued

What We Learned About Spring

Christopher created a flower using oil pastels. He also created a frame for his picture made of rolled paper. He explained, "The flower is growing because the sun is warmer. It is a violet. It is one of the first flowers to appear in the spring."

Olivia created a snowman. She indicated that sometimes it snowed in the spring and that sometimes she could still make a snowman. "My snowman will soon melt. He will slowly disappear."

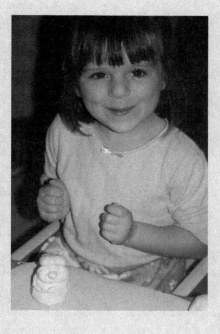

TABLE 6.3 SELF-EXPRESSIVE ACTIVITIES

Type of Activity	Range of Self-Expressive Activities
Art	• Painting—With tools such as brushes or rollers; fingerpainting or foot-painting; painting on different surfaces such as paper, clear surfaces, boxes • Drawing—With tools such as oil pastels, chalk, pencil or wax crayons, markers, sticks, or fingers or hands; on a variety of surfaces: boxes, paper, booklets, lined paper, unlined paper, trays filled with sand or flour, the ground or sand in the sandbox • Sculpting—Clay, playdough, wet sand, papier mâché, boxes; with tools such as knives, spatulas, rollers, hammers or fingers and hands • Decorating—Glue, scissors and materials to decorate with: paper products such as shiny paper, regular or tissue paper in various colours and sizes; collections from nature such as shells, colourful stones, pine cones, grasses or seeds; material such as scraps of fabric, yarn or felt; glitter; wood products such as popsicle sticks or wooden shapes; wire, such as plastic-covered wire or pipe cleaners
Carpentry	Carpentry tools—For attaching, cutting and decorating activities, plus appropriate materials such as soft wood and appropriate-sized nails. Coordinate with art area to encourage decoration.
Music	• Rhythm instruments—Drums, sticks, bells, cymbals, tambourines, maracas, triangles • Musical instruments—Xylophone, keyboards, bells • Music—Appropriate to play along with or move to • Props—Scarves, capes, ribbons
Blocks	Wooden-unit, soft-unit, cardboard, foam and hollow blocks
Manipulative toys	Lego, Duplo, Interlinks, tinker toys
Dramatic play	• Props—Dress-up clothes, scarves, blankets • Role play materials • Combining dramatic area with other areas—Riding toys, sand and water areas, block areas
Writing	• Writing area—Dictionaries, dictionary cards, papers (lined and unlined) and writing tools of various sizes, booklets, books, photographs, alphabet letters • Scribe centre—Area that children can come to in order to dictate a story
Sewing	• Tools—Plastic large-eyed needles, hole punch, scissors, pinking shears • Material—Cardboard, plastic, fabric, yarn, gimp
Wet sand	• Tools—trowels, shovels, containers of various sizes and shapes • Materials for dramatic play—animals, fences, buildings, fabric to create various scenes (ponds, rivers, meadow) • Materials for planting—flowers (plastic, dried); plant materials gathered outside on a field trip • Photograph/pictures—local construction sites, buildings, farms, gardening firms

G) APPROPRIATE SPACE AND ORGANIZATION "When indoor and outdoor learning centres are designed to do the bulk of the direct teaching, children's pretend play in those centres can support and foster the bulk of their learning. When children play without relying on the accomplished skills of an adult, they tackle complex challenges of language skills, perspective taking, representational thinking, problem solving, and turn taking as they work hard to keep their games going" (Perry, 2004:17).

The organization of the learning environment has a great impact on children's ability to participate in active play. The following factors should be considered:

- Visibility—All interest areas should be clearly visible from all areas of the room. This facilitates the ease with which a child can find an area of interest and also helps improve supervision.
- Accessibility—All areas (indoors and outdoors) should be accessible by wheelchair and have unobstructed floors and passageways to prevent tripping, falling or blocking a route of travel. Materials are accessible on low, sturdy shelves and organized by type.
- Labelling system—Materials are labelled by pictures, words, symbols and/or outlines to facilitate retrieval and return of the materials (Figure 6.5).
- Aesthetics—Materials should be arranged so as as to invite the child to touch, explore or handle. For example, in one inclusive setting children spent a lot of time painting. There were several alternative paint centres set up. One centre was set up with new colours: bright pink, dark indigo, lime green, egg-shell white, tangerine

1. Photograph and label

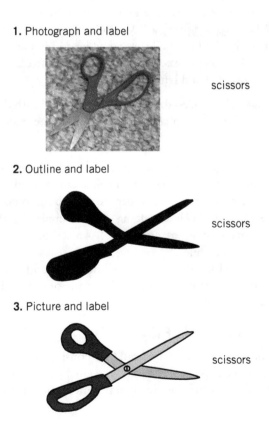

scissors

2. Outline and label

scissors

3. Picture and label

scissors

FIGURE 6.5

Examples of Labelling Systems

and cardinal red. The paint was set up in clear plastic containers set on circular mirrored surfaces. Brushes were placed in a brush container with bristles up. The centre was set up on a rectangular table near a water source to encourage children to clean their brushes after use.

In the hour of free play, this centre was used consistently by most of the children. The children talked about the paint being "mirrored in the glass." Some children put paint on their paper and gently touched the paint with their fingers. One child looked at the paint from many different perspectives. In contrast, areas left messy or dirty tend to be ignored.

- Choices that represent a holistic approach—A full range of choices, including creative, manipulative, dramatic, construction (sand, blocks, carpentry), experimental (water, sand, science, math), language, music, gross motor, fine motor, books and space to be alone—should be available in both indoor and outdoor environments (Harms, Clifford & Cryer, 1998; Crowther, 2007).

H) MEDIATION BETWEEN CHILDREN Young children are at the egocentric stage of life. They see the world from their own perspective. They are also eager to learn and embrace new learning vivaciously. Children may not always understand the signals that are communicated. It is up to the adult to interpret and help children make sense of what they have seen or heard.

For example, Liu, a second-language learner, was playing in the block area. She had built several structures. Mario joined her and started to add to her structure. Liu said, "我想要一個人靜一靜." Mario looked at her with a blank look on his face. Min, the early childhood educator, had heard Liu's comment. She walked over to the two children. She looked at both and said, "Mario, Liu said that she wants to be alone." Mario smiled and left.

I) FOCUS ON PROCESS The process that the child is involved with during play, not the end product, should be the emphasis. Children should be encouraged to extend their play through:

- Asking exploratory questions—Ask a child what he or she will do next, or to explain or demonstrate how a task has been accomplished. "You have worked hard to build the block structure. What are you going to do now?"
- Commenting on what the child is doing—For example, describing the colours, shapes or lines made in an art creation. "I can see that you have made large red circles, and fat blue lines."
- Labelling feelings—Identifying how the child feels and why they are feeling this way. "I understand it is frustrating when someone takes away your toy."

4. Observing Children's Play

There are a number of factors that should be considered when observing play, such as types of play, the child's interests, who the child plays with and attention span. Each is related to play but provides its own pertinent information.

A) OBSERVING TYPES OF PLAY It is important to know what type of play children are involved in, in order to provide the appropriate settings, materials and resources to maintain or expand the play opportunities. Table 6.4 provides an overview of some types of tools that could be used to observe the type of play children are involved in.

How might the observations in Table 6.4 be used? Josh is engaged in age-appropriate types of play. He seems comfortable with other children, especially with Damian. This observation could be used to encourage interactions between the two boys.

Josh's interests include filling and dumping activities. This activity could be encouraged by providing additional materials in both water and sand. Adding a shelf to the water centre (placed in the water centre to provide the child with opportunity to place a container on it and pour water into the container) might facilitate more parallel and/or associative play in water.

B) OBSERVING INTEREST Observations of interest help the care provider to organize settings that encourage children to participate with each other. In addition, it allows the care provider to gain a clear perspective on each of the children's strengths and needs, in order to provide a more emergent and appropriate program for all children. Based on the interest shown by Josh (see Table 6.4), the tool shown in Table 6.5 was used. How might the observations in Table 6.5 be used?

TABLE 6.4 OBSERVING TYPES OF PLAY

Name: Josh (3.6)   **Observer:** Jane
Date(s): November 2, 3, 4, 2004

Type of Play	Setting	Circumstances	Comments
Solitary	Puzzles		Completed a six-part single-piece puzzle by trial and error, put it back on shelf
Solitary, functional	Water	Chose individual water tub	Filled pail with scoop, emptied it; repeated filling and emptying five times; needed reminder to replace toys on shelf
Parallel, constructive	Blocks	Beside Damian	Created a horizontal structure, watched it fall, rebuilt it; Damian built enclosures; stopped building when Damian did; both boys were reminded to clean up
Parallel, functional	Duplo	Beside Damian	Followed Damian to Duplo; attached pieces and took them apart
Parallel, functional	Sand	Beside Hannah	Both used dump trucks and shovels to fill and dump; made appropriate truck noises
Associative	Puppets	With Sharleigh and Damian	Children shared puppets, laughed at funny actions, but continued to use own puppets individually

TABLE 6.5 **OBSERVATIONS OF INTEREST**

Name: Josh

Dates: November 5, 6, 9

Observer: Jane

Key: S = Solitary; P = Parallel; A = Associative

Interest	Frequency	Comments
Play with Damian	PPP AA	Using construction toys–Blocks and Duplo Puppet area, fingerpainting
Filling and dumping	SSS PPP	Water, puzzles, book Noticed shelf in water centre; started to fill and dump

- To confirm previous observations—It would seem that the strategy to use a shelf in the water centre worked. Josh finds it hard to hold a container and fill it at the same time. This strategy eliminated his difficulty. He also seems to play more often with Damian.
- To plan for interactions—Since the two boys are often seen together, this situation can be used by an adult to generate spontaneous interactions with both boys.

C) OBSERVING ATTENTION SPAN Observing a child's attention span gives information about his or her ability to sustain interest over time. The easiest way to do this is to use a graph like the one shown in Figure 6.6. This technique can be combined with types of play and interests. This saves the observer some time and gives the added benefit of recording all the information on one sheet.

How might the observations in Figure 6.6 be used? Inferences can be made about the child's skills and abilities:

- Josh has a normal attention span for activities that he is interested in.
- The type of play Josh engages in is also age-appropriate.
- He has a variety of interests.
- He is interested in filling and dumping activities and taking things apart and putting them together again—mostly functional play activities.

This information could be used to adapt materials in the environment:

- Add the small cubed blocks to the block area. This may encourage more fine-motor control to build towers.
- Add construction vehicles to the block area. This may encourage a different type of building.
- Add building wheels and round peg stackers to the manipulative area to encourage further skill in attachment.

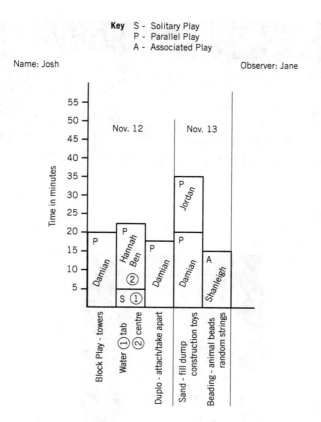

Key S - Solitary Play
     P - Parallel Play
     A - Associated Play

Name: Josh   Observer: Jane

FIGURE 6.6

Obsrvation of Attention Span, Interest, Type of Play

5. Adaptations for Play in Inclusive Settings

Children with special needs may find it difficult to participate in play activities. Special adaptations may need to be made in order to encourage participation in play. Sandall (2004) identifies eight categories for curriculum adaptation: environmental support, materials adaptation, simplifying the activity, using child preferences, special equipment, adult support, peer support and invisible support (Koralek, 2004:44–45).

A) ENVIRONMENTAL SUPPORT To maximize free choice and facilitate positive interactions, a number of adaptations could be made, including:

• Photograph display, to help children find the interest centre that they would like to participate in (see Figure 6.7).
• Posted picture symbols, to help children communicate what they wish to have or do.
• Organization of the environment to, facilitate various types of play, such as individual or small group play (see Figure 6.1, photos 1 and 3, page 189).

Photo 6.4

FIGURE 6.7

Example of a Photograph Display of Interest Areas

Blocks

Art

music

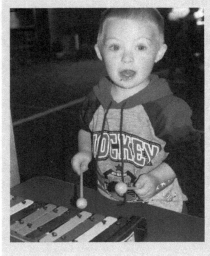

Manipulative

B) MATERIALS ADAPTATION Materials may be adapted to maximize children's ability to manipulate the objects effectively. Several levels of adaptability could occur, including accessibility, comfort and ease of manipulation.

- Accessibility—Children need to be able to freely reach all materials and activities.
- Comfort—Not all children can access materials or activities successfully. For example, putting a wheelchair into a group setting is uncomfortable for the children and for the individual in the wheelchair. Providing a special chair for a child in a wheelchair will enable all children to interact at the same level (Photo 6.6).
- Ease of manipulation—For example, Melanie had only one arm with just two digits on the hand. She liked to play with small vehicles. To pick up small vehicles, she needed to use a tray to trap the vehicles and to have vehicles with open undersurfaces or windows, so that she could grasp them more easily.

C) SIMPLIFIED ACTIVITIES Activities that involve more than one step may be difficult for some children to accomplish. Children may need to have these types of activities simplified. Simplification could be accomplished in a number of ways:

- Reduction of number of pieces or number of steps—Provide puzzles with fewer pieces. Games such as musical chairs could be changed by simply listening to the music and sitting down when the music stops, without removing chairs.
- Changing the timing of activities—Some children may need more time than others to complete an activity such as painting. Songs such as "Head and Shoulders" may need to be sung much more slowly so that children have time to point to the correct body part.

Photo 6.5

Photo 6.6

Photo 6.7

- Scaffolding—For example, Josh and Ted had learned to make their own play-dough. This task was broken down into a number of small steps. These steps were represented pictorially. The boys were able to complete the task with minimal supervision (see Figure 6.8).

FIGURE 6.8

An Example of Scaffolding: Making Playdough

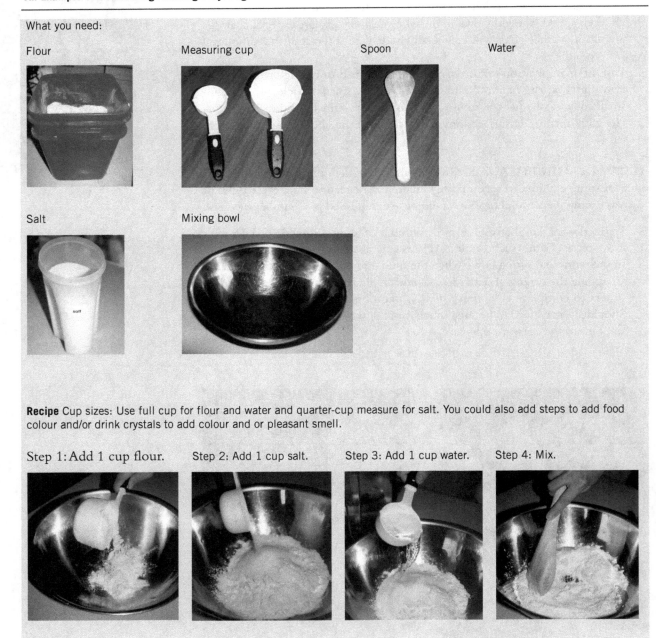

What you need:

Flour   Measuring cup   Spoon   Water

Salt   Mixing bowl

Recipe Cup sizes: Use full cup for flour and water and quarter-cup measure for salt. You could also add steps to add food colour and/or drink crystals to add colour and or pleasant smell.

Step 1: Add 1 cup flour.   Step 2: Add 1 cup salt.   Step 3: Add 1 cup water.   Step 4: Mix.

D) CHILDREN'S PREFERENCES Children who are interested in what they are doing will continue to work on an activity over long time periods. Benjamin enjoyed painting. He was often observed covering paper with paint using tools such as brushes, but also often using his hands. He rarely participated in writing activities or printing. Christopher, his teacher, noticed his interest. He set up a finger-painting activity at one table. Christopher then sat down, covered his page with paint and started to draw designs on the page with his fingers. Benjamin watched for a while, clearly intrigued. He finally covered his paper in red paint. He then proceeded to draw shapes on his paper. He beamed when Jeremy identified the shapes by size, shape or letter name. This activity lasted over several weeks (Photo 6.8). Benjamin's efforts were displayed (see Figure 6.9).

Photo 6.8

FIGURE 6.9

Sample Display of Benjamin's Efforts

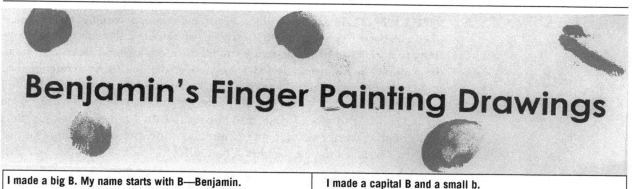

Benjamin's Finger Painting Drawings

I made a big B. My name starts with B—Benjamin.

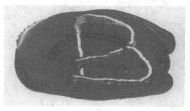

I made a capital B and a small b.

I made a triangle. It's humungous.

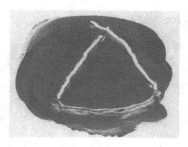

I like making circles. There is one big circle and lots of small ones.

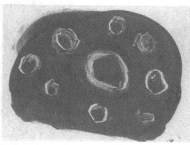

Photo 6.9

E) SPECIAL EQUIPMENT Some children may need special equipment to help them interact appropriately with other children. For example, John is using a weighted bag over his legs to help him concentrate on the music activity he is involved with (Photo 6.9).

F) ADULT SUPPORT Adult support is a critical factor in any children's environment. Adult support includes:

- Encouragement of the activity the child is engaged in—Benjamin was encouraged to continue to fingerpaint by the posting of his results, and by the adult's interest in his activity.
- Joining in—An example would be playing along with the children during musical activities. Harmon was encouraged to join in by providing him with a chair that helped him to be at the children's level (Photo 6.6 on page 211).
- Modelling—Jeremy modelled fingerpainting strategies to Benjamin.
- Commenting—Jeremy made relevant comments about Benjamin's fingerpainting.

G) PEER SUPPORT The early childhood educator uses opportunities to encourage children's peers to join in the play. Jonathan was finding it difficult to find something to do. He had been wandering around the room asking if he could join in. Several times he had been rejected. Susan noticed that Jonathan was walking over to Gracie, who was reading to herself. She walked over to Gracie with Jonathan and said, "Gracie is reading. Would you like to listen?" Jonathan nodded. Gracie looked up and smiled and asked Jonathan if Jonathan's baby liked the story. Jonathan smiled and smacked her hand enthusiastically to indicate his pleasure. The two children continued to play together (Photo 6.10).

Photo 6.10

H) INVISIBLE SUPPORT The environment is organized to maximize children's success. In effect, the environment acts as the third teacher. The choice of materials and equipment and the organization of these materials encourage children to learn interdependently. Materials are stored on low, sturdy, open shelves, easily accessible to the children. The shelves and containers are labelled for easy retrieval and return (Figure 6.5 on page 206). Labelling is used to encourage the child with difficulty in communicating to use the pictures or photographs to communicate (see Photo 6.4, page 210).

Role of the Early Childhood Educator

The early childhood educator's role of encouraging active play in the learning environment requires many skills, including:

- Collaboration with all partners—To set up a learning environment that maximizes children's learning through play, a collaborative process should be established with children, families and other professionals. This process will help identify and utilize children's skills, interests and abilities.
- Creation of an atmosphere of warmth, respect and acceptance—Children need to feel that their interactions, self-expressions and learning are accepted and valued (see Figures 6.7 and 6.9).
- Arrangement of materials and equipment to encourage active play situations within each interest area in the room—Children need to be continually observed to utilize spontaneous "teachable moments."
- Careful consideration of outdoor play spaces—Play spaces outside should reflect a smooth transition from indoor to outdoor play (see Photos 6.5 and 6.8).
- Adaptation—Identification of necessary adaptations to the learning spaces, the materials and equipment in these spaces, and the interactions occurring there is critical (see pages 209–215).
- Use of displays to document children's learning and activities—Displays help to maintain interest and keep all individuals informed about the learning and activities of the children (see Figures 6.7 and 6.9).
- Observing children—Adults observe and document children's activities to enable them to adapt the environment as needed (see pages 206–209).
- Documentation of learning—Adults facilitate in the creation of portfolios (Figure 6.4) or documentation panels (Figure 6.3) that describe children's interests and learning.
- Modification—Play strategies are modified as needed (see pages 209–215).
- Maintaining interest—Materials are added, rotated or adapted to maintain attention and interest over time (Photo 6.3).

SUMMARY

Best practices for all children require that children have the right to learn through play. Through play, children establish positive attitudes toward learning that last a lifetime. Research has identified that withdrawal from play situations has implications for academic success and provides a "strong predictor of peer rejection, social anxiety, loneliness, depression, and negative self-esteem in later childhood and adolescence" (Bergen, 2004:4). Play builds the foundations for all future skills, abilities and learning.

It is therefore critical to foster children's play to develop skills in:

- Social competence
- Communication competence
- Transforming objects and actions symbolically
- Negotiating with peers and adults
- Solving problems
- Learning to take different perspectives
- Learning how to learn

KEY POINTS

Principles that influence play
- Play affects the child's motivation.
- Play affects cognitive decentring.
- Play develops mental representation.
- Play develops deliberate actions.

Types of play in developmental order
- Solitary, parallel, associative, cooperative
- Functional, symbolic, constructive, dramatic, games with rules

Reasons for diverse play abilities in inclusive settings
- Developmental ability, background experiences, family values, family expectations, type of disability, social pressures

Collaborative process
- Families identify interests, monitor progress, mitigate areas of concern, and celebrate successes
- Other professionals: play therapists, occupational therapists, sand play therapists, music therapists— Create appropriate play atmosphere, organize play areas, gain insight into behaviour, gain expert advice, become more knowledgeable about the services specialists provide

Setting the stage for play
- Observation of children's abilities and interests
- Materials and resources—Durable, safe, multi-functional, multi-sensory, avoid frustration, accessible, adaptable, based on children's interests
- Developmental and age appropriateness
- Maximization of self-expression, interactivity, mediation
- Maximization of success—Scaffolding, familiarity, spontaneity
- Program format—Flexible transitions, time to complete tasks, predictability, stability
- Documentation of success
- Organization of learning areas—High visibility, accessibility, labelling, holistic approach

Observations of children
- Types of play, interests, attention span

Adaptations of play in inclusive settings
- Environmental support
- Material adaptations—Accessibility, comfort, ease of manipulation
- Simplified activities—Number of pieces, changed timing, scaffolding
- Use of children's preferences

- Special equipment
- Adult and peer support

Role of early childhood educator

- Collaboration—Children, families, staff and other professionals
- Creating an atmosphere of warmth, respect and acceptance

- Organizing materials and equipment to maintain interest over time
- Smooth transitions from indoor to outdoor play
- Identification of adaptations
- Documenting with documentation panels, portfolios
- Observing and documenting children's interests, skills, progress, successes

EXERCISES

1. Reflect on the following situation: A mother complains that her child is not meeting the goals as set out by her physiotherapist. She feels that the staff is allowing her daughter to play too much. She indicates that she wants to see an IPP set up that addresses her child's needs specifically. She would like to see less involvement in play and more time spent on structured activities such as tracing letters and other manipulative tasks. How would you respond to this mother?

2. Observe a group of preschoolers in an integrated setting. Identify how often you see the children involved in various types of play. Explain why the children might be involved in each type of play.

3. Identify the key individuals in your area whom you might wish to collaborate with to set up an appropriate inclusive play-based program. What type of collaboration would you seek from each individual identified? What are the benefits of this collaboration to the child, the family, the specialist and the staff?

4. Utilize the criteria developed for materials and resources on pages 198. Develop an observation chart. Take the tool to a local toy store and identify which toys would be suitable in inclusive settings. Justify each answer.

5. Utilize the chart below to identify various documentation methods in child care centres in your area. Compare your results with your classmates. Discuss which methods are most effective and why.

6. For each of the adaptive criteria listed, develop specific strategies that will provide for best inclusive play practices:

   - Providing environmental support
   - Adaptations of materials
   - Providing support from adults and peers
   - Simplifying materials and activities

7. Describe the role of an early childhood educator in an inclusive setting. How is that role the same as in other settings? How is it different?

DOCUMENTATION TYPES

Type	Description	Effectiveness
Displays		
Documentation panels		
Portfolios		
Other		

REFERENCES

Bergen, D. (2004). Pretend Play and Young Children's Development. ERIC Digest [online]. Available at www.ericdigests.org/2002-2/play.htm.

Bodrova, E., & Leong, D. (2004). Chopsticks and Counting Chips: Do Play and Foundational Skills Need to Compete for the Teacher's Attention in an Early Childhood Classroom? In D. Koralek (Ed.), *Spotlight on Young Children and Play* (pp. 4–11). Washington, DC: National Association for the Education of Young Children.

Bradway, K. (1999). Sandplay and Children. Sandplay Therapists of America. [online]. Available at www.sandplay.org/sandplay_with_children.htm [06/01/09].

Campbell, C. (2000). *The Mozart Effect for Children*. New York, NY: HarperCollins Publishers Inc.

Canadian Association for Child and Play Therapy (2004). Play Therapy. Canadian Association for Child and Play Therapy [online]. Available at www.cacpt.com.

Canadian Association for Music Therapy (2003). What Is Music Therapy? Canadian Association for Music Therapy [online]. Available at www.musictherapy.ca.

Crowther, I. (2007). *Creating Effective Learning Environments*. Second Edition. Scarborough, ON: Nelson Thomson Learning.

Elkind, D. (2007). *The Power of Play: Learning What Comes Naturally*. Philadelphia, PA: Da Capo Lifelong Books.

Ferland, F. (2005). *The Ludic Model: Play, Children with Physical Disabilities and Occupational Therapy*. Second Edition. Ottawa, ON: CAOT Publications ACE.

Harms, T., Clifford, R., & Cryer, D. (1998). *Early Childhood Environment Rating Scale*. Revised Edition. New York, NY: Teachers College Press.

Jones, E. (2004). Playing to Get Smart. In D. Koralek (Ed.), *Spotlight on Young Children and Play* (pp. 24–27). Washington, DC: The National Association for the Education of Young Children.

Koralek, D. E. (2004). *Spotlight on Young Children and Play*. Washington, DC: National Association for the Education of Young Children.

Landreth, G. (2002). *Play Therapy: The Art of the Relationship*. New York, NY: Brunner-Routledge.

Malaguzzi, L. (1997). *The Hundred Languages of Children*. Second Edition. Reggio Emilia, Italy: Reggio Children.

The National Association for Music Education (2008). Early Childhood Education (Position Statement) [online]. Available at http:menc.blueatlas.com/about/view/early-childhood-education-position-statement.

National Lekotek Centre (2005). Top 10 Tips for Choosing Toys. National Lekotek Centre [online]. Available at www.lekotek.org/resources/informationontoys/tentips.html.

Perry, J. (2004). Making Sense of Outdoor Pretend Play. In D. Koralek (Ed.), *Spotlight on Young Children and Play* (pp. 17–21). Washington, DC: The National Association for the Education of Young Children.

Sandall, S. (2004). Play Modifications for Children with Disabilities. In D. Koralek (Ed.), *Spotlight on Young Children and Play* (pp. 54–57). Washington, DC: National Association for the Education of Young Children.

Tepperman, J., ed. (2007). Play in the Early Years: Key to School Success. Alliance for Childhood [online]. Available at www.allianceforchildhood.net/index.htm [11/21/2008].

7

CHAPTER

Managing Behaviours in Inclusive Settings

Chapter Outline

"Children with challenging behaviours desperately need to learn social skills to protect them in the future. Their socially competent peers, who can act as role models and reinforce their attempts at positive behaviour every day, are the best possible teachers (if there are enough properly trained adults around to support them of course).

"The other children are learning, too. They learn how to help a friend, how to stand up for themselves, how not to become victims. Above all, they learn that people are different and that everyone is a valuable individual" (Kaiser & Sklar Rasminsky, 1999:14).

Learning Outcomes

After studying this chapter, you will be able to:

1. Describe why it is difficult to diagnose challenging behaviours.
2. Identify and describe the types of challenging behaviours of children.
3. Explain why it is important to understand the causes of challenging behaviours.
4. Identify the partners in a collaborative process, and explain why this collaboration is critical with each partner.
5. Identify how and why to observe challenging behaviours of children.
6. Describe the similarities and differences between a standard IPP and a behavioural IPP.
7. Describe the types of environmental adaptations that should discourage the occurrence of challenging behaviours, considering the social context, the overall program, the use of interaction approaches and the child's perspective.
8. Describe the roles of the early childhood educator in organizing a positive learning environment.

Photo 7.1

Introduction

It is often difficult to formally diagnose children with behavioural problems because a challenging behaviour in one setting may not be challenging in another setting. This is a result of the expectations placed on individuals, cultural values and the type of environment a child is in. At age two, Rashawne was an active, curious child. He actively explored the environment, and he especially loved filling and dumping activities (Photo 7.1). But the resulting disarray caused several reactions, depending on where he was playing or whom he was interacting with:

- At home, this activity was acceptable, as long as Rashawne helped clean it up afterwards.
- When he played at a friend's house, he was told it was not appropriate to create a mess—"These beads are meant for stringing, not dumping."
- Within the day care situation, this type of activity was discouraged because it was too noisy, too messy and might cause another child to trip and fall. Additionally, the pieces were deemed too small for toddler use because the toddler might choke on them.

This type of play behaviour would also have been inappropriate in more formal settings, such as a church.

When Rashawne was asked to clean up his beads, his immediate action was to continue to play. When asked again, he said, "No." Again, the reactions to Rashawne were varied:

- His parents calmly ignored his behaviour and made a game of cleaning up the beads. The clatter that the beads made when tossed into a container made a pleasing sound. Rashawne was soon absorbed in the clean-up activity.
- His friend's mother, Janelle, told him not to be naughty, and to help clean up the beads. Rashawne ignored her. When she insisted, Rahawne ran away, kicking the beads in front of him. Janelle's impression was that he was a hard-to-manage child.
- Rashawne visited the preschool room. He found the beads and proceeded to dump them. One of the adults noticed his behaviour and quickly redirected his dumping behaviour by providing alternative containers to dump into.

Each of these settings produced different perceptions about Rashawne's behaviour. At home, he was encouraged to explore freely with some limitation: he had to clean up. His parents realized the value of the activity Rashawne was involved in and encouraged his behaviour. The toddler room did not provide these types of toys because they were considered dangerous. His friend's mother had expectations that were not appropriate for toddlers. It is a natural developmental activity for toddlers to fill and dump, and to assert their independence by refusing to help. The preschool teachers understood the toddler's developmental stage and redirected his behaviour positively so that he could continue to explore actively.

Behaviour should always be looked upon as positive when children are:

- Actively involved in play
- Using materials and toys appropriately

- Interacting positively with each other
- Learning from their interactions with materials and toys
- Enjoying their activities

In contrast, challenging behaviours are behaviours that:

- Interfere with children's learning, development and success at play
- Are harmful to the child or other children
- Put the child at risk for later social problems or school failure (Kaiser et al., 1999:7)

Types of Challenging Behaviour

It is estimated that from 3 to 15 percent of preschool children in Canada are considered challenging (Vitaro, De Civita & Pagani, 1996). Challenging behaviours are varied; they depend on the child's temperament, the circumstances and the setting in which these behaviours occur. Some of these behaviours are frustrating to adults and peers; others may be dangerous to peers or to the child; and some may escape notice as a challenging behaviour. Children who are quiet, shy or withdrawn may not be identified as having challenging behaviours because the behaviours are less obvious and are more socially acceptable. Challenging behaviours may be grouped into several categories: emotional, conduct, hyperkinetic, developmental and diagnosed.

1. Emotion-Related Behaviours

It is often difficult for adults to separate what they think is the imagination of young children from what the young child thinks is real. A shadow on a wall may become a monster; a hot breath of wind may be a lion chasing the child: In the child's mind, these are real. However, many of these instances are based on a combination of correctly observing what has been seen and heard, and using the imagination to fill in the blanks.

Adults are not always able to judge what the incident was that started a train of thought. They tend to judge the child based on the outcome of the imaginary episode. For example, as a young child, my family emigrated from Germany. I overheard my family discussing Hurricane Hazel. I heard them talking about the hurricane's ability to tear the roofs off buildings and to throw cars into the air. I heard them say that the hurricane would arrive tomorrow. I had never heard of a hurricane before. I could not make sense of what they were saying. Nothing in my life had ever exposed me to something that could rip the roofs off buildings and throw cars into the air. The only thing that made sense was that a monster would come and create this havoc. Not wanting to be eaten by this monster, I refused to go to school the next morning.

How do adults separate what is real from what is imaginary to a child? The adult needs to understand the development of children, listen closely to what the child is saying and put what the child has said into the context of what the child is experiencing. Early childhood educators need to gain understanding of the child's world.

Some of the emotional behaviours that children exhibit may stem from:

- Phobias and anxiety states—It is estimated that between 5 and 12 percent of children are affected by phobias or anxiety states. A phobia is a persistent and irrational fear expressed about an object, event, animal or person. Common examples include the young child's fear of the dark. An anxiety state is a fear of something that might happen in the future. Jenna, a four-year-old, was reluctant to go outside. She became very agitated and clung to her caregiver's legs. It turned out that Jenna was afraid of being shot. She had seen a news program about children who had been shot in a school. This had not happened in her community, but she was convinced it would happen to her.

- Depression—There is mounting evidence that some preschoolers suffer from depression. An ongoing five-year longitudinal study found that preschoolers who are depressed may be irritable, grouchy, sad or withdrawn. The child may cease to enjoy activities that had previously been enjoyed and may act out negative feelings during play (Weingarden Dubin, 2001; Winzer, 2008).

2. Conduct-Related Behaviours

Children who seem to be hard to manage because they exhibit a number of extreme behaviours are often diagnosed with conduct disorders. Up to 10 percent of children fall into this category (Weingarden Dubin, 2001). Some of these behaviours are developmentally appropriate for young children who have not yet developed an understanding of their behaviours. One longitudinal survey of children in Canada concluded that physical aggression starts at about nine months and peaks between 27 and 29 months. During these ages, 53.3 percent of boys and 41.1 percent of girls exhibit aggressive behaviours (Kaiser et al., 1999:7). Typical behaviours one might expect of children are listed in Table 7.1.

TABLE 7.1   **CONDUCT-RELATED BEHAVIOURS**

Behaviour	Description
Physical aggression	Biting, hitting, punching, pushing, pinching, kicking
Verbal aggression	Name-calling, swearing, using derogatory terms, shouting
Destructive behaviour	Breaking materials or toys, destroying other children's creations
Lying	Blaming others, refusing to accept responsibility for actions
Refusal to follow directions	Defying attitude when asked to do something, ignoring requests, refusing to follow routines
Running away	Trying to leave if he or she does not want to do something

3. Hyperkinetic-Related Behaviours

Kinetic behaviour is behaviour that is associated with the energy of movement. Hyperkinetic behaviour involves increased energy and movement. It is part of a diagnosed disability such as attention deficit hyperactivity disorder. Depending on the diagnosis used, it is estimated that from 3 to 5 percent of children suffer from this disorder (National Institute of Mental Health, 2003; Winzer, 2008). Typical behaviours exhibited may include all or some of the following, depending on the severity of the condition:

- Overactiveness—Children who exhibit this behaviour are continually on the move, continually talking or interrupting, and flitting from activity to activity. They also tend to have short attention spans.
- Impulsiveness—The child acts without thinking about the consequences. Joseph picked up a stone, looked at it and threw it. The stone hit another child. It had not been Joseph's intent to hit another child. He simply had a stone in his hand and to him the logical thing to do was to throw it.
- Inattention—The child ignores verbal interactions; for instance, he or she is unable to follow directions or answer questions about a story. The child's attention easily wanders from the task at hand.

4. Development-Related Behaviours

Some challenging behaviours would be considered appropriate at a younger developmental age. "Human beings are not born with social skills. Very small children don't have words to express their feelings and needs. They don't yet connect actions to consequences, they are impulsive and self-centred, and even though they may notice others' feelings they don't begin to develop the ability to empathize until they are about two years old. They use any means at their disposal to get what they want and to make themselves understood" (Kaiser et al., 1999:7). Children need to learn which behaviours are appropriate and which ones are not.

From a Mother   **Reflection**

Christy was always an active child. She was continually on the move. I did not associate this with any problems until one day Christy brought me one of her favourite stories to read. During the time I read her the story, she squirmed, fiddled with toys on the floor and ran away. I finally started to watch her more closely and realized that she was not just active but unable to sustain her activity for any length of time.

Reflection   *From an Early Childhood Educator*

Dillon was always eager to learn. I found that he was easily distractible. If he heard something that attracted his interest, he was gone. We finally set up areas in the room that decreased the degree of visual distraction. When Dillon was in these areas, he seemed to be much less distracted.

When children continue to use behaviours that are appropriate for younger ages, this may be indicative of other underlying conditions, such as delays in acquiring skills, or more pervasive conditions such as autism or learning disabilities.

5. Diagnosed Conditions

Some conditions, such as attention deficit disorder (ADD), attention deficit hyperactivity disorder (ADHD), fetal alcohol syndrome (FAS) or fetal alcohol effect (FAE) may be the cause of differences in behaviours. Some typical behaviours include:

- Lack of eye contact
- Lack of response to others
- Self-injury, such as head banging or biting
- Self-stimulating behaviours, such as flicking fingers in front of eyes while rocking back and forth
- Continuous repetitive movements, such as spinning around or running in circles
- Switching from passive to nervous or active behaviours and back to quiet activity again; for instance, sitting quietly rocking, then spinning on the spot, then sitting quietly and then rocking again
- Showing extreme dislike for some stimuli, such as certain sounds
- Finding changes in the environment or routines difficult to cope with

Causes of Various Types of Behaviour

The causes of children's behaviour must be understood in order to provide successful intervention strategies. Not all strategies are successful for all situations. Causes of behaviour may be classified using the following categories: developmental, environmental, functional and psychological.

1. Developmental Causes of Behaviour

To identify possible problems, as well as advanced abilities, it is important to recognize and understand the typical behaviours of children. Like all other domains, behaviour is dependent on interactions with the environment and other individuals, and on normal growth and development. Children learn to control their behaviour along a developmental continuum. Table 7.2 identifies some of the milestones needed to develop self-control. These milestones are helpful in:

- Developing tools to observe behaviour
- Gaining understanding about normal, delayed and gifted behaviours
- Identifying potential problems

2. Environmental Causes of Behaviour

Often, behavioural problems arise from an external source: the learning environment. The organization of the learning environment can lead to either the development of pro-social skills or inappropriate behaviours. Factors to consider are the functionality of the learning spaces, noise levels, choices, use of space, type of organization and type of toys. The factors and resulting possible behaviours are described in Table 7.3. The information can be used to develop a checklist to evaluate the environment and identify if the organization of that environment might lead to challenging behaviours.

In addition to the arrangement of the environment, the interaction between adults and children may also lead to some challenging behaviours:

- When adults pay more attention to negative behaviour than positive behaviour, the negative behaviour itself may become rewarding. The focus of staff interactions with children should be a predominance of positive-behaviour reinforcement.
- When expectations are inconsistent from time to time or between individuals, the children quickly learn to ignore them. This leads to frustration for all individuals, children and adults alike. Expectations should be realistic and consistent for all children.
- Often, frustration occurs because the child was not able to understand what was expected of him or her. Care must be taken to ensure that all interactions are clear and are tailored to fit the comprehension level of each individual child.

3. Functional Causes of Behaviour

When an early childhood educator has identified that a challenging behaviour exists, has eliminated the possibility of a developmental cause, has assessed the environment, has analyzed the child–staff interactions and has still not been able to solve the problem, a functional behaviour assessment should be completed.

TABLE 7.2 DEVELOPMENT OF SELF-CONTROL

Milestone	Age	Importance
Mutual regulation	Infancy	When caregivers recognize and respond immediately to the signals that infants give, the infant gains trust in his ability to communicate and have his communications understood and responded to.
Exploration and observation of body parts	Birth to 3 months	As infants move and touch body parts they start to gain awareness about their own bodies and how they move. This is the first step toward establishing self-confidence.
Recognition of other people	Birth to 3 months	Recognition of others also leads to increased awareness of self as a separate individual.
Expression of emotions	3 months and up	Recognition of and reaction to various emotions expressed is needed in order to gain self-control.
Recognition of own name and response to own name	4–12 months	Recognizing and responding to one's name is a major milestone in the development of self-awareness.
Imitation	1 year	Imitation leads to greater ability to communicate, to act upon the environment and, as a result, to establish greater autonomy.
Self-regulation	1 year	Once infants start to eat by themselves, they are becoming more independent and are starting to do things for themselves—"I eat when I am hungry."
Establishment of cause and effect relationships	1–2 years	As infants and toddlers actively explore the environment, they begin to realize that they have the power to make things happen by their actions.
Acquisition of language	Preschool age	Increased skill in language parallels increased skills in the ability to think and reason, which in turn lead to greater self-control.
Direct independent actions	1–2 years	Toddlers understand simple concepts. They listen to a simple request and comply or do not comply. Toddlers are learning to express their autonomy.
Finding alternative solutions	2 years and up	When children realize that they can control the situation by using a different approach, such as finding a different book to read rather than grabbing a book from someone else, another milestone in self-control is established.
Reaction to personal feelings	About 3 years and up	When children recognize that they are tired and find a quiet activity to engage in, they are learning to respond to and respect personal needs.

TABLE 7.3 **ENVIRONMENTAL FACTORS THAT MAY CAUSE CHALLENGING BEHAVIOURS**

Description of Factor	Description of Possible Behaviours
Overcrowding—Either too many people in a space or not enough room for active play	Children may become frustrated because they cannot get involved in active play. Aggressive behaviours such as throwing materials, grabbing toys or hitting a child who took a toy may occur.
Too many open spaces	Young children like to run. Large open areas encourage running activities such as chasing each other.
Disorganized storage of material	When children cannot find a toy they are looking for, or materials are placed in large containers, dumping will occur. Often this leaves a mess. If children do not have clear guidelines that indicate where materials are found, they tend to leave the area without cleaning up. This may also lead to frustration and non-compliance, because the task becomes too difficult.
Noisy environment or overpowering background noises, such as continuous loud music	When environments become too noisy, the noise level tends to continue to increase. This becomes frustrating and disruptive to some children, because they are unable to concentrate. It is particularly hard for children who are hard of hearing and children with ADD/ADHD or FAS. These children may withdraw from the situation or become even noisier in their attempts to be heard.
Too many choices	When too many choices are provided, children can easily become confused. They typically will get distracted by the variety of choices and flit from one choice to the next. This is particularly true of younger children and many children with special needs.
Too few choices	Too few choices lead to conflict. Children may become aggressive to enable them to play with an activity of choice.
Choices that are developmentally or age-inappropriate	Children may become frustrated because the activity is too easy or too hard. Materials may be destroyed.
Competitive activities	The very nature of competition causes frustration for some children because there is always a loser and a winner.
Provision of violent toys	This often results in aggression against the toy or peers.
Learning experiences not based on the interests or background experiences of the children	Children may not actively engage in play because of a lack of interest, because the activity is inappropriate or because they do not know what is expected.
Too much waiting during transitions	When children are waiting, they become bored and will resort to other activities to entertain themselves. These activities may include aggressive behaviours, withdrawal, non-compliance and noisiness.

"A functional assessment assumes that the behaviour in question serves a purpose or 'function' for the child. Simply put, it 'functions' to get the child something she or he wants, such as attention of staff, access to a favourite toy/activity or escape from a disliked activity. In most cases we find that the behaviour compensates for a skill deficit which is related to the child's special needs" (Orr & Cavallaro, 1997:1-2). For example, when Jade wanted something that another child had, she would simply take it. If an adult noticed, she would sweetly smile at the child and say, "Sorry." The strategy worked; she rarely got a lecture, and she usually got to keep the toy. Jade used the strategy because it had worked in the past, not because she had been able to reason that this was a good strategy to use.

To prevent the challenging behaviour from recurring, it is necessary to find out why the child is engaging in this behaviour. Once that is known, the solutions are usually natural consequences of the behaviour. For example, Jade, a three-year-old, consistently grabbed toys from other playmates. When Jade was observed, it was discovered that she was at the parallel play stage and that there were not enough similar toys to play with. Similar toys were placed in the area. When Jade started to grab, she was told: "Jamie is playing with that toy. Here is another one for you."

4. Psychological Causes of Behaviour

"Although psychological abuse leaves no physical scars, it shakes children's feeling of security and disrupts their development. If Alex, Esther or Ryan is reported to child welfare authorities for suspected physical abuse or neglect, caseworkers will be aware that the child may also be a victim of psychological abuse. Prevention involves working to help these children grow up feeling good about themselves" (Chamberland, Laporte, Lavergne & Baraldi, 2003:1).

Psychological abuse is often an invisible cause of challenging behaviours. Some forms of psychological abuse might include:

- Ridiculing the child
- Ignoring the child or the child's efforts
- Verbal aggressiveness
- Discrediting the child's achievements and efforts
- Comparing the child unfavourably to others
- Making negative judgments about the child's behaviours

"Children who are victims of psychological abuse experience more emotional problems than children who are not victims of this type of maltreatment." Victims of direct psychological abuse are:

- More socially withdrawn
- More depressed
- More insecure
- Much likelier to engage in behaviours that put them at risk (Chamberland et al., 2003:3)

Range of Behaviours in Inclusive Settings

Within any setting, many of the behaviours previously described may be found. The range of behaviours evident depends on the type of special needs, the age of the children, how the environment is organized and the interaction patterns between the adults and the children within the learning environment. Typical behaviours include difficulties in:

- Interacting with peers, resulting in a range of behaviours such as aggression, withdrawal and tantrums
- Attending or interacting in group settings, resulting in behaviours such as interrupting, self-stimulation or fidgeting
- Coping with making choices, resulting in behaviours such as flitting from activity to activity, withdrawal or aimless wandering
- Concentrating, resulting in distractible behaviours such as continually being attracted to a new toy or activity, or taking all toys off the shelf but not playing with any one
- Controlling emotions, resulting in behaviours such as temper tantrums, verbal or physical aggressiveness or defiance
- Accepting praise, which results in low self-esteem and often underachievement: "I can't do this. It's too hard."

Positive Guidance Strategies in Inclusive Settings

1. Establishing a Collaborative Process

Collaboration among all partners is critical. Approaches to guiding children's behaviours must be agreed upon and be consistent to effect any lasting changes in behaviour. Children need to know that expectations are constant. They quickly learn to adjust their behaviour depending on the situation they are in. This is learned behaviour.

For example, Jillian, a three-year-old, had learned to use the phrase "Shut up!" When she used it with her older peers, they thought it was cute and they would burst out laughing. When her teacher asked her to do something, she responded, "Shut up!" and smiled. Her teacher smiled back and said that this was an inappropriate word to use. Jillian thought about it and said, "Shut up, please?" Jillian had obviously had a pleasant experience in the past when she had used this phrase. She was reluctant to give it up. She also knew that "please" was an appropriate word in her preschool. So she tried to create a winning situation.

Children can learn to conform to different expectations in various environments. However, when the expectations are consistent, the child can make better sense of the world and this leads to growth in self-control.

A) COLLABORATION WITH FAMILIES Families share many of the concerns that relate to challenging behaviours. They face the same difficulties at home as are evident in the child care centre. A collaborative process helps deal with the behaviour in the most positive and expedient way for all individuals involved. The collaborative process should include:

- Observations of the child's behaviour
- Development of an IPP
- Evaluation of progress

B) COLLABORATION WITH OTHER PROFESSIONALS Depending on the severity of the problem, other professionals who might become involved with the child include psychologists, psychiatrists, resource consultants, behaviour management experts, mental health workers or play, music or sand therapists. These professionals offer valuable insight into problems. Their collaborative role has many aspects:

- Assisting in setting up an appropriate IPP
- Offering suggestions for positive guidance techniques
- Offering suggestions for how to organize the environment effectively
- Advising on the types of materials and resources that are most effective for dealing with challenging behaviours

C) COLLABORATION WITH OTHER STAFF MEMBERS Dealing with challenging behaviours should be approached consistently by all staff members who may interact with the child. Staff need to be informed of the appropriate strategies to use and should be involved in the evaluation and adaptation process. This gives all staff members opportunities to become more involved and to model appropriate behaviours so that the children can gain from a consistent approach.

2. Observing Children's Behaviours

It is critical to observe the behaviour of the child to try to diagnose the cause of the problem. Does the problem lie in the way the environment is organized? Is it due to the interaction pattern between the children and the staff? Is it a functional behaviour? If the cause cannot be determined and the behaviour continues to exist, it is usually wise to refer the child to a specialist. Observation of children should be conducted in consideration of the following:

A) HOW OFTEN DOES THE BEHAVIOUR OCCUR? The best method for collecting this type of information is through a frequency count. This is most effectively done by making a note of the behaviour each time it occurs (see Figure 7.1).

This type of observation is useful in determining whether a behavioural pattern exists or not. For example, Melanie identified Jordan as being aggressive. She had caught him biting a child once and hitting another child. When she started to count his aggressive behaviours on a regular basis, she found that these had been isolated incidences. If Melanie had discovered instead that Jordan was hitting and biting more often, she should have continued her observations to find out more about his behaviour.

B) WHEN AND WHERE DOES THE BEHAVIOUR OCCUR? Knowing the times of day and how often the behaviour occurs at those times can yield important insights. Is

FIGURE 7.1

Counting Behaviours

Name: Jordan   **Dates:** February 1-10
Observer: Melanie

Behaviour	Frequency
Hitting	I
Biting	I

there a certain routine or activity that might lead to disruptive behaviour? Figure 7.2 provides an example of how this might be accomplished.

This type of observation not only confirms that the child is hitting, it also gives the circumstances under which the child is behaving aggressively. It would seem that Jordan is engaging in functional behaviour. He is using the aggression to get what he wants: a toy. During circle time, he is also getting what he wants. When he bites, he is removed from the activity. Since biting only occurs during circle time, it is safe to assume that Jordan does not want to participate in circle time.

C) HOW LONG DOES THE BEHAVIOUR LAST? For some behaviours, it is not only important to know how often the behaviour occurs, but also how long it lasts (duration count). This type of observation works well for behaviours such as separation anxiety or temper tantrums. Knowing know how long a child may engage in this type of behaviour answers the question of whether intervention is needed or if the child is likely to settle down by himself or herself. The easiest method is to use a graph to document the information. The circumstances and setting can be added to give the detail needed for planning effective intervention strategies.

The information gleaned from the observation shown in Figure 7.3 indicates that Amanda will continue to be upset for a long time. This may cause disruptions to the program and to the other children. This is also a functional behaviour. She wanted a certain book and continued her behaviour until she got it. She did not want to get dressed and continued her behaviour until all the children had gone outside. This seems to indicate that she is willing to cooperate in order to be with the other children.

FIGURE 7.2

Behaviour Occurrence

Name: Jason   **Dates:** February 11–15
Observer: Pritti

Behaviour	Frequency	Setting
Hitting	++++ ++++ III	During free play—hits a child who has a toy he wants, then grabs toy; or if toy taken from him he hits
Biting	++++ ++++	Circle time—bites children sitting near him

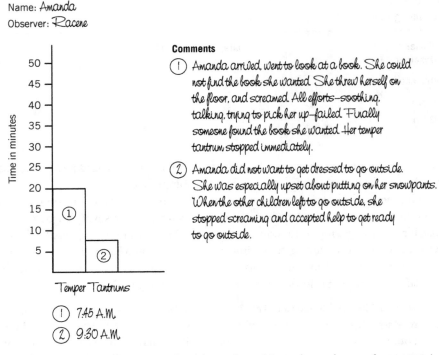

FIGURE 7.3
Duration Count

Name: Amanda
Observer: Racene

Time in minutes

Temper Tantrums

① 7:45 A.M.
② 9:30 A.M.

Comments

① Amanda arrived, went to look at a book. She could not find the book she wanted. She threw herself on the floor, and screamed. All efforts—soothing, talking, trying to pick her up—failed. Finally someone found the book she wanted. Her temper tantrum stopped immediately.

② Amanda did not want to get dressed to go outside. She was especially upset about putting on her snowpants. When the other children left to go outside, she stopped screaming and accepted help to get ready to go outside.

Additional information needs to be gathered in order to learn what strategies have been tried in the past, and which were successful or not (see Figure 7.4). This information will give a better idea about how to plan appropriate intervention strategies for the individual child.

As always, it is better to develop a learning environment and experiences for children by using their interests. Tools for observing interest have been covered in previous chapters (see Figure 5.12 on page 171 and Table 6.3 on page 204).

3. The Behavioural IPP

Once the observation process has been completed, and the staff have some awareness of the types of strategies that may be used to calm individual children, an individual program plan (IPP) can be developed.

FIGURE 7.4
Recording Intervention Strategies

Name: Damian
Observer: Rachelle

Behaviour	Strategy	Result
Temper tantrum	He wanted to eat macaroni and cheese.	It was not available that day. Provided explanation. Showed him that none was there. Unsuccessful; cried harder. Stopped; asked for it the next day.

The development of an IPP for behaviours follows a slightly different pattern from other types of IPPs. The primary purpose of a behavioural IPP is to either increase incidence of a behaviour, such as using words instead of hitting, or decrease a behaviour, such as pushing or pinching. In order for the IPP to be effective, there needs to be some measure against which progress can be measured. This measure is called a base line. A base line is a method used to determine how often behaviour has occurred prior to formal intervention strategies. It is usually established prior to implementing an intervention process. An observation process such as the one shown in Figure 7.1 could be used. However, recording only the number of times that a behaviour has occurred would limit the IPP's potential for success. Gathering of other information, as illustrated in Figures 7.2 to 7.4, needs to be undertaken through observations from all partners: family members, staff and other professionals.

The goal of the IPP is, generally, to increase or decrease behaviours. Objectives are not always stated, but if they are, they usually identify how the incidence of the behaviours should increase or decrease within a particular time frame.

In an IPP for behaviours, children's strengths and needs are usually not stated. Instead, there is a statement about what causes the behaviour (if known) and the strategies that are effective and ineffective. It is critical to avoid using a strategy that the child has already learned to ignore or that may cause the behaviour to worsen. When the best strategies have been identified, similar strategies can be used in the implementation process.

Evaluation of the process should happen daily. A simple method is to use a line graph (see evaluation section of the IPP, Figure 7.5E, pages 239–240). Through this process:

- Success is monitored.
- The need for adaptations and/or revisions can be identified.
- All partners have a record of achievement. This provides opportunities to celebrate success.

The behavioural IPP is usually implemented over longer periods of time than other IPPs and is reviewed weekly to gauge the success of the strategies used. Figure 7.5A–E is an example of a behavioural IPP.

Implementation of the behavioural strategies usually causes behaviours to spike. This is because the child reacts to the new strategies imposed, and the only strategy the child has is the old behaviour: This behaviour worked in the past and therefore will be tried again. With consistent efforts of all partners and with appropriate strategies, there should be a gradual drop in appropriate behaviours or a more modest rise of appropriate behaviours after one week.

Bringing about behavioural change is a long process; it may take weeks or even months. The five-part Figure 7.5 gives an example of an IPP developed for the challenging behaviours of a toddler named Gabriella.

FIGURE 7.5A

Behavioural IPP

Name: Gabriella   **DOB:** February 12, 2000
Date: October 5, 2003

1. **Summary of Diagnosis**
   a. **Summary of Observations by Resource Consultant**
      i. **Attachment**—Separation anxiety caused by traumatic events in the child's life: death of a grandmother, separation of parents and illness of mother.
      ii. **Aggressive Behaviours**—The physically aggressive behaviours seem to be mostly functional, since they occur when she wants something or does not want to follow directions.
   b. **Summary of Observations of Mother**
      i. **Separation**—Gabriella has had a hard time because she has been faced with so many difficulties. I was ill for about a month and was separated from my daughter. She finds it difficult to be separated from me, especially when she visits her dad, and sometimes at day care, and especially if she knows her dad will come to pick her up. She cries and clings to me.
      ii. **Behaviour**—I first noticed her aggressive behaviour when she was one-and-a-half. She would bite, pinch, kick or punch if she didn't get her way or if she was upset. She is an emotional child, which is understandable given what she has gone through.
   c. **Summary of Observations of Day Care Staff**
      i. **Separation**—The staff noted that Gabriella suffered from tremendous separation anxiety. She would cry for at least half an hour when dropped off in the morning, and start to cry right after lunch when she knew sleep time was close. She would wake up, crying for her mother, father or grandmother. When either parent came to pick her up, she did not want to go home.
      ii. **Behaviour**—Her behaviours included kicking, punching, throwing herself on the ground and screaming wildly. Her crying and/or temper tantrums could last up to 45 minutes. She is very sensitive and empathetic toward other children and will try to comfort them.

2. **Observations of Behaviours**
   Observations were conducted at home by the mother and at the day care by one of the child care staff. The process was guided by the resource consultant.
   a. **Challenging Behaviours at Home—See Figure 7.5B.**
   b. **Challenging Behaviours at the Centre—See Figure 7.5C.**
   c. **Interests—See Figure 7.5D.**

3. **Base Line**
   a) Maximum number of aggressive behaviours observed: 12
   b) Separation-anxiety behaviours
      • Four times daily—Arrival, before sleep time, after sleep time and at dismissal
      • Maximum duration—45 minutes

4. **Successful Behaviour-Management Strategies**
   • Provide her with a picture of her family that she can access and hold when she is upset.
   • Provide her with comfort toys.
   • Hold her and cuddle her.
   • Sing to her.

5. **Goals**
   a) Reduce the number of aggressive acts.
   b) Reduce the time spent in separation-anxiety behaviours.

FIGURE 7.5A

Continued

6. **Strategies**
   a) Reduce the number of aggressive acts:
      i. Observe her to try to intervene before the aggressive behaviour occurs and redirect her to a positive behaviour.
      ii. Focus on her positive interactions and reinforce these.
      iii. Model asking for something that is wanted.
      iv. Clearly state the expectations that Gabriella needs to use words.
      v. Prompt her as needed.
      vi. Provide pillows and blankets to scream into and to kick when angry.
      vii. Graph personal success.
   b) Reduce the time spent in separation-anxiety behaviours:
      i. Assign one consistent teacher to Gabriella.
      ii. Provide activities of interest to Gabriella immediately when she arrives.
      iii. Encourage her to use her comfort items as needed.
      iv. Prepare Gabriella for transition times. Focus on positive possibilities with comments such as, "When your mom arrives, you can show her the playdough model you made."
      v. Provide soothing activities such as playdough or books that Gabriella likes to look at.
      vi. Provide a quiet place, safe from interruptions.
      vii. Extend the transition between drop-off and pick-up times—mother stayed 20 minutes during each time slot.

FIGURE 7.5B

Challenging Behaviours at Home

Date: September 30–October 4, 2002
Observer: Mother
Child: Gabriella

Behaviour	Situation
Clingy, crying: IIII	When I tell her she is going with her dad
Hitting: III	When she is upset

FIGURE 7.5C

Challenging Behaviours at the Centre

Child: Gabriella
Observer: Kaya

Dates: Oct. 29, 30

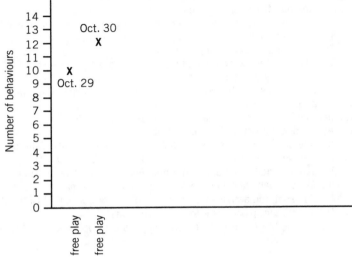

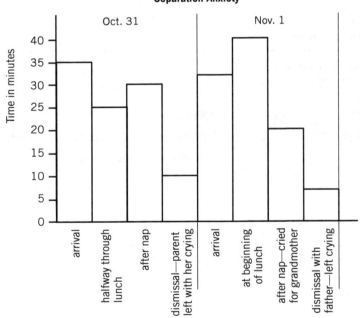

Comments
The only thing that seemed to work was to let her hold her dog and be cuddled. If put down she screams. If teachers switched off, G's behaviour changed dramatically.

FIGURE 7.5D

Interests

A collaborative effort between home and centre

Interests	Description
Dough	Kneading, poking, moulding
Drama	Role-playing, especially grandmother
Books	Likes to be alone to look at books or have an adult read to her
Finger plays	Participated within group or individually

FIGURE 7.5E

Evaluation of Gabriella's Progress

Gabriella's progress was charted daily. The progress was reviewed and adaptations were made to the IPP. Adaptations to the IPP were primarily in the area of removing more adult control and reinforcing Gabriella for her positive interactions. The number of adults in the classroom was reduced to one for as much of the day as possible. Children within the grouping had high problem-solving skills and were good peer role models. Gabriella also attended an art therapy program one morning a week for two months.

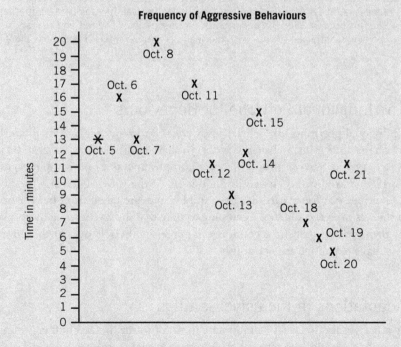

Frequency of Aggressive Behaviours

✱ Transition Days: first and last day of the week (going to a different home)

FIGURE 7.5E
Continued

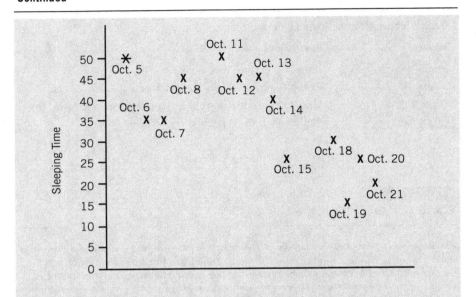

Evaluation Chart of Gabriella's Progress Within two weeks, some positive results were noted, especially with Gabriella's separation-anxiety behaviours. Over the next six months, her behaviour slowly improved. The number and duration of incidences of separation-anxiety behaviours started to gradually decrease. To include Gabriella more in the process, an individual portfolio was begun within seven months of the initiation of the IPP. This offered Gabriella opportunities to discuss how she felt and to start to develop personal strategies to cope with her feelings and her interactions with others.

4. The Individual Portfolio for Behaviours

The individual portfolio for Gabriella was created to reinforce and maintain her positive-behaviour gains. Gabriella was able to share information that was to be put into the portfolio. She was proud of her accomplishments. Some sample pages of her portfolio have been included in Figure 7.6. At the time of starting the portfolio, Gabriella was four years old. The sample pages are taken from her portfolio when she was five years old. It is interesting to note that she has become more aware of her own feelings, that she is confident in expressing herself openly and that her interests have expanded tremendously.

5. Adaptations in Inclusive Settings

There are a number of ways to intervene in order to maximize children's opportunities to be successful: the physical environment can be reorganized, the social context of interactions can be changed, the program can be adapted and interactions

FIGURE 7.6
Sample Pages of Gabriella's Portfolio

Things I like to do:

I like to draw using markers.
I am practising making my name.

I also like to paint, especially flowers.
Flowers need the sun to grow.

Things I am good at:

I am a good cutter.
I folded my paper, and now I am cutting out
pieces to make a snowflake.

FIGURE 7.6
Continued

Doing big puzzles!

I can finish them by myself.

I like it when others help me do the puzzles.
Big puzzles are hard.

I counted the pieces. There are 32 pieces.

I am really good at tracing.

I get angry when . . .

I get angry when my friends tease me.

I get angry when my friends don't let me play with them.

When I get angry I don't hit anymore.

When I get angry sometimes I shout at my friends,
sometimes I shout in my pillow, sometimes I just cry.

with early childhood educators can be reviewed and adapted. The situation should always be viewed from the child's perspective (Kaiser et al., 1999).

A) ORGANIZATION OF THE ENVIRONMENT Effective organization of the indoor and outdoor environments can decrease the incidence of challenging behaviours. Interest areas should be clearly defined in both indoor and outdoor learning areas. This not only serves to provide a defined space for an activity such as water play or block play; in indoor spaces it will also serve to eliminate large open areas that encourage running (Photo 7.2).

Outdoor spaces should have large open areas to encourage running activities. Areas should be set up outside that encourage activities that are similar to indoor activities (Photo 7.3), along with a number of gross-motor activities that encourage gross-motor development at a number of ability and skill levels (Photo 7.4).

Careful consideration should be given to the appropriate size of each area. Some areas, such as the block area, require larger areas to provide ample room for appropriate play. Other areas such as the book area should be in a smaller, comfortable area to encourage quiet reading activities (Photo 7.5). Areas should be set up to encourage individual, small and large group activity (Photo 7.6).

Limits to the number of children in an area should be imposed by the number of pieces of furniture in the area (Photo 7.7), the number of materials available or the sides of equipment such as the water table. If more children are in the area than expected, the area should be monitored closely. If the children continue to play appropriately, there is no need for intervention.

Photo 7.6

Photo 7.2

Photo 7.3

Photo 7.7

Photo 7.4

Photo 7.5

Photo 7.8

Photo 7.9

Photo 7.10

A quiet area that children can withdraw to should be available (Photo 7.8). This area should be protected from intrusion. This can be done by creating a doorway or posting a stop sign when children wish to be left alone.

The room should offer a number of activities that are sensory in nature, in order to provide a calming effect. Examples include sand and water, music, playdough or fingerpainting. These activities encourage children to develop self-control. The child is able to choose to engage in an activity that meets his or her needs at the moment. When upset, the child can find an alternative activity to soothe his or her feelings (Photo 7.9).

Materials and resources should be clearly organized and labelled in order to encourage children to find the materials they need and to return them independently (Photo 7.10).

Photo 7.11

Materials more suitable for children with higher-level skills could be placed on higher shelves. Extra materials should be available for rotation or brought out as needed to maintain interest and create new challenges. This is especially important for children who are gifted.

Areas should be separated into quiet areas and noisy areas. The quiet areas should be removed as far as possible from the noisy areas. Children need to have choices to withdraw from noisier play. Some noise reduction can be achieved by placing shelves or padded dividers around the noisy area. Noisy areas such as blocks should be on a rug to absorb some of the noise. Carpentry areas could have a sound-absorbing surface placed on the carpentry table.

Since the interests and abilities of children in an inclusive setting vary greatly, a large variety of materials should be available for use. Avoid including toys or materials that are related to violent themes, as these may incite aggressive interactions. To help those children who have difficulty focusing, a planning board could be provided to help them make choices prior to participating (see Photo 6.4, page 210). There should be a clear table or surface in the area that children can utilize after they have chosen their activity. Areas that require greater concentration should have some visual barriers around them. This can be achieved with low shelves or dividers (Photo 7.11).

B) CHANGING THE SOCIAL CONTEXT The most important social environment that can be created is one in which all participants will feel welcome and accepted. The centre staff must set a climate that respects all learners, set appropriate policies and times, and be flexible to change as needed.

Reflection

From the Author

I have visited many inclusive environments and make it a point to walk through toy stores and book shops. Within child care settings, I usually see genuine attempts made to try to represent the diversity of the community with very limited resources. Usually there are some books and some photographs or posters representing a diversity of cultures and needs, and some gender-related topics. What I see very little of are toys that represent people with special needs, books about individuals with special needs working in communities or stories including children with special needs. It is also difficult to find available resources of this type. In fact, in most cases you have to order this type of material and equipment from specialized sources, at increased prices. As a result, some centres have created their own resources. Figure 7.7 lists a few of these.

FIGURE 7.7

Ideas for Inclusive Environments

1. Centre-based resource materials were created for display purposes. Photographs were taken of the children engaged in various activities. The photographs were enlarged, mounted and laminated. Not only did these photographs represent the various cultures and special needs, but the children were also engaged in the process.
2. In some centres, the children and staff created their own books. These books were simply made. They involved feelings such as likes or dislikes, and could involve a great many more topics. For example, Dillon created his own book about what he likes to do. A sample page is included.

"I like to draw."

Dillon chose the activities, and the words that are bolded are the words he used or signed. The book was laminated and then coil-bound. An excellent source of ideas for creating books is *Making Books That Fly, Fold, Wrap, Hide, Pop Up, Twist & Turn*, by Gwen Diehn (2006). Additionally, similar techniques could be used to create books about adults with special needs. For books on community helpers, families could incorporate family members and other adults in the community.
3. Broken dolls were used to represent individuals with special needs. These dolls had slings for broken arms, a cane, a crutch or an attached prosthesis for a missing limb.
4. Simple instructions for the creation of toy wheelchairs to use with dolls are found in Figure 7.8.
5. In many cases, the staff approached seniors to help them create special toys (carpentry) or special clothing for dolls or for the dress-up areas, or to help them within the classroom in offering one-on-one activities to children, such as reading to a child or helping a child complete a project.
6. Several centres had borrowed child-sized wheelchairs for children to use from a local hospital. Neither centre had children in wheelchairs.
7. In one centre the dress-up area included child-sized crutches and canes.
8. Several centres had activities children engaged in that involved exploration through only tactile exploration, or visual cues without sound, or sound without visual cues.
9. One centre had developed labelling that included Braille, pictorial symbols and words.

FIGURE 7.8
How to Build a Toy Wheelchair

You need:
- Four pieces of 1/4 plywood large enough to seal one of the dolls
  - Two pieces of the same size for the sides
  - One piece for the bottom
  - One piece for the back
- Four wheels and four nails to fit through the hole in the wheel

Directions:
1. Sand all pieces and all sides of wood until smooth.
2. Nail sides, bottom and back together.
3. Attach nails by sliding through hole of wheel, then hammering the nail into the wood. Make sure that the wheel is not tight. It should move freely.
4. Put some wood glue into wood to cover the nail that has been hammered in.
5. Paint wheelchair.

In collaboration with the staff and families, policies need to be set that describe appropriate child guidance techniques. Policies need to be reviewed at least on a yearly basis and revised as needed. Behaviour policies should stress positive guidance techniques, consistency in managing all behaviours and safety—physical and emotional.

Limits with children should be simple and logical, and based primarily on the safety of the child. Any rules that are set should respect the rights of others, avoid dangerous situations and take care of the environment (Kaiser et al., 1999:19). Rules should be posted pictorially and in writing as well, as a reminder to everyone of what is expected. For example, the photograph of Dillon's signal for quiet had been enlarged and laminated with the word "Quiet" under it, to post in the quiet area (Photo 7.12).

C) ADAPTING THE PROGRAM Program adaptations usually are concerned with routines, transitions, stability, scheduling and flexibility. The routines should be kept consistent and predictable—such as washing hands after using the washroom. Setting predictable, stable routines encourages children to start to accept responsibility for their actions; they can learn to "do the next thing." Behaviours practised over time in different settings, at home and at the centre, will be easier to learn and use, leading to greater child autonomy.

Transitions are often the cause of behaviour problems. Children who wait too long with nothing to do will find alternative ways to amuse themselves. This often leads to inappropriate behaviours. Transitions should be kept to a minimum. When

Photo 7.12

approaching a transition, children should be given a warning so that they can finish what they are doing or save it to finish at another time. Some strategies for more effective transitions include the following:

- Minimize the waiting time—The transition could be staggered so that children who take longer can start to get ready (go outside or get ready for lunch) and the ones who are faster could join them later, so that everyone is ready at the same time.
- Make transitions fun—Provide activities to do during transitions. Good activities include singing songs or doing finger plays.
- Minimize the number of transitions—Group transitions should only need to occur before major scheduled events such as going outside or getting ready for lunch or sleep time.
- Post a pictorial routine of the day—Children will learn to look at it, to see what is coming next.
- Ensure the children know what will happen when they get to the next activity—For example, ask children what they intend to do once they are outside.
- Avoid waiting after the transition—When children get to the lunch table, they may have to wait for everyone to arrive before lunch is served. This might be a good time to read a story or continue with the songs or activities that had been ongoing during the transition.

D) CHANGING INTERACTION APPROACHES The first and most important thing that the staff must learn to do is to carefully observe the children. If a potentially challenging behaviour can be anticipated, it can often be turned into a positive situation. For example, Jennie noticed that Yasmine had a frown on her face as she was playing beside Jenna. Jenna was starting to use the blocks in front of Yasmine. Realizing that Yasmine was not happy, she quickly brought over some more blocks and said, "I noticed that you do not have enough blocks, so I got some more." Jennie prevented a potential negative behaviour episode. She also modelled to both children what they could do if they did not have enough of something. Signals that indicate a potential problem differ from child to child. The adult needs to be observant and to be able to identify these signals. Some common signals include:

- flushed look
- frowning
- angry look
- increased breathing
- sweating
- clenched teeth
- fidgeting
- tears
- thumb sucking
- hair twirling
- rocking

TABLE 7.4   STRATEGIES TO CHANGING INTERACTION APPROACHES

Strategy	Description
Responsive to the intent of the child's message	• Need to be involved in active listening • Clarify message by asking or by observing body language • Check to see if correct interpretation was made
Supportive body language	• Get down to the child's level • Use facial expressions, such as a smile • Respond with gestures, such as nodding • Selectively use hugging or touching with children who like this approach
Open communication	• Involves active listening, responding appropriately to the message received, clarifying the intent of the message, paraphrasing if needed and taking the appropriate action

- whining
- loss of eye contact
- screaming
- loud voices or laughter
- withdrawal

Table 7.4 lists strategies that can be used after caregivers become aware of and subsequently want to change interaction approaches with children.

6. Managing a Challenging Behaviour

If the child's signals have been missed and a challenging behaviour is the result, or if the child does not follow expectations, some different strategies may have to be used. The strategies used are again dependent on the child and his or her reaction to different techniques. Table 7.5 describes some techniques that might work in this situation.

Sometimes, no matter what has been done, the child loses control. In this situation, the following strategy might be used:

- Stand between the child and the rest of the world—but at a safe distance. Don't try to move her.
- Don't confront her. To keep her from feeling trapped, stand sideways, compose yourself, and don't look in her eye.
- Don't talk. She isn't ready to listen yet.
- When she's calm, talk to her quietly. Help her to name her feelings ("You were pretty angry") and to distinguish between feelings and actions ("It's okay to feel angry, but it's not okay to lie on the floor screaming"). Let her know that you love her, and help her to think about how she can solve the problem the next time (Canadian Child Care Federation, 2000:2).

TABLE 7.5 **STRATEGIES TO DEAL WITH CHALLENGING BEHAVIOURS**

Strategy	Description	Example
Keep the statement brief and to the point	• Use words such as stop • Follow up to state expectations • Observe to see if child complies	Jamie has his hand up with a car in it and is ready to throw the car. When asked to stop, he puts the car down and continues to play.
Make the statement only once	• Repetition teaches children that they need not listen the first time	"Please sit down to eat your snack." Lisa did not sit down. "Lisa, I asked you to do something. Tell me what I asked."
Calm, firm delivery of message	• Use a normal volume • Match expression and body language	Nito is throwing sand. Sarah kneels down, looks Nito in the eye and says firmly, "Stop."
Wait for a response from the child	• If the child complies, no further action is needed • Anticipate action and provide a positive outcome	Nito stopped throwing sand until Lisa left. When Lisa looked back, his hand was again up. She quickly put a bucket under his hand and said, "Let's fill the bucket."
Involve child in solving the problem	• Ask questions to help the process	Two children wanted the same toy. Lisa asked, "What can we do?" The children shrugged. "Could we find another toy like this one?"
Provide alternative choices	• Ensure choices are not a punishment • Choices should be something the child enjoys • Choices not liked by the child may escalate the negative behaviour • Provide an opportunity to relieve frustration	Jeremy was grabbing toys from the children at the water table. Lisa finally asked him to go to the sand area to fill his containers there. The sand area was another of Jeremy's interests.
Recognize the child's feelings and respect them	• Label the child's feelings • Discuss behaviour after the child is calm	"I see that you are angry. I will talk to you when you feel less angry."
Restrain the child	• Restraint should only be used when a child is in danger of hurting himself or someone else • It should be used only as a last resort • Talk about the behaviour when the child is calm	Serena sat against the wall and started to bang her head against it, drawing blood. Lisa calmly held her firmly and talked to her soothingly until she quieted down.

TABLE 7.5   **CONTINUED**

Strategy	Description	Example
Ignore other behaviours the child may exhibit if the stated expectations are followed	• Child may shout or complain while he or she is doing the expected task • Ignore these behaviours as long as expectations are followed and the behaviours are not dangerous to the child or the environment	Jamie rode his tricycle off the road and onto the sidewalk as he shouted, "I am not riding on the road."

A) USING THE CHILD'S PERSPECTIVE   All times, the adult should try to understand the situation from the child's point of view. Behind most behaviours there is a reason. If the reason is understood, the solution can be found. Not all children are able to voice or communicate their reasons. It is essential to learn to understand the child's signals and to react to them appropriately and immediately. When warning signals are ignored, behaviours can quickly escalate.

Changing behaviour is difficult. An empathetic, calm and consistent approach should always be taken. Collaboration with family members and other professionals will help produce a greater understanding of a child's behaviour and will help find solutions that can be implemented by all individuals.

B) KNOWLEDGE OF CHILD DEVELOPMENT AND CHILD GUIDANCE TECHNIQUES   Early childhood educators need to have a firm understanding of children, their development and their typical responses to various situations. Challenging behaviours usually do not simply appear in a vacuum. There are usually triggers that cause a behaviour to start. Often, that trigger may be something that is caused by anxiety or frustration. This is the easiest stage in which to deal with the problem. Positive reassurance or active listening will usually solve the problem.

However, if the anxiety is not recognized or the frustration is not noticed, the child often becomes agitated and will seek an outlet for the agitation. Again, if the behaviour is noticed, the adult can use it as a teachable moment. The behaviour should be acknowledged: "I know you find this difficult." Then a solution should be offered: "Do you need some help?" Failure to notice the child's agitation may result in aggressive behaviours or withdrawals. "When children have reached the aggressive state, they are no longer responding from a logical, reasoned state of mind" (Irwin Hope, 1999:81). Children in withdrawal are in a similar state of mind. At this stage, the behaviour is much harder to deal with and the child finds it much harder to revert to his or her normal state. (See Table 7.5 for appropriate guidance techniques.)

If aggressive behaviours are not halted, they can quickly lead to an assaultive state. "In an assaultive state, they begin to take out their anger, hurt, fear, and rage and direct it towards you. There are two primary tasks that you want to accomplish when a child is in this state. You want to protect yourself and those in your care, and you want to move the child out of the assaultive state" (Irwin Hope, 1999:82).

In summary, the consequences of lacking the appropriate knowledge of how to deal with children's behaviours can quickly lead to situations that become difficult to manage for the staff, are extremely detrimental to the emotional health and well-being of the child and lead to frustration for all individuals involved.

Role of the Early Childhood Educator

The early childhood educator actually has several roles: observer, collaborator, planner, manager, supporter, evaluator and researcher. Each role is equally critical in helping the child gain greater self-control.

1. The Role of Observer

Observation is a critical role of the early childhood educator. Observation is an ongoing process that helps the early childhood educator understand behaviours and develop strategies for intervention based on what has been learned through the observation process. This process is an ongoing cycle of observing and interpreting behaviours, implementing strategies, and doing more observing and evaluation in order to adapt strategies as needed (see Figure 7.9).

Early childhood educators need to observe children so that they can learn to understand their behaviours and possible causes of behaviours, as Jennie did by observing Yasmine's frown (page 248). Jennie knew that when Yasmine started to frown, it indicated that she was upset about something. Once there is an understanding of the

FIGURE 7.9

Observation Process

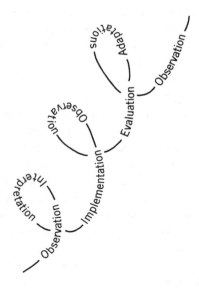

type of behaviour a child uses and the signals that the child exhibits prior to the occurrence of a challenging behaviour, intervention strategies can be developed.

As well, the learning environment needs to be observed and assessed, in order to identify any adaptations that might need to be made to the environment. Interactions between children and between children and adults should also be observed and assessed. For example, is the staff dealing with the behaviour consistently with all children in all settings? Do more problems occur when certain peers play together?

Once an IPP has been established, daily observations and team meetings need to be held to discuss the outcomes of the IPP strategies and to develop new strategies or revise existing ones.

2. The Role of Collaborator

As previously stated, collaboration with partners—families and other professionals—is extremely important. Similar behaviours occur in all settings, and it is very confusing to a child for different behavioural strategies to be acceptable in different settings. Children will adapt to varying expectations, but learning is increased when the expectations are consistent in all settings. This way, children learn to transfer what is expected of them from one situation to another. Gabriella's IPP and portfolio are a good example of what can be achieved if a collaborative process is used.

3. The Role of Planner

The early childhood educator may take the lead in the development of an IPP or portfolio. Planning is an ongoing process. As a plan is implemented, it needs to be evaluated in order to adapt or revise strategies as needed.

An appropriate learning environment needs to be established and organized so that the behavioural needs of all children can be met. Ongoing assessment of the environment will lead to new adjustments as needed.

Routines and policies should be established and revised as needed to create predictability and stability. This will lead to a more secure environment for all children. Children can anticipate what will happen during their day at the centre.

4. The Role of Manager

The early childhood educator acts as a manager. Team meetings need to be organized in order to collaborate with partners. Information needs to be shared with all centre staff, to ensure consistency of programming and implementation of specific strategies. After Gabriella's IPP was completed, for example, Kaya arranged regular meetings with staff to ensure that everyone knew what the expectations were, and could collaboratively implement them. Realistic limits should be collaboratively set and consistently reinforced by all partners. Interactions between children need to be mediated and encouraged.

5. The Role of Supporter

Behaviour is learned. Early childhood educators need to model appropriate behaviours and reinforce appropriate behaviours when they occur. This sets the tone for creating a positive learning environment.

Children and families need encouragement. Inappropriate behaviours take a long time to change. It is easy to give up. Celebrating success, sharing this information and continued acceptance of the child will lead to more positive long-term successes.

Early childhood educators must learn to anticipate challenging behaviours in order to prevent them, or to ignore challenging behaviours whenever possible. For example, Gabriella was asked to find her pillow to scream into. She shouted, "I am not going to use my silly old pillow!" as she was walking over to the pillow. This behaviour can be ignored, since the child is already complying with the expectation. The early childhood educator should focus on positive behaviours and reinforce them; this will help set the tone for more positive behaviours.

6. The Role of Evaluator

The early childhood educator needs to continually monitor and assess the learning environment, interaction patterns and strategies used to cope with all behaviours in order to identify necessary changes or adaptations. When it was noticed that Gabriella needed more positive peer modelling, the staff decided to provide opportunities for her to interact with a group of children who had strong appropriate social skills (see Figure 7.5E, page 239).

7. The Role of Researcher

There is always one child who will challenge the abilities of everyone to find acceptable behaviour-management strategies. Rather than give up on that particular child, acceptable alternatives should be looked for. There are a number of resources listed at the end of the chapter to help the practitioner find alternative solutions.

SUMMARY

Challenging behaviours are difficult to manage for everyone and can be extremely frustrating and emotionally draining for all individuals working with that child. The early childhood educator needs to become part of a collaborative team to help the child, the family and the centre staff cope most effectively with these behaviours. Following the steps outlined in this chapter will help to guide these challenging behaviours. These steps are:

1. Identify the problem behaviour.
2. Gather any pertinent information about the behaviour.
3. Interpret the information at hand.
4. Try to find a reason for why the behaviour is occurring.
5. Develop a plan.
6. Implement the plan.

Review the implementation and adapt as needed. Some strategies that are currently used in Canada include:

- Support and development of an IPP, in collaboration with mental health care workers, families, resource consultants and staff members.
- Referral to a mental health service.
- Referral to a medical team for possible drug treatment.
- Removal of the child from the program.

KEY POINTS

Types of challenging behaviours
- Emotional, conduct, hyperkinetic, developmental, diagnosed conditions

Causes of challenging behaviours
- Developmental, environmental, functional, psychological

Range of behaviours in inclusive settings
- Aggressive, interrupting, low attention span, difficulty concentrating, difficulty with self-control, low self-esteem

Collaboration
- With families, other professionals, staff

Observations
- Frequency counts, duration counts, graphs

Individual program plan
- Summary of diagnosis, observations of behaviour, base line, successful behaviour-management strategies, goals, strategies, evaluation

Individual portfolio
- Reinforce and maintain behaviour, involvement of child

Adaptation to inclusive settings
- Organizing environment, changing social context, adapting program, changing interactive approaches, using the child's perspective

Role of the early childhood educator
- Observer, collaborator, planner, manager, supporter, evaluator, researcher

EXERCISES

1. Reflect upon the challenging behaviours you have seen children engage in within a centre-based program. What were the behaviours? How did they affect the child and the staff? Why do you think these behaviours occurred? Why do you think behavioural disabilities are hard to diagnose?

2. Using the chart provided below, identify some of the behaviours that might fit into each category.

Category of Behaviour	Types of Behaviour
Emotional	
Conduct	
Hyperkinetic	
Diagnosed conditions	

3. Identify the causes of behaviour and discuss how behaviours are similar or different in each case.

4. Discuss why it is important to know the normal development of children, in order to guide behaviour.

5. Using the following table, observe a group of preschool children in a centre-based program to identify the types of challenging behaviours that might occur because of the factors listed on the left side. What adaptations might you suggest to decrease the number of challenging behaviours? If no challenging behaviours were observed, reflect on the information to identify why you did not observe any.

Description of Factor	Types of Behaviour Observed
Overcrowding	
Too many open spaces	
Disorganized storage of material	
Too noisy	
Too many choices	
Too few choices	
Developmentally or age-inappropriate choices	
Competitive activities	
Provision of violent toys	
Organization not based on the interests or background experiences of the children	
Too much waiting during transitions	

6. Define functional causes of behaviour. What strategies might be used to mitigate the occurrence of functional behaviours?

7. Reflect on an experience that you have had that caused you to feel badly about yourself. What was the cause? How did you feel? What strategies did you develop to overcome this situation? How can you help children in similar situations?

8. For each of the following, develop specific strategies that lead to a collaborative process: families, other professionals, other staff members.

9. Identify the purposes of each of the following observational techniques: frequency count, duration count, use of a graph. When might each of the techniques be of the most use?

10. Compare the similarities and differences between a standard IPP and a behavioural IPP, and justify the differences.

11. How is an individual portfolio useful in helping a child learn to control his or her behaviour?

12. Describe each of the possible adaptations to inclusive settings and list at least three strategies for each one.

13. Identify and explain each of the early childhood educator's roles in an inclusive environment.

REFERENCES

Canadian Child Care Federation. (2000). Tips for Parenting Children with Challenging Behaviour. Child & Family Canada [online]. Available at www.cccf-fcsge.ca/docs/cccf/rs048_en.htm [11/21/2008].

Chamberland, C., Laporte, L., Lavergne, C., & Baraldi, R. (2003). Psychological Abuse: Children's Invisible Suffering. Child & Family Canada [online]. Available at www.cecw-cepb.ca/files/file/en/PsycAbuse5E.pdf [11/21/2008].

Diehn, G. (2006). *Making Books That Fly, Fold, Wrap, Hide, Pop Up, Twist and Turn.* New York: Lark Books.

Irwin Hope, S. E. (1999). *Challenging the Challenging Behaviours.* Wreck Cove, NS: Breton Books.

Kaiser, B., & Sklar Rasminsky, J. (1999). *Meeting the Challenge: Effective Strategies for Challenging Behaviours in Early Childhood Environments.* Ottawa, ON: Canadian Child Care Federation.

National Institute of Mental Health. (2003). Attention Deficit Hyperactivity Disorder. National Institute of Mental Health [online]. Available at www.nimh.nih.gov/publicat/adhd.cfm.

Orr, L, & Cavallaro, G. (1997). Interventions for Children with Challenging Behaviours and Special Needs. Canadian Childcare Federation [online]. Avaliable at www.cfc-efc.ca/docs/cccf/00020_en.htm.

Vitaro, F., De Civita, M., & Pagani, L. (1996). The Impact of Research-Based Prevention Programs on Children's Disruptive Behaviour. *Exceptionality Education Canada* 5[105].

Weingarden Dubin, J. (2001). More Than a Mood. *Psychology Today* 34, 21.

Winzer, M. (2008). *Children Exceptionalities in Canadian Classrooms.* Scarborough, ON: Prentice Hall Allyn and Bacon.

8

CHAPTER

Strategies for Facilitating Motor Growth in Inclusive Settings

Chapter Outline

"Movement is a part of everyone's everyday life and has many manifestations. The urge to achieve physical skill mastery and capitalize on the body's capacity for movement is common to all children. They delight in physical accomplishment and enjoy movement for its own sake. Children use movement to express feelings, manipulate objects, and learn about their world" (Sanders, 2002:xiv).

Learning Outcomes

After studying this chapter, you will be able to:

1. Identify the importance of movement to early learning.
2. Describe the connection between perceptual skills and fine- and gross-motor skills, and identify the importance of knowledge of normal perceptual and motor development.
3. Explain the relationship of perceptual and motor development to other developmental areas.
4. Explain the importance of collaborating with families and other professionals.
5. Identify and describe how observations are used to develop an appropriate motor program.
6. Discuss why it is important to have an expert involved in helping to set the direction of a motor IPP.
7. Identify relevant adaptations that should be made to the indoor and outdoor environments to optimize motor development.
8. Describe the various roles of the early childhood educator in helping to develop an appropriate motor program for all children.

Introduction

Movement is innate to all human beings. Movement is evident at birth with the first breath and first cry. Newborns use movements to express themselves. This repertoire of body language continues to grow and become refined as children gain control over their muscles and start to understand the world around them.

Expression through movement is demonstrated in many ways, some more obvious than others. Infants express excitement through a flailing of the arms and legs, or more placidly through increased sucking while feeding or using a soother. Toddlers express their curiosity of the world around them by active exploration of the environment or by observing others and reacting with facial expressions. Preschoolers express their enthusiasm in an increasing number of ways. Their feelings and knowledge about the world can be observed in their actions, language and creations. As children's control over both fine and gross muscles increases, their creative expressions may begin to be expressed in an increasing number of ways, such as through dance, art, writing or music.

Studies of children who have been institutionalized at an early age demonstrate that movement is critical to learning. When infants were placed into an institution and lacked the opportunity to actively explore the environment, their motor development was delayed. Infants in these institutions spent the majority of time in their cribs with no toys to stimulate development. By age three to four, the majority of these infants could not yet walk. However, infants transferred to a more developmentally appropriate environment were all able to walk by age three (Schickedanz, Schickedanz, Forsyth & Forsyth, 2001).

Movement is also critical to all other domains. As children gain increased motor abilities such as walking and the ability to manipulate objects, they also:

- Are increasingly able to act independently
- Make choices about what, when and how they wish to engage in learning activities
- Actively explore the environment to learn about the world around them
- Discover relationships between their actions and the results of their actions
- Develop understanding about themselves, their actions and the materials and experiences in their environments

Motor development is often categorized into perceptual development, gross-motor development and fine-motor development. However, it is important to remember that it is the interplay of all motor domains that leads to healthy growth and development. Children with a challenge in any of these areas often need to learn to compensate by developing skills in another domain. For example, the child with a visual disability will need to rely more on auditory perception, in order to freely explore his or her environment.

Development of Motor Skills

Normal development of perceptual skills and gross- and fine-motor skills occurs in a predictable, universal pattern. Individual differences in reaching milestones may arise from culture or family expectations, early stimulation in milestone development or disability. For example, infants who are born blind will attempt to reach for and try to grasp objects that they can hear. These infants are usually not successful in grasping the objects because they do not know how far away the object is. If this listening and grasping behaviour is not reinforced and guided, these infants will cease to try to grab objects they hear (Schickedanz et al., 2001).

Knowledge of normal motor development will facilitate the adult caregiver's ability to:

- Identify relevant motor skills and milestones, in order to foster further growth and development
- Identify potential motor problems
- Plan appropriate learning experiences for children
- Create appropriate indoor and outdoor environments, in order to encourage optimum growth and development.

1. Perceptual Development

Perceptual development is characterized by visual and auditory perception and by sensory awareness: tactile, body, spatial, directional and time awareness. Knowledge of developmental milestones in these areas will help adults make informed decisions about children's perceptual and motor behaviours and will guide the formation of realistic expectations.

A) VISUAL PERCEPTION Visual perceptual ability involves the physical ability to see and a process of making sense of the information that has been seen. The ability to see is usually referred to as visual acuity. This term "refers to how well the elements of a pattern can be seen by someone at a specific distance" (Schickedanz et al., 2001:95). Development of visual acuity starts at birth and is fully developed by the time a child is three years old. Development of motor abilities hinges on the young infant's ability to see and understand what he or she has seen. The simple act of reaching for a toy involves the ability to see the toy, to centre attention on that toy, to reach toward that toy and, finally, to grasp it. Visual perception is an integral part of the process. As previously stated, if the infant is unable to see the object, other strategies must be used to reinforce the motor behaviours and to help the child continue to develop normal motor behaviours.

Developmental milestones in visual acuity normally follow a predictable pattern:

- Birth—Cannot fixate on an object; poor eye coordination; poor ability to discriminate colour; shows poor visual acuity
- One month—Tracks slowly moving objects; has developed visual preferences for strong contrast, complex designs and human faces; still shows poor visual acuity

- Three months—Can fixate on objects for longer periods of time; can see smaller objects and differentiate colours; pays attention visually by maintaining eye contact; searches for objects visually
- Four months—Shows improved visual acuity; begins to show interest in own body parts; tracks objects moving in all directions
- Five months—Starts to examine things visually; achieves eye–hand coordination (can reach and grasp intended object)
- Six months—Coordinates eye movements smoothly; shows increased ability to differentiate near and far objects
- Two years—Completes myelination of optic nerve: formation of protective sheath that forms around nerve cells to improve transmission of impulses (see Figure 8.1). A myelin sheath can be compared to the coating on an electrical cord. If the wires are left bare, the electricity can still reach the end point, but the signal will be weakened, because the electricity will also be diverted to other points along the bare wire. A weak signal to a light bulb would result in a weak light. The cord protects the wires and provides an efficient means of transmission of signals. Similarly, the impulses travelling along myelinated nerve branches will be faster and stronger.
- Three years—With full maturity of retinal tissue, has ability to see virtually as well as adults

The ability to see is also linked to the child's understanding of what he or she sees, and an understanding of what is seen is closely related to the child's experiences. Understanding is linked both to the growth and development of both motor and cognitive skills. When children actively explore the environment, they learn through touching, manipulating and hearing others describe and talk about their experiences. Infants with motor delays or physical challenges need to experience similar explorations. Adults should be creative in organizing learning experiences that provide opportunities to learn about the world through

FIGURE 8.1
Myelination

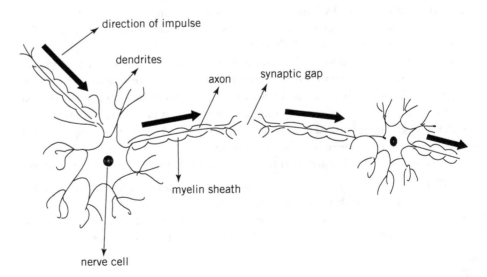

Photo 8.1

Photo 8.2

active physical participation. As children grow and mature, they gradually gain skills and abilities in all domains that reinforce and transform learning:

- Children acquire the ability to use language to identify and describe what they are experiencing—Language ability progresses from differential crying to cooing, to babbling, to first words, and then jumps rapidly to forming sentences and complete ideas.
- Children gain understanding about their personal actions—Infants and toddlers are centred on the self and on the needs of the self. Understanding is based on the individual behaviours and the sensory motor experiences of that child. Hannah has decided to use her hands to paint (Photo 8.1). Notice the intense concentration on her face. She is involved in a sensory-motor experience. She is gaining experience with:
  - How the paint feels (texture, temperature, consistency)
  - What happens when you put paint on paper
  - How to make things change (hands, paper)
  - How to use her fine and gross muscles to retrieve and spread the paint
- Understanding moves from the sensory-motor activity to active exploration of how things work and how things function—Preschool children actively explore the environment to experiment with various techniques of making things happen.

Yasmine is experimenting with different ways of painting (Photo 8.2). She had found a dried flower and was upset because it had "lost its colour." She started out by trying to paint colour onto it. Eventually she switched to using the dried flower to paint with. She was very excited to make various discoveries: the patterns that the flower made on the paper, other things in the environment that she could use, that different materials made different marks, that some materials broke very easily, and another way of representing her experiences—through art. Through this process, Yasmine gained greater understanding of the world around her. She used her perceptual abilities to find the materials needed, and her fine- and gross-motor abilities to represent her experiences on paper.

B) AUDITORY PERCEPTION "Auditory perception is the ability to hear different sounds and to distinguish one from another. Listening, the ability to remember sounds, and sound patterns form a part of auditory perception" (Nyisztor & Rudick, 1995:17). Hearing matures during the fetal stage. The fetus begins to hear during the last two months of pregnancy and is well equipped to hear at birth. Newborns already recognize the voices of their primary caregivers and are soothed by the familiar mother's voice. Over the next two years, the infant gradually develops the understanding of language.

Auditory perception plays a role in movement activities, especially in helping the child to:

- Understand the relationship between movement and language
- Participate in music and movement activities
- Rely to a greater extent on the auditory channel when there are challenges in other domains such as visual

C) SENSORY AWARENESS Sensory awareness develops at the fetal stage and matures over a lifetime of experience in a variety of settings and with a variety of materials. As children actively explore the environment, they gain understanding of many of the sensory concepts, such as spatial and body awareness.

Tactile awareness develops at the fetal stage. The skin is very sensitive to touch because of that area's many receptors. The fetus floats in the embryonic fluid, stretching, bouncing and moving in other ways, and with each movement feels the fluid embrace and flow around the body. Through this sense, individuals learn to detect differences in many variables, such as temperature, texture and consistency. Children with special needs need more sensory motor experiences than other children, in order to gain understanding about their world. Tactile behaviours such as continually putting things in one's mouth may persist for longer periods of time. The caregiver must take note of the development of the child and carefully provide tactile experiences that promote safe and healthy development. Knowledge of developmental guidelines helps practitioners plan appropriate learning experiences. These are some developmental guidelines:

Photo 8.3

- Neonates are extremely sensitive to touch. Touch calms a newborn. A premature infant who has been held and soothed by touching gains weight more quickly than one who has not had this experience (Photo 8.3) (Schickedanz et al., 2001).
- All newborns respond to pain, felt in response to such things as a pinprick or circumcision.
- All infants respond to different tactile stimulation differently and selectively.
- As children start to actively explore their environments, they learn to differentiate between tactile sensations and start to establish distinct preferences for a larger

variety of tactile experiences, such as swimming, rolling down a hill or simply running to feel the breeze around their bodies.

Another type of sensory awareness is body awareness. As children develop an awareness of their bodies and how the different body parts function and move, they also gain a sense of self. There is a developmental sequence to gaining body awareness. Children who do not engage in the following behaviours should be carefully observed to identify if they are at risk:

- As infants kick and move their extremities, they start to gain an awareness of how to move their limbs and the location of these limbs (Photo 8.4).
- Increased mobility brings increased independence and increased ability to practise skills. Toddlers attempt to achieve and maintain balance as they engage in a variety of activities, such as climbing, squatting, running or manipulating objects in various positions (Photo 8.5).
- Preschoolers continue to refine and practise a variety of motor skills; for instance, riding (Photo 8.6), jumping and the manipulation of small parts to put together and take apart (Photo 8.7).

A third type of sensory awareness, spatial awareness, includes the understanding of one's own body, the relationship of one's body to things that are near or far away and the awareness of space between objects. It makes it possible for the child to move freely around a designated space and to identify where his or her body is in relationship to that space and how to appropriately move through that space. Children who lack a good sense of spatial awareness may have difficulty in handling large open areas and may find certain perceptual tasks, such as discriminating similarities and differences, difficult. This may lead to later disabilities in such tasks as reading and writing. Spatial awareness:

- Develops in infancy—As infants are touched, cuddled, played with and hear the language associated with the actions ("I am tickling your tummy") (Photo 8.8), they start to gain awareness about their bodies and the location of body parts.

Photo 8.4

Photo 8.5

Photo 8.6

Photo 8.7

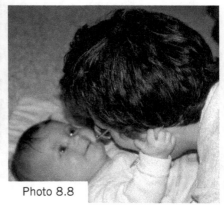

Photo 8.8

- Increases through such activities as dressing, undressing or bathing—Language activities (verbal or signing) should accompany all activities: "Oh, you have bubbles on your nose!" or "Where is that arm? Is it in the sleeve?"
- Increases with maturation, as the infant can start to put body parts into his or her mouth, like fingers, hands or feet.
- Changes dramatically when children start to actively explore the environment— The kind of mobility associated with each stage—crawling, sitting or walking— enables children to see their world from different perspectives. Children are able to place themselves in different positions such as on, inside, outside or under, as they hear or see the appropriate labels that are associated with these actions.
- Changes dramatically with active manipulation—Children can place items in different locations and learn the associated vocabulary that corresponds to the position.

The development of directional awareness, another form of sensory awareness, entails increased understanding of one's own body, such as the knowledge that:

- Each individual body has a front and a back
- The body can move in different directions as a unit
- The different body parts can move separately

Understanding of directionality develops with active movement over the early years. By the time children are about six years old, they develop an understanding of right and left. A healthy development of directional awareness will help children with special needs obtain a better understanding of their bodies. Children who are unable to move efficiently may require help and guidance to gain a normal awareness of how their body moves.

Time awareness is yet another form of sensory awareness. Consciousness of time starts to develop in infancy and continues to grow and expand in the early years. Here are some developmental milestones:

- Reciprocal actions—During infancy, the interactions between caregiver and infant are punctuated by the infant's growing ability to listen, respond, listen and respond again. When an infant engages in an interaction, such as smiling at another individual, and that individual responds by smiling back, the infant gains some awareness of the concept of "after."
- Independence in routines—As toddlers and preschoolers become increasingly independent, they gain further experience in the concepts of before and after: Before I go to bed, I brush my teeth. After breakfast we get dressed and go to day care.
- A general understanding of various times and the sequence of the day—This understanding arrives at the preschool stage. Lunch time, for instance, is followed by a nap. After the outdoor time, Daddy will come to pick me up. A preschooler does not yet have a specific concept of time. Jenny woke up on Sunday morning to get ready to go to day care. Her mother informed her that it was Sunday, and that Sunday was a holiday. Jenny understood the concept of a holiday but, clearly worried anyway, she responded. "Could you phone my day care to see if it is Sunday there too?"

- School-aged children start to develop a more sophisticated understanding of time—For example, they learn the hours of the day and the days of the week.

Children who have not developed an appropriate sense of time will find it difficult to predict what will occur next in their day. These children will need reminders and stable routines to help them make sense of their world.

2. Gross-Motor Development

Gross-motor development is dependent on perceptual development, fine-motor development and maturation. It is also directly related to the experiences and stimulation in a young child's life. Although motor milestones develop in a predictable and universal sequence, there is variation in when individual children reach milestones; these are based on individual characteristics as well as family and cultural expectations. Table 8.1 identifies the major developmental milestones of gross-motor development.

TABLE 8.1   MILESTONES OF GROSS-MOTOR DEVELOPMENT

Age Range	Gross-Motor Milestones
Birth–4 months	• Lifts and clears head from surface when lying on stomach • Rolls over from front to back and back to front • Can be pulled into sitting position
4–8 months	• Sits without support • May pull self to crawling position and rock • Rolls over from front to back and back to front • May push with feet to move backwards • Can be pulled to standing position
8–12 months	• Crawls • Pulls self up to standing position • Climbs stairs • Walks holding onto furniture • Walks independently
12–18 months	• Walks independently • Runs
18–36 months	• Jumps on the spot and jumps down from higher positions • Uses riding toys, first pushing with feet and using pedals by end of period

Sources: Crowther, 2005; Schickedanz et al., 2001

3. Fine-Motor Development

Control over fine-motor skills develops in a process that is smoothly interactive between perceptual and all motor activities. The simple act of picking something up requires an individual to coordinate seeing the object, reaching for the object and grasping it, and using gross muscles to bend and reach for the object. Fine-muscle control develops in a predictable pattern. Children with physical disabilities may continue to use specific grasping skills, such as the palmar grasp, for longer periods of time. Major milestones are included in Table 8.2. One of the important milestone developments in the early years is the ability to grasp and manipulate objects. Figure 8.2 identifies major grasping milestones.

TABLE 8.2   MILESTONES OF FINE-MOTOR DEVELOPMENT

Age	Milestone	Description
Birth–4 months	Hands and feet	Uses hands and feet to wave or kick to express excitement or interest
	Grasp	Reaches for and swats at items with hands or feet, often missing
		Reflexively grasps object when near hand (see Figure 8.2)
4 months–8 months	Grasp	Palmar grasp (see Figure 8.2)
	Transfers objects	Transfers objects from one hand to other
	Release	Starts to release objects voluntarily by end of period
	Exploration of objects	Puts things into mouth
8–12 Months	Release	Uses voluntary release to drop, to transfer or throw, and to place
	Manipulation	Pokes, transfers items from hand to hand, looks intently, starts to stack items
	Grasp	Pincer grasp evolves (see Figure 8.2)
12 months–2 years	Grasp	Releases objects voluntarily—skill well established
	Drawing	Scribbles with whole arm movement
	Feeding	Uses spoon, fork to feed self
2–3 years	Self-help	Undoes buttons and zippers; holds glass in one hand; opens doors; turns pages of book
	Filling and dumping	Fills and dumps repetitively—sand, water or other solid objects such as beads
3 years and older	Increased abilities	Is more independent, feeding and serving self and catching and throwing by self
	Grasp	Performs tripod grasp (see Figure 8.2), leading to increased ability to complete fine-motor tasks such as colouring in lines, drawing, painting, building and printing

Sources: Schickedanz et al., 2001; Crowther, 2005

FIGURE 8.2
Grasping Milestones

Description	Example

Description

Reflex grasp

When something is placed near the infant's hand, the hand reflexively closes

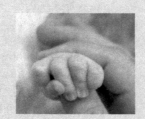

Primitive grasp

When something is placed in an infant's hand, the object is reflexively grasped, but it is dropped when hand becomes tired.

Palmar grasp

The young child uses his or her whole hand to grasp, hold or manipulate objects.

Pincer grasp

The child uses forefinger and thumb to pick up smaller objects.

Tripod grasp

This grasp is used to draw print or write more effectively.

4. Relationship Between Motor Development and Other Domains

Often, when children have a special need, there is an emphasis on just that area of development, to the exclusion of other areas. Such methods are ineffective, however, because they do not recognize the underlying interactions of behaviour (see Figure 8.3).

At two months old, Lara looked at the rattle that was shaken in front of her face. Her attention focused on the rattle because of the its bright colours, movement and sound. When the rattle was placed near her hand, her fingers closed around it in a reflexive grasp. Soon, her hand tired and the rattle dropped to the floor. She did not look for the rattle or seem upset that the stimulation was gone. When Lara was six months old, she was able to initiate her own action. She grabbed the rattle, shook it and then brought it to her mouth (Photo 8.9). When she was placed near the same toys again at another time, she immediately shook the same fish rattle. She had gained greater control over her physical actions, learned to make choices and remembered past actions.

Photo 8.9

FIGURE 8.3

Interaction of Movement and Other Developmental Domains

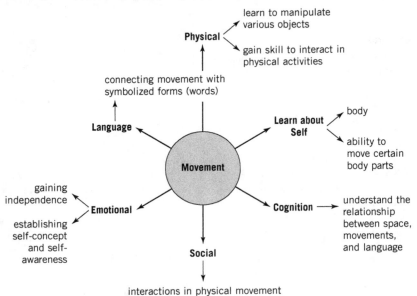

At 12 months old, Lara actively explored the environment. She engaged in filling and emptying activities. She enjoyed taking toys apart, then giving them to someone to put them together again (Photo 8.10). Lara had learned to expand her choices to include others in her play. She remembered what she could do with toys and used her knowledge to interact with other individuals effectively. At 19 months, Lara actively explored her environment. She was able to find her own materials to engage in play. She found the animal beads and the metal bowls, and used these materials to fill and dump. Lara usually retrieved the metal bowls for this activity, because she liked the sound the beads made when they dropped into the bowl. Lara was by this time also attracted to the various colours of beads and often started to find like colours to drop into the bowl (Photo 8.11).

Photo 8.10

Over time, Lara has gained a number of skills. As she interacted with similar materials, she strengthened her knowledge and understanding of the world around her. Initially, her interactions were dependent on adults, and limited to listening and watching. At six months, she used her cognitive skills to remember past actions, and involved gross- and fine-motor skills to reach, pull, shake and manipulate the rattle. At 12 months, she was mobile enough to make her own choices, solve some of her own problems and involve others in social play. At 19 months, Lara had combined many skills: the memory of past actions, increased dexterity to manipulate materials, the ability to take the initiative and the observation of objects to identify detail.

The Ludic Model of occupational therapy exemplifies the effective use of the concept of interacting modalities with children with disabilities. The model is used to "stimulate, develop, and maintain play skills of children, involving the sensory, motor, cognitive, and social sphere" (Ferland, 2005:106). Children are assessed on the criteria listed in Table 8.3. The assessment includes emotional, sensory, motor, cognitive and social components. It is only when all characteristics are considered that a therapy program is developed.

Photo 8.11

Range of Motor Behaviours in Inclusive Settings

The range of motor behaviours in inclusive settings varies greatly from centre to centre in Canada. In most centres, behaviours range from slightly delayed motor abilities to normal and gifted behaviours. However, at times it is necessary to accommodate children who require assistance to be mobile such as children in a wheelchair.

The types of motor behaviours that might be expected include the following:

- Delayed motor abilities—These children will exhibit behaviours that are at a lower developmental level than their chronological age. Since these preschool or school-aged children might still walk with the toddler's unsteady gait or be involved in sensory motor exploration, safety becomes an issue. Organization of the environment must consider the safety needs of all the children, such as putting small parts out of reach and encouraging children to use these with supervision.

TABLE 8.3   DEVELOPMENT OF LUDIC BEHAVIOUR: ATTITUDE AND ACTION

1. Sensory stimulation and response
2. Exploration of objects and space, and manipulation of materials
3. Ludic activity: functional and unconventional use of play materials leading to the acquisition of a personal play repertoire.

Stage 1	Stage 2	Stage 3
	LUDIC ATTITUDE	
	Characteristics	
• awakening of attention • awakening of curiosity • awakening of interest • desire to know	• interest sustained • sensation of pleasure • desire for initiative • desire to explore • desire to act	• interest in action • pleasure in action • initiative • humour • spontaneity
	Emotional Components	
• feelings of confidence	• feelings of control of objects • expression of needs • beginning of autonomy	• feeling of mastery • expression of needs and feelings • autonomy • decision making • self-esteem
	LUDIC ACTION	
	Sensory Components	
• looks • touches • smells • hears • puts in mouth • moves		
	Motor Components	
• grasps • manipulates • maintains a position • moves	• grasps/releases • opens/closes • throws/catches • empties/fills • piles • carries • changes position • moves around	• uses tools (crayon, scissors...) • uses several objects • combines various actions

TABLE 8.3 **CONTINUED**

Stage 1	Stage 2	Stage 3
Cognitive Components		
• experiments with relationships of cause and effect (beginning) • experiments with permanence of the object (beginning) • recognizes basic characteristics of objects	• understands the relationship of cause • understands the concept of permanence of the object • understands how objects work • helps solving problems • understands how activities proceed	• imitates • pretends • creates a play situation • uses symbols (make-believe play, drawing, language) • solves problems • understands symbols
Social Components		
• plays with the adult • plays alone	• plays in parallel • grasps the notion of property	• shares the play materials • plays with other children • cooperates in shared play • knows how to ask for and accept help • can help others • expresses ideas

Source: Ferland (2005)

- Challenges with balance—Some children will find it difficult to maintain their balance while walking or trying to manipulate materials because of spastic movements or rigidity of muscles. Special adaptations need to be made for these children to ensure that they can participate safely and without becoming frustrated.
- Mobility with assistive devices such as a wheelchair—The environment must be made accessible both indoors and outdoors, in order to provide maximum opportunities for independent participation.
- Missing limbs or digits—Adaptive devices must be included, such as toys with lips or hooks and utensils with straps for easier manipulation. In addition, caregivers should develop strategies that encourage full inclusion in all activities.
- Normal range of abilities—These children need to become aware of their peers and develop understanding of their peers' strengths and needs.
- Giftedness—These children usually have exceptional fine- and/or gross-motor skills. Children in this category need to be provided with challenges to avoid potential boredom and inactivity.

Intervention Strategies

Intervention strategies for children with special physical challenges are usually developed by a specialist, such as an occupational therapist or a physiotherapist. It is generally not left to child care providers to offer physical training programs. Their responsibilities are usually more centred on collaboration with specialists and families, to ensure that children are included in programs to their maximum abilities.

1. Collaboration with Specialists

Children who have physical challenges usually attend therapy sessions with a specialist. The specialist develops a program based on his or her assessment and will provide the therapeutic program for the individual child. For example, Simon is a five-year-old with cerebral palsy who uses a wheelchair for mobility. Simon's occupational therapist conducted an assessment of his abilities and used the results, shown here in Table 8.4, to recommend a therapy program based on Simon's strengths and needs.

TABLE 8.4 RESULTS OF SIMON'S ASSESSMENT

1. Sensory stimulation and response
2. Exploration of objects and space, and manipulation of materials
3. Ludic activity: functional and unconventional use of play materials leading to the acquisition of a personal play repertoire.

Stage 1	Stage 2	Stage 3
LUDIC ATTITUDE		
Characteristics		
• **awakening of attention** • **awakening of curiosity** • **awakening of interest** • desire to know	• interest sustained • **sensation of pleasure** • desire for initiative • desire to explore • desire to act	• interest in action • pleasure in action • initiative • **humour** • spontaneity
Emotional Components		
• **feelings of confidence**	• feelings of control of objects • **expression of needs** • beginning of autonomy	• feeling of mastery • expression of needs and feelings • autonomy • decision making • self-esteem
LUDIC ACTION		
Sensory Components		
• **looks** • **touches +** • **smells** • **hears** • **puts in mouth** • **moves**		

TABLE 8.4 CONTINUED

Stage 1	Stage 2	Stage 3
	Motor Components	
• **grasps** • manipulates • **maintains a position** • **moves**	• *grasps/releases* **+** • *opens/closes* • *throws/catches* • empties/fills • piles • carries • **changes position** • **moves around**	• *uses tools (crayon, scissors...)* • uses several objects • combines various actions
	Cognitive Components	
• **experiments with relationships of cause and effect (beginning)** • **experiments with permanence of the object (beginning)** • **recognized basic characteristics of objects**	• *understands the relationship of cause* • *understands the concept of permanence of the object* • *understands how objects work* **+** • helps solving problems • understands how activities proceed	• imitates • pretends **+** • creates a play situation • uses symbols (make-believe play, drawing, language) • solves problems • understands symbols
	Social Components	
• **plays with the adult +** • **plays alone**	• plays in parallel • grasps the notion of property	• shares the play materials • plays with other children • cooperates in shared play • knows how to ask for and accept help • can help others • expresses ideas
Legend: • bold: present • italics: in development	• normal type: absent • + : strong interest	

Source: Ferland (2005)

The results were shared with Simon's day care staff. Regularly scheduled meetings were set up among the occupational therapist, family members and day care staff. In collaboration with the occupational therapist, the staff were able to:

- Develop an individual program plan for Simon
- Share observations on a variety of skills
- Gain expert advice on equipment/material needs to include in the program
- Foster experiences that supported Simon's growth and development in a variety of settings

2. Collaboration with Families

Collaboration with family members helps to identify, evaluate and reinforce learning activities that are implemented in the home, at the centre and at the therapy program. This collaboration is critical to ensuring that:

- The child's program is consistent in all settings
- Information about the child's progress is shared with all partners
- Appropriate revisions and adaptations are implemented as needed
- Evaluations are developed and implemented as a team

Observing Children's Motor Development

Observing children's motor development is important in planning an inclusive environment that provides for the active motor participation of all children. In order to plan the motor experiences and the organization of the materials within the learning environment, child care staff should conduct an observation of children's motor milestones (for examples, see Figures 8.4 and 8.5). This type of observation helps to identify gross- and fine-motor skills and abilities.

How can an observation such as that shown in Figure 8.4 be used? It is evident that Sam seems to participate in gross-motor activity regularly. He seems to like challenges such as walking across tree stumps. But he is also aware of his capabilities—he holds onto the fence and crawls down the stairs backwards. He engages in balancing activities: walking up stairs, on the line and over the stumps. This seems to indicate that more activities—for instance, balance beams, inside and outside—should be set up to enable him to practise various types of balancing activities.

FIGURE 8.4
Observation of Gross-Motor Skills

Child: Sam
Observer: Nadia

Date	Skill	Comments
Oct. 2	Climbing	• Climbed stairs one foot at a time, holding onto rail • Crawled down stairs backwards • Repeated behaviour four times • Refused when encouraged to try to walk down holding someone's hand
Oct. 3	Walking	• Followed line on the floor by moving with one foot on either side of the line; lost his balance and fell twice, but continued to try
Oct. 4	Rolling	• Rolled sideways down hill outside (six times)
Oct. 5	Balancing	• Watched children walk across tree stumps; joined in by holding on to the railing; continued with activity after other children had left

FIGURE 8.5

Observation of Grasping Skills

Child: Sam   **Dates:** Oct. 3–5; 7–11
Observer: Nadia

Type of Grasp	Setting	Description	Intervention
Palmar	Sand	Used shovel frontwards, then flipped it over backwards into the bucket, but most of the sand landed outside the bucket	Provided larger bucket; Sam filled it without spilling
Pincer	Beads	Picked up gimp to thread beads; could not get beads onto gimp; started to frown	Provided some long pipe cleaners; Sam could place beads onto gimp

Observation of fine-motor skills (as shown in Figure 8.5) provides information about the type of grasp that is being used, what type of activity the child is engaged in and intervention strategies that can be used to enhance success of the activity.

A summary of the observations shown in Figure 8.5 could be used to create a tool to observe other characteristics of Simon, such as sensory components, as shown in Figure 8.6. This kind of observation provides valuable information to the therapist about activities and behaviours that are prevalent in other situations, and provides insights into what sensory activities might be organized to encourage Simon's interactions.

FIGURE 8.6

Observation of Sensory Components

Child: Simon
Observers: Combination of family and centre staff

Sensory Component	Setting	Description
Observing	Watched finger play	• Five children and Tracey engaged in Itsy Bitsy Spider finger play as Simon watched from a distance; when asked if he wanted to join, moved wheelchair away • Watched me bake cookies; refused to help but stayed and watched
Tactile activities	Tactile tiles	• Picked up tile and placed it in front of him; rubbed his finger over it several times; repeated process for set of tiles; smiled and continued to rub the ones he liked; placed the ones he liked in one pile—Melanie asked him if she could play; he let her use all tiles, even his favourite ones; she told him that they were her favourite ones too
Listening	Requested to listen to the song and look at the book about Itsy Bitsy Spider	• Listened and looked at book four times

How can an observation such as that shown in Figure 8.6 be used? This type of tool is useful in establishing the child's interests and interactions with both materials and other children. It provides a basis to collaboratively plan experiences in various settings.

The IPP for Motor Skills

Individual program plans are usually not developed by practitioners for motor skills development. Dealing with challenges in motor behaviour is a skill that needs specialized training. Physiotherapists and occupational therapists can provide guidance on the types of motor activities that the child should engage in and the types of specialized equipment that he or she might need.

The individual program set up for Susan was initiated by the physiotherapist. The IPP shown in Figure 8.7 started with a goal set by the physiotherapist. Strategies and materials to reach the goal were collaboratively developed by the family members, the staff, the support staff and the physiotherapist. Progress was tracked by everyone.

Adapting the Environment

General adaptations should be made to accommodate motor abilities of all the children. These general adaptations are usually concerned with accessibility. Adaptations should reflect the ability of any child to access all activities regardless of the mode of movement used, such as a walker or wheelchair. The principles behind the adaptations include the following:

- Movement around the indoor or outdoor environment—Clear passageways should accommodate free movement between various learning spaces.
- Areas free from clutter—Clutter is dangerous, because children may trip and fall. As well, some mobility may be inhibited, because the wheels of devices such as wheelchairs and walkers may become trapped.
- Clear visibility of learning areas—Children should be able to be able to identify the various learning areas from different positions and from various points in the room.
- Access to all learning activities and routine care areas—All areas should be accessible to wheelchairs and other devices.
- Access to the facility—Ramps and automatic door openers should be provided to all entrances to the facility that children use.
- Access to all learning materials and equipment—Materials should be stored on open shelves with height appropriate to all children. Baskets and/or other containers should be available to transport materials to a table.

In addition to the general adaptations, a number of specific adaptations must be made to both indoor and outdoor environments, to reflect individual motor needs. In all instances, these adaptations should encourage maximum autonomy and optimal interactions among children and with learning experiences.

FIGURE 8.7
Individual Program Plan

Name: Susan   **DOB:** Jan. 1, 2001

Overview of Susan's Skills:

Susan has cerebral palsy. She is confined to a wheelchair. She can use her wheelchair independently. She uses a full palmar grasp to manipulate objects. She is persistent in her attempts to pick items up and examine them, but finds it difficult to manipulate objects that are on a slippery surface. She needs to be allowed the time to complete manipulative tasks.

Summary of interests observed in various settings (home, therapy centre and day care):
1. Tactile experiences—tactile tiles, feely bag, tactile books, creative activities with tactile materials
2. Sand—filling and dumping activities; needs help to dump sand out
3. Listening—finger plays and stories told or read

Goal:
To improve manipulation skills

Strategies:
1. Utilize regular play experiences with other children to support goal.
2. Adapt environment to make manipulation easier.
   - Add low, firm pile carpeting to manipulative table to make picking up easier
   - Provide trays in areas with lips and carpeting to prevent toys from falling off surface
   - Provide individual sand containers on tables to encourage filling and emptying activities, with a variety of smaller containers to make it easier to fill and dump the sand
   - Provide large crayons and markers to facilitate palmar grasp creative activities
   - Add basket to wheelchair to facilitate independence in gathering materials of choice

Evaluation:
The following observation form (only a portion of which is shown here) was used to fill in behaviours as they occurred in the centre and at home. The information was reviewed once every two weeks to plan for any needed adaptations or revisions.

Date	Setting	Activity
Oct. 25	Individual sand tray	Solitary play, filled small buckets with a shovel; much of the sand spilled, persisted until pail was full; called teacher over to look at full pail; dumped out sand and repeated activity

1. Indoor Learning Spaces

Indoor learning spaces should provide opportunities for children to actively participate in all learning activities organized with peers using the materials and equipment available. These adaptations can be classed in six categories:

- Environmental control devices—These devices are usually special switches that allow an individual to move around or to access equipment independently. Examples include automatic devices such as door openers, water taps, toilet flushers, light switches or remote controls for such equipment as computers.

Photo 8.12

- Daily living aids—There are a number of assistive devices that encourage independence. Examples include specially designed toilet seats, hand rails beside toilets, tilted mirrors in washrooms and specialized cutlery and dishes to assist independence at meal times.
- Visual aids—These aids are designed to assist maximum participation. Signs should be posted in sign language, Braille and symbolized formats to encourage all children to understand and find the learning activities and materials they wish to engage in (Photo 8.12).
- Alternative communication devices—These devices help children communicate with each other and with adults.
- Mobility devices—These include equipment such as wheelchairs, walkers and adaptive bicycles.
- Positioning equipment—This equipment may be used to maximize children's ability to interact with others and the materials and equipment in their learning environment. Examples include wedges to provide support for various body positions; adjustable chairs, tables and easels; standing frames; and specialized chairs and cots.

2. Outdoor Environments

A number of specific adaptations need to be made to outdoor environments in order to facilitate active participation of all children. These include:

- Clearly defined paths that are paved to allow access to all learning areas with wheelchairs or other mobile equipment (Photo 8.13)

Photo 8.13

Photo 8.14

Photo 8.15

Photo 8.16

Photo 8.17

Photo 8.18

- Ramps to access play equipment (Photo 8.14 and 8.15)
- Adaptive playground equipment (Photo 8.16 and 8.17)
- Play at various levels to encourage a variety of interactions (Photo 8.18)

Role of the Early Childhood Educator

The role of the early childhood educator in the physical environment actually comprises five roles: observer, planner, collaborator, organizer and advocate.

1. Observer

The observer role is critical to helping children with motor challenges participate fully in the learning environment. Children's motor skills and abilities must be observed in order to enable organization of an appropriate learning environment. Ongoing observations need to occur in order to identify:

- Safety issues that affect children of varying abilities—For example, it might be wise to create a one-way system on paths to ensure that children in mobility devices or on riding toys do not bump into each other. Additionally, marked crosswalks and stop signs can be placed at intersection points to avoid collisions and to reinforce safety rules.

- Modifications or adaptations that need to be made in order to allow for active participation by all individuals.
- Modification of activities to help maintain interest and to continue to build capabilities through providing appropriate challenges such as setting up an obstacle course.

2. Planner

Motor activities should be planned to take place in different ways: spontaneously, individually and/or in small or large groups.

- Planning for spontaneous activity—If the environment is organized appropriately, there should be opportunities for children to become actively involved in perceptual, gross- and fine-motor activities. The environment acts as the third teacher. Kyler had watched the children walking across the stumps. He seemed reluctant to try. Claudia noticed his reluctance and asked if he wanted some help. Kyler nodded. He used the stumps several times during outdoor play activities (Photo 8.19).
- Planning for individual skill development—Some skills can be planned for by providing the appropriate equipment and materials. All young children need opportunities to coordinate visual perception skills and motor skills. Jordan was able to manipulate the digger to scoop up snow so that he could load up his dump truck (Photo 8.20).
- Planning for group activity—Children need opportunities to explore activities together. Outdoor water activities often lend themselves to a variety of motor skills through experiences such as these (Photo 8.21):
  - the feeling of water on various parts of one's skin (and the opportunity to share one's impressions)

Photo 8.19

Photo 8.20

Photo 8.21

- awareness of directionality and spatial awareness
- running through water
- splashing other children
- directing the flow of water at others
- blowing bubbles and catching them

3. Collaborator

Early childhood educators need to collaborate with others in order to ensure that programs offered are of the highest possible quality. Through a collaborative process, the early childhood educator can enhance quality by:

- Discussing progress in motor skills and identifying new goals or target behaviours
- Ensuring that a consistent approach to the child's motor needs is used
- Providing opportunities to try motor skills in different settings, which will lead to transfer of skills
- Sharing successes—Nathan was two years old. He had been diagnosed with an overall delay. He had learned to pull himself into a standing position and cruise along with the support of furniture. While at day care, he took his first independent step. The staff member quickly took a photograph, so that this important developmental milestone could be shared.
- Sharing resources—The centre decided that it wanted to replace the indoor playhouse and provide a new setting that was more accessible to all children. A planning meeting with all the families and staff was arranged. One of the fathers was a carpenter. He helped the staff devise plans for a new structure, organized the parent group to procure materials and finally organized all participants to help build the structure.

4. Organizer

Early childhood educators are involved in several organizing roles, including the organization of physical and human resources. The physical environment needs to be set so that it maximizes motor activity for all children. Organization of the physical environment comprises various functions:

- Identifying appropriate resources, materials and equipment to ensure that all children's strengths and needs are met
- Organizing the resources, materials and equipment appropriately, in order to ensure that children have opportunities to practise motor skills on a daily basis
- Providing opportunities to rotate resources, materials and equipment, in order to maintain interest and pose challenges
- Providing toys and play materials that encourage social interactions

- Organizing safe indoor and outdoor environments that encourage children's independence
- Ensuring that an emergency plan is in place that includes children with physical disabilities
- Developing an appropriate schedule that includes regular motor activities
- Organizing displays and materials that showcase diversity, such as pictures, books or photographs

The organization of human resources includes these functions:

- Providing opportunities to children to express their concerns about their physical differences
- Collaborating with families and other professionals to develop IPPs, plan activities and evaluate the program, the environment and the progress of individual children
- Collaborating with staff to identify and develop consistent interaction strategies
- Demonstrating appropriate interaction patterns through modelling behaviours

5. Advocate

Materials and equipment to enhance motor development are often expensive to purchase and to install. Early childhood educators need to learn how to advocate for appropriate funding to procure resources, adaptive technology, equipment and accessibility for all children and their families.

SUMMARY

Gross-motor activities should be seen as a vital component of healthy growth and development. Active movement ensures that children develop:

- Independence skills
- A positive self-image
- Healthy living habits
- Healthy attitudes toward physical activity
- The ability to use their fine and gross muscles in a variety of active play

- The ability to coordinate a number of skills in various domains—sensory, physical, cognitive, social and emotional

Movement and learning are central to the child's healthy development. The interplay between movement and all other domains forms a cornerstone of healthy growth and development. Figure 8.3, page 270, demonstrates the interaction between active motor activity and all other domains. With careful planning and organization of the learning environment, every child can maximize his or her potential. "Our society has an underlying value structure that makes us think of disability in terms of 'tragedy,' having an 'impaired body' or being 'abnormal.' We must change this negative definition. Many things that make a person 'disabled' have to do with not having access to his or her environment. A flight of stairs makes a person who uses a wheelchair disabled. Put in a ramp and the disability disappears—until that person gets to a narrow doorway" (Greenstein, 1998:1).

KEY POINTS

Perceptual development
- Visual perceptual ability—Acuity and understanding of visual stimuli
- Auditory perception—Distinguishing individual sounds and making sense of what has been heard

Sensory awareness
- Tactile awareness—Touch, temperature, texture, consistency
- Body awareness—Function of different parts of the body, self-awareness
- Spatial awareness—Awareness of self in relation to other objects and within a physical space
- Directional awareness—Understanding of own body and how to move body parts in different directions
- Time awareness—Develops through reciprocal actions, independence in routines, daily routines and formal understanding of time such as hours and days of the week

Motor development
- Interaction of gross-, fine- and perceptual-motor development
- Interaction of all domains—Physical, social, cognitive, language and emotional

Fine-motor development
- Grasping skills—Reflex, palmar, pincer, tripod grasps

Range of motor behaviours in inclusive settings
- Normal, delayed, gifted, requiring wheelchair accommodation

Intervention strategies
- Collaboration with specialists
- Collaboration with families

Observing children's motor development
- Observation of gross-motor milestones
- Observation of grasping skills
- Observation of sensory components

Individual program plan
- Overview of motor skills, summary of interests, goals, strategies, evaluation

Adapting the learning environment
- General adaptations
- Adaptations to indoor learning spaces: environmental control, daily living aids, visual aids, alternative communication devices, mobilization devices, positioning devices
- Adaptations to outdoor learning spaces: defined paths, adaptive equipment, various levels of play

Role of the early childhood educator
- Observer—Safety, modifications, adaptations
- Planner—Spontaneous/planned, individual/group activities
- Collaborator—Progress, consistency, sharing successes and resources
- Organizer—Identification of resources, organization of physical resources and environment
- Advocate—Funding, procurement of resources and equipment

EXERCISES

1. Reflect on your personal ability to participate in fine- and gross-motor activity. How does this affect your self-awareness? How does it affect your self-concept?

2. Define each of these terms: perceptual development, gross-motor development and fine-motor development. Why are these developmental areas related?

3. Blindfold yourself in your kitchen. Find a glass and take it to the sink. Fill it with water and have a drink. Describe your experience: How did you feel about this experience? How did your movements change?

4. Explain how the following affect motor development:
   a) Visual perception
   b) Auditory perception
   c) Sensory awareness

5. Describe the changes that occur as grasping behaviour develops. What are the limitations of each type of grasp? What type of material might you provide to encourage children to gain better control over their manipulative abilities?

6. Describe the relationship of motor development to other developmental domains.

7. Describe the importance of each intervention strategy identified on pages 273–276.

8. Observe children in an inclusive setting. Identify the range of gross- and fine-motor behaviours.

9. Compare the IPP developed for motor behaviour to a behavioural IPP. How are they similar or different?

10. Using the chart provided below, identify the adaptations that could be found in inclusive settings to encourage motor development.

11. Identify the key role an early childhood educator should have in order to provide a learning environment that gives children opportunities to optimize their motor development.

Adaptation	Description
General adaptations	
Adaptations in indoor environments	
Adaptations in outdoor environments	

REFERENCES

Crowther, I. (2005). *Child Development Primer*. Scarborough, ON: Thomson Nelson.

Ferland, F. (2005). *The Ludic Model: Play, Children with Physical Disabilities and Occupational Therapy*. Second Edition. Ottawa: CAOT Publications ACE.

Greenstern, D. (1998). Caring for Children with Special Needs. Cornell University [online]. Available at www.ces.ncsu.edu/depts/fcs/pdfs/nc07.pdf [10/01/05].

Nyisztor, D., & Rudick, E. (1995). *Moving and Learning*. Toronto, ON: Harcourt Brace & Company Canada, Ltd.

Sanders, S. (2002). *Active for Life: Developmentally Appropriate Movement Programs for Young Children*. Washington, DC: National Association for the Education of Young Children.

Schickedanz, J., Schickedanz, D., Forsyth, P., & Forsyth, G. (2001). *Understanding Children and Adolescents*. Fourth Edition. Needham Heights, MA: Allyn & Bacon.

9
CHAPTER

Social and Emotional Growth in Inclusive Settings

"No study that has assessed social outcomes for children in integrated versus segregated settings has found segregated settings to be superior. This is important because one of the things that parents of young children with handicaps most desire for their youngsters is to develop friendships with their same-age non-handicapped peers" (Crowther & Sommer. 1997:120).

Learning Outcomes

After studying this chapter, you will be able to:

1. Define and describe social and emotional development.
2. Explain the relationship of Erikson's Stages of Development and how these stages relate to organizing a social–emotional environment that is both inclusive and effective.
3. Discuss how the following factors affect social–emotional behaviours: type of attachment pattern, child-rearing practices, background experiences and temperament.
4. Define and describe social attributes.
5. Describe the types of social–emotional behaviours that might be found in inclusive settings.
6. Explain why it is important to understand the six principles of guiding behaviour in inclusive settings.
7. Identify how to observe children's social–emotional behaviour.
8. Identify and describe the key components of a social–emotional IPP.
9. Identify and describe strategies for guiding social–emotional behaviours in inclusive settings.
10. Identify how to effectively organize the social–emotional environment.
11. Describe the role of the early childhood educator in inclusive social settings.

Introduction

Social development and emotional development are closely linked. As children become more socially competent, they also become more adept at social interactions with peers and adults in their lives and are able to react appropriately to a variety of different social and cultural situations. These interactions build friendships and relationships with others. Positive early social interactions lead to increased self-confidence and increased self-esteem. In contrast, the research clearly shows that negative early interactions leave lasting and sometimes permanent disabilities in emotional and social development that may affect much of the child's success in later academic years (McCain & Mustard, 1999; McCain & Mustard, 2002).

Social skills are also linked to the types of play interactions that children demonstrate at various ages and to the behaviour patterns that evolve. However, it is the interplay of all domains that leads to healthy development (see Figure 9.1).

Healthy social interactions depend on a child's ability to communicate; understand how to interact with others in different situations; form relationships; and express emotions in acceptable ways. The social setting in which children interact has a tremendous influence on how children feel about themselves. When an environment is set up to encourage children to work together and with adults to try new challenges, make appropriate choices and solve problems, children gain confidence in their abilities and skills. When the efforts of children are valued, children receive modelling to learn to respect others. Emotional well-being flourishes in an atmosphere of respect. Children learn to accept each other's varying abilities and learn to function more effectively in a diverse social setting. "Child psychologists, early childhood educators, and others working with young children will readily agree that there is no one factor that can be accredited for determining the quality of children's self-esteem. Rather, many factors interact in shaping the way in which children

FIGURE 9.1

Interplay of Developmental Domains

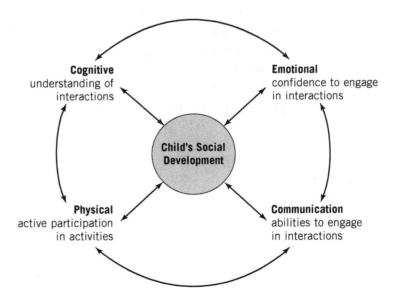

feel about themselves. It is also well known that the nature of this feeling further affects children's motivation, learning, and achievements" (King, Chipman & Cruz-Janzen, 1994). "Primary among the factors frequently identified as being at the core of the children's self esteem are a sense of belonging, feeling of worth, and a sense of competence" (Crowther et al., 1997:84).

When children have difficulties in any one of the developmental domains, they may find it a struggle to engage in appropriate social interactions. To support all children's healthy social and emotional development, a number of areas need to be considered. Adults working in an inclusive setting must have a firm knowledge of social and emotional development, the types and ranges of social and emotional behaviours that young children engage in, how to observe these behaviours and how to develop an emotionally secure and socially responsive inclusive environment.

Social and Emotional Development

Social and emotional development starts at birth. The early interactions between primary caregivers and the infant have a profound influence on all future development. "The evidence from neuroscience and child development studies is clear: The first years of life are crucial in setting a good foundation for each child's future" (McCain et al., 1999:51). As the infants grow and develop, they pass through predictable stages of development. For optimal growth and development to occur, children need to be exposed to a nurturing, stimulating environment at each stage.

According to Erik Erikson's theory of psychosocial development, individuals pass through eight psychosocial stages in their lifetimes. Four of these stages occur between birth and the age of 12 years. At each stage of development, the child achieves either positive or negative outcomes depending on the type of stimulation and interactions that the child is exposed to (Schickedanz, Schickedanz, Forsyth & Forsyth, 2001). Table 9.1 outlines these stages and the outcomes associated with each. Understanding the psychosocial development of children is important, because caregiver-interaction patterns directly affect the optimal development of each child.

Children's social and emotional behaviour progresses along a developmental continuum. Normative data are sensitive to cultural and individual family values. For example, studies have shown that children raised with different parenting styles behaved differently socially. The least competent children were those raised with very permissive or neglectful parenting styles. The children raised with parents with a more authoritative parenting style tended to be the most competent (Schickedanz et al., 2001).

Practitioners need to know and understand social–emotional milestones in order to:

- Plan appropriate social environments for children
- Provide a safe and nurturing environment for all children's skills and abilities
- Identify potential problems
- Provide appropriate social experience to meet all children's strengths and needs
- Nurture appropriate social and emotional development

TABLE 9.1   ERIKSON'S STAGES OF DEVELOPMENT

Stage	Description	Positive Outcomes	Negative Outcomes
Stage 1: **Infancy** **(birth–18 months)**	Infants depend on primary caregivers for food, warmth, affection and stimulation.	**Development of Trust** When the infant's needs are met consistently and immediately, secure attachment with primary caregivers is established. The infant learns to trust that his or her signals are responded to and learns to trust the environment.	**Development of Mistrust** If the infant's needs are not met or met inconsistently, the infant will develop mistrust of the individuals and things in the environment.
Stage 2: **Toddlers** **(2–3.5 years)**	Toddlers learn to do things by themselves, such as walking, talking or feeding themselves. Toddlers start to develop self-control and confidence in their own abilities.	**Development of Autonomy** If toddlers are encouraged to become independent and are reinforced for their efforts, they develop confidence in their ability to make choices and act upon their environment effectively. As a result they develop greater independence.	**Development of Shame or Doubt** If toddlers' independence is discouraged or their efforts are disapproved of or ridiculed, they may develop feelings of shame about their behaviours or may start to doubt their abilities.
Stage 3: **Preschool** **(3.5–6 years)**	Preschoolers have developed a number of skills (motor, cognitive, language, social, emotional) and are able to interact more effectively with others. They are very curious and more independent but are still learning to assume responsibility and self-control.	**Development of Initiative** Preschoolers need to be encouraged to solve their own problems and make their own choices. They need positive and consistent guidance. If preschoolers' choices and actions are valued, they will develop the initiative to try new challenges.	**Development of Guilt** If preschoolers' choices or actions are not valued, or if their activities are mostly directed, they may cease to try and become dependent on the adults in their environment. If their efforts are ridiculed or rejected, they may develop a sense of guilt.
Stage 4: **School-Age Years** **(6–12 years)**	Children at this stage learn academic skills such as reading and writing. Independence increases and friendships proliferate.	**Development of Industry** Children need to be encouraged to become independently productive, to strive for success and to enjoy intellectual activities in order to develop a sense of being a competent individual.	**Development of Inferiority** Children who have become dependent, need continual assistance to accomplish tasks and do not enjoy intellectual activities may develop a sense of inferiority.

Table 9.2 outlines the stages of social–emotional growth in infancy. These social–emotional milestones and those shown in subsequent tables can be used to help early childhood educators and families create observational tools to identify children's behaviour and evaluate their abilities, skills and progress.

Social–emotional growth starts at birth, with interactions between infant and care-givers, and rapidly develops into interactions with others. It is easy to miss the

TABLE 9.2 **SOCIAL–EMOTIONAL MILESTONES: INFANCY**

Age	Milestone	Importance
Birth–6 months	Differential crying	Signals different needs
	Cooing and babbling	Establishes communication patterns between infant and adult
	Attachment patterns formed	Develops sense of trust and security
	Social smiling	Provides opportunity for social interactions
	Differential reaction to different voice tones	Learns to recognize the mood expressed by tone of voice
	Initiating, imitating and maintaining interactions through use of body language and vocalizations	Learns to listen and develops skills of turn-taking
6–12 months	Selective smiling	Controls interactions with individuals of choice
	Social referencing	Opportunities for social interactions between infant and caregivers
	Beginning of stranger anxiety	Leads to selective social interactions
	Responding to stress of others	First indication of awareness of other individuals' feelings
	Using repertoire of gestures to indicate meaning	Initiates and maintains social interactions
	Enjoying attention	Initiates social interactions and expresses feelings through physical acts such as kissing and hugging
	Demonstrating assertiveness by refusing to do something	Development of autonomy
12–18 months	Peak of separation anxiety	Demonstrates increased awareness of own emotional needs and preferences
	Symbolic actions	May be used to initiate and maintain social interactions
18–24 months	Demonstrating empathetic responses to distress	Demonstrating greater awareness of others in the environment
	Using words to interact	Showing greater ability to interact socially with others
	Showing inability to share	May cause some anti-social behaviours

importance of some of these early interactions because of the infant's seeming help-lessness. Caregivers must learn to recognize the interactions for what they are, in order to identify possible problems and to nurture optimal social and emotional growth.

The toddler years are marked with a growth in autonomy. Social–emotional development at this stage is outlined in Table 9.3. Many toddler behaviours may be looked upon as inappropriate, such as the tendency toward non-compliance and the use of aggressive acts to gain what they want. However, these behaviours are developmentally appropriate and arise from the toddlers' inability to adequately express themselves or gain control over their own actions (see author's Reflection). Knowledge of developmental milestones is critical in planning and implementing appropriate social–emotional activities for toddlers.

Reflection

Reflection   *From the Author*

I observed a group of toddlers at play within a physical play group setting. Two of them actively explored their environment. The toddlers were closely observed by the early childhood educator. She seemed to know when she needed to step in. For example, both active explorers continually tried to climb a piece of equipment at the same time. Another two toddlers were lying on a blanket with a number of toys between them. One of these toddlers continually tried to take a toy away from his peer. Another adult quickly intervened to put an identical toy within reach of the "grabbing toddler." Each of these early childhood educators realized that the toddlers' behaviour was not a negative behaviour but simply a result of their developmental competency.

TABLE 9.3 **SOCIAL–EMOTIONAL MILESTONES: TODDLERS**

Age	Milestone	Importance
2 years	Responding verbally to other individuals' stress signals	Increased understanding of the feelings of others
	Starting to include other children in play activities	Start of social play interactions with peers
	Enjoying helping	Creates awareness of some social functions such as chores
	Decrease in physical aggression as communication skills improve	Demonstrates greater awareness of the use of symbolized forms (language) to interact
	Sharing and turn-taking still difficult	Causes anti-social behaviours
	Making demands and expecting compliance	Development of greater autonomy

The preschool years are the start of much pro-social behaviour, as indicated in Table 9.4, such as the formation of friendships and increased independence. Knowledge of social–emotional milestones will help identify possible problems and form the basis of an appropriate social–emotional learning environment.

Effects on Social–Emotional Behaviours in Inclusive Settings

Children's social and emotional behaviours are dependent on a variety of factors, including attachment patterns, child-rearing practices, background experiences,

TABLE 9.4 **SOCIAL–EMOTIONAL MILESTONES: PRESCHOOLERS**

Age	Milestone	Importance
3 years	Starting to share and take turns	Start of pro-social behaviour
	Participating in group activities	Ability to have interest in a group situation
	Defending possessions	Still finds sharing difficult
	Engaging in make-believe play	Start of ability to take on another individual's perspective
	Showing affection to peers	Greater awareness of own feelings in more socially acceptable ways
4 years	Using voice tone to express feelings	Increased ability to express feelings in more socially acceptable ways
	Showing pride in accomplishments	Greater self-awareness
	Ability to label feelings	Greater awareness of personal feelings
	Engaging in role play	Practice of familiar roles
	Rapid mood changes	Reaction to personal challenges such as frustration
	Starting to tell jokes and funny stories	Initiation of alternative reasons for communication with peers
	Striving for independence but easily frustrated	Leads to greater autonomy
	Start of friendships	Leads to ability to maintain relationships
	Possible taunting of peers	Has learned and imitates inappropriate behaviours
5 years	Sudden mood swings	Reacts to personal challenges but also to peer perceptions
	Need of approval from peers and adults	May lead to positive or negative self-image depending on reaction of peers or adults
	Start of moral development	Shows feelings of disappointment and self-criticism

temperament, special needs, social attributes and opportunities in the learning environment.

1. Attachment and Social–Emotional Development

Researchers have measured the attachment behaviours demonstrated in infants' responses to personal needs, potential danger or expectations. "The parent's overall pattern of behaviour toward the baby influences strongly the kind of attachment the baby will develop. Each attachment pattern seems to reflect different histories of parental response. When the parents respond sensitively to the baby's signals, the baby tends to become securely attached. When the parents respond inappropriately, or not at all, the baby tends to form an insecure attachment of some kind" (Schickedanz et al., 2001:236). Four different types of attachment behaviours have been identified: secure, ambivalent, avoidant and disorganized. The latter three categories describe the behaviours of infants who are not securely attached. The impact of attachment patterns in infancy continues to be demonstrated in later years. Expected behaviours of children who are not securely attached might include these:

- Crying more
- Playing less
- Engaging in fewer symbolic activities
- Showing more aggression and destructiveness in interactions with peers
- Showing more dependence on adults for attention and support
- Exhibiting a greater variety of challenging behaviours

2. Child-Rearing Practices and Social–Emotional Development

Child-rearing practices also influence the social behaviours of children. Children who are raised too permissively, without warmth or nurturance, or with high levels of control over their behaviours also exhibit social–emotional behaviours that affect their overall abilities over time. Children raised under these conditions are:

- Less self-reliant
- Less self-controlled
- Lacking in social skills to interact with peers
- More apprehensive of engaging in learning activities
- Likely to experience stress
- Less compliant

3. Background Experiences and Social–Emotional Development

Children are raised in many different environments. The type of social–emotional behaviours children might engage in can depend on the amount and types of stimulation they have previously received. Children who have never been exposed to certain situations, who have never been empowered to use certain tools or utensils, or who are not securely attached to their primary caregivers might find it difficult to adapt to a setting with choices that are foreign to them.

In Western cultures, the ability to read and write is highly valued. Not all children come from backgrounds that nurture this approach. There are a number of cultures, such as many Aboriginal and some Asian cultures, that favour verbal communication. Children from these cultures will not have the background experiences to utilize the many print-based resources within an early childhood setting. Child care providers will need to adjust expectations and strategies to create an enjoyable and positive environment for these children.

Children who have not had the relevant background experiences to engage in some learning activities may exhibit some of the following behaviours:

- Lack of interest in certain things, such as reading books
- Avoidance of certain learning areas, such as the writing, painting or book area
- Developmental lag in certain activities, such as knowledge of the alphabet
- Seemingly inappropriate social behaviours, such as lack of eye contact (considered rude in some cultures)
- Shyness or withdrawal
- Continual talking or interrupting
- Reluctance to initiate social contact
- Reluctance to show emotions

Caregivers need to learn to understand the behavioural expectations of the various backgrounds that the children are from. With this understanding, developmentally appropriate learning experiences can be developed and implemented.

Some children have grown up in backgrounds that are very enriching. These children often seem to be advanced for their age (gifted). The behaviours of these children may vary greatly. Typical behaviours may include:

- Desire to play with older children
- Boredom with activities
- Compassion and empathy for those around them
- Non-compliance
- Challenging of roles or expectations
- Preference for solitary play
- High energy levels
- Intense curiosity about everything
- Impatience with others
- Dislike of routines
- Interactions based on making rules and trying to get others to play by these rules
- Excessive self-criticism (Webb, 1995)

4. Individual Temperament and Social–Emotional Development

"Temperament is a set of in-born traits that organize the child's approach to the world. They are instrumental in the development of the child's distinct personality. These traits also determine how the child goes about learning about the world around him" (Child Development Institute, 2008). Temperament is thought to be an inherited trait. However, expressions of temperament can be modified by maturation, experiences and the environment.

One aspect of temperament that may influence children's behaviours is initiation. When young children are able to initiate their own learning activity, they develop intrinsic motivation (motivation that originates from the individual). Tasks that are intrinsically motivating are more likely to spur children on to learn with enthusiasm. When young children's learning is controlled by adults, children may:

- Become dependent on adults and require attention and encouragement to try different learning activities
- Be unable to regulate their own behaviour and as a result wait for others to initiate activities
- Lack the necessary self-confidence to try some learning activities

Another aspect of temperament that may influence behaviour is fear. Fear inhibits children from actively exploring the environment or activities within the environment. All children have fears; they are considered a normal part of childhood development. Children's fears can be caused by a variety of factors, real or imagined. Some fears are triggered by remembered events, such as falling off a tricycle; others may not have an obvious cause. Toddlers' fears tend to focus on separation from primary caregivers, sudden or unexplained noises, some animals and insects, being in the dark or taking a bath. Preschoolers' fears expand through their imagination to include fears of such things as monsters or ghosts, and potentially more justifiable fears of real-life events such as losing a parent, terrorist activity or war. Children express their reactions to fear through physiological and behavioural signals. Fear reactions could include:

- Physiological signals, such as sweating, increased breathing, increased heartbeat or tense muscles
- Avoidance or withdrawal from situations
- Refusal to participate
- Anxious behaviours, such as continually looking toward the source of the perceived fear or taking a detour around the object of the fear to get to another activity

Frustration is another aspect of temperament that may influence behaviour. Frustration can be caused by a number of social situations that are a normal part of growth and development. Children are exploring different roles and practising various social skills, such as maintaining relationships or showing affection appropriately. During normal social interactions, frustration may arise if the child is not understood, or if the child is rejected from a social situation. Children's frustrated behaviours may range from withdrawal to physical or verbal aggression against other individuals or things in the environment. Jamie had been told that she could not play with a group of her friends. As she stormed away, she shouted, "I hate you. I don't want to play with you anyway." She picked up one of the dolls the group was playing with, threw it and shouted, "Dolls are sissy stuff."

A fourth aspect of temperament that may influence children's behaviours is attention span. A significant factor in any childhood social situation is the length of attention span the children have. Children with long attention spans can maintain play with others over time. Children with short attention spans will find social activity and interactions difficult. These children may continually drift from activity to activity, interrupt interactions, avoid group activities or engage in challenging behaviours at times of stress.

5. Diagnosed Special Needs and Social–Emotional Development

Certain conditions such as attention deficit disorder (ADD), attention deficit hyperactivity disorder (ADHD), fetal alcohol syndrome (FAS) or fetal alcohol effect (FAE) make it much harder for children to engage in social interactions. Children with high needs usually demonstrate all of the socially challenging behaviours already listed.

Social Attributes in Inclusive Settings

There are a number of attributes of social behaviour that need to be considered when interacting with children and when organizing learning environments and activities. These include individual attributes, social-skill attributes and peer-relationship attributes (McClellan & Katz, 2001).

1. Individual Attributes

Individual attributes are those behaviours that children exhibit based on personal temperament, personal learned behaviours or developmental abilities (McClellan et al., 2001). Since all children have different characteristics, it is important to know the individual attributes of the children. This will give early childhood educators guidelines that help them:

- Plan for various social interactions to meet all children's needs
- Identify adjustments or adaptations needed to improve social interactions
- Develop strategies for children with challenges in emotional or social interactions
- Develop sensitivity to creating a social environment suitable for all individuals

Individual attributes include the following:

- Moods of children
- Dependency on adults
- Separation from adults
- Willingness to come to the centre
- Coping strategies
- Capacity to empathize
- Types of relationships with peers
- Types of interactions with peers
- Capacity for humour

2. Social-Skill Attributes

Social-skill attributes determine the types of interactions and skills the children bring to social situations. Through the use of these skills, children learn to interact positively, maintain relationships with other children and assert themselves as needed. Child care providers need to understand what types of skills are used by children, in order to facilitate and maintain positive interactions between individual children and groups of children. Children may use the following social-skill attributes:

- Ability to engage in positive or negative interactions with peers
- Ability to assert self:
  - To express preferences
  - To explain reasons for actions
  - To explain feelings (anger, frustration) effectively and appropriately
  - To be unintimidated by peers

- Ability to initiate contact with peers:
  - To approach peers
  - To negotiate and compromise
  - To seek to join groups successfully
  - To show interest in what others are doing
  - To accept all individuals
  - To engage in appropriate nonverbal interactions as needed

- Ability to maintain interactions:
  - To takes turns
  - To add to interactions by offering comments or suggestions, or asking for information

3. Peer-Relationship Attributes

Peer-relationship attributes refer to other children's interactions with a child. Children are either accepted or rejected by other children. They may be invited to engage in play activities with other children, or ignored. Caregivers need to be able to determine which children have social–emotional strengths and which children are often excluded to help develop strategies for social inclusion. Often, some conditions, such as autism, cause children to have extreme difficulties in developing and maintaining social interactions with peers.

Range of Behaviours in Inclusive Settings

Social and emotional behaviours within inclusive settings will include the full range of specific behaviours discussed already. In terms of their behaviours, children will fall into one of these categories:

- Children with a normal range of social–emotional skills
- Children with advanced social–emotional skills—These children will often act

as models for other children in the program. Identification and assessment of the skills of these children will help caregivers in several ways. Social settings may be organized to encourage peer modelling. They may also be organized to provide opportunities and encouragement for children to initiate contact with peers who may need help or encouragement to participate.

• Children who lack some social–emotional skills—Knowledge of the specific skills that the children do have will help caregivers when planning social settings based on these children's strengths. Caregivers will also be able to respond to spontaneous interactions in accordance with the specific needs of the children.

Interaction Patterns in Inclusive Settings

Guiding children's social and emotional interactions requires that caregivers have a firm understanding of expected social and emotional behaviours and set the stage for positive interactions to occur within the environment. Six principles to setting the stage—recognition of the complexity of social skills, reduction of mistaken behaviours, practices of positive adult–child relations, solution-oriented intervention methods, partnerships with families and a teamwork approach—will be discussed (Gartrell, 2004).

1. Recognition of Complexity of Social Skills

Gaining social–emotional skills is a lifetime achievement. With every new social setting, a new set of expectations and skills is acquired. Adults in children's lives need to recognize that the child is still learning. Adults set the stage on which social learning takes place. "The teacher takes a comprehensive approach. He seeks to understand the problem, modifies the child's program to reduce crisis, intervenes consistently but nonpunitively, builds the relationship with the child, involves the parents, teams with staff and other professionals, and develops, implements, and monitors a long-term plan" (Gartrell, 2004:30).

2. Reduction of Mistaken Behaviours

Many behaviours that children exhibit may be classified as mistaken behaviours, because they arise from the child's limited perspective of how to interact in social settings. Mistaken behaviours are behaviours that are attributed to a child and designated as a problem behaviour. However, these behaviours are not a problem; rather, they can be explained as a natural stage of development or as part of the child's background experiences. Very young children resort to aggressive behaviours such as grabbing or hitting. They have not yet gained the maturity in skills such as language or negotiation to enable them to interact more acceptably. Some children have had models of behaviours such as using inappropriate words in their background experiences. Children will try the social behaviours that they have within their repertoire. Adults need to understand that the child is not "misbehaving" but using behaviours that are based on his or her background experiences and understanding. Guidance needs to focus on modification of the behaviours through positive interactions and modelling. "When children's development, learning style, and family background become the main priority of the program, children become positively involved and feel less need to show mistaken behavior" (Gartrell, 2004:31).

3. Fostering Positive Adult–Child Relations

Photo 9.1

Put toys away.

As Erikson (see Table 9.1, page 292) has identified in his stages of psychosocial development, adults play a key role in setting a positive learning environment. Positive adult–child relations occur when adults:

- Establish limits—Often limits are expressed as rules, which can be stated in the negative—the emphasis is on something that cannot be done. However, limits should be stated in positive terms to guide behaviour. Instead of telling children what not to do, they should be told what to do. This is easily reinforced by placing picture and word messages in various centres as needed (Photo 9.1).
- Ensure that children understand the guidelines—Children need to be given explanations of why they should do something. Guidelines should make sense to them: "We wear a smock so that our clothes don't get dirty."
- Concentrate on reinforcing positive behaviours—Adults should be observing children carefully to anticipate a negative behaviour in order to prevent it. Jamie was watching the children play in the block area. He kept walking around them, getting closer and closer. Jamie usually engaged in solitary play. Other children often told him that he couldn't join their play. Corinne, an adult, had noticed Jamie's interest. She asked Jamie if he would like to play. Corinne told the children, "Jamie and I would like to play, too. What can we do?" The children quickly assigned roles to Jamie and Corinne. Corinne had accurately assessed the situation. She knew that Jamie wanted to join the play. She knew that the children would most likely reject his request. She made it more acceptable to the children because she also joined in their play. She also worded her request in a way that assumed that the children would be happy to include them. In this way, she was able to set up a positive experience for Jamie and the other children.
- Model appropriate behaviours and reinforce them when they occur—Charmaine greeted each of the children as they arrived in the morning. She had a smile on her face, remarked on something personal about each child and inquired pleasantly what he or she was going to do once in the preschool room.

4. Solution-Oriented Intervention Methods

Organization of the learning environment and learning experiences fosters individual and group problem solving. One aspect of organization involves making materials and equipment accessible and available. Storage should be arranged so that children can find the items that they want and use them appropriately. For example, children's dress-up clothes should be stored logically and visibly. Children are already familiar with how clothes are organized at home. Clothes can be put on hooks, hats on shelves and shoes on shoe racks. This offers a consistent scheme. Children are able to transfer information from one setting to another and in the process reinforce expectations in both. This, according to Erikson (see Table 9.1, page 292), will lead to the development of greater autonomy.

Another aspect is helping children find their own solutions to problems. Two children were starting to argue about who could use the cement truck. Corral told the children that she could see that they had a problem. She asked the children to tell her what the problem was. Jordan answered, "We both want the cement truck." Jill nodded. Corral said: "Hmm, that is a problem. You only have one cement truck and two people want to use it. What could we do about this problem?" Jordan thought and said, "We could play together. I'll use the dump truck and Jill can dump the cement into my truck." Jill smiled and nodded again. Corral said, "That sounds like a good solution. You both seem to agree." She continued to watch to see what would evolve.

Corral identified the problem to the children, asked them to help find a solution and then monitored them to make sure that they continued to interact positively.

5. Partnerships with Families

Collaboration with families is critical. Through this process, information can be shared about social behaviours in different settings, emotional adjustments to new experiences and joint strategies to guide behaviour. "Through positive notes home, phone calls, visits, meetings, and conferences, [the child care provider] builds partnerships. It is her job to build partnerships even with hard-to-reach parents" (Gartrell, 2004:32).

6. Teamwork Approach

All individuals who are interacting with the child need to be part of a team effort to reinforce positive social behaviours and ensure that the child's emotional needs are met. Some of the partners in this process might include a social worker, a psychologist, a music therapist or a resource consultant. Strategies should be planned as a team, involve all partners—including staff and family members—and be reviewed regularly.

Observing Children's Behaviours

Observations should be undertaken to identify the existing attributes of social behaviours within a group of children. Anecdotal records are well suited to this work, since most of the behaviours to be observed are related to the affective domain, and effective terminology—such as moods, dependency or separation—is open to interpretation. The terms are non-specific, but the behaviour needs to be clearly described, and therefore anecdotal records are appropriate tools (see Figure 9.2

FIGURE 9.2
Observing Individual Attributes

Name: Joanie   **Dates:** October 15, 16
Observers: Collaborative process between home and centre
Centre: Corral = C   **Home:** Mother = M

Attribute	Description of Behaviour	Setting	Circumstances
Mood	Ran up to Corral and gave her a hug, smiled	Upon arrival	M dropped her off
	Sat in quiet area, quietly reading book, laughed at pictures	15 minutes after arrival	C asked her what was the matter; she shook her head and turned away
Mood	At home—temper tantrum lasted 20 minutes	After we got back from day care	Was upset because I told her she was visiting her dad this weekend
Mood	Cried clung to M, threw self on floor in cloakroom and screamed for 15 minutes	After arrival at day care	Temper tantrum started when mother left
			Temper tantrum ended when Olira came and brought her favourite doll
	Clung to C when M came, refused to look at M, refused to get dressed to leave	At time of dismissal	M indicated that this was the week-end when she was dropping her off at her father's house

for examples). This type of record requires the observer to write down specific information about the child related to the criteria set. Individuals might ask a question such as, "What are the child's moods?" Records of just the moods would give an incomplete picture of what is happening. The particular mood might make more sense if analyzed in the setting and circumstances it occurred in.

This type of tool is useful in gathering information about individual children's ways of handling themselves in various situations. As new attributes are observed, they can be added to the chart as necessary. The chart should yield information about when certain behaviours might be expected and what might be a trigger. Joanie's parents are divorced. Her father has remarried. One of the triggers seems to be when she is told that she will be staying at her father's house. The staff and Joanie's mom continued to observe Joanie's behaviour, in order to confirm this pattern of behaviour or to reject it as an isolated incidence.

Additional information that could be observed includes play behaviours (see Chapter 6, page 206). Play is a form of social interaction. Noting how children play with each other provides caregivers with information on:

- What types of social interaction to plan for
- What types of materials to provide to encourage social interactions
- How to utilize spontaneous activities to encourage children's interactions

Observations of interest should centre on children's social activities (see Figure 9.3). Examples of such activities could include:

FIGURE 9.3

Observing Interests

Name: Liam, age 3.2 **Dates:** April 5, 6
Observer: Shane

Interest Area	Activity	Peers
Block area	Stacked blocks end to end on floor to create a race track; used small cars to push across track; pretended to be race-car drivers	Jonathan and Jake
Sand area	Construction vehicles; pretended to build a road	Jake and Matthew
Tricycles	Raced tricycles around track; pretended to be race-car drivers	Jake and Jonathan

- Pretend play
- Working together to complete a task
- Playing games
- Completing a project

This type of observation reveals some valuable information about Liam's interests and the types of social activities he is engaged in. It would appear that he has formed a closer relationship with two of his peers. The three boys share an interest in racing. This interest could be used to expand their play activity to other areas, such as water; other concepts could also be added to their play, such as different speeds on different surfaces.

Observation tools based on the developmental social–emotional milestones shown in Table 9.4, page 295, could be developed in order to identify milestones reached and also to use as a guide when determining if a referral is needed.

Individual Program Plans (IPPs)

The development of an IPP for education resembles that of the behavioural program plan outlined in Chapter 7, pages 234–240. Desired outcomes are usually used to specify social behaviours that need to be increased or decreased. An IPP (Figure 9.4) was developed for Dillon to help him increase his interactions with peers.

The results of the first week were discussed with the family and resource consultant. It was felt that good progress was being made and that no adaptations needed to be made at this time. Dillon's mother noted that she had set up a creative area on a table at home, and Dillon and his siblings (two boys) had painted a mural together this week. It was decided to bring the mural to the centre and display it to give Dillon a chance to talk about his artwork to other children.

IPP to Increase Interactions with Peers

Name: Dillon   **DOB**: January 8, 2000
Date: April 5, 2004

1. **Summary of Diagnosis**
   a) **Resource Consultant's Observations**
      i. **Type of Play**—Dillon tends to shy away from other children. He is observed mostly as an onlooker or in solitary play.
      ii. **Peer interactions**—If a peer enters Dillon's space, he usually gets up and leaves. He will participate in small group activity at story time and during music and movement activities. He avoids other group activities and will cry if staff tries to encourage him to join in.
   b) **Mother's Observations**
      i. **Peer interactions**—Dillon was always shy. He has had two heart surgeries already and may have to have another one. He spends a lot of time in the hospital recovering. The first operation did not succeed, so they had to do another one. He really doesn't play with any of the kids in the neighbourhood. I have invited the boys over to play with him, but that didn't work. I think the boys were too active. It scared him.
   c) **Day Care Staff's Observations**
      i. **Play Behaviours**—Dillon engages in solitary play in the book area, creative art area, small blocks and puzzles. He often watches the children build with the larger blocks from a distance but resists joining their play.
      ii. **Peer Interactions**—He does not seem to have formed any close relationships with the other children. They tend to leave him alone. He avoids children who are too noisy or too active. He will move to an opposite side of the room to play.

2. **Observations of Behaviours**
   Observations were conducted at home by the mother and at the day care centre by one of the child care staff. The process was also guided by the resource consultant.
   a) **Play Behaviours at Home**

Date: March 27–April 4, 2001   **Observer:** Mother

Play Activity	Description
Reading	Likes Dr. Seuss books; asked to have them read to him; father read book to him
Track and vehicles	Built a track for his small cars; his brother came and asked him if he could play; Dillon agreed, but when Danny started to change the track and move his cars quickly along the track, Dillon left to draw some pictures
Outdoor playground	Dillon's cousins came over and we went to the playground; Dillon sat in the sand and played by himself; he watched the boys play tag on the climbers

   b) **Play Behaviours at the Centre**

Dates: March 27–April 14   **Observers:** Mandy and Kaya

Solitary play	With books, puzzles, small blocks; listened to music; used rhythm instruments (drum, sticks) to play along to the songs on a Raffi CD
Group activity	Participates in music and movement activities: singing (knows all the words of the songs) and rhythm instruments (especially likes the drum); always joins group of children if a story is read or told
Observer activities	If play is too loud or too active will move to quieter spot and may watch the activity; watches large block play

FIGURE 9.4
Continued

3. Interests

Observers: Collaborative effort between home and centre
Dates: March 27–April 14

Interests	Description
Painting	Uses bright colours and covers whole page; creates a shape, then paints it in, very careful not to go over lines; then uses another colour and repeats the process; then fills in the gaps left with a new colour
Music and movement	Always participates in marching-band types of activities, if given a choice always uses the drum; will join a singing group; quickly learns the tunes and words of songs
Books	Likes to be alone to look at books or have an adult read to him; can read several of the simple books
Puzzles	Usually completes at least three puzzles a day
Small blocks	Builds towers and enclosures; sometimes uses his structures with farm animals; will dramatize farm scenarios

4. Number of peer interactions
March 27: 0—participated in rhythm activity but ignored other children
March 28: 1—parallel play with Cynthia with small blocks
March 29: 1—read a book to Cynthia
March 30: 2—sang songs with group of children; continued to sing with Jeremy after the rest of the children left; followed Jeremy to creative area and engaged in parallel painting activity

5. Base Line
Maximum number of interactions: 2

6. Goals
To increase the number of social interactions

7. Objectives
- **Weeks One and Two:** Increase the number of social interactions to two per day.
- **Weeks Three and Four:** Increase the number of social interactions to three per day.

8. Strategies
a) Set up the areas of interest to encourage parallel play (small blocks, puzzles); switch painting from easel to tabletop; provide more drums during rhythm play.
b) Observe Dillon and use spontaneous opportunities to engage him with peers.
c) Use Dillon's ability to read to encourage him to read to peers.
d) Move the small blocks closer to the large blocks to encourage Dillon to participate in large-block structures.

9. Evaluation of Dillon's Progress
Dillon's progress was charted daily.

Continued

Peer interaction: number of times Dillon was involved

	Solitary play	Parallel play	Onlooker	Other
Week 1	IIII	I	II—blocks	
	IIII	II	II—tag outside	
	++++	III	II—water play	
	III	II		Associative with Cynthia
	II	III		Associative fingerpainting

Guiding Social–Emotional Behaviours in Inclusive Settings

Adults need to observe the learning environment and interaction patterns, in order to encourage the active participation of all children. Often children may find it difficult to engage in social interactions because they may be:

- Too timid to join in
- Reluctant to share
- Exhibiting challenging behaviours that make it difficult for other children to join in
- Unwilling to take turns
- Avoiding communication
- Unable to give or read nonverbal messages (Macintyre, 2002:25)

Most children sometimes have difficulties in dealing with social situations. Adults need to be sensitive to these needs to foster social–emotional growth and development and to set up appropriate learning environments.

The first principle of organizing a social–emotional learning environment is to ensure that the environment is a safe and nurturing place in which children can interact in meaningful ways, express themselves freely and be supported in their actions and behaviours. Several steps should be considered when creating an emotionally secure social environment. These include providing opportunities for children to understand and accept individual differences, creating an atmosphere of mutual trust and cooperation, and observing the children to encourage social interactions.

1. Encouraging Acceptance of Individual Differences

It is human nature to perceive each situation and each individual from a personal perspective. Adults have the ability to analyze their perspectives and adjust them as needed. For example, Janine had never taught toddlers before. She was very nervous about her first morning in the toddler room. She planned an interesting welcome circle. She was dismayed when the toddlers were not interested in her activity and engaged instead in what she thought were inappropriate activities. After circle time, she asked her co-worker why her circle had not interested the children. Her co-worker explained that it was really not an age-appropriate strategy for toddlers. Janine researched developmentally appropriate activities for toddlers and changed her group time into an active participation experience. She was pleased to see how much the toddlers enjoyed the activity.

Children lack the ability to analyze and adjust their perceptions. A young child sees the world from his or her perspective. Adults often chuckle at the humorous notions that this creates: "Milk comes from trucks." "Grandmothers borrow other people's children 'cause they don't have any of their own."

Children's attitudes reflect their experiences: what they have heard, what they have seen and how they make sense of these experiences. Jeremy had never seen an individual in a wheelchair before. When Jodi arrived with her wheelchair, he was fascinated. He finally asked Jodi when she would get out of her chair so that she could play with him. Jeremy had not made the connection between the wheelchair and the inability to walk.

Early childhood educators need to create opportunities to involve the children in activities that will increase their understanding of the special needs within their environments. General activities might include:

- Providing books and display materials about children with various special needs
- Providing opportunities to ask questions
- Involving children with special needs in answering questions about their needs whenever possible
- Encouraging children to help find solutions to overcome barriers to active participation
- Involving families and other professionals in planning and reinforcing suitable activities

To help children fully understand the problems that children with disabilities might have, role-playing opportunities should be provided to simulate some disabilities. When children are actively involved, they are much more likely to understand the nature of the problem and to gain a more positive attitude toward the problem. Table 9.5 offers some suggestions for activities that are relevant for some specific needs. These activities should be followed with discussions about how the children felt. Children's efforts should be documented through documentation panels that reflect children's learning. Documentation panels could include photographs, written descriptions and the creative efforts of the children.

TABLE 9.5   ACTIVE ROLE PLAY TO GUIDE UNDERSTANDING OF SPECIAL NEEDS

Need	Description of Activities
Physical disability	Borrow child-sized equipment as needed such as a cane, crutches, braces or a wheelchair. For example, borrow wheelchair to give children an opportunity to explore what it feels like to use one.
Visual impairment	Create opportunities to participate in activities without sight. Simple activities include guessing what an object might be by using a feely box. Children may try to guess what sound they hear or where it came from without seeing the object that made the sound. Asking children to navigate using a blindfold should only be used as a choice activity. This activity may frighten some children. Provide books and signs in Braille.
Hearing impairment	Games could be set up to ask children to distinguish what they can hear when the sounds become very quiet. Involve children in short activities without sound such as watching a short video without sound. Provide some activities that include children in sign language such as singing and using sign language simultaneously.
Challenging behaviours	Provide acceptable alternatives to relieve feelings of frustration or anger, such as a pillow to scream into or punch in a corner of the room. Provide alternative activities that help release stress, such as pounding playdough or a work bench, or soothing activities such as water, finger-painting or sand. Discussions with children could focus on feelings and how to express feelings appropriately, noting that all feelings are appropriate but sometimes how they are expressed is not appropriate.
Low self-esteem	Foster self-esteem through: • Displays of children's creative efforts • Documentation of children's learning • Reinforcement of efforts • Encouraging children to help each other whenever possible • Encouraging discussion of individual abilities—Children need to gain an understanding that all people have things they do well, other things they do not do so well and some things they may need help with.

2. Creating an Atmosphere of Trust and Understanding

Children need to feel that they can express their feelings in a variety of ways, that their expressions of their feelings are respected, that their interactions are valued and that appropriate consistent guidance is provided.

Adults can use a variety of strategies to help them create an environment that encourages trust and respect for everyone. Strategies are outlined in Table 9.6.

TABLE 9.6   **CAREGIVER STRATEGIES TO ESTABLISH TRUST AND UNDERSTANDING**

Strategy	Example	
Learn to recognize and understand the various signals that children communicate	When Venice is unsure of a situation or of new individuals in her environment, she becomes quiet and observant, and puts her hands in her mouth. When her signals are missed, she starts to cry and withdraw from the situation.	
Know when to step in and when to let children solve their own problems	Lauren and Kamaya had been playing together. Kamaya saw Elsa and ran to talk to her. The two girls decided to go and pick daisies. Lauren became upset and ran away. She sat in the playhouse, visibly upset. Kamaya noticed that Lauren had gone. She looked for her and saw that she was in the playhouse and ran to join her. Kamaya asked Lauren if she would like to pick some more daisies with them. At first Lauren refused, but eventually she decided to join the girls. Pritti had observed her charges. She gave the girls an opportunity to try to solve the problem themselves.	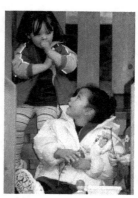
Acknowledge feelings and provide comfort	Michael had been hit by a ball while playing in the sandbox. This was not a serious injury, but Maureen understood that Michael's pain needed to be acknowledged. She put an ice pack on his head and reassured him that he would soon feel better. She also acknowledged his feelings by telling him that she knew that the episode had frightened him and that it hurt.	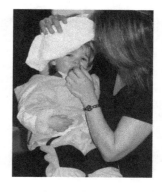
Provide the level of comfort a child needs	Jesse and Kaghu had been arguing about who had a toy first. They were trying to pull the toy away from each other. Kaya's attempts to help the boys solve their own problem were not successful. She said, "I think we should find something else to do. We could read a book or perhaps paint a picture." Both boys decided that they wanted to read a book. Jesse was still upset. He ran to get a book and then sat on Kaya's lap.	

TABLE 9.6 CONTINUED	
Strategy	**Example**
Share a child's accomplishments	Shannon had completed a drawing. She ran excitedly to show the children and Hardeep. Hardeep quickly took a photograph of her drawing. The drawing was framed and mounted on the bulletin board.
Help children as needed	The noise level around the creative table had escalated. Hardeep realized that the children needed some help to calm down. She sat down with them and started interacting. She referred to what they were doing and what colours they were using. The children became more relaxed and the activity continued.
Refer children to each other	Jonathan had built a structure with blocks. He was using some of the toy people and animals to place strategically on and in his structure. Emily watched him from a distance. She moved closer and closer to his activity. Monique noticed what Emily was doing. She said to Jonathan, "Emily is admiring your structure. Can you tell her what you are doing?' Jonathan replied, "I built a city. Now I am strategically placing things like vehicles, people and eventually trees in my city." Emily pointed. Monique said, "Emily would like to know what one of your buildings represents." Jonathan looked at Emily, smiled and said, "An office building. Do you want to get some trees and stuff to plant?" Emily wheeled away in her wheelchair and went to get the required things. Jonathan continued to involve her by asking her to retrieve items and asking her where they should be placed.
Interpret communications	Jocelyn tried to join a group of girls pretending to have a picnic. The girls said no because there wasn't enough room. Jocelyn picked up some toys and said, "There!" as she pointed to another area of the room. Kaya had noticed the interchange and quickly said, "Jocelyn is trying to tell you that there is room over there." The girls looked and said, "OK, let's move."

3. Observing to Encourage Social Interaction

In an environment that provides children with opportunities to engage in active play, make their own choices and interact with peers and adults, many opportunities arise to expand children's learning. If the caregivers have a good understanding of the children, these opportunities may be used as teachable moments. For example, on one occasion the children had built an obstacle course out of the hollow blocks. They were walking along the blocks and then jumping off at the end. Esta noticed that Rachel was watching the children. Rachel had difficulty with balance when walking or running, and so it would have been difficult for her to participate. Esta said

Photo 9.2

to the children, "I wonder how else you could move across the blocks. Do you have any ideas, Rachel?" Rachel said, "Crawl." The idea quickly caught on. Soon all the children were crawling, including Rachel (Photo 9.2).

Organizing the Social–Emotional Environment

The second organizing principle of any social–emotional learning environment is to ensure that the environment maximizes opportunities to engage in social–emotional activities. Inclusive settings need to be organized in a way that considers the familiarity of the children with various social activities, the stability and predictability of the environment and the promotion of independence.

1. Familiarity of Social Activities

Young children's activities should be based on their background experiences. Children need to be able to explore various roles of individuals or activities that they have observed, imitating and refining as the skills involved are practised and gain acceptance by others. Much of children's social play is based on symbolized actions and imitated behaviour. The ability of children to engage in imitative and symbolized play is largely dependent on the materials and learning experiences in their environment.

Very young children's play is dictated by the props around them. A child will use a bucket for filling or a spoon for stirring. Play is more likely to occur when the child is familiar with the objects that he or she is using. Familiar objects for young children include items that are used for everyday activities. To encourage imitative social play, the play environment should include realistic items associated with activities such as eating, sleeping, dressing, cooking, cleaning, driving, gardening and communicating.

Children naturally move from a dependence on props to using other materials symbolically. Children may use a curved block as a telephone, or use a stick to stir. Symbolic activity depends very much on the experiences children have had with real materials. As children manipulate the real materials, they learn about the materials' shapes, sizes and uses. They can then transfer this knowledge to new settings with new materials. The caregiver should take careful note of what materials are in the environment and place alternatives in other areas to increase children's ability to use situations symbolically. Some suggestions are included in Table 9.7.

2. Stability and Predictability

It is essential to establish stability in the environment; this provides children with continuity and comfort, so that they can learn where to find things and what experiences are possible in various settings. Continual changes to the configuration of learning spaces leads to fragmentation and sporadic activity. The emphasis needs to

TABLE 9.7 EXAMPLES OF MATERIALS FOR SYMBOLIC USE

Material	Purpose	Example	
Sticks of different sizes	Drawing, stirring	Benjamin used the popsicle sticks as road graders, the dowelling as the start of telephone poles along a road and logs as the ditch at the side of the road	
Various materials, including plastic sheets and materials from nature	Creating various scenes for dramatic play	Colin and Jordan decided to build a fishing camp in the sandbox. They created a river with blue plastic strips, leaves for an island, logs to sit on, toy boats, fishing poles and plastic shrubs.	
Boxes of various sizes	Encouraging group activity, dramatic play	Petra and Madison used boxes as part of their dramatic house play. They pretended the boxes were cars they used to do their shopping.	

be on children's continued social activity. Changes and adaptations should reflect learning needs and changing interests.

Figure 9.5 shows how, at the centre, the block area was originally organized. It had been observed that children used some of the manipulative materials in the block area. However, although the area received high use, all of the children had tended to use the blocks and the manipulative materials in the block area. The area became overcrowded and some challenging behaviours started to be observed.

The staff discussed some strategies. They realized that the children were actively using the area. The children were finding the materials they needed and were returning materials appropriately. The following changes (see Figure 9.6) were decided on:

• Increase the size of the area, but leave the configuration the same.
• Replace the open-sided shelf with two shelves, in order to limit access to manipulative materials from each side.
• Rearrange the manipulative materials.

The changes were effective. Children continued to actively use the block area. There was increased use of the manipulative area, and the challenging behaviours declined.

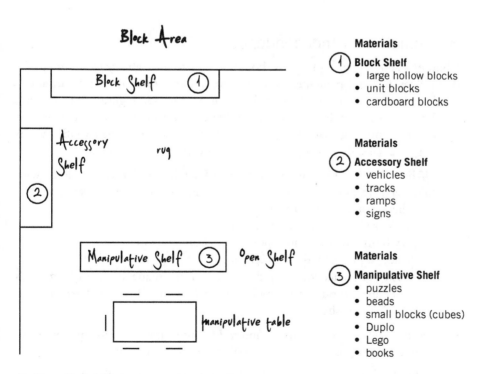

Materials

① **Block Shelf**
• large hollow blocks
• unit blocks
• cardboard blocks

Materials

② **Accessory Shelf**
• vehicles
• tracks
• ramps
• signs

Materials

③ **Manipulative Shelf**
• puzzles
• beads
• small blocks (cubes)
• Duplo
• Lego
• books

FIGURE 9.5

Initial Organization of the Block Area

Problems Observed
• block area became congested with items from manipulative shelf
• overcrowding in block area

FIGURE 9.6
Revised Floor Plan

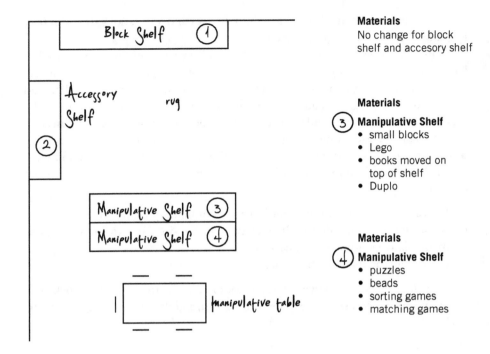

Materials
No change for block
shelf and accesory shelf

Materials

③ **Manipulative Shelf**
• small blocks
• Lego
• books moved on
  top of shelf
• Duplo

Materials

④ **Manipulative Shelf**
• puzzles
• beads
• sorting games
• matching games

3. Promotion of Independence

Children's activities and materials should maximize their ability to do things for themselves. General principles of setting up an environment to nurture independence include using appropriate labelling systems (see Figure 6.5, page 206), installing low, open shelves that are accessible to all children, organizing materials by type and ensuring that all areas remain free of clutter. Some specific factors relating to social skills directly influence the growth of independence:

• Self-help skills—Children love to help with adult tasks. Provide children with child-sized cleaning materials so that they can help in routine clean-up activities. These materials could include:
  ○ Child-sized brooms, dustpans and mops
  ○ Spray bottles of water and sponges to clean tabletops
  ○ A place to put dirty dishes after eating
  ○ A posted sequence for doing things, such as the sequence of washing hands
  ○ A container to put dirty supplies in, such as toys that have been sneezed on or dirty brushes

• Dressing skills—Children often find it difficult to put on dress-up clothes. To make it easier to use dress-up materials, try these strategies:

  ○ Put Velcro tabs on dress-up clothing to make it easier to fasten.
  ○ Cut down clothes to child's size so that there is less danger of tripping.
  ○ Avoid providing adult-sized shoes. These can cause tripping.

- Add elastics to waists of pants or skirts. This will make it easier to slip them on and keep them on.
- Provide similar clothes for dolls, in order to encourage children to use an actual sequence of dressing.

The third principle of organization for any social–emotional learning environment is to make any needed adjustment to the individual interest centres to maximize social–emotional activities.

4. Dramatic Play

Dramatic play activities lend themselves to social–emotional development. All levels of dramatic play provide for opportunities to plan for social–emotional growth (Crowther, 2007:176–177). Table 9.8 identifies the levels of dramatic play, the types of interactions to expect and specific examples of learning activities.

5. Music and Movement

Music is also particularly suited to social–emotional growth and development. Music can be used in a variety of ways, at individual levels of comfort and skill development, and in individual or group settings. Musical activities involve active interaction with materials, can involve interactions with others and can be used for different purposes, including relaxation, mood changing, skill development, active listening, active participation, concept learning (language, beat, rhythm, volume, tone and pitch), creativity development and, of course, simple enjoyment. "Music builds and strengthens bonds of trust and communication between adults and children. Music gives children a reference point, a way to respond appropriately. Simple songs, incorporated into daily activities, communicate without nagging or endlessly repeating directions. Since the children are already 'tuned in' musically, singing will capture their imagination. Transitions will be smoother and children will be more likely to remember the daily routines. Better yet, the children will begin to help each other by singing the songs together, as they anticipate the planned activity" (Ensign Baney, 2002:7).

- Music for relaxation—In the Loyalist College Curriculum Lab, music was used to calm children down when the activity level was too noisy. When soft background music was played from a variety of CDs (Gibbon & Gibbon, 1991; Gibbon & Gibbon, 1992; Milner, 1993), the children immediately calmed down, play became less noisy and harmony within the room was restored.
- Music to change the mood—It is an acceptable practice to play soothing music during sleep time. This technique can also be used to help children calm down or cheer up. Jeremy, a toddler, was very upset. Someone had taken his toy away. He was sobbing and clinging to the caregiver, Jennifer. Jennifer picked him up and sat on a rocking chair with him. She knew that he was too upset to listen

TABLE 9.8 **STAGES OF DRAMATIC PLAY**

Stage/Age	Interactions	Examples of Learning Activities
Stage 1: prop-dependent, imitative (1–2 years)	Imitation of facial expressions and actions	Play imitation games with objects or actions: "Put the cup on your head, on your head." Children can initiate the activity or follow the lead.
	Mirror play, parallel play	Set up dress-up activities (scarves, blankets) in front of mirrors to encourage imitation, interactions and self-awareness.
Stage 2: familiar roles (2–3 years)	Play involving roles that children have observed, such as those associated with household activities (cleaning, food preparation, meal times, personal care routines) trips or visits to doctor's office	Coordinate adjacent learning areas such as blocks and dramatic play to encourage use of materials in both settings. Josh had built a simple school bus with the blocks. He is the bus driver to pick up children to go to school. Other ways to coordinate learning areas include putting books in every area to encourage looking up information or to use as sources of ideas for extending play. Water and sand could be combined to encourage exploration of mixtures. Or provide mobile creative units that encourage social activity by encouraging drawing and painting in various areas of the room, such as making signs or documenting activities.
Stage 3: diverse roles (4–5 years)	Play that involves less familiar roles that children might have read about, heard about or seen on TV or in a movie. These include adventure roles, less frequently observed roles of familiar adults or roles from favourite stories.	Provide materials that can be easily converted to assume a variety of purposes, such as blankets, scarves and other dress-up clothes, fabric flowers, pieces of hose, pillows or boxes. Children will be creative in their interpretations. Emily, for instance, is a bride.
Stage 4: communicative-cooperative (5 years and up)	Various forms of dramatic play in which children create their own characters, scripts and props	After a visit from a police officer, the children re-created their own version of what to do if "some bad people" wanted to come into their house. They used a cage from the veterinarian's office dramatic-play area to act out their story.

to her words. She quietly sang his favourite songs to him. He gradually calmed down as he listened. Eventually he sang along with her.

- Music for skill development—"Each component of music affects a different part of the brain, e.g. a familiar song activates the left frontal lobe, timbre the right frontal lobe, a pitch the left posterior. One side of the brain processes the word while the other processes the music—activating the whole brain to ensure retention. Short-term memory has the ability to hold onto seven bits of information. If bits of information are bonded together as in a song, it can be processed as one piece. By condensing the information, the brain is able to receive and process more" (Harman, 2002:1). Thus, when we sing with children to encourage them to engage in activities, skill development is enhanced. Examples of songs are listed in Figure 9.7.
- Music for active listening—Listening is the first stage of music development. Involve children in various types of listening activities, such as singing a book (Siomades, 1999); listening to music or a song and playing along on a rhythm instrument; or listening to the words of a song such as "If You're Happy and You Know It, Clap Your Hands" and doing the actions.
- Music for active participation—Music is a natural combination with movement. It gives the child specific signals for how to move, such as fast or slow, or the type of movement, such as heavy or light. Children may move to an instrument played (drum, piano, guitar), to music played on a CD or to songs that are sung ("This Is the Way We Walk Indoors"). Providing props such as scarves, banners or flags encourages children to also become creative in how they move.
- Music for concept learning—Examples of concepts that could be learned include language concepts, speed and volume, self-awareness, responses to feelings or relaxation.
- Music for enjoyment—Children naturally enjoy music. In one preschool setting, the teachers used music in many ways to help children through transitions and

FIGURE 9.7

Examples of Songs to Sing During Activities

Pick an easy song that the children are familiar with. Adjust the words of their activity to the melody.

"Clean-up"
(sung to the tune of "Mary Had a Little Lamb")
[Child's name] picking up the blocks, up the blocks, up the blocks. [Child's name] picking up the blocks, and stacking them up high.

"Counting"
(sung to tune of "One Little, Two Little, Three Little Indians," during activities such as climbing stairs or setting the table)
One fork, two forks, three forks, four forks. Five forks, six forks, seven forks, eight fork. Nine forks, ten forks, put them on the table. Now we have ten forks.

to learn new concepts. One child, a four-year-old named Ted, was curious about everything around him. One day he was heard humming to himself, "I just love insects, I just love grass and I just love my friends." The children heard him and soon imitated him. Soon this became a regular part of the program.

6. Activities to Encourage Group Play

Alternative arrangements of standard activities such as sand and water may encourage more interaction between children. For example, when the sand was placed in shallow containers on a table, children interacted with each other to describe what they were doing. Raven said, "The sand is flowing through my fingers. I love the feel of it." Kamaya, who was busily decorating her sand with glass beads, responded, "I know. I like doing it at the beach. It's cool 'cause the sand is nice and hot." Lauren said excitedly, "Look! I made a weird face." The other girls stopped and looked at Lauren's creation and told her that it was "cool" and "weird" (Photo 9.3).

Creative activities can be set out on a table or the floor to encourage more children to participate and interact with each other.

Some strategies are listed here:

- Place a long piece of paper on a wall or the floor to encourage children to create a mural together.
- Provide large boxes and encourage children to decorate them and use them as playhouses.
- Take large papers along on field trips and ask children to record their impressions.

Photo 9.3

Learning areas in the room should be carefully monitored, so that caregivers can identify when changes or adaptations need to be made. Areas may need to be increased or decreased in size, depending on the interests or activites of the children. Caregivers may have to provide additional materials to maintain interest. The adaptation of the learning area should be based on the activities and interactions that children engage in.

7. Develop Social Stories

Social stories are used to provide children with details about social situations that are confusing. A confusing situation is explained in detail. Children gain information about a specific social situation through learning about:

- The social cues needed
- The events that typically occur
- The reactions of all the characters
- Responses that an individual might make

Many children's books are examples of social stories. Stories that deal with going to a doctor or going to the hospital, or stories about toilet training, are some typical examples. Caregivers could create a book that is personalized about events within a child care setting such as arrival, greeting time or snack time. The story could be illustrated with photographs of the individual child.

Role of the Early Childhood Educator

The role of the early childhood educator in organizing a social–emotional environment is primarily to create an atmosphere that provides children with safe and secure learning spaces and experiences, so that they can express their feelings and interact positively with each other and other adults. The early childhood educator's role comprises these functions:

- Being an active listener and encouraging active listening skills—Kaya listened to the children's interactions and interpreted what Jocelyn wanted to do. She was able to communicate Jocelyn's intent to the other children in order to involve Jocelyn in their interactions.
- Observing children's body language in order to respond appropriately—Children may not always express themselves with words. They may communicate using body language, as was evident with Emily's behaviour, when she observed Jonathan's play but needed Monique's help to join in the play.
- Providing opportunities for children to initiate and maintain activities—A table was set up outside for creative art activities (Photo 9.4). This provided opportunities for children to engage in creative activities, to share ideas and to set their own pace to complete what they wished to do.

Photo 9.4

- Observing children to identify behavioural causes such as fear or frustration. Kim was afraid to go outside because she was afraid of flying insects. She uses crutches to walk and finds if difficult to get away. But Kim agreed to go outside with her teacher, Melina, when Melina promised to make sure that none of these insects would land on Kim.
- Observing children to identify teachable moments—Esta utilized a teachable moment when she challenged the children to use alternative methods for crossing their obstacle course. This involved Rachel in a physical activity with the other children.
- Coordinating team efforts—The activities of the IPP were coordinated by Dillon's teacher. She set up regular meetings with staff, family and the resource consultant.

SUMMARY

Social and emotional behaviours are closely linked. When a child participates successfully within social settings, his or her emotional well-being is also improved. Caregivers must be aware of all the factors that influence social–emotional behaviours of children in order to:

- Understand each individual child's behaviour
- Plan an effective social–emotional environment for children
- Implement effective social interactions
- Be sensitive to children's emotional needs
- Collaborate effectively with families and other professionals

KEY POINTS

Healthy social interactions—Communicate, understand interactions, form relationships and express emotions

Social–emotional development
- Starts at birth
- Has predictable stages

Erikson's psychosocial stages
- Trust versus mistrust
- Autonomy versus shame or doubt
- Initiative versus guilt
- Industry versus inferiority

Effects on social–emotional behaviours
- Attachment
- Child-rearing practices
- Background experiences
- Temperament

Social attributes
- Individual attributes
- Social-skill attributes
- Peer-relationship attributes

Range of behaviours in inclusive settings
- Normal range
- Advanced social–emotional skills
- Delayed social–emotional skills, or lack of them

Guidance principles
- Recognition of complexities of social skills
- Reduction of mistaken behaviours

- Positive adult–child interactions
- Solution-oriented intervention methods
- Partnerships with families
- Team approach

Observing behaviour
- Anecdotal records
- Interests
- Checklist to observe milestones

Individual program plan—Background information, summary of diagnosis, observations, base line, goals, objectives, strategies, evaluation

Guiding behaviour
- Accepting individual differences
- Creating an atmosphere of trust and understanding
- Observing children

Organize the social–emotional environment—Familiarity, child developmental levels, stability and predictability, promoting independence

Learning activities
- Dramatic play—Prop-dependent, imitative, familiar roles, diverse roles, communicative-cooperative
- Music and movement—Relaxation, change mood, skill development, active listening, active participation, learning concepts, enjoyment

EXERCISES

1. Using the information developed in Tables 9.1, 9.2, 9.3 or 9.4, develop a screening tool for one age group that would help identify potential problems in social–emotional development.

2. In a small group, discuss and record major points about factors that affect social–emotional behaviours. Utilize the chart provided to facilitate your discussions.

Factor	How the Factor Affects Social–Emotional Behaviour
Attachment	
Child-rearing practices	
Background experiences	
Temperament	
Attention span	
Diagnosed special need	

3. Utilize the individual, social and peer relationship attributes on pages 299–300 to develop a screening tool for observing children. Implement the tool with two different age groups. How are the results different? What social behaviour differences did you observe in the two groups? Explain the differences.

4. Define mistaken behaviour. What type of mistaken behaviours might you find in a group of infants, toddlers or preschoolers?

5. Amy is a four-year-old. She has been diagnosed with ADD. She rarely interacts with other children. Describe a solution-oriented model that you might use to increase her peer interactions.

6. You are a staff member in a toddler program. You suspect that one of the children has a social delay. How would you confirm or deny your supposition?

7. You have been informed that a new child is to be admitted to your program. This child has cerebral palsy and is confined to a wheelchair. What steps might you take to prepare the children and the environment for the new child?

8. What strategies might you use to help a child who has been identified as gifted become more socially active?

9. Reflect on the roles of an early childhood educator in an inclusive setting. How are the roles similar to or different from settings that have not included children with special needs? Explain your answer.

10. Develop a social story about one routine within the day care centre.

REFERENCES

Child Development Institute. (2008). Temperament and Your Child's Personality [online]. Available at www .childdevelopmentinfo.com/development/temperament_ and_your_child.htm [11/24/2008].

Crowther, I. (2007). *Creating Effective Learning Environments.* Scarborough, ON: Nelson Thomson Learning.

Crowther, N., & Sommer, M. (1997). Building Social Relationships. In K. E. Kilbride (Ed.). *Include Me Too: Human Diversity in Early Childhood.* Toronto, ON: Harcourt Brace & Company Canada Ltd.

Ensign Baney, C. (2002). Wired for Sound: The Essential Connection Between Music and Development.

Earlychildhood.com [online]. Available at www.gym-boreeturkey.com/pdf/wired_for_sound.pdf [15/1/2005].

Gartrell, D. (2004). *The Power of Guidance: Teaching Social–Emotional Skills in Early Childhood Classrooms*. Clifton Park, NY: Thomson Delmar Learning.

Gibbon, D., & Gibbon, G. (1991). *Solitudes: The Classics*. Toronto, ON: Solitudes Ltd.

Gibbon, D., & Gibbon, G. (1992). *Solitudes: Peaceful Classics*. Toronto, ON: Solitudes Ltd.

Harman, M. (2002). Music and Movement: Instrumental in Language Development. Earlychildhood.com [online]. Available at www.earlychildhoodnews.com/earlychild-hood/article_view.aspx?ArticleID=601 [11/1/2005].

King, E., Chipman, M., & Cruz-Janzen, M. (1994). *Educating Young Children in a Diverse Society*. Boston: MA: Allyn and Bacon.

Macintyre, C. (2002). *Play for Children with Special Needs*. London, UK: David Fulton Publishers.

McCain, M., & Mustard, F. (1999). *Early Years Study Final Report*. Toronto, ON: Publications Ontario.

McCain, M., & Mustard, F. (2002). *The Early Years Study*. Toronto, ON: The Founders' Network.

McClellan, D., & Katz, L. (2001). Assessing Young Children's Social Competence. ERIC Clearing House on Elementary & Early Childhood Education [online]. Available at www.vtaide.com/png/ERIC/Social-Competence-Checklist.htm [12-8-2004].

Milner, D. (1993). *Mystical Call of the Loon*. Plymouth, MN: Metacom.

Schickedanz, J., Schickedanz, D., Forsyth, P., & Forsyth, G. (2001). *Understanding Children and Adolescents*. Fourth Edition. Needham Heights, MA: Allyn & Bacon.

Siomades, L. (1999). *The Itsy Bitsy Spider*. Honesdale, PA: Bell Books.

Webb, J. (1995). Nurturing Social–Emotional Development of Gifted Children. The ERIC Clearinghouse on Disabilities and Gifted Education [online]. Available at www.ericdigests.org/1995-1/social.htm [27/01/05].

10

CHAPTER

Cognitive Growth in Inclusive Settings

"Play is the way children learn what no one can teach them. It is the way they explore and orient themselves to the actual world of space, time, of things, animals, structures, and people. By engaging in the process of play children learn to live in our symbolic world of meaning and values, at the same time exploring and experimenting and learning in their own individual ways" (Landreth, 2002:10).

Learning Outcomes

After studying this chapter, you will be able to:

1. Identify and discuss the importance of Howard Gardner's theory of multiple intelligences.
2. Identify stages of cognitive development in the various age groups.
3. Identify the variations of children's cognitive behaviours in an inclusive setting.
4. Explain how variations of children's cognitive behaviours may affect children's abilities.
5. Discuss the importance of forming partnerships.
6. Identify and discuss various methods of observing cognitive behaviours.
7. Explain why a portfolio is an appropriate tool to document cognitive behaviour.
8. Identify and discuss how to set up an environment to enhance cognitive growth.
9. Describe the role of the adult in fostering children's cognitive development.

Introduction

How intelligence develops has been disputed for a long time. For many years, it was thought that intelligence was inherited and could not be altered. John Locke (1632–1704) believed that a child was born with an "empty mind." He compared the mind of a newborn to an empty slate (tabula rasa) that experience writes on (Landry, 2004). In the 1960s, it was believed that most behaviours were learned through a system of rewards and punishments (behaviourist theory; Berk, 2009). This theory was followed by social learning theory, built on the behaviourist theory but including the use of imitation and modelling. Jean Piaget (1896–1980) developed the constructivist theory, which was based on the notion of learning through stages of cognitive development (Piaget, 1962). Piaget's theory clearly recognized the interplay between nature and nature. Stanley Greenspan sees intelligence as routed in emotional well-being. He states that "the emotions are in fact the architects of a vast array of cognitive operations throughout the lifespan. Indeed, they make possible all creative thought." Modern theorists believe that intelligence is shaped by both heredity and the environment.

One modern theorist, Howard Gardner, proposed that there is no single entity of intelligence but that there are seven different types of intelligences: linguistic, logical-mathematical, musical, bodily kinesthetic, spatial, interpersonal and intrapersonal (see Table 10.1). Although Gardner's theory has been disputed by many academic psychologists, it has received wide acceptance by educational theorists, teachers and policy-makers within the educational system. This acceptance reflects the fact that "the theory validates educators' everyday experiences: students think and learn in many different ways. It also provides educators with a conceptual framework for organizing and reflecting on curriculum assessment and pedagogical practices. In turn, this reflection has led many educators to develop new approaches that might better meet the needs of the range of learners in their classrooms" (Smith, 2002:20).

Gardner's theory of intelligence clearly focuses on the change in thinking today. Children need to learn within inclusive environments that foster opportunities to grow in all domains: social, emotional, physical, communicative and cognitive. Cognition is the underlying glue that binds all development together. "We know that learning and memory are strongly connected to emotions, and thus, the learning environment needs to be both stimulating and safe. Classroom experiences can be designed to allow children to investigate, reflect, and express ideas in a variety of ways that are increasingly complex and connected. Gardner proposed that each individual draws on multiple intelligences and generally relies on some more than others (Gardner, 1993). Thus, learners need ample opportunity to use and expand upon their preferred intelligences as well as to adapt and develop other intelligences which are all interdependent within one brain" (Rushton & Larkin, 2005:21).

Cognitive Development

Cognitive development is evident through the interactions of children with others and the materials and equipment within their learning environments. The stages of cognitive development may be inferred through these interactions. Although children tend to go through similar stages in cognitive development, the timing and rate of progress through these stages is varied and depends on background experiences. It is important to know what some of the typical behaviours of the various age groups are in order to learn:

- What types of behaviours might be demonstrated by each age group
- How these behaviours might be interpreted
- What types of observation tools might be developed
- How to encourage cognitive growth and development

TABLE 10.1 **GARDNER'S THEORY OF MULTIPLE INTELLIGENCES**

Intelligence Type	Description
Linguistic	• Learns and uses language effectively • Understands and uses verbal and symbolized language such as body, signed and written language • Uses language creatively Example: Yasmine's story—see Figure 10.1.
Logical-mathematical	• Performs mathematical operations such as addition and subtraction • Explores materials and the environment to find out why or how things work • Solves problems • Uses reasoning in an orderly, sensible fashion Example: Billy decided to see which pail of sand was heavier. The scale that was in the room was too small. He decided to bring his bathroom scale from home to see which pail was heavier. He could not read the numbers on the scale but was able to explain, "It's heavier if the little line goes more this way" (pointing to the right).
Musical	• Follows musical patterns such as beat and rhythm • Recognizes differences and similarities in musical elements such as pitch, tone, mood, tempo and rhythm • Creates simple rhythms, songs or tunes • Learns to play a musical instrument Example: Wolfgang Amadeus Mozart played the harpsichord by age three, composed solos for the harpsichord by age four and produced his first symphony by age eight.
Bodily/kinesthetic	• Uses body or parts of body to solve problems in gross-motor activity such as climbing, moving or moving around obstacles • Coordinates mental abilities and bodily movements Example: Madison started formal gymnastic classes at age three. By age four, she could walk across the balance beam, somersault and swing on the bars, jump from the trampoline to land on various parts of her body and hang upside-down from the rings.

TABLE 10.1 **CONTINUED**

Intelligence Type	Description
Spatial	• Uses different sizes of spaces appropriately for movement • Recognizes and uses spatial terminology correctly Example: As Josh was putting the animals in different containers, he signed "in," "out," "on top of" and "beside" correctly.
Interpersonal	• Uses effective social skills that include understanding of the desires, motivations and intentions of others Example: Melanie, age four, saw that Jamie, one of her peers, was crying. She correctly interpreted the situation to mean that Jamie was sad because she wanted the same toy as another child's. Melanie got her a pail that was the same colour and size and said, "See, now you have a pail 'xactly the same."
Intrapersonal	• Understands self: fears, feelings and personal motivations Example: Joanie, a five-year-old, created a book of drawings inspired by her personal feelings. She used the book to "get rid of my sad and angry feelings."

FIGURE 10.1

Yasmine's Story

Yasmine decided to create a storybook by dictating a story on most days. The following is an example of one of her stories.

I feel like being creative today.
I am going to illustrate my story with lots of pictures.

My mommy and I are in this picture. The small one is me and the large one is my mommy. We look alike because we have red dresses on.

1. Infant Cognitive Development

Infants are at the sensory motor stage of development. Learning during the sensory motor stage involves exploring the learning environment through the use of all the senses. In the first few months, much of the infant's behaviour is reflexive. As the reflexes disappear, the infant's behaviours become more deliberate and purposeful. Infants learn about their world through manipulation, listening, observing and interacting with individuals in their environment (see Table 10.2). Learning is cumulative. Skills and knowledge gained at one level will continue to be used and refined at subsequent levels of development.

TABLE 10.2 INFANT COGNITIVE DEVELOPMENT

Age Range	Skill	Description of Behaviour
Birth–1 month	Random manipulation	Swats at items; grasps reflexively at items near hand
	Observation	Follows objects slowly if held close to face
	Preferences	Prefers familiar voices, sweet tastes; turns away from strong, unpleasant odours
	Memory	Turns toward familiar voices
1–6 months	Visual perception	Looks at various parts of face—eyes, mouth
	Preferences	Prefers high contrasts such as black- and -white patterns, familiar faces or voices, soothing music such as Mozart, Vivaldi and Brahms; familiar odours
	Memory	Remembers familiar objects, individuals, voices; demonstrates understanding of how to keep toys in motion, such as hitting mobile to make it move
	Imitation	Imitates familiar gestures such as waving bye-bye, sticking out the tongue, making sounds
6–12 months	Imitation	Imitates new behaviour if it is familiar, e.g., pat-a-cake
	Interactions	Repeatedly drops item, looks for it, then waits to have item returned
	Object permanence	Searches for completely hidden object
	Preferences	Prefers to look at things that have more detail, such as scrambled faces
	Trial-and-error learning	Tries a variety of ways to make something work, such as trying to place a circular shape into each hole of a shape sorter until it fits
12–18 months	Reciprocal play	Includes others in play activity, such as an adult building a block tower and the child knocking it down
	Pointing	Points to objects or pictures to request information or answer question, e.g., "Bring the ball, please."
	Following simple directions	Child brings ball when requested to get ball
	Pretend play	Pretends with familiar objects such as stirring with a spoon
	Understanding causality	Starts to understand cause and effect, such as banging on a lid will make a noise

2. Toddler Cognitive Development

Toddlers actively explore their environment in order to learn about people and things and how to make things work. They demonstrate their new understanding of their world through unique mental representations. These representations start to be expressed in various ways, including:

- Actions, such as shrugging their shoulders if they don't know something
- Language, such as giving labels to items or using language to express thoughts
- Symbolized play, such as the use of a hand and appropriate noises to represent a digger in the sand
- Body language, such as jumping for joy or dancing to music

Toddlers continue to build on the skills and knowledge gained throughout infancy to practise new tasks and or refine existing ones (see Table 10.3). Toddlers view their world from their own perspective, and consequently many of their skills reflect the absence of a skill in another area, such as an inability to share.

3. Late Toddler/Early Preschool Cognitive Development

As toddlers gain more control over their bodies and learn more communication skills, their cognitive development also becomes more evident. They start to remember and use background experiences to solve problems. They begin using the

TABLE 10.3 **TODDLER COGNITIVE DEVELOPMENT**

Age Range	Skill	Description of Behaviour
18–24 months	Object permanence	• Continues to look for an object even if the location is unknown; for instance looking for a favourite toy in common places such as a drawer or toy box
	Deferred imitation	• Copies behaviours previously seen, such as scratching head to indicate puzzlement or smacking the lips to indicate that something is delicious
	Pretend play with familiar objects	• Pretending to do such things as use a phone or drive a car
	Functional relationships	• Demonstrates understanding of common relationships between things, for instance placing a spoon with a bowl or standing up a doll beside a chair
	Functional play	• Takes thing apart and puts them together
	Matching	• Finds things that are the same, such as two red cars
	Sorting	• Starts to put like things, such as red cars, together, but easily confused and may switch—For example, Jamie was lining up cars. But as he lined up a red car, he noticed a red plastic bear and switched to lining up bears.
	Inabilities	• Unable to share ideas and or materials, or to take another person's perspective—For example, Jordan held up a painting he had done to show his teacher, but he held the painting facing him.

TABLE 10.4   **LATE TODDLER/EARLY PRESCHOOL COGNITIVE DEVELOPMENT**

Age Range	Skill	Description of Behaviour
24–36 months	Symbolic activity	• Increased use of objects to represent other, unrelated objects, such as a block to represent a telephone
	Theme play	• Pretend play is related to known activities such as washing babies, cooking or cleaning
	Prop-dependent play	• The props available give direction to the type of play engaged in—For example, Jenna was in dramatic play area. She saw a whisk and some bowls. She immediately pretended to make scrambled eggs.
	Sorting	• Objects are grouped together by function, such as things we eat or things we wear
	Inabilities	• Unable to understand different perspectives from their own; to think in abstract thoughts; or to distinguish what is real and what is not—For example, Jonathan noticed a stone tumbling down a stream and was upset because he thought it was getting hurt.

names of other individuals and labelling objects in their environment. They also learn to recognize other means of communication, such as books and music.

Toddlers' play is rich in symbolic and imitative actions. As toddlers mature, they increasingly substitute objects for other things in pretend play. Actions are used to represent ideas and/or communicate intent. As toddlers grow into the preschool years, they move from sensory motor activity into preoperational thinking—they begin to demonstrate their knowledge of the world around them through symbols such as words. Thinking during this stage is inflexible and tied to the situation the child is involved in. For example, Christopher saw a harvest moon in the evening sky. He said excitedly, "Look, my mommy. There is the sun." His mother replied, "It's the moon, Christopher." Christopher thought about it and said, "No, my mommy, it is the sun. It is big, round and orange. It is the sun. OK, my mommy?"

Cognitive development is dependent on the experiences and interactions that children are exposed to. As children grow and develop, differences in their cognitive abilities become more individualistic and varied. Typical abilities are listed and described in Table 10.4.

4. Preschool Cognitive Development

Preschoolers continue to practise preoperational thinking. Children at this stage see the world mostly from their own perspective, but by the end of the preschool period they gradually become aware of different viewpoints. Preschoolers continue to build on previous skills. Play activities become more social, and children expand upon their abilities to engage in symbolic activities. As children continue to actively explore their learning environments, emergent skills are practised and refined. Table 10.5 outlines some of the additional cognitive skills children gain during the preschool years.

TABLE 10.5   PRESCHOOL COGNITIVE DEVELOPMENT

Age Range	Skill	Description of Behaviour
3 years	Counting	• Uses conventional words • Counts to five by rote
	Comparison/Seriation	• Solves nesting cup problems by comparing each size and placing it in or on top of the next size; may miss some cups in the process
	Labelling	• Starts to recognize and name geometric shapes: circle, triangle, square
	Dramatic play	• Pretends with realistic scenarios such as dressing a doll and taking it for a walk in a stroller
3.5 years	Counting	• Counts five objects without error
	Drawing	• Draws shapes (triangle, square, circle) and letters
	Sorting	• Sorts by single dimensions: colour, size or shape
	Comparison	• Identifies size differences: larger or smaller
	Inabilities	• Has difficulty distinguishing false beliefs; understanding different perspectives; classifying by more than one attribute; and patterning such as forming a consistent pattern (e.g., red bear, blue bear, red bear, blue bear). Also has difficulty with seriation, such as consistently ordering items by size; observation, such as recognizing that quantities remain the same even when the container changes; and abstract thinking (thinking is restricted to situation)
4 years	One-to-one correspondence	• Uses one-to-one correspondence to form rows of objects of equal length
	Reading	• Recognizes name in print
	Writing	• Prints name; recognizes some printed words; may read simple books
	Seriation	• Stacks up to five objects in increasing order of size
4.5 years	Counting	• Counts up to 15 by rote
	Patterning	• May start to create simple patterns but is inconsistent
	Different perspectives	• Starts to understand false beliefs—may say, "This is just pretend"; identifies feelings in others
	Classification	• Classifies using more than one attribute
	Inabilities	• Unable to understand conservation of mass, volume or weight, or to think abstractly
5 years	Classification	• Classifies using one defining attribute, e.g., food, animals, vehicles
	Concepts	• Combines shapes to create new shapes, such as putting two triangles together to form a square
	Number and letter recognition	• Identifies similarities and differences in items, for instance, matching letters that are the same • Orders objects, for instance by size or identification of first or last • Recognizes written numbers to 10

TABLE 10.5 CONTINUED		
Age Range	**Skill**	**Description of Behaviour**
5.5 years	Conservation	• Recognizes that sets of numbers are the same even when arranged differently
	Counting	• Counts 20 objects without error
	Concepts	• Understands mathematical concepts such as half, more, less
	Patterning	• Forms consistent simple patterns
	Inabilities	• Unable to understand conservation of mass, volume or weight, or to classify using more than one attribute; incapable of abstract thinking

5. School-Age Cognitive Development

Children in their school years, aged six to twelve, demonstrate concrete operational thinking. "Children begin more and more to use logic and mental operations to understand situations and to think about how things work" (Schickedanz, Schickedanz, Forsyth & Forsyth, 2001:439). For example, Janine, a seven-year-old, counted 10 birds sitting on a telephone wire outside. She also counted three birds that flew away. She then identified that there were only seven birds left.

During the school-age years, children make dramatic gains in cognitive development. They learn to:

- Think more logically—For instance, they may decide not to do something because the consequences of the action are not desirable.
- Use abstract reasoning—This is most evident in their ability to add, subtract, divide and multiply, and to take on and understand different viewpoints and perspectives.
- Gain increased ability to use symbolized forms—Examples include increased reading and writing skills, and greater facility with mathematical symbols.
- Begin to recognize and use time appropriately—John found the quickest way to get to school by timing himself to see how long it took him to get there.
- Use rehearsal strategies to increase ability to remember, such as repetitive practice of skills
- Play strategy games—Examples include Monopoly and Scrabble.
- Summarize information without including irrelevant information (for an example, see Figure 10.2)
- Understand conservation
  ◦ Six-year-olds: conservation of number
  ◦ Eight-year-olds: conservation of area
  ◦ Nine-year-olds: conservation of weight
  ◦ Eleven-year-olds: conservation of volume

Christine's Book Report (age 9)

The book I read was The Three Little PUA'A written by Sherry Forkum.

This story is really the story of the Three Little Pigs. It takes place in Hawaii. Instead of a wolf, there was a scary creature Mo'o. A Mo'o is like a giant lizard. The rest of the story is the same except that the Mo'o was tricked into falling into a trap filled with hot lava rocks. He disappeared after eight hours.

I read this book because I like different versions of fairy tales.

In summary, cognitive development is demonstrated through children's actions and behaviours. Although predictable stages can be identified, children pass through these stages at varying rates and at different ages. Cognitive development is dependent on the experiences children have in various tasks, such as problem solving, interacting with others to identify solutions or to explain a process used in collaborating with other children and adults. It is also affected by various experiences and conditions, such as individual life experiences, degree and type of disability, individual attitudes toward learning. cultural expectations and exposure to learning opportunities.

Range of Cognitive Behaviours in Inclusive Settings

Within any inclusive setting, a wide range of cognitive behaviours will be evident. Ranges in cognitive behaviours include children's ability to understand the world around them, to act on the learning environment and to interact with others.

1. A Child's Understanding of the World

Children's ability to understand the world around them is based on their knowledge, skills, interests, background experiences and abilities. Specific behaviours that might be observed include:

- Inability to find appropriate learning activities—Jamie wandered around from area to area. He had roamed around the room twice before he decided to stay in the water area. There, Jamie grabbed one of the bubble wands from one of the girls. Instantly an argument erupted. The girl tried to grab back the wand, shouting, "I had it first." Jamie had a tight grip on the wand, and as the two children struggled, the wand broke. Jamie fell down and started to cry. Sue, the early childhood educator, came over. She checked to see if Jamie was hurt and consoled him. She brought out two new wands for the children to use. When Jamie tried to create bubbles with his wand, he was not successful. He tried to

Photo 10.1

grab another wand from another child. Sue quickly came over and indicated that he already had a wand, but in frustration he threw his wand on the floor. He was redirected to another activity. Jamie obviously had difficulty trying to find something to do. He was attracted to the bubble play but lacked the skill to use the materials successfully.

- Inappropriate use of materials—Jordan was trying to fit a puzzle piece into the appropriate slot. He was unsuccessful. He ran over to the carpentry area and grabbed a hammer. He proceeded to try to hammer the puzzle piece into place. The vibration of the hammer hitting the puzzle caused the puzzle piece to shift and land in the correct slot. Jordan immediately tried another piece. When he hit this one it broke.

Photo 10.2

- Inappropriate use of equipment—Samantha was five. She had been in this particular day care since she was two. The playground was used by all age groups. Samantha climbed up the slide instead of climbing up the stairs. She was redirected. She went over to the climber and climbed on top of the tube tunnel connecting two areas. She was again redirected. Samantha obviously had excellent motor abilities. The existing climbing structures no longer challenged her abilities, so she created her own challenges.

Photo 10.3

- Lack of understanding of how to use materials—Michael picked up a pair of scissors and looked at them. He watched the other children cutting. He picked up a piece of paper and tried to cut it without opening his scissors. Eventually he gave up and put the scissors down.
- Frustrated behaviours—Michael came back to pick up the scissors again. Once more he tried to cut without opening his scissors. Finally he threw the scissors on the floor and ripped up his paper. Alice, another child, was at the puzzle area. She took out all the puzzles and put them on the table. She gave a big sigh. Her caregiver asked her why she didn't pick one puzzle. She replied, "I can't find one I like. They are all too easy."
- Self-expression through various forms at various levels of ability:
  - Art (Photos 10.1 and 10.2)
  - Movement (Photos 10.3 and 10.4)
- Creation of intricate structures or scenarios—Ben, a four-year-old, created a structure of three towers in the block area. He placed toy insects according to types on the various towers (see Figure 10.3).

Photo 10.4

2. Acting on the Learning Environment

Children demonstrate their cognitive abilities through their interactions with the environment. Their acts represent their knowledge about the world:

- Various ability levels—Mikayla (see Photo 10.1) and Michael (see Photo 10.2) demonstrate their ability to draw at different skill levels.
- Various degrees of problem solving—Dillon wanted a toy, so he tried to take the toy from someone else. In contrast, Nick wanted to expand his

FIGURE 10.3

Observation of Ben's Insect Towers

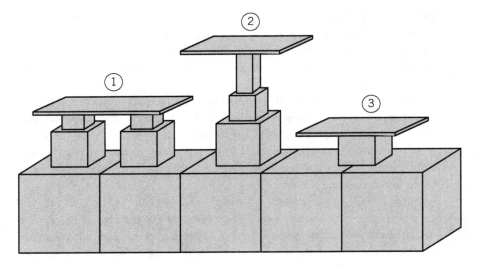

Ben organized the insects according to the following criteria:

(1) Large flying insects—dragonfly, butterfly, moth, bumblebee

(2) Small flying insects—bees, ladybugs, flies, flying grasshopper

(3) Crawling insects—ants, aphids, walking sticks

flower garden, so he asked to go to the storage room to find materials for his garden.

- Varying ways of utilizing the space—When the children went to the large gym, they behaved in various ways. Some children immediately started to run around the room. Others picked up a piece of equipment, such as a hoop or a ball, and started to play with it in a more confined area.
- Varying ways of using materials—Kim played in the sand by creating various structures with moulding containers, whereas Jodi used similar containers to fill and dump the sand.
- Varying approaches to learning—Timmy completed a six-piece puzzle through trial-and-error learning (learning by trying different techniques until one that works is found). Tammy completed the same puzzle by looking at each piece, finding the shape of the piece on the puzzle board and placing the piece into that slot.
- Background experiences—Braelyn could name all the shells in the collection in the room. Michael had difficulty finding two shells that looked the same. Braelyn had just returned from a holiday at the beach. She had not only added additional shells to the collection but also brought a book to identify them. Michael had not had any past experience with shells, nor had he expressed an interest in them or manipulated them.

3. Interactions with Others

Children's understanding may also be expressed in the way they interact with others. Children range in their ability to interact through:

- Type of play engaged in—Solitary to cooperative
- Ability to follow directions—Ranging from inability to follow simple directions to ability to follow complex directions
- Ability to initiate and maintain interactions—Ranging from inability to exceptional ability

Children may also experience difficulty in these areas:

- Knowing what to do
- Being able to make suggestions to take the game forward
- Short-term memory—not remembering what happened before, poor verbal skills (e.g., limited vocabulary), remembering what was said
- Ability to follow the rules of the game (Macintyre, 2002:25)

Effects of Various Cognitive Behaviours in Inclusive Settings

The presence of varying ranges of cognitive abilities affects all learning areas in the room. It may affect children's ability to do certain things:

- Understand directions—Therefore children may have difficulty remembering routines
- Play effectively with peers or the materials within the learning environment
- Negotiate for themselves
- Solve problems
- Find appropriate challenges
- Sustain activity over time

The learning environment needs to be structured and organized in order to address the range of abilities of all the children. This requires that there are enough materials to interest and challenge all abilities. The materials must be organized to maximize children's ability to find and succeed in self-directed tasks.

Caregivers must model and scaffold appropriate interaction patterns. Scaffolding refers to "verbal interaction between teacher and child that helps the child to solve a problem, carry out a task or achieve a goal beyond efforts that are unassisted" (Genisio & Drecktrah, 2002:43). "Modelling" means "physical demonstration, showing the child what needs to occur, while demonstrating the activity to the child" (Genisio et al., 2002:43-44). When scaffolding and modelling are combined in any circumstances, learning is nurtured and enhanced. For example, Jonathan noticed that Michael was having difficulty trying to use the scissors. He showed and explained to Michael how to open and shut the scissors. Michael was delighted to try. Next, Jonathan cut a piece of paper. He then held up a piece of paper to Michael. Michael made a few snips on the paper. Jonathan scaffolded the task. He broke it down into manageable parts to help Michael gain success with the cutting activity.

Early childhood educators must therefore carefully observe children to identify when they need help or become frustrated, or when adult intervention is needed.

Forming Partnerships

Caregivers should form partnerships with family members and other professionals to coordinate learning activities effectively. Partners play a critical role in helping to:

* Observe children
* Provide expert advice
* Provide help and resources
* Ensure that consistency for the child is maintained in all settings

Observing Children's Behaviours

Careful observation and documentation is the cornerstone to building a quality program. Observations have many uses:

* Developing an IPP or portfolio for individual children
* Understanding and interpreting children's behaviours
* Providing appropriate adult-intervention strategies
* Providing appropriate materials and interactions to encourage cognitive development
* Assisting with preparation of progress reports and referrals
* Enabling the appropriate organization of learning environments

Since cognitive behaviour cannot be observed directly, techniques need to be developed to identify and collect information about various demonstrated behaviours that can be interpreted. Some of these techniques include collections of children's work, photographs or diagrams of their products, checklists of specific skills and anecdotal records of specific behaviours.

1. Collections of Children's Work

Collections of children's efforts could include artwork, writings, and photographs of structures made or video recordings of specific episodes. Examples of pieces of children's efforts could be collected periodically in individual portfolios (see page 156). Each specific item collected should be accompanied with an interpretation (see Figure 10.4 for an example). Information gathered from this type of process provides opportunities to:

* Interpret aspects of children's cognitive development
* Document changes over time

- Determine appropriate challenges to encourage further development
- Select materials, experiences or equipment to foster sustained interest and development over time
- Explain and illustrate changes in cognitive behaviour

2. Photographs

Photographs provide wonderful opportunities to record the achievement of milestones in children's cognitive activities (see Figure 10.5). Photographs can also be placed in a child's individual portfolio. The caregiver should include descriptions and interpretations of the event.

3. Diagrams of Children's Products

Sometimes it is not possible to take a photograph or adequately describe a child's actions or accomplishments. A quick diagram may best capture the child's efforts. These can then be interpreted (see Figure 10.6). Diagrams can also be placed into a portfolio.

FIGURE 10.4

Observations of Mikayla's Work

Date: May 2004   **DOB: January 22, 1999**

Circumstances: Drawing reflects follow-up of a field trip to look for signs of spring

Description	Comments	Interpretation
"My flowers are in front, so they are bigger. My house is in the background, so it's smaller."	Uses symbols to represent recognizable objects.	Able to take on a different perspective: size. Schematic stage of art development. Creative in recreating past experiences.

FIGURE 10.5

Explore to Discover Meaning

Date: April 2, 2004   **DOB: June 5, 2001**

Circumstances: Jordan had discovered the "Tornado in a Bottle." He had difficulty creating the tornado. Colin noticed and came to help him. Colin showed Jordan how to "make the tornado spin." Jordan eventually was successful.

Description	Comments	Interpretation
	J: "I can't." C: "Sure, you can. See, it's easy. Just turn the bottle." J: "The water's going around." C: "It's not really a tornado. It's a water spout." J: "Water spout." C: "Now you try!" J: "I did it, I did it. I made a water spout."	Jordan is at the math and science stage of exploration to discover meaning. He was able to interpret his discovery with Colin's help.

FIGURE 10.6

Interpretation of Ben's Insect Tower

Date: September 21, 2004   **DOB: April 22, 2000**

Circumstances: Ben was fascinated with the various kinds of insects. He often looked up information in books. He could name most of the collection of plastic insects that were available in the room. He built a special tower for his insects.

Description	Comments	Interpretation
[See Figure 10.3 for diagram.] He named the categories he had created—large and small, flying insects and crawling insects. He named all the insects he used.	Ben is able to classify using more than one attribute. Structures show his grasp of balance and order.	He placed blocks in order of size to effectively build his structure.

4. Checklists of Specific Skills

A number of checklists can be created to interpret cognitive behaviours. Checklists lend themselves to the identification of skills, such as matching, sorting, seriation or patterning. Skills need to be observed more than once and in various settings in order to be sure that the skill has been acquired. These checklists give valuable information to ensure that children's developmental levels are being addressed and

FIGURE 10.7

Samples of Checklists

Sample 1: Matching

Name: Josh   **DOB:** 12/03/1999

Skills	Date	Evidence
Colour	02/02/04	Matched vehicles by colour into egg carton container—yellow, red, blue, orange
Shape	03/04/04	Paired animals that were the same in the sandbox

Sample 2: Seriation

Name: Josh   **DOB:** 12/03/1999

Skills	Date	Evidence
Ordering items	05/02/04	Placed three nesting cups in order from smallest to largest
	05/04/04	Placed three rings in order from smallest to largest on sorter; used three of the six rings

Sample 3: Patterning

Name: Marlene   **DOB:** 10/05/2001

Skills	Date	Evidence
Colour	05/02/04	Created red-and-blue pattern with round beads
Size	05/04/04	Created large-fish, small-fish pattern with pattern cards

Sample 4: Sorting

Name: Marlene   **DOB:** 10/05/2001

Skills	Date	Evidence
Colour	05/04/04	Created necklace of all red beads from round beads of various colours

that appropriate challenges are provided for children. Figure 10.7 provides a few examples of appropriate checklists.

5. Anecdotal Records

Anecdotal records may be used to identify behaviours that need more explanation or do not occur very often. One example would be the child's use of language that demonstrates understanding. These types of records are useful, because they preserve the total incident, making the information easy to interpret (see Figure 10.8).

Individual Portfolios

Since cognitive behaviour is very difficult to observe, building a portfolio with the help of the child is an excellent way to document cognitive abilities. This works particularly well with children who are very verbal or who have been identified as gifted. Portfolios should be built in partnership with children, families and other professionals. Sample sections—reports, collections and personal reflections—are included in a sample portfolio (Figure 10.9 A–E). Portfolios are excellent ways to:

- Keep track of individual interests and skill development
- Maintain a record of progress over time
- Provide ongoing documentation that the child and family can keep as a record
- Provide a record of demonstrated cognitive skills and abilities
- Provide documentation that is easy to interpret and share

FIGURE 10.8

Sample Anecdotal Record

Name: Jill   **DOB:** 09/30/2000

Jill's Dialogue	Interpretation
"I hurted my finger. I cried. Mommy didn't cry. She is brave."	Has recognized that verb endings change when talking about the past. Sees the world from her perspective.

FIGURE 10.9A

Christopher's Portfolio: Introductory Page and Reports

Date: July 2, 2004

My name is Christopher.
I am almost four years old.
My birthday is on September 30. I will be four then.
The picture I drew is of me and my mommy.

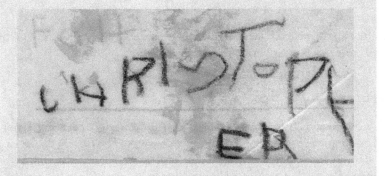

FIGURE 10.9A
Continued

Psychologist's Report

Christopher took part in a research study at Braceton University.

The purpose of the study was to test young children from three to five years of age who had an extensive vocabulary to see if this was an indicator of overall proficiency. Christopher's test results put him in the high superior range, overall.

Preschool Report

1. **Social adjustment:** Christopher gets along with all the children and adults in the program. He is very popular with all the children.
2. **Creativity:** Christopher is very creative in everything he does. His abilities in art far surpass the normal expectations of his age group.
3. **Overall Abilities:** Christopher excels at everything he does. He continually keeps the staff on their toes with his unique questions. He always seems to want to know everything. He can read most of the books on the shelf, and sometimes reads to other children.
4. **Summary of Observations:** Christopher is at an advanced level in all skill levels observed.

FIGURE 10.9B
Christopher's Portfolio: Collections

Christopher's Report
What I Can Do

I am good at painting, drawing and music.
I am good at sports like skiing, swimming and gymnastics.
I like preschool. I like pretend playing with my friends.

1. Art

I really like to draw.

I really like trucks. They can go anywhere. I wish my mommy would drive a truck.

I like to use paint. I experiment to create interesting designs. I mixed the colours blue and green to get turquoise. I used really thick paint to create dots and thin paint to create lines.

FIGURE 10.9B
Continued

2. Projects

I especially like to use clay.

I decided to make a dinosaur. I formed it out of clay. Then I decided to make it be two different things, like my transformers. So, I made a dinosaur rabbit. Then we took it down to the kiln to be fired. We then painted it and glazed it and next it was fired again.

This is my dinosaur.

This is the dinosaur transformed into a rabbit

3. Stories

I love to write stories. I still need help to write them.

Dictated Story: "My Pets"

We have a pet cat and some fish. I love them. I think that I am lucky. I have four fish. They like to swim in an aquarium. I feed the fish.

I like to play with our pet cat. I love her. Her name is Simsim.

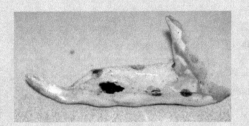

FIGURE 10.9C
Christopher's Portfolio: Personal Reflections

1. What I Like to Do

I like to play the piano. We had a concert and I got to play a solo.

I like all kinds of sports.

I love the art lessons. I take them at the Art Gallery. We got to see a show about South American art. It was cool. I liked the colours the artists used.

I like to play with my friends.

I like the rooftop playground at our nursery school, and I like to roll down the big hill with Darren when we go to the nursery school.

FIGURE 10.9C

Continued

---

2. What I Don't Like

I don't like to sit and wait to go outside. Some kids are so slow.

I don't like spinach. I don't care if it's good for you.

I don't like to be always interrupted when I'm busy.

3. What Makes Me Sad

I was really sad when my grandfather died. I still miss him.

4. What Makes Me Happy

I'm really happy when people give me presents, like on my birthday and at Christmas.

I like to make my mommy happy. I draw her pictures.

My mommy tickles me.

5. What Makes Me Angry

I get really mad when people hurt animals.

I get annoyed when people won't leave me alone when I tell them to.

6. What Scares Me

Sometimes I get scared that a plane will drop bombs on us.

FIGURE 10.9D

Christopher's Portfolio: Samples of Observations of Christopher's Skills

All information was gathered by the staff and family members.

Name: Christopher   **DOB:** 09/30/00

Skills	Date	Evidence
Matching **missing pieces**	02/05/04	Matched set of cards
Interior detail	03/04/04	Matched identical pieces hidden in a background of many pieces
Seriation	02/29/04	Ordered 10 shells from smallest to largest
	03/02/04	Built set of 15 towers, each getting larger
	03/04/04	Helped Josh to order stacking cups from smallest to largest several times
	03/04/04	Used clay to create series of dinosaur eggs from largest to smallest

Patterning Skills

Name: Christopher   **DOB:** 09/30/00

Skills	Date	Evidence
Colour	03/02/04	Created turquoise-and-blue pattern of sponge print
Shape	03/04/04	Used toy animals to create a pattern of mother, baby animals
Size	04/06/04	Used beads to create two-small, two-large pattern

Sorting Skills

Name: Christopher   **DOB:** 09/30/00

Skills	Date	Evidence
Colour	05/04/04	Sorted all the beads (which had been dumped) by colour
Classification	06/07/04	Placed the toy animals into two groups, then asked teacher to guess the groups; teacher was unable to do so; had correctly separated animals with and without hooves.

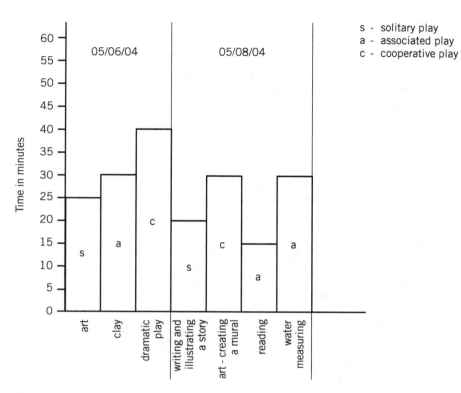

FIGURE 10.9E

Observation of Interests and Attention Span

Comments
Dramatic play involved planning and creating a zoo in the block area. Christopher was the
"engineer" and later the "veterinarian." All five children assumed different roles.

Organizing the Cognitive Environment

The indoor and outdoor environments should be organized in a way that maximizes
children's opportunities to solve problems, make decisions, experiment, transfer
knowledge and skills from one situation to another and engage in self-reflective
activities. There should be a smooth flow of activities from indoors to outdoors.

1. Opportunities to Solve Problems

Opportunities for children to solve their own problems should be available in
every centre. Caregivers should ensure that materials at the appropriate level are
available and accessible (see Table 10.6).

2. Opportunities to Make Decisions

Organization of the materials in the environment should ensure that materials
are accessible, categorized with an appropriate labelling system (see Chapter 4,

TABLE 10.6   SUGGESTIONS FOR CREATING OPPORTUNITIES TO SOLVE PROBLEMS

Learning Area	Description of Opportunities
Dramatic play areas • **Housekeeping** • **Role play** • **Pretend play**	• One-to-one correspondence when setting the table: one spoon for every plate • How to mix ingredients to make a meal • How to dress for certain roles • How to interact when role-playing • How to set a table
Music area	• Counting the beat • How to play an instrument • Learning words of songs, or names of instruments • Matching sounds to different instruments • Keeping time to music
Manipulative area	• How things fit together • Matching shapes to put them into a puzzle or shape sorter • How to create patterns • One-to-one correspondence: one bear in one container • How to fit nesting cups together
Creative arts	• How to mix colours • How to create different designs • How to create different shapes • How to use different tools such as brushes or scissors • How to make things stick
Sand area	• How to create moulds • When to use wet or dry sand • How to build structures in sand • Which tools are most effective for digging or filling • How to measure: heavy, light, full, empty
Water area	• Which tools are most effective to pour or fill with • How to create flow • How to make bubbles • Identifying what sinks or floats
Math and science area	• How to make things sink • How to notice detail • Counting to find out what has more or less • One-to-one correspondence • Sorting objects by size or colour or shape • Identifying which items are attracted to a magnet
Carpentry area	• How to attach things together • Identifying appropriate tools to use for different tasks • Identifying which size of nails to use • How to shorten pieces of wood • How to use tools safely

TABLE 10.6 CONTINUED

Learning Area	Description of Opportunities
Book area	• How to use books for different purposes • How to read • Answer questions • How to retell a story using props such as felt pieces • Finding an appropriate book
Block area	• How to build stable structures • How to fit blocks together to form different structures • How to build to different heights • How to transport blocks effectively • How to represent different ideas such as tunnels, platforms or towers
Gross motor play	• How to get to the top of a climber • How to stop • How to balance on a balance beam • How to ride a riding toy • How to move around obstacles

pages 111–114) and are easily visible from various areas of the room. Materials should reflect the following criteria:

• Open-ended—Children should be able to make decisions about how to use the materials (see Photo 10.5).

• Multi-purpose—Materials should be usable in a variety of settings for a variety of purposes. Children can make the decisions about where or when the materials might be used (see Photo 10.6).

Photo 10.5

Photo 10.6

Photo 10.8

Photo 10.7

Photo 10.9

- Providing choices—Children should be able to choose materials from a variety of alternatives (Photo 10.7). This provides opportunities to make decisions about when or which materials will be used.

3. Opportunities to Experiment

Children learn about their world through active participation. They need to explore their learning environments in order to discover many important things:

- How things work (Photo 10.8)
- What will happen as a result of certain actions (Photo 10.9)
- How things change or can be changed for different purposes (Photos 10.10 and 10.11)
- How to work together or independently (Photo 10.12)

Photo 10.10

Photo 10.11

Photo 10.12

4. Opportunities to Transfer Knowledge and Skills

Learning occurs as children explore and learn about their environment. However, learning is reinforced and strengthened when learning can be transferred from one situation to another. Children learn that similar actions can be used in similar ways in different circumstances. Table 10.7 offers some suggestions of how different materials may be used in similar ways in different settings.

5. Opportunities to Engage in Self-Reflective Activities

Children need to learn to reflect on what they have learned, what they still wish to learn, and the value of their activities. Self-reflection activities might include discussion, writing, or drawing.

TABLE 10.7   SUGGESTIONS FOR CREATING OPPORTUNITIES TO TRANSFER SKILLS

Skill	Transfer Opportunities
Pouring	• Sandbox—Dry sand • Water—Filling and emptying • Snack—Pouring own drink • Manipulatives—Pouring gems or beads into containers
Pouring	• Blocks—Transporting blocks in construction vehicle toys and dumping them where needed • Water—Creating mixtures with various things, such as soap or food colour • Sand—Adding alternatives, such as scraps of materials or paper
Stacking	• Blocks • Manipulatives—Duplo, Lego or small blocks • Dramatic play—Dishes, bowls • Outdoor play—Rocks
Mixing	• Sand—Making wet sand • Water—Creating mixtures with various things such as soap or food colour • Painting—Creating new colours • Dramatic play—Creating meals • Sand—Adding alternatives such as scraps of materials or paper
Reading	• Blueprints for creating carpentry projects • Recipes for making own playdough or snack • Books to read for pleasure • Books placed in all learning areas to look through for ideas, expand knowledge
Drawing/painting	• Block area—Create maps, signs, roads, scenery • Creative area—Free exploration of materials • Outdoors—Natural extension from indoor to outdoor activity • Field trips—Recording what has been observed • Carpentry—Decorating projects • Sand—Mixing sand and paint to create sand pictures

A) DISCUSSION Discussion opportunities should be provided that help the children reflect. Children might be asked the following questions:

- How do you feel about what you have done/created?
- What did you like about what you have done/created?
- How might you do things differently next time?
- What other materials might you need to continue working on what you are doing?
- How did this experience make you feel?

B) WRITING AND DRAWING Children could be encouraged to create personal booklets in which they can record their reflections. A scribe (someone who listens and writes down exactly what the child says) should be provided to aid younger children with this process. The advantage of a booklet is that children can refer back to their reflections over time and also share them with others. Reflection booklets should be personal and should only be shared if the child wishes to share them.

Role of the Early Childhood Educator

The role of the early childhood educator is to observe, monitor and organize developmentally and age-appropriate learning activities to meet the learning needs of all children within the group (see the author's Reflection). Some specific strategies have been adapted from Genisio and Drecktrah (2002); see Table 10.8.

Reflection | *From the Author*

One of my most memorable incidents concerning facilitator interactions occurred during a practice teaching occasion. The children had been very interested in dinosaurs. Much of this dinosaur play had occurred in a large sandbox on the floor. One of the student teachers, Tammy, decided that since it was spring, she should change the activity to reflect the season. She collected a number of plastic flowers and created a flower garden in a corner of the sandbox.

When Benjamin and Damian arrived, they immediately went to the sandbox. "Where are our dinosaurs?" Tammy explained that it was springtime and wouldn't they rather plant a garden? "No!" was the instant reply. "Let's go and get the dinosaurs!" Tammy responded that she did not know where the dinosaurs were kept. "Come, we will show you!" The two boys took her to the storage room to retrieve the dinosaurs. They also showed her where to find the other things they needed for their dinosaur play.

When they got back to the sand area, Benjamin asked Tammy to tell them the names of the dinosaurs. Tammy responded with phrases like "That is a ferocious looking dinosaur," or "That one is a green one." Benjamin finally looked at her, put his hands on his hips and said, "Don't you know any of their names?

Even I know some of them." He pointed to the dinosaurs and said, "This is a tyrannosaurus rex, this is a triceratops and this is a pteranodom."

The next day Tammy was ready. She had brought appropriate books, expanded the dinosaur collection and brought in some tall grasses that the children could use in creating the dinosaur play. Benjamin and Damian were enthralled with the new activity. This time when they asked her the names of the dinosaurs she knew some of the names. If she did not, she offered to find the dinosaur in the book and read about it.

When Tammy reflected on the experience she said: "I never realized how smart the kids could be or how important it was to follow their lead. I know you always told us how important it was to know more about the child's play and know the names of the materials they are playing with. I now realize just how important that is. This has been a great learning activity for the children, but a much more powerful one for me!"

TABLE 10.8   ROLE OF THE EARLY CHILDHOOD EDUCATOR

Strategies	Description	Example
Focus on child's activities	Observe the child's interest and actions	Jamie observed the dinosaur play without interacting.
Guided dialogue	Based on the observation, interact with the child and engage him in the activity	Tammy: "I see you are interested in the dinosaur. I wonder what he feels like."
Modelling	Model the activity that could be encouraged	Tammy ran her fingers over the back of the dinosaur. "It feels bumpy." She extends the dinosaur to Jamie and he touches the dinosaur's back.
Label the child's actions or feelings	Observe the child and describe what he or she is doing or feeling	"You are running your fingers over the dinosaur's back. His back feels bumpy."
Guided actions	Expand the play by offering suggestions	Tammy: "Let's put the dinosaur in the sand." She holds out the dinosaur, and Jamie takes it and places it in the sand. Tammy continues to observe his actions and guide his behaviour. Jamie eventually plays with the dinosaur in the sand by himself.

TABLE 10.8 **CONTINUED**

Strategies	Description	Example
Use concrete examples	Build children's understanding of the real world	After a visit to the zoo, Tammy provided photographs, books and toy animals of the animals observed. The children matched the toy animal to the photograph or the picture in the book.
Provide practice	Engaging in repetitive actions in more than one setting	Dillon emptied and filled containers with water, sand or plastic gems.
Provide time	Allow enough time to practice; may occur over more than one day	Samuel walked over the balance beam out-side at least ten times. An indoor balance beam was set up to allow Samuel to con-tinue practising this skill.
Range of materials and equipment	Provide materials that allow children to practise skills in different settings	Small pitchers and containers in the water, sand and housekeeping centres help chil-dren practise pouring
Encourage activities	Maintain attention by providing opportunities to continue play outdoors or indoors and over more than one day	The children had been developing a garden in the sandbox. They were encouraged to bring materials outdoors to continue the gardening activity.
Flow from indoor to outdoors	Encourage activities to continue or provide similar opportunities outdoors	Children take books out to the outdoor reading area
Observe and document	Observe and document children's activity, skills and interests	Figures 10.9B and 10.9D
Modify learning activities	Scaffold learning activities and learning experiences	Josh tried to bead but found it difficult. He was able to bead using long pipe cleaners. When he was able to manage beading with the pipe cleaners, some gimp was left out. He tried and was successful.
Arrange for choice to meet a variety of needs	Provide materials that encourage different skill levels	Book area Simple dictionaries Picture books Storybooks Illustrated poetry books

TABLE 10.8 CONTINUED

Strategies	Description	Example
Supportive feedback	Relate feedback to what the child is doing or what has been accomplished	Intermittent feedback results in keeping children on task for longer periods of time (Macintyre, 2002:3)
Model skills: Patience		Jamie consistently held the scissors with both hands. He could cut when the paper was held for him. He learned that he could do the task his way and be successful.
Persistence	Children need to learn that sometimes things do not go as expected the first time	Dillon was trying to fit a puzzle piece into a slot. He put the piece down and tried a different piece. Thomas noticed his efforts and quietly said, "What a good idea to try another piece. I wonder if it will fit." Dillon smiled and tried the piece, but it did not fit. He looked up at Thomas and frowned. Thomas smiled and said, "What are you going to do now?" Dillon smiled and picked up another piece. This time it did fit.
Encourage independence	Observe in order to encourage individual independence	A child may not be able to start a zipper but may be able to pull it up once started.
Strategies to encourage independence	Encourage independence through observation and knowledge of child's abilities and skills	Consider the following questions before helping: Is this is an important task for the child to master at this time? Does the child have the skills to do this task? Can the task be broken down to make it easier to accomplish? Are there alternative activities that can be used to reinforce that skill?

Provide challenges	Lack of challenge can lead to boredom. Boredom can lead to inappropriate behaviours.
	
	Provide opportunities to:
	  Extend play
	  Transform learning
	  Build skills
		When Dillon filled and emptied his containers in the sand, water and with gems, he learned to extend his knowledge about the behaviour of objects as they were poured: water and sand flowed, and the gems tumbled and made loud noises. He built his skills in pouring. He learned that you can pour solids and liquids.

SUMMARY

To interpret cognitive behaviour, children's activities must be carefully observed. The actions of the children provide clues about their understanding of the world. Children demonstrate their understanding of the world around them by the way they interact with the materials in their learning environment, the way they interact with others and what they communicate about these interactions. Children need opportunities to engage in active play that includes solving problems, making decisions and becoming increasingly independent.

KEY POINTS

Cognitive development
- Nurture versus nature
- Multiple intelligences—Linguistic, logical-mathematical, musical, bodily/kinesthetic, spatial, interpersonal, intrapersonal
- Infant—Sensory motor, reflexive, manipulative, imitative
- Toddler—Sensory motor, start preoperational stage, symbolic play, deferred imitation
- Preschool—Preoperational, inflexible thinking, increased refinement of cognitive skills
- School age—Concrete operational, appearance of abstract thought, increased ability to use abstract concepts

Range of cognitive behaviours—Related to ability to understand the world, act upon the environment and interact with others.

Effects of range of cognitive behaviours—Affects children's understandings, abilities, skills and organization of the environment

Observations—Collections, photographs, diagrams, checklists, anecdotal records

Individual portfolio—Introduction, reports, collections, personal reflections, observations

Organization of the environment—Opportunities to solve problems, make decisions, experiment, transfer skills and knowledge, reflect

Role of early childhood educator—Focus on important activities, use concrete examples, provide practice, observe and document, modify, scaffold learning, provide supportive feedback, model a variety of skills, encourage independence, provide challenges

EXERCISES

1. In a small-group discussion, discuss Gardner's theory of multiple intelligences. Reflect upon which of the listed intelligences best represents you.

2. Utilize one of the developmental charts listed in Tables 10.2–10.5 (pages 331–335). Develop an observation tool to identify cognitive milestones. Implement the tool. Discuss what behaviours you have observed that demonstrate cognitive behaviour.

3. Discuss why there is a great deal of variation of cognitive behaviours in any setting. What adaptations need to be made to accommodate these differences?

4. Discuss the importance of forming partnerships.

5. Utilize two of the observation tools listed on pages 340–344. Implement the tools with an individual with special needs and an individual without special needs. Compare the results.

6. Reflect on the individual portfolio on pages 344–349. What makes the portfolio a useful tool to the child, the teacher and the family member?

7. Observe an inclusive environment. Identify what adaptations have been made to:
   a) Accommodate individual cognitive needs
   b) Caregiver interaction patterns
   c) The materials and equipment within the centre

REFERENCES

Berk, L. (2009). *Child Development.* Toronto, ON: Pearson Education Canada.

Gardner, H. (1993). *Multiple Intelligences: The Theory in Practice.* New York, NY: Basic Books.

Genisio, M., & Drecktrah, M. (2002). Emergent Literacy in an Early Childhood Classroom: Center Learning to Support the Child with Special Needs. In K. Freiberg (Ed.), *Annual Editions Educating Exceptional Children,* 40–47. Guilford, CT: McGraw-Hill/Dushkin.

Landreth, G. (2002). *Play Therapy: The Art of the Relationship.* Second Edition. New York: Brunner-Routledge.

Landry, P. (2004). John Locke (1632–1704) The Philosopher of Freedom. Blupete [online]. Available at www.answers.com/topic/tabula-rasa [4-10-2005].

Macintyre, C. (2002). *Play for Children with Special Needs.* London, UK: David Fulton Publishers.

Piaget, J. (1962). *Play, Dreams, and Imitation in Childhood.* New York, NY: Norton.

Rushton, S., & Larkin, E. (2005). Shaping the Learning Environment: Connecting Developmentally Appropriate Practices to the Brain Research. In K. Cauley, F. Linder & J. McMillan (Eds.), *Educational Psychology.* Dubuque, IA: McGraw-Hill/Dushkin.

Schickedanz, J., Schickedanz, D., Forsyth, P., & Forsyth, G. (2001). *Understanding Children and Adolescents.* Fourth Edition. Needham Heights, MA: Allyn & Bacon.

Smith, K. (2002). Howard Gardner, Multiple Intelligences and Education. Infed [online]. Available at www.infed.org/thinkers/gardner.htm [9/4/2005].

11
CHAPTER

Issues Concerning Inclusive Care in Canada

"In 1982, under Canada's Charter of Rights and Freedoms, children with special needs finally gained the right to attend school in all provinces and territories.

"In signing the UN Convention on the Rights of the Child in 1991, Canada made additional commitments to children with special needs. Today it is a matter of urgency that children with special needs finally gain the right to attend child care programs in all provinces and territories with their non-disabled peers, and that these programs be adequately resourced to meet their needs. These children must no longer be excluded and segregated" (Hope Irwin, Lero & Brophy, 2000:xiv).

Learning Outcomes

After studying this chapter, you will be able to:

1. Discuss the issues associated with equitable access—lack of space, the need for proportionate care and the need for appropriate policies.

2. Define the 11 components of quality care.

3. For each of the 11 components of quality care, identify associated problems.

4. Describe issues associated with diagnosis and assessment of children with special needs.

5. Describe how culture may influence the treatment of children with special needs.

6. Identify the barriers that exist to funding programs for children with special needs.

7. Describe the issues related to the education of individuals working with children with special needs.

8. Describe the effects of poverty on children with special needs.

Introduction

All provinces and territories have some legislation that provides for the care and education of children with special needs. However, the definitions of inclusive care and education vary. On the one hand are simple statements, such as, "Inclusion is based on Wolfensberger's principle of normalization (i.e., all persons regardless of ability should live and learn in environments as close to normal as possible). The basic idea behind normalization is that people with special needs should be viewed in the ways in which they are the same as other people rather than in the ways in which they are different" (The Centre for Inclusive Education, 2008). Other definitions are multidimensional: Child Care Association of Canada identifies that inclusive practices include:

- Zero rejection
- Full participation
- Same range of program options
- Maximum feasible parent participation
- Pro-action for community inclusion. (Child Care Association of Canada, 2004).

A definition of inclusiveness provides a starting point from which the dialogue that is necessary to the establishment of appropriate philosophies and the creation of proactive policies for inclusive care can begin. Without a common definition, it is not surprising that a number of approaches and a variety of policies or a lack of policies have been implemented across the country.

The absence of a universally acceptable definition of inclusive care is but one of the issues that can be identified in Canada. Issues concerning inclusive care in Canada have been clearly articulated in the research (Hope Irwin et al., 2000; Hope Irwin, Lero & Brophy, 2004; Goleman, Doherty, Lero, LaGrange & Tougas, 2000; Valentine, 2001) and by many individuals who work with children with special needs.

In this chapter, a summary of the prevailing issues will be presented through the eyes of individuals who are involved with the education of children with special needs. A series of interviews was conducted with individuals involved in ongoing research: family members, staff, supervisors, directors, consultants, board members, licensing officials and faculty involved in training programs for special needs certification.

Those interviewed were asked to identify what they perceived to be the outstanding issues concerning the care of children with special needs. The issues identified can be grouped into several categories, including access, diagnosis and assessment of special needs, funding, family concerns, staff concerns, the effects of poverty and legislative policies. A final category of issues, quality care, comprises many aspects: the learning environment, equipment and materials, the role of the director, support for staff, training of staff, provision of therapy, individual program planning, inclusion of families as partners, facilitation of social interaction among children, support from board members, and establishing a smooth transition from centre to elementary school.

From the Author   Reflection

Reflection

I have always spent a lot of time reading the research about the care of children with special needs in Canada. Reading about the issues and problems is always a very abstract experience. You might reflect upon what you have read, but after you have put the readings aside, the information gleaned quickly recedes. It is only when you actually become involved with the children, families and professionals caring for children with special needs that the issues become more personal, real and understandable.

I wanted to bring this more personal perspective to the readers of this text. That is why I decided to conclude by interviewing individuals working with children with special needs. I thought it would be valuable to catch a personal glimpse into the issues and problems associated with working with children with special needs.

Equitable Access

Equitable access involves the inclusion of children with special needs within community care settings of the family's choice. All individuals interviewed identified equitable access as a concern. Research clearly supports this viewpoint: "The Canadian Council on Social Development's original survey of 112 Canadian agencies demonstrated that . . . there are many barriers to services for these children and families. This results in a number of unmet needs. In their report, The Canadian Policy Research Network has concluded that 'full citizenship demands the easy access to inclusive supports, services and community settings. They argue that the provision of a package of portable and flexible supports targeting the particular needs of children with disabilities and their families must be readily accessible in local communities (Valentine, 2001:68). This is clearly not the case." (Canadian Council on Social Development, 2000:53). The issues of equitable access identified included the lack of child care spaces, the need for proportionate care and the need for appropriate policies.

1. Lack of Child Care Spaces

A common problem identified was an overall lack of child care spaces. It was estimated that approximately one out of every eight child care centres in Canada do not include children with disabilities.

Many individuals reported that they could not meet requests to accommodate more children either with or without special needs. One centre reported a huge waiting list that included 250 space requests for children not identified as special needs and 40 requests for supported spaces. All centres reported that they had waiting lists for children with special needs.

The number of available spaces has also decreased because many of the part-day and nursery school programs have closed in many jurisdictions. For example, with the opening of junior kindergarten in Ontario, many preschool programs were closed. Children with special needs often attend programs part-time, in order to accommodate the many other services that they are involved with. Without available half-day or part-time programs, these children now compete for spaces within full-day settings. Many centres cannot afford to offer part-time services to their clients, even if spaces did exist.

One director of a full-day child care centre, Susan, reported that children with special needs could not be accepted into the program. The reasons for refusal included these:

- The staff was already overburdened with a number of challenging behaviours exhibited by children enrolled in the program. These children had not been diagnosed with a behavioural problem, but Susan felt that in reality the program should be receiving funding to help with these problems. She did not feel that the centre could accept more children with special needs.
- The staff, Susan felt, did not have adequate training to provide quality programming for children with special needs.
- Additionally, Susan felt it was difficult if not impossible to access appropriate expertise to help with programming for children with special needs.

What can you do to address the lack of child care spaces? Here are some suggestions:

a) Become informed about equitable care issues. Talk to individuals involved with the care of young children with special needs to find out what the issues are.
b) Learn to advocate for better care for children with special needs. Attend workshops on how to become a better advocate.
c) Join community groups that meet regularly to discuss issues concerning children with special needs, such as the Canadian Council for Children with Exceptionalities.
d) Read appropriate resources (see references at end of chapter).

2. The Need for Proportionate Care

One of the principles of inclusion is that the care of children with special needs should be in naturally occurring proportions, in proportion to their occurrence in the general population. This is generally about 10 percent of the group size. When the number of children with special needs within a program is higher than 10 percent, the resources of the program often become stretched. It becomes more difficult to meet the needs of individual children and their families, and to access appropriate resources. Care for children with special needs varies across Canada.

Individuals interviewed indicated that special needs care ranged from proportionate to disproportionate.

June, a staff member in an inclusive setting with a higher number of children with special needs, summed up the situation in the following way:

- Nine of our sixteen children have special needs. This is too high a proportion for us to provide a high-quality program.
- Sometimes I feel that our typical children lose out because they do not get the same individual attention. We seem to spend more time with the children with special needs because they often need the one-on-one approach to cope.
- We have a support worker in the room, so we do have an extra pair of hands, but it never seems enough.
- I realize the importance of the social interactions that take place. All our children benefit from these interactions. However, sometimes children pick up inappropriately modelled behaviours, and it is hard to explain to a young child why the behaviour is not appropriate.
- I believe in inclusion, but I do think that all the children and the staff would benefit more from a more balanced approach.

What can you do to address the need for proportionate care?

a) Become informed about the benefits of proportionate care.
b) If more help is needed on the floor, encourage volunteer support in the room: family members, senior citizens or community members.

3. The Need for Appropriate Policies

All individuals interviewed identified that there was a need for proactive policies. All were concerned that there were no proactive policies consistently in place in Canada. The lack of proactive policies makes it essential that practitioners working with children with special needs engage in proactive activities. This activity is defined in another principle of inclusive practices: the inclusive program actively promotes legislative and policy change, encourages enrolment of children with disabilities and involves parents at the level they choose.

Interviewees agreed that appropriate proactive policies provide the framework for quality inclusive care. One director indicated that these policies should not be linked to the need to label children but should be tied to providing adequate resources to inclusive child care centres, such as funding for higher staff–child ratios, resources (human, physical and material) and training.

Concerns were also expressed by several individuals that often there are provincial or territorial pressures to reduce standards. One supervisor indicated that "There have been pressures to reduce standards in BC. During a review of legislation in BC, care has been made more affordable by reduction of standards. We should strive toward national policies that will drive local applications."

What can you do to advocate proactive policies that support inclusive child care?

a) Become informed about the policies concerning children with special needs in your jurisdiction.
b) Identify what proactive policies may be needed in your area.
c) Participate in public forums or internet-based forums.
d) Write letters to your MLA or MPP to indicate your concerns.

Quality of Inclusive Care

All those interviewed expressed concern about the generally low overall quality of care for children with special needs in Canada. This concern is clearly supported by the research. The results of a national research study, *Inclusion: The Next Generation in Child Care in Canada* (Hope Irwin et al., 2004), clearly support this concern. Based on the Early Childhood Environmental Rating Scale—Revised (ECERS-R) (Harms, Clifford & Cryer, 1998) and reports from the 32 participating centres, the study reached these conclusions:

- Three centres (9.4%) had quality scores that indicated inferior program quality.
- Fourteen centres (43.8%) had scores in the minimal-to-mediocre range.
- A similar proportion (46.9%) had scores in the good-to-excellent range (Hope Irwin et al., 2004:158).

Aspects of quality inclusive environments include the physical environment, equipment and materials, the role of the director, support for staff, training of staff, provision of therapy, individual program planning, inclusion of families as partners, facilitation of social interaction between children, supportive board members and a smooth transition from centre to elementary school (Hope Irwin et al., 2004:151). Some individuals raised concerns about the quality of at least one of these aspects.

1. Physical Environment

All individuals expressed concern about the impact of the physical space on the quality of the learning experiences for the children. Specific concerns included these:

- Lack of space to make necessary adaptations—One staff member reported that she felt the quality of the program for the children had decreased because of the modifications that had to be made to the physical environment. The environment had been changed to include wheelchair access. To accommodate access, a number of learning areas had to be removed. These learning experiences were now offered on a rotational basis. "I do not think that this is ideal. We had to make the adjustments because we all wanted to accept the child in the wheelchair. The consequences are that children now have fewer choices and the adults are working harder to rotate a variety of experiences that have similar outcomes. It has been both challenging and frustrating. We simply need a larger space."

- Lack of funding to make the relevant modifications—A number of directors and board members indicated that they would like to make modifications that would make the centre more inclusive but that they lacked the necessary funds. Sandy, an executive director, reported: "We found it quite easy to make some of the physical adjustments, such as adding an elevator to the building, ramps and accessible washroom spaces because we received a one-time grant to make modifications to the physical space. What has been most difficult is to receive funding for ongoing equipment needs such as standing frames, communication boards, adaptable devices and switches, or adaptive playground equipment. The grants given provide only access. There is no consideration given toward ongoing funding to provide for quality experiences for the children once they are in program."

2. Equipment and Materials

Most individuals interviewed indicated that it was difficult to obtain specialized materials and/or equipment to encourage independent choices and abilities. These specific difficulties were mentioned:

- Finding specialized equipment and materials can be difficult. Material may have to be purchased at a distance from specialized suppliers, such as adaptive eating utensils or adaptive switches.
- Much of the highly specialized equipment, such as standing frames, is needed by only a few children.
- Equipment may require a lot of storage room. Many centres may not have adequate storage space.
- These materials and equipment may be too expensive to purchase.

3. Role of the Director

Directors interviewed were very conscious of their role in supporting inclusive care. There was a general concern that related to attracting suitable staff. One director commented: "I realize that training is one way to enhance the quality of the program. Trained individuals have presumably learned the relevant skills and knowledge necessary to interact with children with special needs. However, there are also other dynamics at work. I have noticed that standards of practice may change with the dynamics of the group. Often when a new staff member is hired, there is a change in practice. If we have selected the individual carefully, we may find that quality actually improves. Unfortunately, some of the factors I look for in individuals are generally not things we can teach: good people skills, passion, respect for children, nurturing attitudes and knack for creative programming."

Kim, another director, found that much of her time was involved in supporting and challenging the staff to continually find new ways of doing things, to help find various ways to resolve conflicts and to actively provide real choices to all children.

Directors who were in centres with a high degree of support for inclusive care had very low staff turnover. The opposite was true of centres with low support. In one instance, the director reported that within a single year there had been a continual need to hire new staff, and that sixteen new individuals had been hired. She also indicated that the behaviour of the children changed drastically with the constant staff turnover.

All staff members interviewed readily identified that the director was a key individual in advocating and maintaining quality inclusive care.

4. Support for Staff

Staff concerns centred on these issues:

- Child–adult ratios—Often, enhanced support is provided for individual children with a diagnosed need. One staff member, Vivian, stated that "Since funding is usually tied to diagnosed need, only children with high needs tend to get support. There are many children within our inclusive setting who have not been diagnosed and have similar high needs but do not get any support. In these cases we rely on a resource consultant who comes in once in a while to offer suggestions. This is really helpful, but what we need most is an extra pair of hands on the floor to help us cope. What do you do when you have three children who are throwing temper tantrums and another child who needs your help, and you have only four hands to cope? It can become very frustrating."
- Time relief—All staff members interviewed indicated that it was difficult to address the needs of all the children, confer with consultants or other specialists to help provide better programming for the children, meet the families' needs and meet the needs of regular programming during the daily schedule. One staff member, Charmaine, noted that "There are not enough hours in the day to do all the things we need to do. Also, we never have time to meet as a team. We need to find some way to function without continually spending our own time to meet. This can very quickly lead to resentment and to burnout."

5. Training of Staff

All interviewees were aware that getting training to work with children with special needs was not something that was universally mandated across Canada. All individuals expressed the belief that specialized training should be mandatory for all those who work with children with special needs. They identified these areas of concern:

- Education—Vivian stated that "I feel that I do not know enough about how to deal with a child with special needs. I had only one course about special needs in my college diploma program. That was not enough to prepare me for this job.

Don't get me wrong—I love what I do, but I wish I could get more training to help the kids more."

- Additional training—Another staff member summed up the lack of supplementary training as follows: "I know that education is important. I have participated in training. I have obtained a certificate to work with children with special needs. I financed the additional training by myself. It does help me to do my job better, but do I get more money? Of course not! Quite frankly, I am getting tired of the lack of acknowledgment for my additional skills. I keep saying that I won't take any more training, but you know what? I always do."
- Ongoing training—As new children with special needs are accepted within programs, ongoing training may become necessary. Staff members indicated that they needed ongoing training in order to help them plan an appropriate environment, gain expertise to know what types of materials or equipment are needed and manage the group dynamics of a wide range of abilities and skills.
- Consultative support—Most staff members identified that the support received from a resource consultant or other specialists was very valuable. However, they identified a need for a more gradual transition to move from consultative support to independent handling of children within the program.

6. Provision of Therapy

Parents interviewed clearly identified the high need for resources to help the family cope with a variety of therapy needs. They noted the following issues:

- Difficulty in obtaining assessments—Janine and Rob suspected that there was a problem with their daughter. She seemed delayed in all her milestones. When they attempted to have their child assessed they were told that they should be patient and that the child was too young to be accurately assessed and would probably outgrow the problem.
- Long waiting lists—Janine and Rob believed that their child needed to be assessed immediately. They felt that the longer they waited, the more behind their daughter would be. They insisted on a referral to a child psychologist. They were referred but were told that the next available appointment was in nine months.
- High cost and lack of choice—Janine and Rob did not want to wait nine months. They decided to see if they could get a private referral. They found someone who could see their daughter within one week. When they inquired if they could get funding to pay for the private consultation, they were refused. They could not afford the cost themselves.

Children in regular care often need additional therapy, such as physical or speech therapy. In most cases, it is up to the family members to bring children to the various required therapy sessions. Several problems were identified with this approach:

- Disruption of family schedules—Many families were often unable to take time off work to take their children to the required doctors, specialists or therapists.

As a result, some of the children were not receiving all the help they needed. Other families found that the schedule added continual stress to their family's life.

- Disruption of program schedules—In some instances, staff reported that the children found it difficult to settle into the program because of the periodic absences of children who required additional therapy.
- Isolation—Some staff members indicated that they felt that the child's program seemed fragmented. Information sharing between agencies was often incomplete or non-existent. The staff felt that this made quality programming difficult.

7. Individual Program Planning

There was consensus that individual programming was needed for children with special needs. Several individuals pointed out that this should be a standard policy for all children. Some of the problem areas identified included:

- Time—Many staff members indicated that while the development of an individual program plan was important, there was little time to develop an individual plan and to implement it.
- Nomenclature—Several individuals felt that a common professional vocabulary seemed to be lacking. Rachel summed up this point well: "We get very concerned about what to call a special plan for children with special needs. I have worked in the system for a long time. I have heard a number of terms used: functional program plan, developmental service plan, individual training plan, family service plan and so on. I think it is time that we get more concerned about the quality of what is in the plan and how it is implemented than what it is called. Additionally, it gets very confusing for non-professionals to sort through all the acronyms: IPP, IFP, FSP . . . "
- Access to resource consultants—Interviewees noted that collaborative access to a resource consultant was not consistently available. Children who had been identified with special needs were most likely to receive help.

8. Families as Partners

All interviewees agreed that families needed to be involved in developing appropriate programs for children with special needs. However, disagreements were expressed about the ideal degree of involvement:

- Treating families as partners—Some felt that the family members did not have the experience or the knowledge to know what was best for their child. Nancy, a parent of a child with special needs, vehemently disagreed: "I do not understand the patronizing attitude of some professionals toward me and, I am sure, other parents. Who better than I to know what my child needs? I have been traipsing to every specialist conceivable since my son was an infant. I have read their reports, have disagreed with some, have sought second opinions, have read a lot about my child's disability and I live with my child for most of his day. I am truly the greatest expert on my son."

- Regular information sharing—All individuals agreed that information sharing was critical. In all cases, information sharing was done in writing and through meetings. However, some professionals did not include family members in professional team meetings in the belief that family members would not understand the information presented. Some of the family members interviewed wanted to be included in professional meetings, while others did not.
- Program planning—The individuals interviewed, both family members and professionals, varied in their responses to the issue of involving parents in program planning. Some felt that family members should be full partners in all aspects of the child's program, while others felt that the professionals should handle programming, sharing only progress reports.

9. Social Interactions

All individuals interviewed agreed that social interactions among all children were critical. The identified problems focused on how to handle three particular issues:

- Diversity—Concern was expressed about how to meet mandated diversity requirements within the child care setting. For example, some staff and directors identified the difficulty in providing appropriate role models for children with special needs. One commented: "Children with special needs often grow up in 'normal' families and attend care with children of 'normal' abilities. These children continually live in situations that identify them as different. It is sometimes difficult to foster a nurturing attitude among peers and adults that fosters the uniqueness of the child without the continual focus on the special need."
- Abilities—Some difficulty was identified among staff members in meeting the increased range of needs. This difficulty translates into the need to provide a greater range and variety of learning materials, take more care in organizing materials to challenge the developmental needs of all children, provide safety to actively explore the learning opportunities and gain additional skill in providing opportunities for active social interaction for all children.
- Communication—Staff noted that it was often difficult to receive appropriate training, resources and materials to meet the needs of various children. They expressed the belief that training outcomes should include increased competency in signing and augmentative communication techniques and devices.

10. Supportive Board Members

Board members are critical individuals to involve in efforts to achieve quality practices for inclusive care. Supportive board members are able to initiate the development and implementation of an appropriate philosophy and proactive policies that value and support quality inclusive care. Several issues were identified by staff, directors and board members interviewed:

A) STAFF MEMBERS' PERSPECTIVE Staff members identified that often the philosophy developed and the policies set had little connection with the realities of working with children and families on a daily basis. Jeremy, one staff member, summed up this viewpoint: "It is one thing to set a philosophy and policies, and it is another to try to work in this situation. So, sure, we advocate inclusive care and will not turn away any children. The reality is that we have turned away children because we do not have the training or resources to help the child and family. For example, we had a child that needed to be tube-fed. None of us knew how to do this, nor was any training opportunity available to learn the process. Additionally, our centre is very small. There is no room to set up an area in which we can do this. The child was turned away. I think it is too easy to state wonderful things in writing, but not so easy to follow up and actually implement them. Part of setting philosophies and polices should include strategies and resources to make sure that it is feasible to actually implement the expectations implied."

B) DIRECTORS' PERSPECTIVE Some of the directors indicated that it was difficult to get "good" board members and keep them. It was particularly difficult to encourage family members with children with special needs to participate on the board because they were already overwhelmed with the burden of coping with the demands made on their time. A failure to include family members could leave the board structure lacking in adequate representation of the perspectives of children with special needs.

C) BOARD MEMBERS' PERSPECTIVE The common problems identified by the board members interviewed were time, expertise and expectations:

- Time—All board members interviewed noted that they did not regret the commitment made to sit on the board. Most, however, stated that they found it difficult to balance their family, work and volunteer commitments.
- Expertise—Several board members indicated that they wished that more parents and professionals dealing with children with special needs could be part of the board representations. One board member stated that "Although I have a child with special needs, I am continually astounded at the variety of special needs that are evident in my daughter's program. My child has a physical disability. My husband and I have learned how to make adaptations to her learning environment and are very happy to interact with the staff and board to offer our help. However, most of the needs in this program seem to be social and emotional. I wish I had more experience to help. As a board, we have tried to recruit individuals with that expertise but have been unsuccessful. As a result, I sometimes think that we set philosophies and policies that may not be in the best interests of the children or the families."

- Expectations—Board members often seem to feel that too many expectations are placed on their time. Jonathan, another board member, commented: "I agreed to sit on the board to develop policies, help evaluate the program to ensure congruency between the program and our mission statement, and possibly volunteer for committee work as needed. I now find that it seems expected that I am at the bingo hall to raise funds every month and that I am on a program review committee to identify needed program adaptations identified in the last evaluation of the centre. I have also been asked to assume an executive position because one of our board members resigned. My one evening a month for three hours is now four evenings a month and sometimes more. Most meetings last for more than three hours. I do not have time for this in my schedule. I will not be able to return to the board for another term."

11. Transition from Centre to Elementary School

Most individuals interviewed indicated that there was a complete break in the child's life from the early childhood setting to the elementary school. In most cases, the information about the child's diagnosis, progress and treatment strategies was lost. Most school boards re-evaluated the child upon entry into the elementary school system. Family members were concerned about the time this took. Mary, a mother of a child diagnosed with ADD, indicated that it took six months before any action was taken. Mary tried to share previous assessments with the teacher but was told that the school board would initiate its own diagnosis. Mary said, "By the time they got around to it, Jimmy was worse than he had ever been. He had adjusted so well at the day care. He was actually making progress. Now it seems nothing helps. I think that by the time he got help, it was too late. They moved him into a special class for kids with behaviour problems by the middle of grade one. It was so frustrating and we felt so helpless. He is now in grade three and has been identified as a problem child."

What can you do to play a greater role in obtaining high-quality inclusive care?

a) Utilize opportunities to get information from different perspectives. Attend board meetings, staff meetings or parent groups.
b) Become skilled in active listening skills. Learn to listen to the intent of the message rather than from a personal perspective.
c) Become knowledgeable about quality issues through reading, courses or workshops.
d) Utilize the resources in your community to become more knowledgeable about the issues of quality care. Resources could include libraries, faculty at colleges or universities, family members with children with special needs, local support groups or resource consultants and other professionals.

Diagnosis and Assessment

The survey identified several problems related to labelling the type and number of disabilities, misdiagnosis, assessment strategies and cultural expectations.

1. Labelling

The process of labelling a child involves two aspects:

- Assessment or diagnosis—The child is assessed in order to identify the level of functioning in all developmental domains, or to identify specific medical or psychological problems.
- Application of a label—The label is applied as a result of the assessment or diagnosis. Examples of labels include learning disability, ADD, mental retardation and autism.

In most jurisdictions in Canada, the process of assessment and labelling may result in funding or programming for the child. Funding depends on the label applied. Additional purposes of labelling include:

- Providing a direction to programming
- Identifying appropriate resources or ideas
- Identifying potential approaches to implement

In addition to the problems of labelling identified in Table 3.1 (page 72), the following disadvantages were identified by interviewees:

- From a teacher: "The label provides you with a general idea about what difficulties the child may have, such as reading disability. You may suspect that the child will find it difficult to learn to read. [The label] does not tell you where the difficulties lie or what strategies to use to teach the child to read. You still need to observe the child in order to utilize appropriate strategies that will work for that individual child."
- From an early childhood educator: "I have found that the label can be used to excuse our inability to cope with the child's behaviours. For example, I remember one child who had a number of behaviour problems. He was referred for assessment and diagnosed as ADHD. Once it was identified that he had a disorder that could be diagnosed, the attitude seemed to change from trying to cope with the behaviour to using the label as an excuse for not being able to cope. I have actually heard a staff member say, 'How do they expect us to cope with this child? He is impossible to deal with. He needs specialized help.' The child's behaviour had not changed but the staff attitude toward him had."
- From a psychologist: "I think there is too much attention paid to labels. Often the label sticks and follows the child through life. We should emphasize that a child is a child and that every child has some special needs. We need to deal with the child, not the label."

From the Author   Reflection   Reflection

I had returned to work after a maternity leave, having obtained a new position as a learning resource teacher. I remember my first case conference. Everyone used a number of acronyms, such as DAP, IEP and IFP. I didn't have a clue what they were talking about. I felt so stupid. After the conference, I did some research on the new terminology so I wouldn't be in a similar position again.

- From a resource teacher: "Early childhood educators and family members already know the child's needs best. Sufficient documentation on a child's needs already exists for a diagnosis (IPP/IFSP). This should be adequate to provide needed resources to help the child, the family and the centre without trying to label the child."

2. Misdiagnosis

Several individuals expressed concern about the increased number of children diagnosed with behavioural types of disabilities. One director of a program identified that there had been an increased number of children diagnosed with autism. She said that half of the children within their program had been diagnosed with this disability. Other individuals—both staff members and directors of programs—noted that more children were being diagnosed with ADD or ADHD. They expressed concern about the correctness of these diagnoses and wondered if a mere diagnosis of mistaken behaviours might be have been more accurate in some cases.

Cindy, one director, observed: "I have had several children diagnosed with autism in my program. Two children certainly demonstrated behaviours consistent with autism. However, two of the boys did not. Initially both boys demonstrated very high activity levels. Once they had settled into the program, the activity levels dropped, and I really saw very little evidence of any behaviour that even remotely resembles autism. Both boys maintained consistent eye contact, used language appropriate to their age group, sat on an adult's lap to read a story, interacted socially in a similar manner to their peers and maintained activities of choice for age-appropriate periods of time. These are not normal behaviours of children with autism. I think this diagnosis was definitely based on mistaken behaviours."

Some of the individuals interviewed also addressed the controversial issue of medicating children to control their behaviour. Generally there was agreement that medication at times was necessary, such as for childhood depression. However, individuals expressed concern that medication was an external control—it did not help the child achieve self-control.

3. Assessment Strategies

Formal assessment is usually provided by professionals who are trained to assess young children, such as psychologists, psychiatrists, speech and language pathologists, occupational therapists or pediatricians. These services are often hard to access for families with children with special needs. Penelope, a mother of twins with special needs, stated that "I knew something was wrong with my twins. They were just not developing as they should. At first I thought that I was not doing something right. But when I saw my doctor he agreed [with my parenting approach]. Then began the long search for answers—we went from specialist to specialist. I was lucky because my doctor referred us, so the services were free. Nothing conclusive was discovered, however. We were told that perhaps it was a developmental delay and that time and stimulation might mitigate the problems. On the advice of our physician we started an infant stimulation program. I am so thankful that we had such a good doctor."

Appropriate assessment tools for staff members to use are based on observation. These tools, such as the Brigance inventory, the Portage guide or the DISC assessment, are expensive to purchase and require some training to successfully implement and interpret. Additionally, the tools compare the subjects with children of normal development. The comparison does not indicate the type of treatment that is required. Often, as a result, the child's program becomes based on meeting special needs rather than active play. Janice, a mother, noted: "It really bothers me when the teachers tell me all about my son's needs and how they will ensure that the program is built to strengthen his needs. He is just a little boy. He needs to actively play. I feel that learning through play is much more appropriate for him. He will learn to make choices, solve problems, play with his peers and build on his strengths."

The most appropriate assessment strategies to use in early childhood settings are observations. Interviewees identified the problems that prevent adequate observation:

- Insufficient time—Many of the staff members felt that they did not have time to observe and record children's behaviours because they were too busy interacting with children.
- Insufficient experience—Staff members identified that they needed training to help them select appropriate tools and interpret what they had observed.
- Insufficient staffing—Staff felt that ideally all children should be observed, not just children with special needs, but given present resources this was felt to be an unrealistic expectation.

What can you do to improve the assessment process?

a) Become more knowledgeable about the various assessments that are implemented—Ask questions of the individuals doing the testing. Ask them to explain why they are using a particular tool and what the advantages and disadvantages might be.

b) Increase your skill in personal observations—You can do this by utilizing the variety of tools presented in the various chapters of this text.

4. Cultural Expectations

As it does in all experiences, culture plays a large part in how children are diagnosed and treated. One executive director indicated that Italian cultures are much more tolerant of active children, and as a result fewer children in Italy are labelled as ADHD or ADD than in the United States and Canada. In fact, there has been an increase of 200 to 300 percent in the number of prescription medications, such as Ritalin and Prozac, used by preschoolers in the United States (Science Friday, 2000). Individuals interviewed indicated that they felt that similar increases have taken place in Canada.

In some areas in Canada, there is a refusal to label young children. It is felt that as children grow and mature, their behaviour may change. However, often in these jurisdictions, funding is not available without the labelling.

What can you do to determine the extent to which culture influences diagnosis and treatment in your community?

a) Become informed about the incidence of various types of disabilities diagnosed in your community. Are the numbers comparable to national averages? If they are different, ask questions to identify why there are differences.
b) Become informed about the advantages and disadvantages of labelling children.
c) Interview the family of an older child with special needs. What challenges have they faced? What recommendations would they make?

Funding of Programs

In Canada diversity is celebrated, but this attitude is not evident in early childhood settings. Early childhood programs are not funded for optimal growth and development. As discussed previously, there are a number of barriers to obtaining funding to ensure equal access for children with special needs. Because of insufficient funding for programs, necessary adaptations of equipment and modifications of the environment are often not undertaken. But worse yet, the time children with special needs spend in centre-based programs is often reduced. Many programs offer half-day services only. One director stated: "We have a large waiting list for children with special needs. To accommodate that need, we offer half-day programs for these children. It is not ideal, but at least we can provide services to more children with special needs."

What can you do to advocate better funding for programs?

a) Become informed about how children with special needs are funded in your area and in other areas.
b) Develop advocacy skills to advocate for increased funding.
c) Participate in fundraising events in your community.

Education of Staff

Training standards across Canada vary greatly. Interviewees identified an overall lack of training concerning accommodation, adaptation, social–emotional disabilities and how to include family members as partners. Lack of training for staff was seen to lead to a variety of problems:

- Higher burnout rates
- Decreased capacity for coping with diverse abilities of children
- Inability to identify relevant resources and materials
- Decreased ability to manage the variety of behaviours demonstrated in child care settings
- Higher frustration levels
- Inability to interact appropriately with families
- Diminished overall self-confidence in personal child guidance techniques

What can you do to attain adequate training and avoid these problems?

a) Search out opportunities to gain additional education, such as courses at universities or colleges, conferences and workshops.
b) Develop a resource library containing articles, newspaper clippings, journals and internet references.

Poverty

Poverty has a long-lasting detrimental effect on children's growth and development. In recent years, child poverty has increased in Canada. "The child poverty rate is almost at what it was in 1989 when Parliament unanimously resolved to end child poverty by the year 2000. Nearly one out of every nine children lives in poverty." (Campaign 2000, 2006) Children with special needs living in poverty are doubly affected. According to the Urban Poverty Consortium of Waterloo Region:

Poverty brings with it many costs that have a long-term influence on children:

- Poor nutrition, hunger
- Family stress, parental depression, reduced supports and family conflict
- Fewer resources for learning, lower quality child care, financial barriers for activities
- Crowded and dilapidated housing problems, homelessness, problem neighbourhoods, frequent moves, lack of safe places to play (The Urban Poverty Consortium of Waterloo Region, 2000:3)

The result of poverty on children is evident in children's abilities to learn. Most often, this is a long-term effect, unless the conditions of poverty can be reversed. Poverty itself may be a contributing factor to special-needs diagnoses.

Poverty has a negative influence on learning. In comparison with other children, children living in poverty have:

- Lower IQ levels
- Lower math and reading abilities
- Shorter attention spans
- Greater speech delays
- Vocabulary limitations

Poverty during childhood is related to poor intellectual outcomes and general learning or overall educational attainment. This means:

- Lower average grades
- Fewer years of education
- Lower rates of going to college or university
- Lower adult productivity (as measured by annual earnings, wages and work hours) (The Urban Poverty Consortium of Waterloo Region, 2000:7)

In addition, children who live in poverty take part in fewer recreational activities. Children rarely have opportunities to participate in organized activities such as swimming, physical-activity programs for family members and children, organized sports or clubs, or community groups such as Beavers or Guides. As a result, poverty often acts as an exclusionary factor in the child's life.

What can you do about the effects of poverty on childhood development?

a) Learn about the effects of poverty on children.
b) Research ways in which the effects of poverty can be mitigated, such as providing nutritious meals throughout the day.
c) Join community groups to advocate against poverty.
d) Become aware of and support programs to mitigate the effects of poverty, such as Better Beginnings and Healthy Babies Initiatives.

Aboriginal Children

According to Indian and Northern Affairs Canada (Campaign 2000, 2006), there was a 70 percent increase in child welfare cases between 1995 and 2003. One in four children living in Northern communities live in poverty. "The plight of First Nations children in their local communities and the conditions of urban Aboriginal children require sustained action to ensure that children will thrive, and not merely survive" (Campaign 2000, 2006:4).

Aboriginal children face the same debilitating results of poverty as other children, but are more vulnerable because many live in isolation and often there are a lack of resources within Northern communities. There is a strong need for awareness of the plight of Aboriginal children and sustained action against child poverty in First Nations and Aboriginal communities (Campaign 2000, 2006).

From the Author

I wanted to end the text on a positive note. I wanted to share many of the positive feelings and attitudes that individuals talked about across Canada. I believe that with increased awareness, we will also forge change. I have seen many families, professionals and community members striving to make Canada a better place for children with special needs. In my lifetime we have seen the demise of the horrific institutions that children with special needs were once placed in. I believe that the future will bring additional positive changes.

Attitude

In this section, I will provide quotes from various individuals who have cared for, or lived with, children with special needs.

Parents of child born with Down syndrome:

"We were so excited about our son's birth. I couldn't wait to hold my new son in my arms. It was a profound shock when the doctor told us that there was something wrong with our baby. After the first shock wore off, I just wanted to hold him. I remember that first time I held him. I remember the strong feelings of joy to look on my son's face. So what if he wasn't perfect? As the years passed, we have never regretted having Darren. He has taught us many lessons, such as patience, tolerance for others and acceptance of individual differences. Darren has been a blessing in our lives."

Staff member:

"I find it highly rewarding to work with children with special needs. It gives me a sense of accomplishment and a sense that I am making a difference."

Director:

"I have worked in many different settings, but I must admit that I most enjoy working in inclusive settings. The rewards are so rich. I love to see the acceptance and tolerance of individual differences that grow between the children and the families who attend the centre. It is such a win, win and win for everyone."

School-aged child:

"I knew that there were children around who didn't act or look the same as the rest of us, but I had never really met one. We had a new classmate, Sheilagh, who had cerebral palsy. At first, I tended to avoid her. She looked so different. Our teacher was really great. She noticed that some of us were rather hesitant. She helped Sheilagh explain to us about her condition. I never had really thought of her as a person like me. After she had told us about herself, I began to realize how funny and brave she was. We became good friends. I began to realize that she wasn't so different from me after all."

Licensing professional:

"I have been so pleased to see a gradual change in our community. Twenty years ago, when I first started my position as a licensing officer, children with special needs went to one preschool for children with special needs. When the centre first closed, there was a lot of resistance to including these children. Today I am proud to say that all of our centres accept children with special needs. I am not aware of one instance in which a child has been refused access to centre-based care in our community."

Learning Resource Consultant:

"I just love my job. It is so great to go into a centre and support the staff, family and child with special needs. I have found most staff members very open to suggestions and very willing to try new things. It is refreshing to see all children play together. After all, we are a society that embraces diversity."

SUMMARY

Although there are still many issues involved in caring for children with special needs, great strides have been made over the last century. For the most part, segregated preschool settings have disappeared. Most jurisdictions in Canada embrace the concept of inclusive care. This means that children can attend the centre of their choice, with the peers from their community, in a community setting. Additionally, there is abundant research available that increases awareness about the benefits of inclusive care. As a result, more proactive policies are being developed in some centres and jurisdictions across Canada.

KEY POINTS

Equitable access

- Lack of space—One out of eight child care centres in Canada does not accept children with special needs; long waiting lists
- Proportionate care—Children with special needs in proportion to their occurrence in general population
- Appropriate policies—Lack of proactive policies

Quality care

- Physical environment—Lack of space for adaptations; lack of funding to make relevant modifications

- Equipment and materials—Difficult to obtain; specialized equipment for few children; problem to store bulky equipment; expensive to purchase
- Role of director—Attracting and maintaining suitable staff; supporting role to staff; leadership role
- Support for staff—Concerns about child–adult ratios; need for time relief from meetings and planning
- Training of staff—Lack of training opportunities; no support for additional training
- Provision of therapy—Difficult to initiate assessment; long waiting lists; few choices; disruption of

schedules; lack of coordination between therapy and child care program

- Individual program plan—Need time to develop; standard nomenclature; access to resource consultants
- Families as partners—Attitudinal differences with respect to degree of involvement, type and manner of information sharing and family involvement in program planning
- Social interactions between children—Difficult to implement because of lack of role models, large diversity of skills and abilities and various communication methods
- Supportive board members—Lack of connection between setting policies and philosophies and daily program implementation; difficulty in attracting and maintaining board members; time involved in volunteer role of a board member; lack of expertise on board; too many expectations of board members
- Transition from centre to elementary school—Re-evaluation of child upon entry to school

Diagnosis and assessment

- Labelling—Tied to funding; labels fail to provide programming strategies and provide excuses for lack of programming; child stuck with label; focus on disability, not programming needs
- Misdiagnosis—Increased number of ADD/ADHD children diagnosed; controversy of medicating children
- Assessment strategies—Formal assessment by trained professionals; training needs of staff to use

informal tools and observation; lack of time and experience to implement and interpret

Cultural expectations

- Role of culture in determining how children are diagnosed and treated
- Variation among cultures in diagnosis of behavioural disorders

Funding of programs

- Need to provide equality of access to children with special needs

Education of staff

- Lack of training leads to burnout, decreased coping ability, decreased ability to procure relevant resources, decreased ability to manage a variety of behaviours effectively, higher frustration levels, decreased ability to interact with families and overall lack of confidence

Poverty

- Compounded influence on children with special needs
- Influences development—Through poor nutrition, increased stress, access to fewer resources and poor living conditions
- Negative effect on learning—Lower IQ, lower math and reading abilities, shorter attention span, greater speech delays, limited vocabulary
- Fewer recreational opportunities

EXERCISES

1. Review the definitions of inclusive care on page 362. Identify how each definition might place limits on or enhance inclusive care.

2. Conduct a survey of your community. Consider the following questions:
   a) How many centres accept children with special needs?
   b) How many spaces are available to children with special needs?
   c) What is the ratio of children with special needs to other children in the program?
   d) What policies are in place to ensure equal access to programs for children with special needs?

3. You are a staff member of a program that has previously not had children with physical disabilities enrolled. Therefore, no physical adaptations have been made to the play spaces. You are on a ground floor and ramps are provided for all entries into the building. You are going to accept a child who is in a wheelchair. What types of adaptations need to be made to the playrooms, washrooms and play yard to accommodate this child?

4. Look over some of the resources listed for children with special needs, such as those found at www. toronto.ca/children/pdf/sn_resources.pdf. Identify some additional resources you might need for:
   a) Physical disabilities
   b) Social–emotional disabilities
   c) Cognitive disabilities
   d) Communication disorders

5. What types of support are needed to increase the effectiveness of child care centre directors? Staff? Board members?

6. Identify strategies that might be used to overcome barriers to accepting families as partners within all aspects of the program.

7. What are some strategies that could be developed in order to help provide appropriate social interactions in settings of diverse abilities and skills?

8. What strategies might be developed in order to decrease the lack of transition from centre-based care to the elementary school system?

9. Describe some of the problems associated with diagnosis and assessment of young children.

10. Explain why the effects of poverty are compounded for a child with special needs.

11. Reflect on the attitudinal statements made by the various individuals on pages 380–381.
    a) Which reflections strike a chord with you? Identify why.
    b) Are there any reflections that you do not understand? Explain why not?

REFERENCES

Campaign 2000 (2006). Oh Canada! Too many Children in Poverty for Too Long. Campaign 2000 [online]. Available at http://www.campaign2000.ca/rc/rc06/06_C2000NationalReportCard.pdf [5-3-2008].

Canadian Council on Social Development (2000). *Children and Youth with Special Needs.* Ottawa, ON: Canadian Council on Social Development.

Child Care Association of Canada. (2004). What Do We Mean By Inclusion [online]. Available at www.specialinkcanada.org/resources/factsheets.html [11/24/2008].

Goleman, H., Doherty, G., Lero, D., LaGrange, A., & Tougas, J. (2000). *You Bet I Care! Caring and Learning Environments: Quality in Child Care Centres Across Canada* Guelph University, ON: Centre for Families, Work and Well-Being.

Harms, T., Clifford, R., & Cryer, D. (1998). *Early Childhood Environment Rating Scale.* Revised Edition. New York, NY: Teachers College Press.

Hope Irwin, S., Lero, D., & Brophy, K. (2000). *A Matter of Urgency: Including Children with Special Needs in Child Care in Canada.* Wreck Cove, NS: Breton Books.

Hope Irwin, S., Lero, D., & Brophy, K. (2004). *Inclusion: The Next Generation in Child Care in Canada.* Wreck Cove, NS: Breton Books.

Science Friday. (2000). Hour One: Medicating Preschoolers/ADHD. Science Friday [online]. Available at www.sciencefriday.com/pages/2000/Mar/hour1_030300.html - 13k [11/24/2008].

The Centre for Inclusive Education. (2008). Inclusions Defined [online]. Avalilable at www.edu.uwo.ca/Inclusive_Education/inclusion.asp [06/01/09].

The Urban Poverty consortium of waterloo Region (2000). Let's Talk about Poverty Fact Sheet 6 [online]. Available at www.waterlooregion.org/poverty/talk/6.html

Valentine, F. (2001). *Enabling Citizenship: Full Inclusion of Children with Disabilities and Their Parents* (Rep. No. F/13). Ottawa, ON: Canadian Policy and Research Network.

Glossary

Active listening Listening to the content of a message without personal bias and clarifying the intent of the message when the meaning is unclear or to ensure that the meaning is clear.

Addictive behaviours "Habits that are out of control, with a resulting impact on a person's health" (Insel, & Roth, 1999:312).

Age-appropriate Appropriate for the chronological age.

Age-appropriate practices Practices that are appropriate for the chronological age of the child, regardless of his or her developmental level. For example, a four-year-old with a developmental delay of two years should be playing with toys that are appropriate for a four-year-old. The toy should also be appropriate for child's developmental skill level.

American Sign Language A visual–spatial language that uses gestures, facial expressions such as eyebrow and lip movements, and the surrounding space to communicate.

Anti-bias "An anti-biased approach means taking a stand against unfair treatment associated with one of the areas of diversity where bias may exist" (Saderman Hall et al., 1995:2).

Anxiety state A fear of something that might happen in the future.

Aphasia An inability to communicate effectively using verbal language because of difficulty in comprehension or production difficulties.

Apraxia An inability to communicate verbally because the individual cannot effectively use the muscles that control speech sounds.

Associative play Play in which children share materials and ideas but may continue to be engaged in individual play activity.

Asthma A condition that obstructs the bronchial passages by narrowing or swelling of the tubes or by clogging of the tubes with mucus.

Attention deficit hyperactivity disorder (ADHD) This behaviour is characterized by a short attention span, distractibility, inattentiveness, impulsiveness and increased physical activity.

Augmentative devices Devices that help an individual communicate a message, such as symbol boards and talking computers.

Augmentative/alternative communication (AAC) "Any device or method that improves the ability of a child with communication impairment to communicate effectively" (Ballinger, 1999:1).

Autism Pervasive developmental disorder leading to social and communicative problems.

Base line A method used to determine how often behaviour has occurred, prior to formal intervention strategies.

Bias "Bias is a point of view or inclination that manifests itself through favoritism, dislike, or fear toward someone because of that person's particular looks, behaviour, or lifestyle. A bias can be conveyed to another through nonverbal, verbal, and physical interactions. In other words, one's point of view is clearly reflected by one's attitude and actions" (Saderman Hall et al., 1995:2).

Childhood schizophrenia "Unlike children with autism, those with schizophrenia typically have a later age of onset of their problem, show less intellectual impairment, display less severe social and language deficits, develop hallucinations and delusions as they get older, and experience periods of remission and relapse" (Mash & Wolfe, 1999:411).

Closed materials Materials that usually provide only one effective solution to completing a task, such as puzzles, dominoes and nesting cups.

Complex units Activity units containing four play spaces in order to encourage group play, such as sand, water or carpentry activities.

Concrete operational thinking "Children begin more and more to use logic and mental operations to understand situations and to think about how things work" (Schickedanz et al., 2001:439).

Conduct disorders Patterns of behaviour characterized by, for instance, aggressiveness toward other children or materials; disruptive behaviours, such as constant interruptions; throwing temper tantrums when thwarted; or withdrawal from the situation.

Constructive play Play in which children use materials or objects to create something.

Cooperative play Play toward a common goal that involves planning, role designation and sharing of ideas and materials.

Critical periods of brain development Times when "the developing brain is best able to absorb language, any language . . . . This ability to learn a language will be more difficult, and perhaps less efficient or effective, if these critical periods are allowed to pass without exposure to language" (National Institute on Deafness and Other Communication Disorders, 2001: 2).

Cystic fibrosis A genetic condition that affects the respiratory and digestive systems.

Decibels The smallest measurable difference in loudness intensity between sounds.

Deictic gestures Gestures used by infants to communicate intent, such as pointing to or reaching for a desired object.

Developmentally-appropriate practice "Refers to applying child development knowledge in making thoughtful and appropriate decisions about early childhood program practices—the understanding that "programs designed for young children be based on what is known about young children" (Bredekamp et al., 1997:v; Gestwicki, 1999:6).

Divergent thinking Ability to think of a variety of ways to solve a problem.

Dramatic play Play in which children create imaginary roles and situations with or without props.

Duration count A record of how long a behaviour lasts.

Easy reading books Books with large pictures and few words; the pictures illustrate the meaning of the words.

Emergent curriculum A program for children based on the observations of children's interests, strengths and needs. The learning experiences emerge from these observations.

Emotional and behavioural disorders Children with these disorders may exhibit feelings such as sadness, fear, anger, guilt or anxiety that may alter the way they behave and interact with others.

Expressive language Expressing thoughts, desires or ideas through verbal language, signing, body language, or by using symbols such as pictures.

Eye-hand coordination Ability to reach and grasp intended object.

Fetal alcohol syndrome Brain disorder involving physical and mental birth defects developing during pregnancy, caused by mother's consumption of alcohol during pregnancy—central nervous system involvement, growth retardation and characteristic facial features.

Finger spelling A spelling method in which each letter of the alphabet has a corresponding sign, and words are spelled out letter by letter.

Full-spectrum fluorescent lighting with ultraviolet enhancement The type of artificial lighting that closest to natural sunlight.

Functional play Play in which children practise skills through repeatedly interacting with objects, other individuals and language.

Holophrastic speech One-word utterances representing questions or statements; dependent on the inflection pattern used.

Hyperactivity Condition characterized by higher motor activity levels than normal for individuals of a given age.

Hyperkinetic Behaviours that involve increased energy and movement.

Hypertonic Excessively tense muscle tone.

Impaired health Describes a disease or condition—such as diabetes, asthma, allergies, cystic fibrosis or muscular dystrophy—that affects the daily functioning of the individual's life.

Intrinsic motivation Motivation that originates from the individual.

Joint attention Occurs when a child looks at an object, points to it and then looks back at the adult to focus the adult's attention on the desired object.

Kinetic Behaviours associated with the energy of movement.

Labelling Labelling comprises two aspects: assessment or diagnosis (the child is assessed to identify level of functioning in all developmental domains, or to identify specific medical or psychological problems) and application of the label (the label—for example, "learning disability," "ADD," "mental retardation" or "autism"—is applied as a result of the assessment or diagnosis).

Matching activities Exact duplicates of objects are placed side by side, such as two large bears or two dominoes.

Mental representations Mental pictures.

Morphology Description of how words are built in language.

Multimodal communication Using more than one method of communication, such as verbal and signing.

Muscular dystrophy An inherited condition, typically occurring in boys, that is associated with the degeneration of muscle fibre.

Myelination Formation of a protective sheath around nerve cells to improve transmission of impulses.

Non-compliant oppositional defiant disorder A consistently negative pattern of behaviour in which children may act with hostility—physical, verbal or both—and openly refuse to comply with expectations.

One-to-one correspondence The process of assigning one object to another, such as one spoon to one cup.

Onlooker play Play in which the child watches others play without interacting.

Open-ended materials Materials that provide children with a variety of ways to use them, such as blocks, paint and beads.

Orthopedic condition A condition resulting in difficulty in movement that involves the skeleton, joints and muscles.

Overextension Using single words to represent broad categories such as "dog" for all animals that have a tail and four legs.

Parallel play Play in which children play side by side, using similar materials but without interacting with each other.

Paraphrase To repeat what has been said in one's own words. Paraphrasing often starts with statements such as "I understand that . . . " or "I believe you said . . . ."

Pararead To repeat to oneself in one's own words what one has read. If in doubt, check what has been read with the author. Check what you have written against the original. If in doubt, clarify your perception in person.

Patterning The creation of a pattern that is repetitive, such as ABAB or red bear, blue bear, red bear, blue bear.

Phobia A persistent and irrational fear about an object, event, animal or person.

Phoneme The smallest unit of speech sound.

Phonetics A language system that breaks spoken language down into vocal sounds; used to read and spell.

Phonology The system that builds sounds into words.

Physical communication An individual's ability to transmit signals by facial expressions and other body language, such as shrugging the shoulders or using hand movements. Physical communications are culturally determined.

Pragmatics Refers to how language is used. Language usage changes with the context of a situation.

Prefixes The part of speech placed in front of a word to change the word's meaning, such as in- or re-.

Preoperational thinking When children begin to demonstrate knowledge of the world through symbols such as words. This type of thinking is inflexible and tied to situations.

Proto-words Verbalizations that sound like words and are accepted as words, such as "da-da-da" for "daddy."

Read-aloud books Books that adults read to children.

Receptive communication An individual's ability to understand what has been transmitted through verbal communication, body language and/or other means such as symbolized messages or signing.

Receptive language Understanding the message that has been communicated through speech, signing or symbols such as written words.

Representational gestures Gestures used to symbolize an object, a request or an event, such as supporting the side of the head with two hands to indicate tiredness.

Representational study Study conducted on a sampling of day care centres in pre-selected regions as opposed to all day care centres in all regions. The outcomes of the study are then generalized as representative of all of Canada.

Research books Books that encourage children to find information for themselves.

Risk factors Include biological and environmental conditions that may increase the likelihood of problems in development—physical, social, emotional and cognitive.

Scaffolding The process of providing and gradually removing external support for learning.

Scribe Someone who listens to and writes down exactly what the child says.

Scribe centre Area to which children can go to dictate a story.

Semantics The meaning of words.

Sensory motor stage Stage in which learning involves exploring the learning environment through the use of all the senses.

Seriation Activity in which materials are lined up in order according to size (such as small bears to large bears).

Signed English Every word in the English language has a corresponding sign. Signed English is similar to spoken English.

Simple units Single play spaces to encourage individual play, such as working on a puzzle, reading a book or painting activities.

Sociodramatic play Occurs when two or more children are engaged in dramatic play.

Solitary play Play alone without interacting with others.

Sorting Activities in which a number of materials with similar characteristics are placed together, such as collecting all the red bears on a red tray.

Spastic cerebral palsy Refers to children who have suffered damage to the motor cortex of the brain. These children will have difficulty controlling voluntary movement. The condition is characterized by slow and difficult movement, poor coordination and weak, hypertonic (excessively tense) muscle tone.

Spina bifida A defect in the vertebrae that protect the spinal cord. Effects include neurological damage that results in delays in or impairment of growth and development, paralysis of the lower body, inability to walk without assistive devices, and some perceptual and cognitive disabilities.

Suffixes Parts of speech placed at the end of a word, such as -ly or –ness.

Super units Activity units containing eight play spaces to encourage individual or group play, such as dramatic or block play.

Symbolic play Play in which children use an action or object to represent something else.

Syntax The way words are put together to form phrases, clauses or sentences and the connection of the elements of language into an orderly system (grammar).

Telegraphic speech Utterances that resemble sentences but are expressed only in essential two-to-three-word phrases such as "Want milk!"

Tourette's syndrome A condition characterized by involuntary muscle movement, such as sporadic twitches or tics.

Trial-and-error learning Trying different techniques until one that works is found.

Underextension When one word is used to represent many meanings, such as "hat" as a general term to mean all types of hats.

Visual acuity "Refers to how well the elements of a pattern can be seen by someone at a specific distance" (Schickedanz et al., 2001:95).

Visual figure ground Ability to pick out individual items from a background.

SECTION 1

The SpeciaLink Child Care Inclusion Practices Profile

"The *SpeciaLink Inclusion Child Care Practices Profile* and the *SpeciaLink Child Care Inclusion Principles Scale* are tools for assessing inclusion quality in child care centres. Used together, they provide a picture of sustainable and evolving inclusion quality— an emerging issue as more children with special needs attend community-based centres and as inclusion pioneers leave their centres and a new generation of directors and early childhood educators take on the challenge."

The SpeciaLink Child Care Inclusion Practices Profile and the SpeciaLink Child Care Inclusion Principles Scale (Final Workshop Version, May 2005) by Sharon Hope Irwin (SpeciaLink: The National Centre for Child Care Inclusion). Reprinted with permission. Recommendations for Inclusive Care, from Sharon Hope Irwin, Donna S. Lero and Kathleen Brophy: Highlights From Inclusion: The Next Generation in Child Care in Canada *(SpeciaLink: The National Centre for Child Care Inclusion), pp. 23–25. Reprinted with permission.*

Practice 1: Physical Environment and Special Needs.

Inadequate 1	Minimal 3	Good 5	Excellent 7
1.1 □Y □N No modifications for children with special needs.	**3.1** □Y □N Minor modifications (e.g., placement of furniture).	**5.1** □Y □N Major permanent modifications (e.g., ramps, step-up changing table).	**7.1** □Y □N Universal design principles are evident throughout*
1.2 □Y □N Building entrance and/or classroom entrance not accessible.	**3.2** □Y □N Some classroom areas are accessible.	**5.2** □Y □N Many classroom areas are accessible.	**7.2** □Y □N All classroom areas are accessible, as are washroom, coatroom and hallways.
1.3 □Y □N Classroom is too noisy and/or too bright or too dim.	**3.3** □Y □N Some efforts made to soften noise and light.	**5.3** □Y □N Many efforts made to ensure that noise and light are appropriate.	**7.3** □Y □N Sound and light are at appropriate levels.
1.4 □Y □N Playground entrance not accessible.	**3.4** □Y □N Some playground areas are accessible.	**5.4** □Y □N Many playground areas are accessible.	**7.4** □Y □N All playground areas are accessible.

Score: 1   2   3   4   5   6   7

* Universal design principles are part of a concept of design, right from the beginning, that embodies characteristics that make a physical environment accessible to all people. Hallways are wide enough for wheelchairs, bathrooms are accessible and kitchen counters are reachable. At its best, universal design is so well done that adaptations are invisible. There is no ramp, because the threshold of the building is at ground level. The field of universal design is opening up rapidly, as a large proportion of our adult population ages and wants to remain active and independent. We should expect no less for our youngest children. "Some" means at least 3 interest areas are accessible; "Some efforts" means at least 3 examples are evident. "Many" means at least 5 interest areas are accessible; "Many efforts" means at least 5 examples are evident.

Comments: _____

Practice 2: Equipment and Materials.

Inadequate 1	Minimal 3	Good 5	Excellent 7
		Score: 1 2 3	4 5 6 7
1.1 ☐ Y ☐ N No adaptations or special equipment for children with special needs.	**3.1** ☐ Y ☐ N Some* adapted typical toys and specialized equipment for children with special needs.	**5.1** ☐ Y ☐ N Many* adapted typical toys and specialized equipment for children with special needs.	**7.1** ☐ Y ☐ N Equipment and materials are individualized to meet unique needs. Universal design principles are evident throughout.
1.2 ☐ Y ☐ N No adapted gross-motor equipment available for children with mobility, coordination and sensory issues.	**3.2** ☐ Y ☐ N Some gross-motor equipment is adapted for children with limited mobility, coordination, and sensory issues.	**5.2** ☐ Y ☐ N Many items of gross-motor equipment adapted for children with mobility, coordination and sensory issues.	**7.2** ☐ Y ☐ N Substantial gross-motor equipment adapted for children with mobility, coordination and sensory issues.
	3.3 ☐ Y ☐ N At least one example of assistive technology is evident.**	**5.3** ☐ Y ☐ N At least 3 examples of assistive technology are evident.	**7.3** ☐ Y ☐ N At least 5 examples of assistive technology are evident.
	3.4 ☐ Y ☐ N Adapted and assistive equipment occasionally*** used in regular routines and activities.	**5.4** ☐ Y ☐ N Adapted, specialized and assistive equipment frequently*** used during regular activities.	**7.4** ☐ Y ☐ N Adapted, specialized and assistive equipment integrated into all regular activities.

As universal design principles are applied to equipment and materials, items such as door handles, kitchen utensils (such as "Good Grips"), pens and pencils, forks and spoons, and hair brushes are designed so that people with motoric problems can use everyday items. In a child care centre you would look for specialized equipment, adapted equipment and well-designed regular equipment that allow children with motoric issue and other issues to participate fully in routines and activities. Look for visual cue systems (such as PECS), knobbed puzzles, crayons with good grips, two-person scissors, sensory materials for children with high needs, touch screens and head switches for computers, and touch switches for mechanical toys. Note whether the height and design of tables, housekeeping area, and easels allow access by children who use walkers, standing braces or wheelchairs, is respectful of children and convenient for staff.

* "Some" means 3 or 4; "Many" means 5 or more.

** "Assistive technology" refers to equipment such as specialized computer software, input devices (such as head switches, touch screens, voice recognition software), output devices (such as speech simulation software), cause-effect switches, and FM switches.

*** "Occasionally" means 25% of the time; "Frequently" means over 50% of the time, as appropriate.

Comments:

Practice 3: Director and Inclusion.

Score: 1 2 3 4 5 6 7

Inadequate 1	Minimal 3	Good 5	Excellent 7
1.1 ☐ Y ☐ N Director expresses no interest in inclusion.	**3.1** ☐ Y ☐ N Director expresses willingness to include children with special needs.	**5.1** ☐ Y ☐ N Director takes an active role in inclusion program.	**7.1** ☐ Y ☐ N Director is an inclusion leader** within the centre.
1.2 ☐ Y ☐ N Director plays no advocacy role regarding inclusion.	**3.2** ☐ Y ☐ N Director is an advocate in at least one area—the community, the ECE field, education system or with government.	**5.2** ☐ Y ☐ N Director is an advocate in at least two areas—the community, the ECE field, education system with government.	**7.2** ☐ Y ☐ N Director is an inclusion leader*** within the community, in the ECE field, with the education system, and with government.
1.3 ☐ Y ☐ N Director does not encourage staff to become knowledgeable about inclusion.	**3.3** ☐ Y ☐ N Director allows staff to attend yearly workshops or conferences on inclusion with either lieu time or some funding.	**5.3** ☐ Y ☐ N Director promotes staff participation in courses/workshops/conferences related to inclusion, with lieu time and funding.	**7.3** ☐ Y ☐ N Policies are developed that reward staff development, skills and credentials related to inclusion.
1.4 ☐ Y ☐ N Director does not encourage board to be supportive of inclusion.	**3.4** ☐ Y ☐ N Director passes along information on inclusion to board members.*	**5.4** ☐ Y ☐ N Director promotes board* knowledge of inclusion through speakers at meetings and/or information sessions.	**7.4** ☐ Y ☐ N Director actively recruits board members* who are supportive of inclusion and educates them on issues, policies and trends in inclusion.
1.5 ☐ Y ☐ N Director does not work with related early childhood intervention agencies.	**3.5** ☐ Y ☐ N Director attends occasional meetings with agencies related to inclusion.	**5.5** ☐ Y ☐ N Director is a partner in at least one agency or community group related to inclusion.	**7.5** ☐ Y ☐ N Director collaborates with many community agencies related to inclusion.

*   Or other similar unit, such as parent committee.
**   Providing in-services on inclusion and modelling participation in advocacy activities to staff.
*** Provides workshops in community, ECE field and to government; participates in task forces, committees and working groups; promotes broad participation in advocacy for inclusion.

Comments:

Practice 4: Staff Support.

Inadequate 1	Minimal 3	Score: 1 2 3 Good 5	4 Excellent 7 5 6 7
1.1 ☐ Y ☐ N There is little or no consultative assistance available to staff on inclusion.	**3.1** ☐ Y ☐ N Scheduled consultative assistance is available during period when children with special needs enrolled.	**5.1** ☐ Y ☐ N Consultative assistance plans are developed collaboratively.	**7.1** ☐ Y ☐ N Level of consultative assistance flexible to centre's needs.
1.2 ☐ Y ☐ N There is no in-centre staff, in addition to ratio, to support the children with special needs.	**3.2** ☐ Y ☐ N There is at least a part-time support staff, in addition to ratio, to support the children with special needs.	**5.2** ☐ Y ☐ N Reduced child-to-staff ratio to include children with special needs or one-to-one staffing, as needed.	**7.2** ☐ Y ☐ N Reduced child-to-staff ratio to include children with extra needs, and one-to-one staffing, as needed.
	3.3 ☐ Y ☐ N Resource support staff have some training in ECE, special needs or the individual child's issues.	**5.3** ☐ Y ☐ N One permanent staff (in-house RT) in addition to ratio; facilitates inclusion (at least part-time).	**7.3** ☐ Y ☐ N In-centre RT, in addition to ratio, facilitates inclusion (full-time position).
		5.4 ☐ Y ☐ N In-centre Resource Teacher has ECE diploma and post-diploma special needs certificate, or BCE diploma and at least 10 years' experience with children with special needs and 10 workshops in special needs/inclusion.	**7.4** ☐ Y ☐ N In-centre RT has degree in ECE or related field and post-diploma certificate in special needs/inclusion.

Comments: _____

Practice 5: Staff Training.

Inadequate 1	Minimal 3	Good 5	Excellent 7
		Score: 1 2 3	4 5 6 7
1.1 □Y □N No regular staff with special needs/inclusion training.	3.1 □Y □N One staff partially trained in special needs/inclusion.*	5.1 □Y □N One staff has certificate in special needs/inclusion.	7.1 □Y □N More than one staff has certificate in special needs/inclusion.
1.2 □Y □N Staff not encouraged to attend workshops, conferences or in-services on special needs issues.	3.2 □Y □N Some** staff attend periodic*** workshops, conferences or in-services on special needs issues.	5.2 □Y □N Many*** staff attend periodic workshops, conferences or in-services on special needs issues.	7.2 □Y □N Most staff attend periodic workshops, conferences or in-services on special needs issues.
1.3 □Y □N Director does not participate in inclusion training.	3.3 □Y □N Director either participates in inclusion training or encourages staff to do so.	5.3 □Y □N Director participates in inclusion training.	7.3 □Y □N Director provides inclusion training at in-services, workshops or conferences, or at community college.
			7.4 □Y □N Some inclusion training provided as in-services, with topics developed collaboratively.
			7.5 □Y □N Director/board promote inclusion training through funding of workshops, lieu days, career laddering, etc.

* "Training" means a diploma or certificate in special needs/inclusion beyond basic ECE training.
** "Some" means less than 25% of staff.
*** "Periodic" means at least once a year; "Many" means over 50%.

Comments:

Practice 6: Therapies: Physiotherapy (PT); Occupational Therapy (OT); Speech & Language (S&L); Behavioural Consultation.*

Inadequate 1	Minimal 3	Good 5	Excellent 7
Score: 1 2	3	4 5	6 7
1.1 ☐ Y ☐ N Director has little or no knowledge of therapeutic interventions and goals for children with special needs.	**3.1** ☐ Y ☐ N Director has information about therapeutic interventions and goals for some of the children with special needs.	**5.1** ☐ Y ☐ N Director is knowledgeable about children's therapies and encourages liaison between therapists and staff.	**7.1** ☐ Y ☐ N Director successfully promotes collaborative goal setting among therapists, parents and staff.
1.2 ☐ Y ☐ N Staff has little or no knowledge of therapeutic interventions and goals for children with special needs.	**3.2** ☐ Y ☐ N Staff has information about therapeutic interventions and goals for some of the children with special needs.	**5.2** ☐ Y ☐ N Staff are knowledgeable about children's therapies and meet occasionally with therapists for most of the children.	**7.2** ☐ Y ☐ N Staff are knowledgeable about children's therapies and participate collaboratively with therapists and parents in developing and assessing therapeutic interventions for all of the children.
	3.3 ☐ Y ☐ N Therapies may be provided at clinics or at the centre.	**5.3** ☐ Y ☐ N Some therapies are provided at centre, in group settings; when therapies are provided at clinics, staff periodically attend therapy sessions.	**7.3** ☐ Y ☐ N Most therapies are provided in group settings.
	3.4 ☐ Y ☐ N Staff sometimes carry out follow-up activities suggested by therapists.	**5.4** ☐ Y ☐ N Staff are consistent in carrying out follow-up activities.	**7.4** ☐ Y ☐ N Staff are creative, as well as consistent, in implementing follow-up activities.
	3.5 ☐ Y ☐ N Follow-up activities may be carried out outside of classroom or within activities and routines.	**5.5** ☐ Y ☐ N Follow-up activities are often carried out within group activities.	**7.5** ☐ Y ☐ N Goals are embedded into regular routines and activities.

* Since the availability of therapeutic interventions, their adequacy, frequency and duration are issues beyond the control of child care centres, we do not address this issue in Practice 6. Obliquely, however, we do address the issue under "advocacy" in the SpeciaLink Child Care Inclusion Principles Scale.

Comments:

Practice 7: Individual Program Plans (IPPs).

Inadequate 1	Minimal 3	Good 5	Excellent 7
Score: 1	2 3	4 5 6	7
1.1 ☐ Y ☐ N Children with special needs are present, but none have Individual Program Plans (IPPs).	**3.1** ☐ Y ☐ N Children with special needs are present, and some* have IPPs.	**5.1** ☐ Y ☐ N Most* children with special needs have IPPs.	**7.1** ☐ Y ☐ N All children with special needs have IPPs.
	3.2 ☐ Y ☐ N IPPs may be carried out in one-to-one pull-out sessions and/or within regular routines and activities.	**5.2** ☐ Y ☐ N IPPs are generally used in either small group pull-out sessions or in regular group sessions.	**7.2** ☐ Y ☐ N IPP goals are embedded in regular group activities.
	3.3 ☐ Y ☐ N IPP goals of the children with special needs are known by at least the one-to-one workers and/or the RT.	**5.3** ☐ Y ☐ N IPP goals are shared with all staff at staff meetings and/or planning sessions.	**7.3** ☐ Y ☐ N IPP goals are posted at interest centres so that all staff can access them.
	3.4 ☐ Y ☐ N IPPs are developed by therapist or consultant/RT.	**5.4** ☐ Y ☐ N IPP goals are developed by consultant/RT, with staff and/or parent input.	**7.4** ☐ Y ☐ N IPPs are developed collaboratively by consultant/RT, staff and parents.
		5.5 ☐ Y ☐ N IPPs goals and objectives are reviewed periodically.	**7.5** ☐ Y ☐ N Children's progress is monitored to document acquisition toward IPP goals, and ineffective practices are modified.

* "Some" means at least 25%; "Most" means at least 75%.

Comments:

Practice 8: Parents of Children with Special Needs.

Inadequate 1	Minimal 3	Score: 1 2 3	Good 5	Excellent 7 / 4 5 6 7
1.1 ☐Y ☐N Director makes no additional effort to involve parents of children with special needs in the regular activities of the centre, beyond attendance at mandatory IPP meetings.	**3.1** ☐Y ☐N Director makes minimal effort to involve parents of children with special needs in the regular activities of the centre.*	**5.1** ☐Y ☐N Director encourages involvement of parents of children with special needs in the regular activities of the centre.*	**7.1** ☐Y ☐N Director actively promotes involvement of parents of children with special needs in IPP meetings, regular activities of the centre, collaborative meetings with therapists for goal setting, committees, board membership.*
1.2 ☐Y ☐N Parents are not treated as sources of information about their children with special needs.	**3.2** ☐Y ☐N Parents are treated as sources of information about their children with special needs.	**5.2** ☐Y ☐N Parents are seen as contributors to program planning and goal setting.	**7.2** ☐Y ☐N Parents are encouraged in their role as advocates for their children.
1.3 ☐Y ☐N Parents of children with special needs are not given information concerning progress of their child on IPP goals, unless they ask for it.	**3.3** ☐Y ☐N Parents of children with special needs are given information concerning progress of their child on IPP goals, at least twice a year.	**5.3** ☐Y ☐N Parents of children with special needs are encouraged to participate in regular planning sessions and reviews of their child's progress, at least twice a year.	**7.3** ☐Y ☐N Parents of children with special needs are encouraged to develop greater knowledge about IPP processes, transition to public school procedures, therapies and/or disability organizations.
1.4 ☐Y ☐N Parents of children with special needs are not encouraged to join committees, the board or other governance/specialty groups.	**3.4** ☐Y ☐N Parents of children with special needs are told about opportunities to join committees, the board or other governance/specialty groups.	**5.4** ☐Y ☐N Parents of children with special needs are encouraged to join committees, the board or other governance/specialty groups.	**7.4** ☐Y ☐N Parents are encouraged to participate in panels, workshops, staff training and advocacy.

* To achieve a "3" rating, the centre must provide at least 2 supports, such as transportation, babysitting, translation, meeting at site convenient to parents, time convenient to parents, encouragement to bring relative or trusted friend/advocate. To achieve a "5" rating, the centre must provide at least 4 supports. To achieve a "7", all must be available.

Comments:

Practice 9: Involvement of Typical Children.

Note frequency and intensity of play that involves children with special needs and typically developing children—especially in housekeeping area, block area, and out of doors, during free play times.

Score:	1	2	3	4	5	6	7
	Inadequate 1		Minimal 3		Good 5		Excellent 7
	1.1 ☐ Y ☐ N Typically developing children rarely interact with children with special needs.		**3.1** ☐ Y ☐ N Typically developing children sometimes* interact with children with special needs in group social play situations. (That means that during at least 25% of the time when children with special needs are in group play situations such as the Dramatic Play area and the Block area, they are not ignored and left out of the play.)		**5.1** ☐ Y ☐ N Children with special needs are often* included in group social play.		**7.1** ☐ Y ☐ N Children with special needs are included in group social play most of the time.*
	1.2 ☐ Y ☐ N Staff take no active role in encouraging social inclusion.		**3.2** ☐ Y ☐ N Staff make comments or gestures to promote social inclusion.		**5.2** ☐ Y ☐ N Staff suggest appropriate roles or dramatic situations that are inclusionary.		**7.2** ☐ Y ☐ N Staff systematically use techniques of scripting, cooperative learning, valued object sharing, etc., to promote social inclusion.
	1.3 ☐ Y ☐ N Competition is used frequently to motivate children to perform.		**3.3** ☐ Y ☐ N Cooperation is motivated occasionally, by adult requests.		**5.3** ☐ Y ☐ N Cooperation is stressed, through planned activities that require more than one child to accomplish.		**7.3** ☐ Y ☐ N Staff receive specific training in the promotion of inclusive social play.
							7.4 ☐ Y ☐ N Cooperation is motivated frequently by adult verbal statements and by activities that need more than one child to accomplish.

* "Sometimes" means 25% of the time; "Often" means 50% of the time; "Most of the time" means over 75% of the time.

Comments:

Practice 10: Board of Directors and Other Similar Units.

In privately owned centres, inquire about parent committees. Replace the word "board" with "committee."

Inadequate 1	Minimal 3	Good 5	Excellent 7
Score:		1 2 3	4 5 6 7
1.1 □ Y □ N Board of directors (or parent committee) has not addressed the issue of inclusion.	**3.1** □ Y □ N Director occasionally provides information about inclusion issues to board of directors (or parent committee).	**5.1** □ Y □ N Board of directors (or parent committee) has adopted a written policy on inclusion.	**7.1** □ Y □ N Board of directors (or parent committee) actively promotes inclusion in the community.
1.2 □ Y □ N Board of directors (or parent committee) includes no parents of children with special needs.	**3.2** □ Y □ N Board of directors (or parent committee) occasionally* includes a parent of a child with special needs.	**5.2** □ Y □ N Board of directors (or parent committee) always includes at least one parent of a child with special needs.	**7.2** □ Y □ N Board of directors (or parent committee) actively recruits parents of children with special needs for board positions.
1.3 □ Y □ N Board of directors (or parent committee) given no orientation/information about inclusion of children with special needs.	**3.3** □ Y □ N Board of directors (or parent committee) given orientation/ information about inclusion of children with special needs.	**5.3** □ Y □ N Board of directors (or parent committee) receives regular report about inclusion/special needs.	**7.3** □ Y □ N Board of directors (or parent committee) continuously updated about inclusion issues at meetings, written information, speakers.

* "Occasionally" means 25% of the time.

Comments: _____

_____

Practice 11: Preparing for Transition to School.

	Inadequate 1	Minimal 3	Good 5	Excellent 7
Score:	1	2 3	1 2 3	4 5 6 7
	1.1 ☐ Y ☐ N Centre has not addressed this issue.	3.1 ☐ Y ☐ N Director and/or staff actively seek information about school system practices related to children with special needs. 3.2 ☐ Y ☐ N School system staff may telephone or visit centre in regards to individual children with special needs in preschool year.	5.1 ☐ Y ☐ N Staff implement suggestions from school system—from kindergarten teachers or special educators. 5.2 ☐ Y ☐ N Centre staff meet with some school staff (e.g., special education staff, resource teachers, principals, teachers, classroom assistants) regarding many* children with special needs in spring of preschool year.	7.1 ☐ Y ☐ N Staff actively collaborate with teachers and parents to design and implement transition strategies during preschool year. 7.2 ☐ Y ☐ N Centre holds regular case conferences with school staff, in spring of preschool year, about all children with special needs. 7.3 ☐ Y ☐ N Centre shares information with school system, only as requested by parents, and only after discussion with parents about potential pros and cons of such disclosure.

* "Many" means at least 50%.

Comments: _____

The SpeciaLink Child Care Inclusion Principles Scale

Principle 1: Zero Reject.

In fully inclusive child care centres, *all* children are welcome, regardless of type or level of disability. Many child care centres that are referred to as "inclusive" actually integrate only children with mild to moderate disabilities, or children with a single disability. Children who are not toilet-trained, who are not ambulatory, who have behavioural disorders or who have special health care needs are most likely to be excluded. (Read this statement to the director as you begin to discuss Principle 1 in a non-judgmental tone. Then use probe questions, as necessary, and record comments.)

<u>Some probe questions</u>: (1) Have you, or would you be unable to, accept children with any particular level or type of disability? If "yes," what type of disability(ies) or level(s) are these? (2) How many children with what disabilities and levels of disability (mild/moderate/severe/profound) have you been able to accommodate in your centre? Record under "Comments."

	Inadequate 1	Minimal 3	Good 5	Excellent 7
Score:	1	2 3	4 5	6 7
	1.1 ☐ Y ☐ N Director describes previous and present inclusion of children with disabilities in terms of very subjective criteria, such as "very nice parent," "seemed easy to include," "we were forced to."	**3.1** ☐ Y ☐ N Director specifies some* types and levels of disability** that the centre can accommodate.	**5.1** ☐ Y ☐ N Director specifies many* types and levels of disability that the centre can accommodate.	**7.1** ☐ Y ☐ N Director specifies that the centre will enroll children with all levels and types of disability—actively following the principle of zero reject.
	1.2 ☐ Y ☐ N Lead ECE is not aware of previous or present enrollment of children with disabilities in her classroom.	**3.2** ☐ Y ☐ N Lead ECE is aware of previous or present enrollment of some* children with disabilities in her classroom.	**5.2** ☐ Y ☐ N Lead ECE is aware of many* children with disabilities, previously and presently enrolled, including some specifics about accommodations and modifications made to include them.	**7.2** ☐ Y ☐ N Lead ECE, another ECE, a support staff (such as secretary or cook), and a parent*** all articulate zero reject principle as their own and as the centre's.
	1.3 ☐ Y ☐ N The centre has no written or verbal policy on inclusion.	**3.3** ☐ Y ☐ N The centre has an informal policy on inclusion (evidenced by Director's comments and supported by such evidence as accessible materials on diversity including pictures, books, dolls with disabilities, or by the presence of information and training opportunities on inclusion being available to staff).	**5.3** ☐ Y ☐ N The centre has a written policy statement that supports inclusion.	**7.3** ☐ Y ☐ N The centre has a written inclusion policy statement that affirms the zero reject principle, with a phrase such as "*all* children."

* "Some" means three or fewer; "Many" means four or more.

** "Types of disability" refers to diagnosis, such as autistic, intellectual, physical, visual, auditory. "Levels" refers to intensity, such as mild, moderate or severe.

*** "A parent" means the first parent (or close family member) of a child with special needs whom you see—in locker room, at arrival or departure, or identified through probe question.

Comments: _____

Principle 2: Natural Proportions.

In fully inclusive child care centres (those with a "7" rating), **the proportion of children with disabilities is roughly that of their natural proportion in the general population (10-15%).** Many child care centres referred to as "inclusive" enroll only one or two children with special needs at any one time. Other child care centres that are referred to as "inclusive" are actually programs with a very high proportion of children with special needs. Sometimes called reverse mainstreaming, these programs typically enroll a few typically developing children as role models, or include 50% typically developing children and 50% children with disabilities. (Read this statement to Director as you begin to discuss Principle 2 in a non-judgmental tone. Then use probe questions, as necessary, and record comments.)

Probe questions: (1) What percentage of children with disabilities do you think you could enroll (or do you enroll) in your centre? (If they answer with a number, convert this to a percentage by using the licensed capacity figure.) (2) Do you think that there is a percentage that would be too high? What is it? (3) If she says, "It depends on the child/ren," ask what she means. Record as "comment."

Inadequate 1	Minimal 3	Good 5	Excellent 7
Score: 1	2 3	4 5	6 7
1.1 ☐ Y ☐ N Centre never enrolls a child/ren with disabilities.	3.1 ☐ Y ☐ N Centre occasionally* enrolls at least a few (less than natural proportions, which is roughly 10-15%) children with disabilities,	5.1 ☐ Y ☐ N Centre usually* enrolls nearly a natural proportion of children with disabilities (roughly 10-15%).	7.1 ☐ Y ☐ N Director actively follows "natural proportions" as a working principle in the centre, enrolling a natural proportion of children with disabilities nearly all of the time.*
1.2 ☐ Y ☐ N Centre mainly enrolls children with disabilities, with a few typically developing children as role models.	3.2 ☐ Y ☐ N Lead ECE is aware of the number of children with disabilities currently in her classroom because she is involved in arranging and/or carrying out accommodations and adaptations to support these children.	5.2 ☐ Y ☐ N Lead ECE is aware of the number of children with disabilities currently in the centre because she is involved in developing and carrying out IPP goals and because inclusion strategies are discussed at staff meetings.	7.2 ☐ Y ☐ N Lead ECE, another ECE, a support staff (such as secretary or cook) and a parent articulate the principle of natural proportions as their own and as the centre's.
1.3 ☐ Y ☐ N Centre enrolls 50% children with disabilities and 50% typical children.	3.3 ☐ Y ☐ N The centre has an informal policy on inclusion (evidenced by director's comments and supported by such evidence as accessible materials on diversity including pictures, books, dolls with disabilities, or by the presence of information and training opportunities on inclusion being available to staff).	5.3 ☐ Y ☐ N The centre has a written policy statement supporting inclusion.	7.3 ☐ Y ☐ N The centre has a written inclusion policy affirming the principle of natural proportions.
1.4 ☐ Y ☐ N Lead ECE is not aware of number of children with disabilities currently in her classroom.			7.4 ☐ Y ☐ N The centre's policy statement is visible to visitors and available to staff, parents, community.
1.5 ☐ Y ☐ N Centre has no written or verbal policy on inclusion.			

* "Occasionally" means at least 25% of the time; "Usually" means at least 75% of the time; "Nearly all of the time" means around 90% of the time.

Principle 3: Same Hours/Days of Attendance Available to All Children.

In fully inclusive child care centres, all attendance options (such as full day, mornings, two days per week, etc.) that are available to typically developing children are also available to children with special needs. Many child care centres referred to as inclusive only include children with special needs for part of the day. The centre may be open until 5:30, but the child with special needs is required to leave early. Funding is often cited as the limitation, because too often what is being funded is not "child care" but rather "development."
(Read this statement to Director as you begin to discuss Principle 3 in a non-judgmental tone. Then use probe questions, as necessary, and record comments.)
<u>Probe question:</u> (1) Are there any limitations on the hours or number of days that children with disabilities can attend your centre? For example, if the parent is not employed, can the child with a disability attend five days per week, until closing time? (Record as "comment.")

Inadequate 1			Minimal 3			Score: 1 2 3	Good 5			4	Excellent 7		
1.1 ☐ Y ☐ N Director states that many* children with disabilities attend limited hours per day, or limited number of days per week, despite parent preference—not the same options that other children have.			3.1 ☐ Y ☐ N Director states that at least some* children with disabilities attend the same hours and days that other children attend—with the same options that other children have.				5.1 ☐ Y ☐ N Director states that most* children with disabilities attend the same hours and days that other children attend—with the same options that other children have.			7.1 ☐ Y ☐ N Director actively follows the principle of "same hours of attendance available for all children." No children with disabilities are limited to schedules that do not apply to typically developing children.		
1.2 ☐ Y ☐ N Children with disabilities are often** required to stay at home when particular staff members are absent.			3.2 ☐ Y ☐ N Occasionally** a child with a disability <u>may be asked to stay at home</u> because a particular staff member is absent.				5.2 ☐ Y ☐ N Children with disabilities are never asked to stay home because a particular staff member is absent.			7.2 ☐ Y ☐ N The absence of a particular staff member does not have a major impact on the child with disabilities, because s/he is accustomed to interacting with several members of the staff.		
1.3 ☐ Y ☐ N Lead ECE is unaware of centre policy on "not same hours/days of attendance" for children with disabilities.			3.3 ☐ Y ☐ N ☐ N/A Lead ECE is aware of centre's policy on attendance options for children with disabilities.				5.3 ☐ Y ☐ N Lead ECE recognizes inequity in a hypothetical policy that does not provide same hours/days of attendance option.			7.3 ☐ Y ☐ N Lead ECE, another ECE, a support staff (such as secretary or cook) and a parent articulate their support and the centre's support of the principle of "same hours/days of attendance available for all children."		
1.4 ☐ Y ☐ N Parents are required to be present to perform related health procedures—such as tube-feeding or catheterization—as a condition of enrollment.			3.3 ☐ Y ☐ N Parents are requested to be present to help with training of staff in related health procedures, such as tube-feeding or catheterization. (N/A is possible.)				5.4 ☐ Y ☐ N Parents are invited to participate in the development of a Special Health Care Plan for their child with special health care needs, and to collaborate in related staff training.			7.4 ☐ Y ☐ N Parents are acknowledged as experts in their child's health care needs, and are fully accommodated so that they can participate in training and information sessions.		
1.5 ☐ Y ☐ N Centre has no written or verbal policy on inclusion.			3.5 ☐ Y ☐ N The centre has an informal policy on inclusion (evidenced by director's comments and supported by such evidence as accessible materials on diversity including pictures, books and dolls with disabilities, or by the presence of information and training opportunities on inclusion being available to staff).				5.5 ☐ Y ☐ N The centre's written policy statement affirms the centre's support of inclusion.			7.5 ☐ Y ☐ N The centre's written inclusion policy statement affirms the principle of "same hours/days of attendance available to all children."		

* "Some" means at least 25%; "Many" means more than 50%; "Most" means at least 75%; ** "Occasionally" means 3–4 times a year; "Often" means more than monthly.

Principle 4: Full Participation.

In fully inclusive child care centres, children with special needs have their needs met within the regular group activities and routines, through accommodations, modifications, and extra support where necessary. They are celebrated, not simply tolerated or accepted. Many child care programs that are referred to as inclusive are actually programs that merely *physically* include children with special needs, but that make insufficient provision for their full participation. These children often are "observers" rather than "participants" for a large part of the day, or are engaged in pull-out activities rather than those of the group. (Read this statement to Director as you begin to discuss Principle 4 in a non-judgmental tone. Then use probe questions as necessary and record comments.)

Probe questions: (1) Does the ability of a child ever cause exclusion from certain activities? (2) If not, what sorts of accommodations and modifications have you made to include children with disabilities in all activities? (3) If it does, what exclusions have been necessary for which children? (Record as "comment.")

Inadequate 1	Minimal 3	Good 5	Excellent 7
Score: 1 2	3 4	5 6	7
1.1 ☐ Y ☐ N — Children with disabilities are never included in *all* activities and routines.	**3.1** ☐ Y ☐ N — Children with disabilities participate in *some* regular activities and routines, at least a substantial part of the day.*	**5.1** ☐ Y ☐ N — Children with disabilities participate in *most* regular activities and routines, most of the day.*	**7.1** ☐ Y ☐ N — Director actively follows and promotes the principle of full participation, assuring that children with disabilities can participate in *all* activities and routines *all* of the time.
1.2 ☐ Y ☐ N — Children with disabilities and resource support staff are an obvious "pair," not part of the group, almost all of the time.	**3.2** ☐ Y ☐ N ☐ N/A** — Resource support staff enhance ratios or ratios are reduced by enrolling fewer children, so that all staff have additional opportunity to interact with and support children with special needs.	**5.2** ☐ Y ☐ N ☐ N/A** — While enhancing ratio, resource support staff also bring specialized knowledge (or reduced ratios provide time for regular staff to become familiar with additional resources) about individual children and inclusion strategies to staff and community.	**7.2** ☐ Y ☐ N — Resource support staff are "invisible"—all staff work as a team and demonstrate a positive, *celebratory* attitude in their modifications and adaptations for children with special needs. Expertise is shared, not hoarded.
1.3 ☐ Y ☐ N — Lead ECE verbalizes no strategies for including children with disabilities in regular activities and routines of classroom.	**3.3** ☐ Y ☐ N — Lead ECE verbalizes *some** strategies for including children with disabilities in activities and routines.	**5.3** ☐ Y ☐ N — Lead ECE verbalizes a wealth of experience and knowledge about disabilities and about inclusion strategies.	**7.3** ☐ Y ☐ N — Lead ECE, another ECE, a support staff (such as secretary or cook) and a parent articulate their support and the centre's support of the principle of "full participation."
1.4 ☐ Y ☐ N — Centre has no written or verbal policy on inclusion.	**3.4** ☐ Y ☐ N — The centre has an informal policy on inclusion (evidenced by director's comments and supported by such evidence as accessible materials on diversity including pictures, books, dolls with disabilities, or by the presence of information and training opportunities on inclusion being available to staff).	**5.4** ☐ Y ☐ N — The centre's written policy supports inclusive child care.	**7.4** ☐ Y ☐ N — The centre's written inclusion policy statement affirms the principle of "full participation."

* "Few" means 2 or 3; "Some" means more than 3; "Most" means more than 5; "A substantial part of the day" means at least 1/3 of the time that all children are there (generally 9–3); "Most of the day" means 75% or more.

** If there are fewer than 4 children with disabilities in the centre, if the disabilities are mild, if the staff are experienced at including children with disabilities, and if high-quality consultation and therapeutic support is available, there may be no need for either additional staffing or ratio reduction. Use N/A for this situation.

Principle 5: Maximum Feasible Parent Participation at Parent's Comfort Level.

In fully inclusive child care centres, adjustments are made by the centre to encourage attendance at IPP planning meetings, committee meetings, and training sessions, arranging times convenient to parents; transportation and babysitting when necessary; translators at no cost to parents; encouraging parents to bring relatives and/or trusted advisors to meetings and/or observations, etc. With these adjustments in place, parents participate in IPP planning meetings, committees, training sessions, etc., to the maximum extent of their comfort level. Many child care programs that are referred to as inclusive report that parents of children with special needs are just too busy to participate. (Read this statement to Director as you begin to discuss Principle 5 in a non-judgmental tone. Then use probe questions, as necessary, and record comments.)

Probe questions: (1) Do you have difficulty in getting parents of children with special needs to participate in meetings and training sessions? (2) If you do, what have you done to try to increase such participation? (3) If you don't, to what do you attribute your success? (Record as "comment.")

Inadequate 1	Minimal 3	Good 5	Excellent 7
Score: 1	2 3	4 5	6 7
1.1 ☐ Y ☐ N Parents of children with disabilities almost never participate in meetings or trainings at the child care centre.	**3.1** ☐ Y ☐ N Parents of children with disabilities sometimes** participate in meetings or trainings.	**5.1** ☐ Y ☐ N Parents of children with disabilities often** participate in meetings and trainings at the centre.	**7.1** ☐ Y ☐ N Director actively follows the principle of maximum feasible parent participation. Parents of children with disabilities are active on board or committees, and very frequently** participate in IPP meetings and trainings. Parents are not "guilted" into being involved.
1.2 ☐ Y ☐ N Centre has made no adjustments to encourage greater parent participation.	**3.2** ☐ Y ☐ N Centre has made at least one adjustment to encourage greater parent participation.*	**5.2** ☐ Y ☐ N Centre makes some adjustments to encourage greater participation, such as providing transportation, babysitting, translators or parent-sensitive scheduling.***	**7.2** ☐ Y ☐ N Centre encourages participation through many adjustments such as providing transportation, babysitting, location, translators, parent-sensitive scheduling.****
1.3 ☐ Y ☐ N Lead ECE is unaware of any adjustments made to encourage maximum feasible participation.	**3.3** ☐ Y ☐ N Lead ECE is aware of an adjustment made to encourage maximum feasible participation or spontaneously articulates at least one reason why this is important.	**5.3** ☐ Y ☐ N Lead ECE is aware of some adjustments made to encourage maximum participation and spontaneously articulates at least one reason why this is important.	**7.3** ☐ Y ☐ N Lead ECE, another ECE, a support staff, and a parent list several adjustments made to encourage maximum parental participation and articulate at least two reasons why this is important.
1.4 ☐ Y ☐ N Centre has no verbal or written policy on inclusion.	**3.4** ☐ Y ☐ N The centre has an informal policy on inclusion (evidenced by director's comments and supported by such evidence as accessible materials on diversity including pictures, books and dolls with disabilities, or by the presence of information and training opportunities on inclusion being available to staff).	**5.4** ☐ Y ☐ N Centre has written policy on inclusion	**7.4** ☐ Y ☐ N Centre has written policy on inclusion that affirms the parent-participation principle.

* Must list at least one adjustment (such as transportation, babysitting, location, translators, parent-sensitive scheduling) to achieve a "3" rating. **"Sometimes" means roughly 25% of the time; "Often" means roughly 50% of the time; "Very Frequently" means 75% of the time. Two factors are combined in this item—percentage of parents of children with disabilities who participate and frequency that each participates. If 25% participate 25% of the time, 3.1 applies. (Add the two percentages and divide by 2). If 10% participate 40% of the time, 3.1 still applies. ***Must list at least 3 adjustments to achieve a "5" rating; ****Must list at least 5 adjustments to achieve a "7" rating.

Principle 6: Leadership, Pro-active Strategies and Advocacy for High Quality, Inclusive Child Care.

Even when the regular child care program is available and adequate, many families of children with special needs are excluded by reasons such as staff training, support staffing, transportation, funding and therapeutic support. In fully inclusive child care centres, these limitations are not passively accepted by the director, board, parents or staff. Advocacy activities on behalf of high-quality inclusive child care include appeals to civic organizations, work with government officials to change rules that limit the inclusion of children with special needs, and presentations on inclusion to staff, associations and community—these types of actions exemplify fully inclusive child care centres. (Read this statement to Director as you begin to discuss Principle 6 in a non-judgmental tone. Then use probe questions, as necessary, and record comments.)

Probe questions: (1) Does your centre try to change policies and funding arrangements that impede full inclusion? (2) If it does, what sorts of actions have you taken? (3) Who is involved (such as the director, staff, board, and/or parents)? (Record as "comment.")

	Inadequate 1	Minimal 3	Good 5	Excellent 7
Score:	1	2 3	4 5	6 7
	1.1 ☐ Y ☐ N Neither director, board, staff nor parents participate in advocacy activities or in providing workshops on inclusion.	**3.1** ☐ Y ☐ N Director participates in advocacy activities or in providing training for inclusion.	**5.1** ☐ Y ☐ N Director and lead ECE staff participate in advocacy activities or in providing training for inclusion. (either/or for each person).***	**7.1** ☐ Y ☐ N Director takes a leadership role in *both* advocacy *and* providing training for inclusion.
	1.2 ☐ Y ☐ N Centre passively uses funded supports, and doesn't seek additional supports such as summer grants, service clubs or volunteers.	**3.2** ☐ Y ☐ N Centre uses funded supports, and once in a while* seeks additional supports, such as summer grants, service clubs and volunteers.**	**5.2** ☐ Y ☐ N Centre uses funded supports and often* seeks additional supports such as summer grants, service clubs, volunteers, students, in-kind donations, fund-raising, other government programs.**	**7.2** ☐ Y ☐ N Lead ECE staff, and board or some parents participate in advocacy activities and in providing training for inclusion (staff—both; others—1).
	1.3 ☐ Y ☐ N Centre does not have a verbal or written policy on inclusion.	**3.3** ☐ Y ☐ N The centre has an informal policy on inclusion (evidenced by director's comments and supported by such evidence as accessible materials on diversity including pictures, books and dolls with disabilities, or by the presence of information and training opportunities on inclusion being available to staff).	**5.3** ☐ Y ☐ N Centre has written policy supporting inclusive child care.	**7.3** ☐ Y ☐ N Centre uses funded supports, constantly* seeks additional supports and is creative in obtaining additional resources, both human and financial.**
				7.4 ☐ Y ☐ N Centre has written inclusion policy that affirms leadership/advocacy principle.

* "Once in a while" means less than yearly; "Often" means at least yearly; "Constantly" means as integral part of administration, at least several times a year.

** For "Additional Supports" (such as summer grants, service clubs, volunteers, students, in-kind donations, fund-raising and other government programs), the centre must score at least 2 for "3"; 5 for "5"; and 7 for "7".

*** In 5.1, 2 out of 3 must participate for a "yes" answer.

Comments: _____

Notes on Rating and Scoring

1. Read the entire scale carefully, including the Items, Notes for Clarification, and Questions. In order to be accurate, all ratings have to be based exactly as possible on the indicators provided in the scale items.

2. Examples that differ from those given in the indicators but seem comparable may be used as a basis for giving credit for an indicator.

3. Scores should be based on the current situation that is observed or reported by staff, not on future plans. In the absence of observable information on which to base your rating, you may use answers given by staff during the question period to assign scores.

4. When scoring an item, always start reading from 1 (inadequate) and progress upward till the correct score is reached.

5. Ratings are to be assigned in the following way:

    *   A rating of 1 must be given if any indicator under 1 is scored Yes.
    *   A rating of 2 is given when all indicators under 1 are scored No and at least half of the indicators under 3 are scored Yes.
    *   A rating of 3 is given when all indicators under 1 are scored No and all indicators under 3 are scored Yes.
    *   A rating of 4 is given when all indicators under 3 are met and at least half of the indicators under 5 are scored Yes.
    *   A rating of 5 is given when all indicators under 5 are scored Yes.
    *   A rating of 6 is given when all indicators under 5 are met and at least half of the indicators under 7 are scored Yes.
    *   A rating of 7 is given when all indicators under 7 are scored Yes.

6. The total mean scale score is the sum of all the item scores for the entire scale divided by the number of items scored.

7. Transfer your ratings to the score sheets on the following pages.

Score Sheet
SpeciaLink Child Care Inclusion Practices Profile

Observer: _____

Centre/School: _____

Room: _____

Teacher(s): _____

Number of Staff Present: _____

Number of Children Enrolled in Class: _____

Number of Children Present: _____

Any Unusual Occurrence During Observation: _____

Date of Observation: _____

Number of Children with Identified Disabilities: _____

Check Type(s) of Disability: □ Physical/Sensory   □ Cognitive/Language   □ Social/Emotional   □ Other

Birthdates of Children Enrolled: Youngest _____   Oldest _____

Time Observation Began: _____ : _____   □ AM   □ PM

Time Observation Ended: _____ : _____   □ AM   □ PM

---

1. Physical Environment and Special Needs

1 2 3 4 5 6 7

Y N	Y N	Y N	Y N
1.1	3.1	5.1	7.1
1.2	3.2	5.2	7.2
1.3	3.3	5.3	7.3
1.4	3.4	5.4	7.4

Notes:

---

2. Equipment and Materials

1 2 3 4 5 6 7

Y N	Y N	Y N	Y N
1.1	3.1	5.1	7.1
1.2	3.2	5.2	7.2
	3.3	5.3	7.3
	3.4	5.4	7.4

Notes:

---

3. Director and Inclusion

1 2 3 4 5 6 7

Y N	Y N	Y N	Y N
1.1	3.1	5.1	7.1
1.2	3.2	5.2	7.2
1.3	3.3	5.3	7.3
1.4	3.4	5.4	7.4
1.5	3.5	5.5	7.5

Notes:

---

4. Staff Support

1 2 3 4 5 6 7

Y N	Y N	Y N	Y N
1.1	3.1	5.1	7.1
1.2	3.2	5.2	7.2
	3.3	5.3	7.3
		5.4	7.4

Notes:

---

5. Staff Training

1 2 3 4 5 6 7

Y N	Y N	Y N	Y N
1.1	3.1	5.1	7.1
1.2	3.2	5.2	7.2
1.3	3.3	5.3	7.3
			7.4
			7.5

Notes:

---

6. Therapies: PT; OT; S&L; Behavioural

1 2 3 4 5 6 7

Y N	Y N	Y N	Y N
1.1	3.1	5.1	7.1
1.2	3.2	5.2	7.2
	3.3	5.3	7.3
	3.4	5.4	7.4
	3.5	5.5	7.5

Notes:

7. Individual Program Plans (IPPs)   1 2 3 4 5 6 7   Notes:

	Y N		Y N		Y N		Y N
1.1		3.1		5.1		7.1	
		3.2		5.2		7.2	
		3.3		5.3		7.3	
		3.4		5.4		7.4	
				5.5		7.5	

8. Parents of Children with Special Needs   1 2 3 4 5 6 7   Notes:

	Y N		Y N		Y N		Y N
1.1		3.1		5.1		7.1	
1.2		3.2		5.2		7.2	
1.3		3.3		5.3		7.3	
1.4		3.4		5.4		7.4	

9. Involvement of Typical Children   1 2 3 4 5 6 7   Notes:

	Y N		Y N		Y N		Y N
1.1		3.1		5.1		7.1	
1.2		3.2		5.2		7.2	
1.3		3.3		5.3		7.3	
						7.4	

10. Board of Directors and Similar Units   1 2 3 4 5 6 7   Notes:

	Y N		Y N		Y N		Y N
1.1		3.1		5.1		7.1	
1.2		3.2		5.2		7.2	
1.3		3.3		5.3		7.3	

11. Preparing for Transition to School   1 2 3 4 5 6 7   Notes:

	Y N		Y N		Y N		Y N
1.1		3.1		5.1		7.1	
		3.2		5.2		7.2	
		3.3				7.3	

Total and Average Scores

	Total Score	Average Score
Physical Environment and Special Needs	_____	
Equipment and Materials	_____	
Director and Inclusion	_____	
Staff Support	_____	
Staff Training	_____	
Therapies	_____	
Individual Program Plans	_____	
Parents of Children with Special Needs	_____	
Involvement of Typical Children	_____	
Board of Directors and Similar Units	_____	
Preparing for Transition to School	_____	
TOTAL	_____	
	# of Items Scored _____	_____

Score Sheet
SpeciaLink Child Care Inclusion Principles Scale

Observer: _____
Centre/School: _____
Room: _____
Teacher(s): _____
Number of Staff Present: _____
Number of Children Enrolled in Class: _____
Number of Children Present: _____

Observer Code: _____
Centre Code: _____
Room Code: _____
Teacher Code: _____

Date of Observation: _____
Number of Children with Identified Disabilities: _____
Check Type(s) of Disability: ☐ Physical/Sensory   ☐ Cognitive/Language
                              ☐ Social/Emotional   ☐ Other

Birthdates of Children Enrolled: Youngest _____
                                 Oldest _____

Time Observation Began: _____ : _____   ☐ AM ☐ PM
Time Observation Ended: _____ : _____   ☐ AM ☐ PM

Any Unusual Occurrence During Observation: _____

---

1. Zero Reject   1 2 3 4 5 6 7

Y N	Y N	Y N	Y N	Y N	Notes:
1.1	3.1	5.1	7.1		
1.2	3.2	5.2	7.2		
1.3	3.3	5.3	7.3		

2. Natural Proportions   1 2 3 4 5 6 7

Y N	Y N	Y N	Y N	Y N	Notes:
1.1	3.1	5.1	7.1		
1.2	3.2	5.2	7.2		
1.3	3.3	5.3	7.3		
1.4			7.4		
1.5					

3. Same Hours of Attendance Available to All Children   1 2 3 4 5 6 7

Y N	Y N	Y N	Y N	Y N	Notes:
1.1	3.1	5.1	7.1		
1.2	3.2	5.2	7.2		
1.3	3.3	5.3	7.3		
1.4	3.4	5.4	7.4		
1.5	3.5	5.5	7.5		

4. Full Participation   1 2 3 4 5 6 7

Y N	Y N	Y N	Y N	Y N	Notes:
1.1	3.1	5.1	7.1		
1.2	3.2	5.2	7.2		
1.3	3.3	5.3	7.3		
1.4	3.4	5.4	7.4		

5. Maximum Feasible Parent Participation   1 2 3 4 5 6 7

Y N	Y N	Y N	Y N	Y N	Notes:
1.1	3.1	5.1	7.1		
1.2	3.2	5.2	7.2		
1.3	3.3	5.3	7.3		
1.4	3.4	5.4	7.4		

6. Pro-active Strategies and Advocacy for High Quality, Inclusive Child Care   1 2 3 4 5 6 7

Y N	Y N	Y N	Y N	Y N	Notes:
1.1	3.1	5.1	7.1		
1.2	3.2	5.2	7.2		
1.3	3.3	5.3	7.3		
			7.4		

continued

continued

Total and Average Scores

	Total Score
Zero Reject	_____
Natural Proportions	_____
Same Hours of Attendance Available to All Children	_____
Full Participation	_____
Maximum Feasible Parent Participation	_____
Pro-active Strategies and Advocacy for High Quality, Inclusive Child Care	_____
TOTAL	_____

# of Items Scored	Average Score
_____	_____

Recommendations for Inclusive Care

From *Highlights from Inclusion: The Next Generation in Child Care in Canada*

A Focus on Leadership

Inclusion: The Next Generation confirms the critical role of the child care centre director as inclusion leader. Some of the programs in this study lacked resource teachers, some lacked regularized funding for the extra costs of resource supports and some lacked strong boards, but none of the successful programs lacked strong, committed directors. Activities and programs that enhance that role are critical. Fully inclusive child care centres are still rare, and their sustainability is in question as founding directors retire or move on. We strongly recommend that:

1. **Governments must target inclusive directors as key change agents, and fund projects that enhance their impact on the broader child care community.**

   This can be achieved through projects that:

   - Bring key people from successful inclusive child care sites together to share learnings and best practices, and to strategize about practical initiatives;
   - Sponsor inclusion leadership training institutes for directors, and for potential directors, with demonstrated commitment to inclusion;
   - Support networking opportunities for directors/supervisors of inclusive centres;
   - Create a national mentorship program for inclusion, with successful directors/supervisors of inclusive centres as mentors, nominating in-province leaders who are "ready to include";
   - Support field-based speakers' bureaus on inclusion, with directors/supervisors—credible practitioners—as key figures;
   - Promote a career ladder and encourage existing successful inclusion practitioners to become trainers.

   There is a tremendous reserve of "practice wisdom" that should be widely shared and utilized to enhance inclusive practice and to encourage the next generation of directors and child care professionals.

2. **Governments must fund a variety of opportunities (using in-person presentations, print materials, videos, and web-based resources) to share with others knowledge acquired by leaders in inclusive child care programs.**

A Focus on Training

3. **Provincial and territorial governments must ensure that there is a variety of courses, conferences and workshops on inclusion that are accessible, affordable and available to staff and directors on an ongoing basis, addressing the range of topics and issues that are important for successful inclusion.**

4. **College and university programs in ECE must incorporate more materials about inclusive practices in their curricula and in post-diploma and graduate courses.**

5. **Practical and placement courses in ECE and related programs must be strategically developed to ensure that students have the opportunity to learn about inclusion by participating in successful centres.**

6. **Colleges and universities must reconceptualize (in consultation with the field) post-diploma/graduate programs for resource teachers and special needs workers in early childhood education.** These should reflect the multiple roles of direct service, collaborative practice, consulting and adult education. They should also address the needs of short-term contract workers who work in inclusive child care settings, often without training.

7. **Intensive inclusion quality-enhancement programs, such as *Keeping the Door Open* in New Brunswick; *Measuring and Improving Kids' Environments (MIKE)* in Prince Edward Island; and *Partnerships for Inclusion* in Nova Scotia, must be offered to centres in all provinces.**

A Focus on Policy

Provincial/territorial/municipal policy must support effective inclusion practice. Funding must be provided to ensure that centres and their staff have access to the resources (both financial and human) they need to continue to be effective and to expand their capabilities, and that they are compensated for the valuable work they do. Among policy concerns to be addressed are:

8. **Child care centres that enroll children with special needs must have timely access to child assessments, both to determine eligibility and to help child care staff in their planning efforts.**

9. **Child care centres must have additional funds to enhance ratios (or employ an in-house resource teacher) when four or more children with special needs are enrolled, or when any children have extremely high special needs. Funding should be stable and adequate to recruit and retain trained and experienced ECEs for this work.**

10. **Itinerant resource teachers must be available to child care programs to support the effective inclusion of children with special needs.**

11. **Child care centres must have appropriate levels of support from therapists and other related specialists in the community when they enroll children with special needs.**

12. **Child care centres must have additional assistants when they enroll children with more challenging needs.**

13. **Since accessibility and physical structure are so closely related to both inclusion quality and global quality, all new centres must be purpose-built to meet current standards, and older centres must be eligible for capital grants to increase accessibility.**

A Focus on Planning for Transitions

Provincial/territorial policy must support a collaborative, interdisciplinary approach among early years' professionals, including school personnel.

14. **Early years' personnel must develop protocols and strategies for effective planning and coordination of efforts to assist with child care transitions (from home or early intervention/infant development to child care, and from child care to school).**

A Focus on Research

15. **Governments must fund thorough evaluations of the effectiveness of different models of inclusion support.**
16. **Governments must fund the monitoring of progress toward inclusiveness in child care programs.** Instruments for monitoring inclusion quality, such as the *SpeciaLink Inclusion Profile* and the *SpeciaLink Inclusion Practices Scale*, are available and are familiar to the field.

A Focus on the Profession

Wide variance exists in the roles, training, caseload size, duration and frequency of visits, focus of service, etc., of resource teachers in child care.

17. **As an emerging profession, leaders in the field of resource teachers/ specialists in Early Childhood Education must define their own code of ethics, mandates, appropriate caseloads and standards of training and practice.** Funding must be allocated for research and development projects oriented toward this goal.

Toward a System of High-Quality, Affordable, Accessible and Inclusive Child Care Programs Across Canada

The continued underfunding and undervaluing of child care professionals is a serious concern that will affect the recruitment and retention of skilled individuals in this field.

A renewed commitment to a national child care program must consider the quality of early learning and child care, along with issues of affordability and expansion of spaces.

18. **Federal/provincial/territorial governments must strengthen the funding component of the *Multilateral Framework on Early Learning and Child Care* to build a national Canadian child care system that includes career ladders with graduated salaries, and assures a continuing infrastructure to support high quality, inclusive programs.**

Index